CONSCIOUSNESS AND TRANSCENDENCE

CONSCIOUSNESS AND TRANSCENDENCE

The Theology of Eric Voegelin

by

MICHAEL P. MORRISSEY

UNIVERSITY OF NOTRE DAME PRESS

Notre Dame   London

Library of Congress Cataloging-in-Publication Data

Morrissey, Michael P., 1953–
    Consciousness and transcendence : the theology of Eric
Voegelin / Michael P. Morrissey.
        p.   cm.
    Includes bibliographical references and index.
    ISBN 0-268-00793-4
    1. Voegelin, Eric, 1901–   —Religion.   2. Theology,
Doctrinal—History—20th century.   3. History (Theology)—
History of doctrines—20th century.-   I. Title.
    B3354.V884M677   1994
    193—dc20   92-50159
                                                                CIP

  ∞ *The paper used in this publication meets the minimum requirements*
of the American National Standard for Information Sciences—Permanence of Paper
for Printed Library Materials, ANSI Z39.48-1984.

FOR TONI

There is no truth of *kosmos* and *akosmia* in man other than the truth emerging as the Word from the divine–human movement of the loving quest. The word of truth, "the tale that saves" as told by Socrates-Plato, is not a piece of information available to everybody. The tale has to be found by the man who is suffering the death of reality and, in the cave of his death, is moved to turn around toward the divine light. The turning-around from death to life, then, must not remain a mute event in the soul of the man who was touched by grace, or it will be lost. It must become Word. . . . The tale that saves must itself be saved from the death from which it emerges, if it is to become the living Word with the magic power of salvation. . . . The man who returns from the light to the cave will speak the Word to those who cannot hear what they hear; he will be mocked, persecuted, and like Socrates be put to death. When the living are dead, the dead who are living have no audience. So it was in the time of Socrates; so it was in the time of Christ; and so it is today. . . . The magic of the saving word is as dependent on man's openness to the order of love as is the magic of the disordering word on his inclination to resist and hate truth.

—Eric Voegelin
from "Wisdom and the Magic of the Extreme:
A Meditation"

CONTENTS

PREFACE   xi

INTRODUCTION   1

1. TOWARD A PHILOSOPHY OF CONSCIOUSNESS:
   THE EARLY WRITINGS, 1928–50   17

   Voegelin's Background   17
   The Writings   25

2. THE HISTORICAL DIMENSION:
   THE MIDDLE WRITINGS, 1951–59   37

   The New Science of Politics   37
   Order and History   44
   Israel and Revelation   51
   The Polis and Philosophy   56
   Plato and Aristotle   67

3. THE THEORY REFINED:
   THE LATER WRITINGS, 1960–74   81

   A Period of Transition   81
   The Ecumenic Age   91
     Expansion of the Spiritual Horizon   91
     Historiogenesis   93
     The Ecumenic Age   97
     The Pauline Vision of Transfiguration   101
     The Unity of Humankind   106
     The Balance of Consciousness   109

4. THE THEORY ACHIEVED:
   THE LAST WRITINGS, 1975–85   115

   The Meditative Search for Transcendent Order   117
   The Paradox of Consciousness   118
   The Symbolic Ambiguities of Divine Presence   122
   "Imaginative Oblivion" in the German Context   127
   Hesiod and Remembrance   132

The Ambiguities of Bonaventure and Leibniz   134
The Return to the Platonic Myth   136
Faith and Vision in the Christian Context   150
    Voegelin's Theological Method   151
    The Christian Vision   163

5. LONERGAN'S FOUNDATIONAL THEOLOGY   171

The Anthropological Turn   172
Transcendental Method   178
Freedom and the Human Good   184
Conversion   187
Theological Method and Foundations   194
Doctrines   203
Lonergan and Voegelin Compared   209
    Comparative Abstract   223

6. THE THEOLOGICAL IMPLICATIONS OF
   VOEGELIN'S PHILOSOPHY OF CONSCIOUSNESS   227

Voegelin's Reconstruction of Christian Philosophy   227
    The Meaning of Christ   235
Principles of a "Voegelinian Theology"   247

NOTES   255

BIBLIOGRAPHY   319

INDEX OF NAMES   333

INDEX OF SUBJECTS   337

ABOUT THE AUTHOR   355

PREFACE

The thought of a great philosopher is a major challenge. Whether a philosopher's works are ancient and time honored or contemporary and relatively unknown, his thought brings us into uncharted regions and challenges us to reach beyond ourselves, to broaden our intellectual and spiritual horizons. But the attribute of greatness is the judgment of history. When a new major thinker comes along we are at first suspicious. We subject his works to critical investigation, as of course we should, calling to bear the historic resources of our civilization's rich traditions. Only in time will the label of greatness be judiciously bestowed, for only after concerted years of absorption, interpretation, analysis, critical commentary, and debate by scores of scholars who begin to take seriously a serious thinker's work will we come to recognize the presence of greatness in our midst. Such recognition usually occurs only after the philosopher has long departed. But those of his followers who carry on the work left unfinished remember with great esteem the one they believed initiated a renaissance of thought.

In my view Eric Voegelin is such a philosopher. If any contemporary thinker has challenged us to alter our habitual ways of thinking and to shift our perspective away from our prevailing modernist views toward an enriched, universal comprehension of reality, it is surely he. But not by doing away with the old has he tendered the new. On the contrary, Voegelin is the one contemporary thinker who, through an extraordinary recovery of the experiential roots of our intellectual and spiritual history, has allowed us to see with fresh eyes the formative sources of our Western heritage. In our wayward journey through time he has in effect called us back to ourselves, if we only risk the "anamnetic venture" that he invites us to take.

The breadth and depth of Voegelin's study of history is startling. Among contemporaries his knowledge and insight into the entire sweep of Western history is virtually nonpareil. For this reason alone his voluminous works have appeared forbidding to many, and thus he is not widely known beyond a small, faithful, but ever increasing readership. It is my hope that this study of this important thinker will help increase his audience beyond the cadre of political scientists and philosophers where it has up to now been generally confined. For those who are nonspecialists and altogether unfamiliar with Voegelin, I hope this presentation and analysis of his basic insights and concepts will bring his thought out of obscurity and into the light of day. Therefore, I intend this study to serve as an introduction to, and an explication of, Voegelin's extensive work, especially in light of its significance for theology. Because of his singular importance to theology, I hope my interpretation and analysis of Voegelin's thought will be of particular benefit to those whose interests and labors, like my own, are in that domain.

Any explication of Voegelin's massive corpus is apt to involve some misrepresentation. In following the necessary precaution of sticking as close as possible to Voegelin's own language in the course of presentation, I only hope that my effort at "popularization" has not slipped beyond the range of admissible flaws. In this regard I can only invite the readers to take up Voegelin's challenging texts for themselves and thereby embark on a philosophical apprenticeship with a true master. I believe the success of this study can be measured by the degree to which such a response is inspired.

I wish to acknowledge with heartfelt gratitude all the persons who have supported me in this project. Without what Plato called "the community of pathos" which I have been graced with, this labor of love would have long ago degenerated into mere labor. Most of all I wish to thank Paul Caringella, who was Eric Voegelin's personal assistant in the last years of his life. I am indebted to him not only for his many helpful criticisms of an earlier version of this work but also for the many conversations with him that have helped me understand Voegelin's work so much more.

I particularly wish to thank all those other individuals who have aided me over the years in the completion of this project through their intellectual inspiration and conversation, especially Ted Peters, Bob Hurd, Bill Slottman, Fred Lawrence, Patricia Codron, Frank Turner, Arthur Kennedy, Terry Nichols, Kelly Donovan, Tatha Wiley, Mark Sinnett, and Bill Thompson. Among these gracious souls I am particularly indebted to those who contributed by reading in part or in whole an earlier draft of the manuscript and giving me their helpful comments.

I also wish to extend my gratitude to the very helpful staff at the Hoover Institution Archives Library at Stanford University where I was able to research Eric Voegelin's papers.

For material support in the completion of this study I wish to thank my own institution, the University of St. Thomas, for a Research

Assistance Grant, and also the Earhart Foundation for a Fellowship Research Grant.

Finally, I wish to extend my great appreciation to Jeannette Morgenroth, my editor at the University of Notre Dame Press, for her very skillful work in bringing this volume to production, as well as to Richard O'Keeffe for his very meticulous and indefatigable labors in preparing the index.

I dedicate this work to a very cherished person in my life. I am eternally grateful for her love and support without which this book would never have seen the light of day.

INTRODUCTION

The deeper the roots of a man's inner nature, the better will he take the past into himself; and the greatest and most powerful nature would be known by the absence of limits for the historical sense to overgrow and work harm.

—Friedrich Nietzsche

This is one of the puzzling observations of the young and impassioned Nietzsche in a tract protesting "the burden of history," which was published in a book aptly titled *Thoughts Out of Season.*[1] Of course what Nietzsche meant by the "historical sense" we would call the relative, insignificant, and fleeting. To this notion of the "historical sense" he contrasted two other notions: the "unhistorical," by which he meant forgetting the insignificant and drawing a manageable horizon of meaning around oneself; and the "superhistorical," or the power to turn one's eyes away from the endless process of becoming toward the eternal and transcendent, to that which gives human existence a constant and ultimate character, to art and religion.[2] Nietzsche claimed that only by striking a balance among these approaches to history, could history serve life and not overwhelm it. Taking into account the explosion of the historical sciences of his day and the concomitant rise of historicism, as well as the breakdown of spiritual order in the Christianity of nineteenth-century Europe, it becomes clear why Nietzsche held some bold views about history. In spite of the radical historicism and voluntarism that characterize his philosophy as a whole, I believe that in this early work Nietzsche was calling for a spiritual regeneration of Western culture. By this I mean a kind of conversion by which we moderns, who are overburdened by the radical vicissitudes and sufferings of recent history, may once again marshal the necessary intelligence, reason, and will needed for a truly critical appropriation of the great minds and spiritual events of the past. It is predominately a call to take one's bearings on the eternal, to live in light of what is highest and noblest in human nature.

1

Over a hundred years after Nietzsche wrote these words, we find ourselves still caught in the throes of "the burden of history." On the one hand, our century is marked by the vast expansion of the historical and interdisciplinary fields of the human sciences. The interpretative and theoretical enterprise in philosophy and scholarship cannot keep pace with the growing empirical data in the fields of history, politics, psychology, sociology, anthropology, archeology, and religion. This burgeoning wealth of knowledge has wrought not a modicum of disorder in the modern academy. The climate of specialization so thoroughly permeates our institutions of higher learning that it is now no longer fashionable to decry the loss of purpose and meaning of the university. The university has become the multiversity where contemplation of the permanent questions and the unity of knowledge are lost in the now-routine bustle of specialized academic pursuits and research. In large measure, the proliferation of commentary, speculation, and opinion has replaced science understood in the classical sense as the quest for truth, goodness, and wisdom. Contemporary philosophy and theology are especially prone to this disorder, as marked by the plethora of ideological "isms" under which they continue to operate, such as positivism, relativism, historicism, and, more recently, deconstructionism and postmodernism.

Moreover, ours is also a century of unprecedented violence. The numerous modern ideologies underpinning the political mass movements of our time have left a mass of destruction and horror in their wake, which makes our century appear incommensurable to any prior age. Only in the past few years with the breakdown of numerous totalitarian societies and the spread of democratic regimes, particularly in Eastern Europe and what was once the Soviet Union, does the decades-long madness on the world political scene seem to be finally subsiding, marking the end of an era that traces its ideological roots two to three centuries before the beginning of this century's Cold War. But the breakthrough to a new world order is precarious, for the roots of the modern crisis are still ever present and deeper than the social and political institutions that shape our lives. The roots of the crisis are personal and spiritual. Thus, the intransigent chaos that exists in the academy is just a mirror of the general disorder in society and history, which in turn reflects the perennial disorder in the human soul.

It is upon this scene that the work of Eric Voegelin stands out as a monument of order, clarity, and passion for truth in a world of unrelenting crisis and violence. The breadth and depth of his scholarship have been directed toward a lifelong philosophical effort to recover the true order of humankind as revealed in history by coming to terms with the history of order and disorder. I believe Voegelin's philosophy of order, with its vast historical grounding and deep spiritual sensitivity, is the most sophisticated and incisive study of human existence in our time. It not only answers Nietzsche's call for spiritual regeneration, but goes beyond Nietzsche in illuminating the movement of a philosophical consciousness that makes sense out of the drama of history and humanity's role in the drama. In addition to achieving this task, Voegelin has elucidated for us, by a process of recovery or anamnesis, the therapeutic conditions that make self-transcendent living possible in our personal, social, and historical lives.

In view of these considerations, I believe no other contemporary thinker fits so suitably Nietzsche's description of the singular man, whose deep inner nature and transcendent, superhistorical vision allows him a vast and an unequaled appropriation of human historical experience, than Eric Voegelin. It is Voegelin whose masterful, and ultimately mystical, reappropriation of history and the spirit has countered those purveyors of civilizational decline whom Nietzsche called "the abusers of history," or those Schleiermacher called "the cultured despisers" of religion. Voegelin's work is a recovery of the permanent order of human nature, a philosophy that is executed in the service of life and the spirit. If Nietzsche is the preeminent philosopher of disorder whose work foreshadowed this century's civilizational crisis, then Voegelin is the preeminent philosopher of order whose work can be said to herald a civilizational renaissance.

Voegelin's corpus has been praised as a scientific and scholarly work of the highest order. In essence, his philosophy of order has encompassed an almost unparalleled expanse in his encyclopedic attempt to capture the whole drama of human history as the substance of his investigations. Voegelin has also incited a minirevolution of sorts in contemporary philosophical and political thought by his turn to consciousness and its structure as the interpretative key for understanding the human engagement with reality and the process by which humans order the meaning of their experience personally, socially, and politically. Accordingly, Voegelin, building on the formative discoveries of the classical philosophers, has provided us with nothing less than a major retheoretization of human existence centered on the order of consciousness and its ground. In his response to the various crises of our time, he has attempted to base the intellectual discourse of philosophy and politics on a new and more adequate foundation. This has entailed the return to the originating experiences in human history that gave rise to the ordering insights, worldviews, and symbols which together tell the unfinished story of human existence in time. The emergence of these differentiated experiences or "theophanies" and their symbolizations form the constitutive episodes in the mysterious, ongoing drama of human being and divine being that *is* history itself.

This story, whose warp and woof is eminently spiritual, Voegelin's lifelong study of history has sought to tell. It is the story of the transcendent ground of human existence breaking through into consciousness, thereby transfiguring the nature of the human being by the order of love and grace. As such it is a story that can be told, and a meaning that can be interpreted and communicated, only in a language inherent to theology. And yet, ironically, throughout Voegelin's writings almost every reference to theology is pejorative. The irony lies in the probative view of some admirers of his work, this writer among them, that his thought represents perhaps the most important contribution to theology on the contemporary scene, for no contemporary thinker can surpass Voegelin's prodigious and critical furnishing of philosophical and historical foundations for theology. With the recent publication of Voegelin's final writings, along with a number of his previously unpublished essays, scholars are now in a position to offer a more complete assessment of the thought of this great philosopher.[3] Now, almost a decade after his death, the impact of Voegelin's work in the areas of philosophy and political science has been notable and will continue to be so. However, the attention paid to his work by theologians has been relatively slight, though ever increasing. For me there is no doubt that Voegelin's later work is essentially a theological endeavor, or is the kind of work that should properly be called theology. Whatever one makes of his work it is a major achievement that the theological community can ill afford to ignore.

In this book I will explicate the substance of Voegelin's work, with a particular focus on his contribution to theology, a contribution which I believe is actually a radical challenge that calls theology back to its roots after centuries of deformation. This challenge lies not only in the results of Voegelin's scholarly labors over the years but in the nature of his "method." While Voegelin always remained at heart a philosopher in the deep, transcendental sense of Plato, his thorough integration of theological themes was profound and was present from the very beginning of his intellectual career. I believe Voegelin's work, in both substance and method, provides a guide by which theologians as well as philosophers can take their bearings in the future.

Certainly Voegelin would dispute the notion that his work followed some foundational "method," philosophical or theological. He was very suspicious of the modern interest in method (a concern associated today with foundationalism—so called by the antifoundationalists). However, I argue that there is indeed a foundational method that Voegelin employed and developed throughout his work which he explicitly elucidated only in his later writings. It may not have been a systematically formulated method; however, it comes into relief by Voegelin's very execution of it. Voegelin's method does not follow an externally imposed set of rules yielding certain objective truth, the bane of the antifoundationalists. Rather, it is a method based in the meditative confrontation with the great texts of history and the great experiences of transcendence that underlie them. Because such a confrontation is in turn based on the reader's awareness of, and responsiveness to the ground of existence, a confrontation which generates such attunement in one's soul, this method becomes a quest for truth and wisdom with the virtual power to yield, not certain knowledge, but personal, social, and historical order. Because of this transcendent orientation, and the convergence of faith and reason that such a quest requires, Voegelin's method is an implicitly theological one which no one to my knowledge has yet to explicitly discern and appraise (I shall do so in chapter 4).

The basic contention of this study is that Voegelin's monumental work, especially his later writings, is as germane to theology as it is to philosophy and political science. Although he is generally regarded as a political theorist and a philosopher of history, his work embodies numerous fields of study and unites them all, for his sole devotion is to truth alone, wherever it may lead. Voegelin is not easily pigeonholed. For example, philosophers think he is a theologian and theologians think he is a philosopher. Though the latter may be less disheartening than the former, this confusion says much about the disordered state of contemporary philosophy and theology which Voegelin often chided. He has tackled a number of theological issues although not in any fashion that one would deem conventional. His original (some would say unorthodox) treatment of traditional Christian doctrines contributes to his being of remarkable interest to theologians as well as a unique challenge to them. In spite of his generally negative (though, as we shall see, oftentimes warranted) depiction of theology and theologians as a whole, I believe Voegelin has provided theology with a profound analysis of human existence that spells out its genuine philosophical foundations. Indeed, of no other contemporary thinker could one say as unhesitatingly that the distinction between philosophy and theology, for all practical and theoretical purposes, virtually disappears. I believe Voegelin's entire philosophical enterprise is actually a veiled reconstruction of theology that I think theologians have by and large yet to recognize. In the name of philosophy Voegelin has reproached and renewed, rebuked and rebuilt, theology. In any case, since both philosophical and theological components are necessarily contained in any critical inquiry of reality, evoked by, and grounded in, the religious horizon of the inquirer, one could, therefore, call Voegelin's whole project a "theological philosophy" or a "noetic theology."

It must be said from the outset that any attempt to identify the theological significance of Voegelin's work must resist the temptation to turn him into a Christian theologian.[4] He was not a confessional Christian believer in the traditional sense and he held no ecclesial attachments. Indeed, he found most "church theology" to be philosophically lame if not intellectually bankrupt; and of course as a philosopher he never felt beholden to the party line of any ecclesial authority. Nonetheless, by successfully annexing faith and reason, reason and revelation, philosophy and theology, Athens and Jerusalem, in a critical theory of consciousness, he has reconstructed the authentic foundations of theology. Furthermore, his own meditative exploration of reality has been executed in a language that thwarts the hypostatizing doctrinalization that kills the spirit of both philosophy and theology as well as faith itself. Because of his careful precision in formulating his analyses of experiences and texts, Voegelin's own texts should effectively impede the onslaught of future ideological construal. An astute reader of Voegelin will discover that he is simply not an apologist for any doctrinaire "position," a quality of his mind which has provoked not a little consternation among even his most ardent admirers who see him as supporting their cause. As a scientist Voegelin rejects dogmatisms in all forms, whether political or religious, of the Right or of the Left. Any truth that claims to be absolute and final, and any club, sect, school, social movement, thinker, or believer who claims to possess such a truth, is anathema to Voegelin's sensitive, "skeptical," mystical mind.

On this matter of dogma and its deforming tendency can Voegelin's pejorative view of theology be explained. The problem with traditional Christian theology, according to Voegelin, lies in its origin in the Middle Ages. It first arose under the peculiar confluence of revelation and philosophy and was given the name "metaphysics," a term which was introduced into the Western vocabulary by the Arab translators of Aristotle's *meta ta physica*, and popularized by St. Thomas in his commentary on that work. The *Metaphysics* was the Aristotelian "first philosophy" or "theology," which for Aristotle was no more than a general pointer to the area beyond the categories that apply to physical phenomena.[5] Under the influence of Thomas, however, philosophy and revelation, the two differentiated modes of knowing reality, were transformed into doctrinal propositional form, thus creating a derivative language that became divorced from the originating experiences and their symbolization, the primary language that gave the theophanic events in history substance and meaning. Thus "metaphysics" became the rubric for denoting what medieval philosophers did when they theologized, i.e., spoke of the transcendent order and ground of things. It entailed a complicated new language, propositional in form, which separated it from the primary philosophical language of Plato and Aristotle. This development of course also separated reason from revelation, turning them into the two independent sources of truth with the Church gaining a monopoly on revelation while converting Plato's *nous* to "natural reason," thus eliminating the transcendent ground and end of reason itself. This "natural reason" later became the utilitarian reason of Enlightenment rationalism, the mode of intramundane knowing of things, of Cartesian clear and distinct ideas, of modern verifiable scientific truth, of cognitive consciousness divorced from any revelatory character.

The historical roots of this deformation are further explained by the fact that the problem confronted in the early medieval context was the fundamental tension between faith and reason that has its origin in the two different ethnic cultures of Israel and Hellas. In these diverse cultures the Israelite prophets and the Hellenic philosophers had a differentiating experience of the divine Beyond that was focused, respectively, on the revelatory appeal and the human quest. According to Voegelin, these "two types of consciousness had to face new problems when the political events of the Ecumenic Age cut them loose from their moorings in their ethnic cultures and forced their confrontation under the multicivilizational conditions of an ecumenic empire."[6] With the introduction in the twelfth century of Aristotle's epistemology as the new foundation for thought, the problems of faith and reason were faced once again. A solution of sorts was reached in the medieval synthesis of scholastic philosophy and theology that followed, but still they were inadequately solved, leading to the disintegration of faith and reason in modern thought.[7]

Voegelin's diagnosis of the disintegration is acutely captured in the following passage:

> Christian theology has denatured the Platonic *Nous* by degrading it imaginatively to a "natural reason," a source of truth subsidiary to the overriding source of revelation; by an act of imaginative oblivion the revelatory tension in Plato's vision of the *Nous* as the "third god" was eclipsed, in order to gain for the Church a monopoly on revelation. But history has taken its revenge. The nonrevelatory reason, imagined by the theologians as a servant, has become a self-assertive master. In historical sequence, the imagined nonrevelatory reason has become the real antirevelatory reason of the Enlightenment revolt against the Church. The resistance to the social

power of intellectually inert, self-assertive institutions has motivated the acts of imaginative oblivion that eclipse the noetic-revelatory truth preserved in ecclesiastical doctrines that have become inflexible.[8]

Accordingly, the formulations of medieval theology in a doctrinal mode, whatever their existential value in the history of Christianity,[9] have today become an inadequate method of analysis and exploration of reality. To correct this deformation, Voegelin spent a lifetime recovering the primary languages of myth, philosophy, revelation, and mysticism with their respective noetic and pneumatic structures in consciousness.[10] Through a process of dedoctrinalization and experiential rejuvenation Voegelin attempted to regain the authentic roots of theology in Plato and Aristotle, and in his late essays, as we shall see, even in the great theologian of the Middle Ages, St. Anselm.

In Voegelin's view the primary problem of theology, then, has been its centuries-long tendency to adopt the "metaphysical" language of the medieval thinkers. The transformation of primary symbols which emerge from myth, philosophy, and revelation, into hypostatized entities which can then serve as the subject of propositional, doctrinal state-ments and be given various predications, is a deformation because no reality, certainly no transcendent reality, can become an independent, autonomous reality apart from the consciousness that explores its truth.[11] The fateful dogmatisms and ideologies of modernity, which separated humans from the ground of true order, often violently, were the logical consequence of the intellectual *scotosis* that followed in the wake of the so-called medieval synthesis. Having become socially dominant over time, such a dogmatic/ideological enterprise and its attendant language still forms to this day the manner of discourse that real philosophy and theology must continually struggle against. When consciousness hardens in such a fashion, reality is eclipsed, supplanted by "second realities," projections of human will to power, and even the "death of God." The catastrophic results of this antitheistic development tell the dire history of the modern age. This hardening of consciousness can corrupt even the greatest minds who attempt to resist its linguistic deformation. Among the moderns Voegelin finds in Hegel the greatest ignominy, but this "trauma of the Orthodox environment," as he calls it, has victimized even Hegel's greatest predecessors and successors, the whole gamut of German thinkers from Leibniz to Feuerbach, Nietzsche, Jung, and Heidegger.[12] In a passage summarizing this development, Voegelin declared that it was the bias of the Enlightenment thinkers to

arrogate the authority of noetic truth for their resistance to it; in the form of the various ideologies, resistance to noetic truth, understanding itself as resistance to "irrationality," has become the ultimately legitimizing source of truth revealed. The usurped monopoly of revelation has migrated from the ecclesiastic institutions to their ideological successor establishments, down to the revelatory "statements" through acts of violent destruction in the contemporary movements of terrorism.[13]

This deformation of consciousness which culminates in the murder of God leaves a number of deformed symbols of God in its wake. The enlightened debate about God, says Voegelin, is comic:

> The God who is declared dead is alive enough to have kept his undertakers nervously busy by now for three centuries. Yet the life he is leading, before and after his death, is troubled and complicated. When interrogated by eminent thinkers, he does not seem to be sure whether he is a substance or a subject (Spinoza/Hegel), or perhaps both, or whether he perhaps does not exist at all, whether he is personal or impersonal, whether conscious or unconscious, whether rational or irrational, whether spirit only or matter too (Spinoza), whether he is perhaps only a regulative idea (Kant), whether he is identical with himself, or not, or whether he is the identity of identity and nonidentity (Hegel), whether he is an ontological or a theological being, or both, or whether he is something entirely different (Heidegger). What is absolute in this ambiguous debate about the Absolute is its deadly seriousness. The only one permitted to laugh in the situation appears to be God.[14]

Thus marks a centuries-long process of deculturation. In an earlier essay Voegelin remarked about this process that

> the grotesque rubble into which the image of God is broken today is not somebody's wrong opinion about the nature of man but the result of a secular process of destruction. . . . And least of all can anything be achieved by pitting right doctrine against wrong doctrine, for doctrinization precisely is the damage that has been inflicted on the movement of the search. There would be no doctrines of deformed existence today unless the search of both philosophy and the gospel had been overlaid by the late-medieval, radical doctrinization of both metaphysics and theology.[15]

Voegelin often mentions the *Parmenides* as the Platonic text written to combat this hardening of consciousness in antiquity. In the sophistic context of Plato's time, a context not too dissimilar to the dogmatic one of the Middle Ages and modernity, the question concerning "the One" took on various misunderstandings. In this dialogue Plato explored in detail the various predicates that the One can be given when a soul is not attuned to its transcendent mystery. For Plato the One signifies the Beyond, the *epekeina*, that is even beyond the predicates "existence" and "Being," and thus it would be as true to say that the One has no being and does not exist as it would be to say that it exists and has being. The paradoxical conclusion of the last sentence of the dialogue, therefore, is not an aporietic statement as conventionally interpreted, but a precise rendering of the reality of the One which for a philosopher is beyond any predication. Therefore, such questions as, "Does the One exist?" "Does it have Being?" "Is it past, present, or future?" "Is it like or unlike, equal or unequal, greater or lesser than itself or anything else?" etc. (which Plato probably heard all the time in the Academy and in frustration was motivated to write the dialogue) are rendered silly. As Voegelin often reminds us, Plato himself warned that anyone who interpreted him as having doctrines about anything did not understand what he as a philosopher was up to. Indeed, doctrines about ultimate reality are ultimately fruitless since Mystery can never be captured in propositional terms.

What Plato was up to, for Voegelin, was not "metaphysics" but a way of investigating reality that entailed a meditative exploration of one's experience articulated in language symbols, a quest motivated by the erotic response to the divine pull on one's soul. This method of exploration that carries the name philosophy also under certain contexts can be called theology, not in the medieval sense of propositional metaphysics but in its truly original, classical sense, as the faithful, meditative inquiry into the whole of reality mediated by experiences of transcendence. It was this understanding of theology that was first formulated by Plato in the Greek fourth century. In fact it is Plato who invents the word "theology" (*theologias*) in the second book of the *Republic* (379a) to describe both the positive and negative types of propositions about the gods. These *logoi* describe one of the two possible responses to the divine appeal, either formative response or deformative resistance. The truth or falsity of the *typoi peri theologias*, the types of theology, lie not in the propositions as such but in the existential state of the one who utters them. The truth of the positive propositions is neither self-evident nor provable. They are as empty as the negative propositions if they are not supported in experience by the actual reality of human assent to the divine appeal. But more than simply a symbolization or verbal mimesis of divine truth, the positive propositions, or doctrinal statements if you will, act as a defense against the negative ones.[16] In its origin, in Plato's discussion of "theology," this was the primary function of true propositional statements: to counter the false ones.[17] If these "doctrines" are taken as embodying the truth in themselves, they will derail into the foolishness of believing that their truth is ultimate.[18] The word of human beings that struggles to express the Word of God is ultimately penultimate.[19] To believe otherwise is to rank among the fools that both Plato, and later St. Anselm, found themselves resisting. Thus, "theology" in its Platonic origins denotes the philosophical attempt in speech to discriminate between "the response or non-response of divine presence in personal, social, and historical existence,"[20] the noetic response of the soul to the divine appeal that is a potentiality in the metaxic existence of every human being. It is therefore the attempt to regain the divine order of human existence in truth in resistance to the falsehood of deformed existence. Thus, "theology" is Plato's philosophical neologism that emerges out of a decaying social context where philosophy is ordered to die the death of its destruction by sophistic, dogmatic, atheistic corruption (the fate of Socrates) in order to be reborn like a phoenix with its divine foundation renewed in the true stories of divine–human *metalepsis,*[21] the very same "old truth" compactly articulated by the pre-Socratic poets and philosophers. Consequently, theology is an inquiry into reality that inevitably has as its existential context social, religious, and educational structures that inadequately, even deformatively, mediate the divine. Indeed, theology, as a search for transcendent order, was born in the confrontation with these defective structures in ancient Greece. Its authoritative status is timeless.

Based on this discovery, Voegelin's work not only eradicates the conventional dichotomy between philosophy and theology but also seeks to recover the original theological enterprise in the mind of Plato. In gist Voegelin has identified and overcome the deforming inadequacies of the medieval synthesis through the retrieval of Platonic "theology," the method employed to investigate reality in its transcendent fullness that is essentially no different from philosophy, the quest for truth via the meditative exploration of theophanic experiences and their symbolizations in history. Theology, like philosophy, is constituted by the quest for the ground of one's existence motivated by faith, hope, and love (the Christian theological virtues); it is the love of divine wisdom through an endless search for its truth. This quest does not yield definitional concepts that can easily, and inevitably, lose their mooring to the original experiences from which they arose but, rather, bears language symbols that are the imaginative product of a seeker of truth. Of course a philosopher/theologian in his or her own exploration of reality will always seek ever-greater symbolic adequacy but, nevertheless, will also realize that no symbol loses its relative truth wherever it may lie on the historically ascending scale of compactness and differentiation.

How can theology be fundamentally identified with philosophy? Is this view of their essential oneness really legitimate? What about the traditional, time-honored methods and categories that for centuries have kept them distinct, that is, philosophy proceeding from wonder and natural reason and theology from revelation and faith? Voegelin has persuasively argued that philosophy in its classical formulation also proceeds from revelation and faith. Furthermore, given what we know about the rich diversification of divine presence in history and its structural manifestation in human consciousness, these traditional dichotomies must now be deemed obsolete. "We can no longer ignore," he says, "that the symbols of 'Faith' express the responsive quest of man just as much as the revelatory appeal, and that the symbols of 'Philosophy' express the revelatory appeal just as much as the responsive quest."[22]

In fact the real philosopher, as Voegelin argues, must necessarily (1) begin from the standpoint of faith (a claim most philosophers today would deny), (2) be open to revelation (indeed, the reflective quest for truth is initiated by revelatory events), (3) find his or her intellectual quest rooted in a community of fellow believers and inquirers (who if not lovingly present in one's own life are vicariously present through their historic texts), and (4) be motivated above all by personal experiences of conversion or "vision" which require anamnetic recovery (an interpretive exercise based in a reflective meditation that borders on prayer). Given these principles, how does such an inquiry differ from theology? Take away theology's traditional dogmatization and enlarge its scope to include the totality of human experience in its depths wherever or however it is symbolized, and they become virtually identical. This is the essential insight I believe that select texts of Voegelin's later writings make transparently clear, his most explicitly "theological" texts, which this study will eventually examine in chapter 4. There I will attempt to illuminate the essence of his method as a philosopher's *fides quaerens intellectum*.

If Voegelin's cryptotheological enterprise has been constructed in resistance to traditional theology (among other sources of deformation), it would follow that it has also been largely executed in defiance of the Church. Much of Voegelin's criticism of the Church[23] stems from the fact that through the centuries it neglected to teach the faithful that the soul remains the site of the unfolding process of divine revelation in history. In other words the soul is the direct locus of divine mediation, not an earthly institution, which at best can only invite and facilitate such mediation. This is a basic tenet of the gospel, the principle which authoritatively counters the Church's possessive control of revelation as a past event captured in canonized scriptures, dogmatic propositions, and reified symbols, thus making divine presence opaque to contemporary believers. To assent to spiritually empty formulas in the name of faith and authority, Voegelin believed, amounted to the abandonment of reason and not the proper intellectual humility (the *sacrificium intellectus*) before Mystery which faith is always in search of understanding.[24] The truths of faith are experiential and only secondarily symbolic and propositional. Faith cannot be assent to dogmatic propositions about "objective" events. Revelation is not information, not an "objective" event in the external world. For Voegelin the Church has for centuries been mired in hypostatic distortions and their puissant propagation. When creeds and doctrines become divorced from their experiential source in Mystery, one loses sight of reality. The result is blind belief, mindless fideism, fundamentalist perversion, and spiritual decay, which Voegelin seeks to abolish by his therapeutic emphasis on experience.

An illustration of this hypostatic distortion and ecclesial hegemony can be seen, for example, in Voegelin's repudiation of the idea of salvation history established by the Church and its theologians. Briefly, Voegelin's reproach of this doctrine is best explained by his theory of historiogenesis: the gnostic enterprise of constructing a unilinear image of history that culminates in the life of the author, a construct that Voegelin's historical science found to be absent in the differentiating events of revelation.[25] The upshot of Voegelin's critique of such an enterprise is his conclusion that there is no essentially Christian meaning of history, the false supposition among Christian theologians going back to Augustine and even Paul. No religious tradition, including Christianity, has a monopoly on revelation. The totality of human existence in history, and the irruptions of saving events experienced therein, is irreducible to a single, chronological course of development. Such imperialistic theologizing is today untenable, indicative of a metastatic enterprise. Voegelin's philosophy of history confronts any claim to a finality of meaning, even the Christian one. Voegelin would likewise reject the Christian doctrine of the Second Coming as a metastatic distortion of history or "an immanentist hypostasis of the eschaton,"[26] though he would support the truth of the eschatological hope and transfiguring process that the symbol represents, but only in the nonapocalyptic, nonphenomenal sense. The saving tale of saving Love being revealed in the mystery of history is not a salvation history with a definitive historical beginning and a definitive historical end with definitive episodes in between that can be unilaterally discerned and directed by historians, theologians, philosophers, priests or prophets, or any human being. Rather, the movement of history is an unfinished drama that human beings participate in and comprehend only from their limited vantage point in the middle, that is, in the present moment between an inadequately knowable past and an unknowable future.

Since reality is an unfinished process its meaning can never be expressed definitively. If this is so then what is the contribution of Christianity in understanding the process of history? This book will eventually attempt to answer this question, but for now let it suffice that in Voegelin's mind Christianity seems to be nothing other than a fuller differentiation of life in the *metaxy*.[27] It is that simple and yet that profound. That "there is no history other than the history constituted in the Metaxy of differentiating consciousness"[28] is a characteristically compact Voegelinian statement which surely portends significant theological overhaul. This study will attempt to unpack the meaning of this provocative declaration.

This book comprises six chapters. Chapters 1, 2, 3, and 4 elucidate the substance of Voegelin's thought. This exposition of Voegelin's work attempts, not only to articulate the thrust of his historical investigations, but, more importantly, to explain the theory of consciousness that underlies all of his extensive studies. This theory of consciousness, which he spent a lifetime developing, is the framework for all of his philosophical and historical inquiries. The development of this theory can be traced through three distinct periods in his career. Tracing this development gives some chronological structure to this study. Thus, chapters 1 and 2 focus on the early and middle periods of Voegelin's work, while chapters 3 and 4 concentrate on Voegelin's later period when he produced his mature philosophy of history. Chapter 4 will specifically examine Voegelin's final work, especially the volume *In Search of Order*, which brings to a conclusion his masterwork, *Order and History*. Although unfortunately attenuated by his death, this unfinished volume marks the culmination of his philosophical labors. A careful reading of this text by any serious student of Voegelin's work will certify that it actually marks a fourth and final stage in Voegelin's lifelong quest for truth. This text sets the standard by which to read his whole corpus.[29] Along with Voegelin's other late essays, some of them only recently published as the inaugural volume of his collected works, *In Search of Order* comprises perhaps the most penetrating and most demanding philosophical meditations of our time. The theological significance of these writings abounds. I hope to show how they consummate Voegelin's singular importance and prominent challenge to contemporary theology and how his theory of consciousness bears upon a reconstruction of theology. For these reasons, and because these last writings are now beginning to be reviewed and analyzed by the scholarly community, this relatively small body of work merits extensive and detailed study.

Because I believe Voegelin's contribution is found primarily in his theory of consciousness, his grand hermeneutical and historical investigations, and his noetic analysis of transcendent experiences and their symbolizations, which together comprise the direction for a methodical theology, some comparison with another foundational and methodological thinker in theology, whose work has also been grounded in a theory of consciousness, would be quite salutary. Therefore, I devote chapter 5 of this work to an exposition of one of the most important foundational theologians today who has had particular impact in contemporary Catholic theology, namely, Bernard Lonergan. Lonergan has worked out a differentiated account of human consciousness and its cognitive structure in a manner quite different from Voegelin. Lonergan's theological method, based on his analysis of cognitional intentionality, has gone a long way in meeting the quest for an adequate foundational theology for the contemporary world. An analysis of Lonergan's theological method, which came to the fore in his latter thought, followed by a dialectical mediation of his work with Voegelin's, will punctuate the diverse quest for foundations in contemporary philosophy and theology, as well as bring Voegelin into a theological community of discourse.

Voegelin's work, though quite unique, actually penetrates to the very same important issues raised by Lonergan and foundational theologians as a whole. Like Lonergan, the major importance of Voegelin's contribution is foundational. Both of them have provided theoretical principles and a critical linguistic framework for doing philosophy and theology that will keep generations of scholars busy. And both have frequently expressed the magnitude of work that remains to be done along the lines they have developed. This alone attests to their stature, for we are forced to acknowledge that these great thinkers did not write for the age but for the ages. This is not a chapter that compares the thought of these two major thinkers point by point.[30] In spite of their common concern with the nature of consciousness and their respective efforts to achieve a viable, universal method or foundational theory for handling the global totality of human experience and its symbolizations in history, there are real divergences in their thinking on some fundamental matters. These differences will be pointed out in the final section of chapter 5. However, my basic purpose for drawing on Lonergan's foundational thought is to present a complementary work in philosophical theology that will help illuminate the theological significance of Voegelin's religious philosophy. Indeed, to use such terms as philosophical theology, religious philosophy, and foundational theology may well obfuscate the single quest for truth that Voegelin epitomized throughout his life. Following Plato, he believed that the name for this quest is to be called quite simply "philosophy," the love of wisdom.

Chapter 6 draws together the most important facets of Voegelin's thought in light of the foundational quest in theology. The implications of Voegelin's thought are applied to certain pressing and still-unanswered questions that his work evokes, particularly his controversial treatment of Christianity and its christological underpinnings. I conclude this final chapter with a summary of principles that make up the heart of a "Voegelinian theology."

If it is true that Voegelin's philosophical work is equivalent to a foundational theology, then contemporary theologians have much to learn from Voegelin and may even find themselves being transformed if they take his work seriously.[31] His hermeneutical method can be construed as a theological method minus the conventional theological apriorities. Though his work is radically oriented to religious experiences and their symbolizations in history, mediated by memory, language, and texts, it is also based on the personal appropriation of these experiences through one's meditative, anamnetic, and philosophical consciousness. He is as emphatic as Lonergan on the centrality of personal conversion as the immanent source of transcendent order, and his writing deliberately invites the reader into such a conversion through the self-appropriation of intellectual and spiritual interiority. As this whole study demonstrates, Voegelin's mind, like Lonergan's and any true theologian's, is engaged in "faith seeking understanding." Indeed, whatever one makes of Voegelin's thought, it is hard to dispute the profound employment of *fides quaerens intellectum* in his work.

I conclude this introduction to the work of a great philosopher by repeating my own appreciation for his work. The order of human consciousness in its search for transcendent order has, for me, found no greater expression in our time. I hope that this study of Eric Voegelin will inspire a like appreciation.

1

TOWARD A PHILOSOPHY OF CONSCIOUSNESS: THE EARLY WRITINGS, 1928–50

The development of Eric Voegelin's thought progressed by some inner necessity through three distinct stages, and his last writings hark towards another phase. His work began with the study of political science and law, shifted toward political philosophy and its history, and culminated in a philosophy of history grounded in a philosophy of consciousness. The last phases cover about a thirty-year period in which he produced his *magnum opus, Order and History*.[1] This body of writing represents the hallmark of his work and provides the most theologically relevant material for this study. But before we embark on an analysis of Voegelin's work, a brief review of his personal background will shed some light on the evolution of his thought.[2]

Voegelin's Background

It should not surprise us that a person's philosophy, insofar as it is marked by a return to the concrete, would be motivated by some very concrete experiences. For Voegelin, these experiences were political in nature. In his later years he remarked that "the motivations of my work . . . are simple. They arise from the political situation."[3] The political situation of Voegelin's early life was a world in crisis: the First World War, the collapse of the Austro-Hungarian Empire, the Bolshevik revolution in Russia, the rise of political ideologies in Europe both Left and Right, such as communism, socialism, fascism, and national socialism, and the totalitarian, murderous regimes of Stalin and Hitler. Since his student days in Vienna the world was his classroom. By these troubling events his political and intellectual formation was procured by the hardest of schools. As a result, his scientific quest for truth had to find its way through a miasma of conflicting ideologies and methodologies. The philosophical search for order in the midst of disorder was well grounded in Voegelin's personal experience. In the midst of disaster his search led to a wisdom born of suffering.

In large part, the motivation behind Voegelin's analysis of consciousness can be pinpointed to one very prevalent phenomenon of the twentieth century. It is probably the most concrete and the most horrible problem of our time: mass murder. In an autobiographical statement written two years before his death, Voegelin tells us that

> this reality of murdering through inspired idiocy was a fundamental problem that induced me to deal with experiences of the social structures within which human experiences move, and the results of them. . . .
>
> Concrete experiences like this motivated the direction in which my research headed, and I should perhaps say the strongest influence is my perhaps misplaced sensitivity toward murder. I do not like people just shooting each other for nonsensical reasons. That is a motive for finding out what possibly could be the reason someone could persuade somebody else to shoot people for no particular purpose. It is not simply an academic problem, or a problem in the history of opinion and so on, that evokes my interest in this or that issue in the theory of consciousness, but the very practical problem of mass murder which is manifest in the twentieth century.[4]

How can interest in the theory of consciousness be motivated by the practical problem of murder? To answer this question, one must first understand concrete influences, both existential and intellectual.

Voegelin's early years were lived in direct confrontation with, and defiance of, national socialism, one of the more grotesquely murderous ideologies run amok in the modern world from which Voegelin himself barely escaped with his life.[5] During this formative period of the 1930s Voegelin published four books in German, all growing out of his opposition to the pseudo-religion of nazism.[6] Two of these works, *Rasse und Staat* and *Die Rassenidee in der Geistesgeschichte von Ray bis Carus*, dealt specifically with the idea of race, its deformation by the race theorists behind Aryan nationalism, and the inherent connection of these theories with biological scientism, pseudo-religious ideologies, and totalitarian regimes.[7] Upon the books' publication in 1933 they were almost immediately suppressed by the Nazis. This act of courage on Voegelin's and his publisher's behalf had the consequence of putting him on the Nazis' list of enemies, so that after the Anschluss in 1938 he had to flee for his life.

But the Nazi menace was not the only ideology that motivated Voegelin's search for an adequate theory of consciousness, for there were other mass movements that "threatened, and still threaten, to engulf Western Civilization in their political prison culture."[8] As Voegelin tells us, all the school-philosophies of the time failed to come to terms with them:

> The analysis of the movements of Communism, Fascism, National Socialism, and racism, of constitutionalism, liberalism, and authoritarianism had made it clear beyond a doubt that the center of a philosophy of politics had to be a theory of consciousness: but the various academic institutions of the Western world, the various schools of philosophy, the rich manifold of methodologies, did not offer the intellectual instruments that would make the political events and movements intelligible.[9]

And further on he tells us why: "The default of the school philosophies was caused by a restriction of the horizon similar to the restrictions of consciousness that I could observe in the political mass movements."[10] By this "restriction of the horizon," Voegelin means the refusal to ask questions about sectors of reality that were intentionally prohibited by the intellectual Zeitgeist of the 1920s and 1930s,

> such as the neo-Kantianism of the Marburg school, the value philosophy of the Southwest German school, the value-free science of Max Weber, the positivism of the Viennese school, of Wittgenstein, and of Bertrand Russell, the legal positivism of Kelsen's Pure Theory of Law, the phenomenology of Husserl, and, of course, Marx and Freud.[11]

Nevertheless, Voegelin informs us that there was no absence of revolt against the school-philosophies and their restrictive deformations.[12] He became greatly interested in all those who attempted to recover the content of consciousness through historical restoration and original perception. Among those who strongly formed his own horizon were the French philosophers of revolt: Camus and Bergson; the restorers of the German language: Stephen George and his circle; the existentialists: Jaspers and Kierkegaard; the European literary giants: Proust, Valéry, Joyce, Mann, Musil, and Kraus; the civilizational historians: Meyer, Spengler, and Toynbee; and especially the restorers of Platonic phi-losophizing and Platonic myth: Friedlaender, Hildebrandt, and Salin.[13] From these people Voegelin appropriated an understanding of concrete consciousness, whose quality depended upon the unrestrained horizon of the concrete human being, and on the flourishing of the individual's desire to know. It was a consciousness that could not be restricted to a transcendental ego or to an *a priori* structure whose horizon was given. Rather, he discovered consciousness to be a ceaseless process of questioning, ordering, expanding, articulating, and correcting itself—an event in the reality of which it partakes, a continuous effort to respond, lovingly, through an "open soul" to the appeal of reality:

What I discovered was consciousness in the concrete, in the personal, social, and historical existence of man, as the specifically human mode of participation in reality. At the time, however, I was far from clear about the full bearing of the discovery because I did not know enough about the great precedents of existential analysis in antiquity, by far surpassing, in exactness and luminosity of symbolization, the contemporary efforts. I was not aware, for instance, of the Heraclitian analysis of public and private consciousness, in terms of the *xynon* and the *idiotes*, or of a Jeremiah's analysis of prophetic existence, before I learned Greek and Hebrew in the 1930s.[14]

During this period, Voegelin found in the classic philosophers, particularly Plato and Aristotle, the appropriate language for analyzing the state of order and disorder in both the soul and society. He discovered that Plato was the first to ask and answer adequately the central questions pertaining to the essential problems of human existence, which are as applicable today as they were in fourth-century Greece.

The richly textured analytical insights he gained from Plato could be reduced to two: "The polis is the human being writ large," and "God is the measure of the human being." The first is Plato's anthropological principle articulated most emphatically in the *Republic*.[15] The second is Plato's theological principle found principally in both the *Republic*[16] and the *Laws*.[17] Neither of these principles is a self-evident truth. They are insights acquired through the differentiation of the *psyche* as the seat of transcendent experiences in the human being. They arise by a process of conversion, which is the great subject of the *Republic*. At the center of this dialogue, Plato placed the parable of the cave with its description of the *periagoge*, or conversion, the turning around from the untruth of existence in sophistic society to the truth of the transcendent Measure, which is to say, to the new truth about God.

From these principles Voegelin was able to build upon Plato's philosophy of order in his own study of order and history. In brief, the validity of the Platonic and Aristotelian standards of political order rests on the conception of an individual who can be the measure of society because God is the measure of his or her soul (*Laws* 716c–d). The true authority in a society is located in the one whose soul is attuned to the divine measure, the ultimate source of order. For Plato this is represented by the *daimonios aner*, the spiritual person; for Aristotle it is the *spoudaios*, the mature, virtuous person. If the parallel can be drawn with the appropriate caution, it could be said that the enemies of Plato, the sophists who engage in eristics and other intellectual trickery (as against dialectics or true inquiry), become, for Voegelin, the ideologues who engage in propaganda and mind control, whether it be in the form of positivism and behaviorism, or nazism and communism. Whatever form the destructive deformation takes, Voegelin was convinced from the beginning that the ruinous disorder in the individual human soul, which is always writ large in society, is essentially a problem of consciousness.[18]

For Voegelin, as for Plato, the only recourse one has at hand to combat the various deformations that surround one is philosophy itself, or, more precisely, reason or noetic consciousness. It is the life of reason that brings one into attunement with the divine ground of being. Reason is the dimension of the *psyche* that orders human existence intellectually, spiritually, and politically. However, Voegelin also shares Plato's rather pessimistic view of the positive and efficacious function of philosophy in the world. If Voegelin appears to avoid practical politics by not offering specific policies and encouraging direct political action to cure society of its ills, it is because he has been so impressed by the destruction caused by the modern-day messiahs and their programs of annihilation that his first concern is to recover the sense of creatureliness and finitude that constitute one's humanity. His priority has been to teach the inherent limits of existence in the *metaxy*.[19]

As Plato fought the sophistic forces that led to the inevitable decay of the polis, Voegelin, as a philosopher, believed that the first action to take is to resist the forces of chaos by illuminating the forces of order and disorder in the soul and society. To this end, then, the recovery of philosophy is paramount because it alone has the capacity to bring to consciousness these very forces of good and evil. The philosopher, thus, as a rule, does not prescribe specific policies of political action on the institutional level. In the midst of a corrupt society, the philosopher's role is primarily one of resistance:

> Philosophy is not a doctrine of right order, but the light of wisdom that falls on the struggle; and help is not a piece of information about truth, but the arduous effort to locate the forces of evil and identify their nature. For half the battle is won when the soul can recognize the shape of the enemy and, consequently, knows that the way it must follow leads in the opposite direction.[20]

In this sense, Voegelin believes that philosophy has no utilitarian purpose beyond itself, since the love of wisdom is practiced for its own sake. Furthermore, it is nearly powerless in effecting the course of ideological movements which require centuries to disintegrate. This is inevitably the case since the *modus operandi* of philosophy is always persuasion (*peitho*), not force, and so it can only hope to influence the few. But if philosophy can be said to have a positive social aim, it would be to make reason an ordering force in society by producing, through education or *paideia*, enough reasonable and mature people who would assume positions of rule, or at least have a governing influence on society at large. Though not utilitarian, this should be considered philosophy's therapeutic function in society at large.[21]

Disorder in society is rooted in what Plato called the *anoia* or *amathes*, the ignorant and dull-witted fools who invariably hold positions of power. Of course it is not only those in political institutions who cause the decay of the polis or the disintegration of culture; it is the managers of the "climate of opinion," the "philodoxers"[22] who refuse to engage in noetic consciousness or *nous*. The *nous*, as the classic philosophers understood it, is the human capacity for seeking true knowledge, as opposed to *doxa* (opinion), under the guidance of attraction toward the transcendent. Reason in search of divine wisdom was given such a sublime valuation by Plato that he considered it the divine substance itself, immanent in human being; so much so that Plato in the *Laws* called *nous* "the Third God" who will rule after the age of Kronos and the age of Zeus.[23] This experience of *nous* was the central experience of Platonic politics. It inspired the consciousness of epoch: the age of the people's myth was drawing to a close only to be superseded by the new age of the philosophers, the sons of Zeus. It was the age initiated by Socrates and Plato. This experience of epoch found its expression in Plato's new myth of the soul, articulated first and foremost in *Gorgias* and the *Republic*, as well as in the triadic symbolism of history developed in the *Laws*.[24]

Since reason is what attunes us to God, then reason, properly speaking, is not the instrumental rationality of the Enlightenment thinkers who did indeed endow reason with a utilitarian purpose, i.e., progress or "enlightenment." Reason, however, is not "natural" or "merely human" but revelatory and divine. Therefore, Voegelin insists on using reason as Plato and the pre-Socratic philosophers understood it:

> Reason . . . was formulated in the Greek fifth century denoting the tension between man as a human being and the Divine ground of his existence of which he is in search. The consciousness of being caused by the Divine ground and being in search of the Divine ground—that is reason. Period. That is the meaning of the word "reason." That is why I always insist on speaking of noetic and use the term *nous*: in order not to get into the problems of the ideological concept of reason of the eighteenth century.[25]

We can begin to see why Voegelin's emphasis through the years shifted from politics to history to consciousness, although from the beginning he knew full well that these three dimensions of reality were inseparable. In his book of 1952, *The New Science of Politics*,

Voegelin opened with the sentence, "The existence of man in political society is historical existence; and a theory of politics if it penetrates to principles, must at the same time be a theory of history."[26] In *Order and History*, volume IV, *The Ecumenic Age*, the work that contains his mature philosophy of history, Voegelin drew out the logical extension of this formula. It is the unstated principle that already greatly informed his theoretical work *Anamnesis*: the existence of the human being is conscious existence; and a theory of history, if it penetrates to principles, must at the same time be a theory of consciousness. This formula has now become the foundational precept that undergirds his latest work, particularly *Order and History*, volume V, *In Search of Order*.[27]

This procedure of uniting a theory of politics with a theory of history and consciousness, however, must not be construed as an innovation. As Voegelin reminds us, it is a restorative enterprise since these components of reality were inseparably united when political science was founded by Plato.

To epitomize by way of introduction, then, it can be said that the core of Voegelin's achievement rests on his theoretical analysis of the emerging truth of reality and its structure, as this truth manifests itself to human consciousness in history. For Voegelin, this analysis must be derived from the historical materials themselves, not superimposed upon them. This precept is certified by his famous theoretical principle which opens his *magnum opus*, *Order and History*: "The order of history emerges from the history of order."[28] This is the fundamental canon that guides his hermeneutics of history from beginning to end.[29]

What, then, is the fundamental order that emerges in history? For Voegelin, the process of history reveals a certain order that is inescapable. This order, which he continually calls to our attention, is the tension of human existence, the Platonic *metaxy*, which structures our experience of reality and which the utopian dreamers in their libidinous construction of "second realities" must deny. It is a tension which comes to illumination through the theophanic experiences, both compact and differentiated, that reveal the divine ground of being. History, therefore, is structured by this movement from compact to differentiated experience, from a less adequate to a more adequate awareness of being. These are the experiences which are symbolized by those who undergo them and which reveal a concomitant differentiation of consciousness. A return to these experiences of reality, particularly to the most differentiated experiences of transcendence, would not only give new life to old symbols, deadened by a process of hypostatization and dogmatization, but also point us in the direction of true authoritative order by which we can take our bearings personally, socially, and historically.

So by way of a hermeneutics of recovery, Voegelin has worked out his own theory of history and consciousness. The task of this and the next three chapters, then, will be to analyze Voegelin's theory of consciousness, tracing its development from his early writings to his mature statement found in *The Ecumenic Age*, a few subsequent major essays, and his final work, *In Search of Order*. The development of Voegelin's theory can be followed according to three distinct phases. The first phase (roughly 1928–50) begins with his initial wrestling with the nature of consciousness in his first book of 1928. Something of a climax occurs with his theoretical breakthrough in 1943 which stemmed from his correspondence with Alfred Schutz. This phase must also include Voegelin's German works (1930s) and his history of ideas period (1940s). The second phase (about 1951–59) is the period between *The New Science of Politics* (1952) and the first three volumes of *Order and History* (1956–57), where he worked out the historical dimensions of his theory of consciousness. The third and final phase (1960–85) begins with the essays he published in the 1960s which led up to his last major book *The Ecumenic Age* (1974). This final period culminates in Voegelin's last work: *In Search of Order* (1987).[30]

It should be noted that these are not arbitrary divisions of Voegelin's intellectual career. The phases are clearly marked by a pronounced shift in his thinking that is exhibited in his work and to which Voegelin himself has attested in his autobiographical statements. The first shift was a result of his two years of study in the United States (1924–26), when he abandoned the Kantian idealism and legal positivism under which he had been trained in his youth, and adopted the commonsense philosophy represented by American thinkers like James, Dewey, Peirce, Santayana, Whitehead, and John Commons, as well as the Scottish philosopher of the eighteenth century, Thomas Reid.[31] The second shift was an abandonment of his nearly completed "History of Political Ideas" in the late 1940s. This was precipitated by a reading of Schelling, from whom he learned the secondary and derivative status of ideas and the need to penetrate to the experiences that underlie them. Consequently, Voegelin turned away from the history of ideas approach to an ambitious study of the foundational experiences of order and their symbolization in history.[32] The third shift was a result of his ongoing studies in gnosticism and pertained to his understanding of history. This is best reflected in *The Ecumenic Age*, where he abandoned the last vestiges of a historiogenetic conception of history in his thought, which he considered to be a gnostic symbolism, and espoused a radically nonlinear, eschatological conception of history.[33] Along with this turn came a more radical differentiation of the *metaxy* as the prime focus of his philosophy of history and consciousness.[34]

The Writings

One admirer of Voegelin has stated that "ever since his book *The New Science of Politics* was published in 1952, Eric Voegelin's reputation has been located among those thinkers we are prone to call 'well known' but not 'known well.' "[35] This is so mostly because readers of his work have failed to grasp the theory of consciousness that undergirds all of his writings.

The nature of consciousness was thematic in the very first book Voegelin wrote: *Über die Form des amerikanischen Geistes*, 1928. In the first chapter, written after his time of study in the United States, he embarked on a critical analysis of the current theories of time and perception.[36] Already he knew that the prevailing theories of consciousness were inadequate and would have to be overhauled. He rejected the materialistic and idealistic theories in vogue at the time because the former could not explain the existence of consciousness and the latter could not adequately account for the reality that transcends it. Also current were theories that conceived consciousness as a "stream" of perceptions, and on this basis analyzed its temporal structure in relation to objects of the external world. Voegelin criticized the theorists who represented this analysis of consciousness, particularly Hume, Brentano, Husserl, and Hodgson, as proposing, not an actual description of the phenomena of consciousness, but speculative constructions. He reproached the stream theorists because they understood all knowledge of reality according to the model of knowledge of external objects and neglected experiences of participation that are the prime source of knowledge. Voegelin believed that the concern of these English and Continental thinkers arose from a fundamentally skeptical position.[37] They reduced the fullness of consciousness to the problem of cognition, adhering particularly to the question of the unitary subject and that subject's transcendence into the external world. The American thinkers whom he admired (especially James and Peirce) did not consider this question to be a problem. Rather, they considered the issue of a cognitively self-transcending self a given, upon which to explain other more important matters.

It is to William James that Voegelin owed a real debt at this time. What influenced him most was James's conception of pure experience developed in his *Essays on Radical Empiricism* and *A Pluralistic Universe*.[38] The thrust of James's thought was to break down the wall of concepts so as to arrive at concrete experience. He attempted to recover the whole of experience behind the cloud of intellectual systems, dialectical abstractions, and philosophical constructs. According to James, consciousness as an entity does not exist. Instead, what exists as the stuff of reality is pure experience, of which knower and known are the inseparably linked parts of a whole. This means that mind or consciousness cannot be viewed as a distinct reality apart from the material world. There is only the one reality of experience which is immediately apprehended in the flux of existence. Only in reflection is this pure experience seen in its objective and subjective elements. Only in the experience itself, however, is reality "known" in its stark presence. This applies also to the relational aspects of experience. Against Hume and his successors, James argued that the relations within and among experiences are just as real as things experienced. Thus he made the point of saying that

> to be radical, an empiricism must neither admit into its constructions any element that is not directly experienced, nor exclude from them any element that is directly experienced. For such a philosophy, *the relations that connect experiences must themselves be experienced relations, and any kind of relation experienced must be accounted as 'real' as anything else in the system.*[39]

Perhaps here we can already discern a confirmation of the relational poles of experience that Voegelin would later come to emphasize in his analysis of noetic consciousness in Plato and Aristotle. In any case, there is in James to be found the fullness of experience and the warning against any hypostatizing reduction into subject and object that is prevalent in materialism and rationalism.

Voegelin's disdain for dogmatism found its intellectual roots in James. But more particularly, it was his return to personal, concrete experience, open to the divine reality beyond the self, that Voegelin found so appealing in James. In response to James's reliance on the normal, sympathetic relation to the universe that each person has in the intimacy of his or her experience, Voegelin coined the terms "open self" and "closed self."[40] Because of their skepticism, Voegelin considered the English philosophers "closed" within their atomized private existence, whereas he considered the American thinkers "open" because of their attunement to the mysterious whole of reality disclosed in pure experience. These symbols were a great factor in the formation of Voegelin's theory of consciousness. It found great resonance in Bergson's notion of the "open society" and the "closed society" articulated in his *Two Sources of Morality and Religion* which had a great influence on Voegelin when it appeared in 1932.[41]

In James's analysis of experience we can find the incipient features of Voegelin's later account of consciousness. At this point in Voegelin's career he had not yet seriously encountered Plato, but many of the symbolisms he would later stress in deference to Plato were already present in inchoate form in James, such as: consciousness as participatory, the consubstantiality of being, the flux of existence, the tensional poles in experience, and the self-reflective awareness of the beyond of existence.[42]

Voegelin, in this first book, did not go beyond his penetrating criticisms of the stream theory. At the time, he did not have the philosophical and historical knowledge necessary to develop a more adequate theory of consciousness, as he later admitted.[43] His only positive conclusion was that the mystery of the transcendence of consciousness into the world cannot be reduced to rational categories, nor can the being in which consciousness participates be divided into being that is symbolized and being that is not (such as Kant's "thing-in-itself"). To consciousness all being is symbolic; all of reality is subject to symbolizing consciousness and known therein, including consciousness itself when consciousness reflects on consciousness. An analysis of consciousness must maintain the tensional unity of the two aspects of being (symbol and symbolized). Since consciousness as activity is existential being and not symbolic being, the mystery of the transcendence of consciousness can be understood in depth only by the intimate examination of one's personal experiences, of one's own concrete consciousness.

This conclusion is what eventually led Voegelin to undertake his own "anamnetic experiments" in 1943.[44] But only after he gained the fundamental insights by way of a sustained critical confrontation with Husserl's philosophy did he experience the breakthrough to his own theory of consciousness expounded mostly in three letters to his friend Alfred Schutz in the same year.[45] In reflecting back on this struggle to formulate an adequate theory, Voegelin asserted in 1966 that

> the most important result of these efforts was the insight that a "theory" of consciousness in the sense of generically valid propositions concerning a pre-given structure was impossible. For consciousness is not a given to be deduced from outside but an experience of participation in the ground of being whose logos has to be brought to clarity through the meditative exegesis of itself. The illusion of a "theory" had to give way to the reality of the meditative process; and this process had to go through its phases of increasing experience and insight.[46]

This phase of 1943, in which he began to embark on the "meditative process," can be analyzed as follows:

Voegelin believed that the phenomenological investigations into the inner consciousness of time and existence, which became prevalent only in the nineteenth century, occupied the place that was held by meditation before the disintegration of Christian categories of thought. He claimed that "the analysis of the time-consciousness of world-immanent man is the laicist residue of the Christian ascertainment of existence in meditation with its spiritual climax of the *intentio animi* toward God."[47] The destruction of the traditional Christian symbolism, beginning in the seventeenth century with Descartes and culminating in the "radical philosophy of consciousness" of Husserl's transcendental subjectivity, was for Voegelin not a necessary progression but one in need of explanation. He found an explanation in the recurrent historical phenomenon of "reaction": a centuries-long reaction to a civilization in decline, a civilization whose traditional symbols had become questionable and even meaningless. The attempt to withdraw consciousness from its ontic context, its world and its history, and to reconstruct it out of the subjectivity of the I, he argued, is an attempt to provide a new foundation of the world, one grounded in the radical starting point that a transcendental consciousness offers. The need for this new beginning, this desire to make a *tabula rasa* out of consciousness, "will be felt when the symbolical language, in which the ontic contexts are couched, has become questionable, or—historically speaking—when a civilization with its symbols has fallen into a crisis."[48] Voegelin claimed that such a reaction is legitimate if the old symbolism can no longer communicate its value. Indeed, then there occurs "the indispensable requirement for the development of a new, more adequate symbolism."[49] However, the reaction against the crisis of the spirit in any age, no matter how legitimate, says nothing about the value of the new beginning as a positive spiritual reconstitution. What emerges as a reaction may be more corrupt than the tradition it attempts to replace. This was precisely how Voegelin judged the reaction of the nineteenth century:

> The development of the transcendental critique down to Husserl is characterized by the dissolution not only of traditional symbolic systems but also by the exclusion of the underlying areas of experiences and problems from the orbit of philosophical reflection. It is the fate of symbols in the history of the mind that transparence turns to "appearance". But that the reality they illuminated comes to be, if not downrightly denied, at any rate rejected as a motive of philosophizing, is a desperate move, a bankruptcy of philosophy. Transcendentalism has had magnificent successes in the clarifications of consciousness-structures in which the objective order of the world is constituted; but these successes cannot gloss over the abandonment

of philosophy as the creation of an order of symbols through which man's position in the world is understood. The creation of the transcendental I as the symbol of philosophy implies the destruction of the cosmic whole within which philosophizing becomes at all possible. The basic subjectivity of the egological sphere, Husserl's philosophical and nondiscussable ultimatum, is the symptom of a spiritual nihilism that still has merit as a reaction, but no more than that.[50]

The "abandoned philosophy" to which Voegelin alludes in this passage is the classic philosophy of Plato, which itself was a reaction against the first great crisis of Western civilization in the fifth century B.C. The merits of that reaction lie "in Plato's breadth of spirit, which enabled him to supplant the dying world of the polis with a new spiritual world based on the fundamental experiences of *thanatos, eros,* and *dike,* and that he had the creative imagination to develop a symbolic language adequate for the expression of the new psychic experiences."[51] A return to these experiences and their symbolic language enabled Voegelin to work out his own theory of consciousness in opposition to the inadequate theories of the time, and particularly as a counterposition to the "apodictic beginning" of Husserl's restrictive phenomenology.

What has been mentioned so far is chiefly Voegelin's conclusions to the problem of consciousness as he saw them in 1943. It remains to be seen in greater detail the exact nature of his critique of the stream theories and of Husserl's egological transcendentalism to which he responded with his own positive steps toward a theory of consciousness as illuminative.

First of all, the stream theory of consciousness conceived consciousness as a flow of perceptions experienced as the vanishing point of the present moment. This conception is false, for there is no stream of consciousness, except when a person's attention is focused upon a certain kind of simple perception. This focused perception, then, becomes a limit-experience, which for Voegelin was no basis upon which to construct an adequate theory. The example used unanimously by Brentano, Hodgson, and Husserl to depict this experience of the flow of consciousness was the experience of hearing a tone. The awareness of the tone is marked by the initial perception of its sound which glides into the past but is continuously remembered. But what we are aware of here in this limit-experience is not the nature of our consciousness but merely our consciousness of a continuing perception, which has its own peculiar structure.[52] If we considered instead another example, such as the experience of a painting, we would see that consciousness involves much more than a stream of isolated momentary perceptions.

In understanding a painting, one cannot turn one's perception to the flow of time which passes in the experience of looking at it. When one is trying to grasp the totality of the artwork and its meaning, time passes without being noticed. The perception of a painting has the function of a bodily entry into a spiritual realm that is not intrinsically conditioned by the flow of time. The experience itself is actually "timeless." It occurs in external time indeed, but without itself being temporally constituted. The choice of simple sense perception as a model for understanding the nature of consciousness is inappropriate because it is not true to the nature of experience. In fact, Voegelin saw it as a convoluted and artificial abstraction from our normal experiences. The vanishing point of the present moment seemed to carry fascination for these thinkers, because in it they saw a mode of transcendence from which they could derive a foundation of consciousness, which they could not attain through other spiritual means. A reliance on this sphere as a model of consciousness leads not to an adequate description of consciousness but to speculative constructions. It was Voegelin's contention that "the function of consciousness [is] *not* to flow but rather to constitute the spaceless and timeless world of meaning, sense, and the soul's order."[53] The ego which Husserl postulates as an agent in the constitution of consciousness seems rather to be a phenomenon *in* consciousness. Voegelin believed the I to be no given at all, but rather a complex symbol of certain perspectives of consciousness.[54]

The analysis of consciousness based on the stream theory Voegelin thought to be a dead end. Thus he embarked on his own analysis based on "the dimensions of inner illumination." Like the stream theories, his analysis began with the relationship between consciousness and time, but unlike them, his quickly led to the consideration of what those theories neglected: the historical dimension in the constitution of human consciousness, which for Voegelin required a critical assessment of the relationship between consciousness and myth.

First of all, he argued, consciousness experiences itself as having two dimensions of awareness, past and future. These dimensions of awareness are not the past and future of external time. Time does not exist "as such" apart from the process of a substance. I do not remember something that lies "in the past"; rather, I have a past because I can make present a completed process of consciousness through memory. Likewise, I do not "project" into the future. I have a future because my consciousness can imagine future possibilities. "Past and future," thus, become "the illuminatory dimensions of the process in which the energy center is engaged."[55] These illuminatory dimensions of past and future are not empty spaces but the structure of a finite process between birth and death. This is the only experience of process we can know "from within." All other processes, including the cosmological world-process, we can know only through extrapolation of this immanent process of consciousness. Since the process of consciousness is finite, we cannot know what transcends consciousness. There is an inherent conflict between the finite model of consciousness and the extrapolation of that model to account for the infinite beginning and end of world-process. This is the problem of the antinomies of infinity in Kant's sense. We have no experience of processes transcending consciousness, such as a causal beginning. As Voegelin put it, "the only time of which we do have an experience is the inner experience of the illuminated dimension of consciousness, the process that drops away, at both ends, into inexperienceable darkness."[56] In other words, consciousness can never experience a radical beginning or end. It always finds itself in the middle. Subsequently, the only adequate expression in extrapolating finite process to include the structure of infinite world-process is the myth. In this early articulation of the irrevocable function of myth Voegelin explained a mythical symbol to be "a finite symbol supposed to provide 'transparence' for a transfinite process."[57] Some examples are the myth of creation, the immaculate conception, speculations about the preexistence and postexistence of the soul, the fall, and original sin, all of which illuminate the mystery of finite existence in an infinite spiritual realm beyond birth and death. The myth is the symbolic language in which consciousness articulates itself. It illuminates the ontic context in which consciousness is always situated, that is, between birth and death, time and eternity, mortality and immortality, fall and redemption. Since the problem of consciousness is intrinsically related to this transfinite context, a theory of consciousness must attend to the symbolic language of the myth. Voegelin finds in Plato's use of the myth the only recourse a philosopher has in articulating experiences of transcendence.[58] Where others would engage in instruments of speculation, Voegelin in his early exploration adhered to the symbolic language of illumination in analyzing the nature of consciousness.

In the expression of consciousness in the myth, however, he discerned a very important problem, i.e., the conflict between the philosopher's deliberate myths and the prevailing myths of the cultic community. Since human consciousness occurs in a multitude of successive and simultaneous paradigms, there is always a wide range of experiences of transcendence and a variety of expressions for them. Every community has its own myth reflecting the prevailing image of the human being and the divine ground transcending the human being. Since there is no agreement on the truth of the prevailing myths there arises the problem of a mythical tension of a conflict of myths between different communities. Such is the problem of a plurality of gods in a polytheistic community, or of idolatry in a monotheistic community such as that of the Hebrews.

But a more relevant aspect of this problem relates to the destruction of the myth through the demythologization of Western rationalism. Voegelin illustrates the impact of this far more odious development in the following passage:

> For ever-increasing masses of people, the sensual myths of the Christian tradition are being dissolved, while the spiritualized expressions of the experience of transcendence in intellectual mysticism and philosophical speculation are accessible only to a small minority. The inevitable result is the phenomenon of "being lost" in a world that has no more fixed points in the myth. People, of course, do not cease to have experiences of transcendence, but these experiences remain in the psychic strata of shudder and fear; they cannot productively contribute to the creation of an order of symbols through which the transfinite processes can be made comprehensible in the transparency of the myth.[59]

It is at this point that Voegelin mentions another problem area besides the cosmological antinomies and the myth. It is the problem evoked by the question classically formulated by Leibniz and Schelling: "Why is Something, why is there not rather Nothing?"[60] It is the question of the mystery of existence over the abyss of a possible nonexistence which every being experiences. Since no being creates itself, the relationship between a being and the mysterious ground that transcends it must be accounted for. Voegelin believed that only a process-theology which seeks to express the relations among consciousness, the transcending intraworldly classes of being, and the world-transcending ground of being, in the language of immanence, can interpret the world order in a comprehensible fashion. He said, "I am inclined to believe that the process-theological attempt and its expansion, a metaphysics that interprets the transcendence system of the world as the immanent process of a divine substance, is the only meaningful systematic philosophy."[61] Such a process-metaphysics is the only construction that can adequately comprehend transcendence in immanence.

Voegelin cites two experiential complexes, the consideration of which lead to what he called a "process-theology."[62] The first has to do with the ontic structure of human being in relation to other immanent structures in the hierarchic order of being. Human consciousness occurs in integral relation to other processes. It is based on animalic, vegetative, and inorganic being. As consciousness finds itself transcending into the world, it also discovers other levels of being which constitute its very foundation. The order of being is differentiated along different levels of which consciousness is one. Even though the levels of being are clearly distinguishable in their respective structures, they must have a common basis which makes possible the continuum of all of them in human existence. For example, the phenomenon of maturing and growing old is obviously part of our biological organism, but it is also a process in our consciousness. This interrelationship of processes in the order of being, in which one participates with one's body as well as with one's consciousness, incites our imagination to comprehend the ontological structure of the cosmos.

The second experiential complex is the experience of meditation. It is in meditation that "the intention of consciousness is directed toward the contents of the world, not objectively through the *cogitata*, but rather nonobjectively toward the transcendent ground of being."[63]

Based on these complexes of experience, Voegelin claimed that an ontologist can infer a substantive identity of the levels of being. This identity forms the background of all the differentiations of being which unfolds through a series of phases, the process of which culminates when this substance attains the illuminative phase of human consciousness. Ontologically then, the meditative complex of experience reveals the necessity of seeing the world-immanent process of being conditioned by a process in the ground of being. No one can read these pages of Voegelin without being struck by the close parallel that his theory of consciousness, along with its metaphysical foundation, seems to have with Whitehead's process–metaphysics.[64]

This thematization of consciousness as a process "from within," as a meditative process, and as a process of illumination, points to a conception of consciousness not as phenomenal but as noumenal. But even the *noumena* of consciousness is not the *noumena* of being as a whole. That being, which is the ground of all experienceable particular being, is an ontological construct without which the experienced reality of our ontic context remains incomprehensible. This ground is nowhere a datum of consciousness. Rather, it is always strictly transcendent and approachable only through meditation. It cannot be drawn from the beyond of finiteness into finiteness itself. For this reason, neither an idealistic nor a materialistic metaphysic is tenable, since both attempt to reduce the totality of being to the level of an immanent particular being. Nor is a phenomenologically oriented metaphysic tenable for the same reason. It, too, attempts to derive the whole out of a part.[65]

On this point it will be apt to stress the fact that in Voegelin's approach to a philosophy of consciousness he is truly an independent thinker. He pays no debt to any school of psychology or philosophy. His inquiry into the nature of consciousness strove to include all relevant data. He took his cue from the conscious experience of reality and there alone. Already we can recognize his commitment to an economy of analytical terms in his study of consciousness. The study of consciousness must limit itself to the symbols that emerge in the process of its exegesis. All extraneous concepts or secondary symbolisms must be excluded. Voegelin did not develop a mature theory of consciousness until the 1960s when he employed the symbols of classical *noesis*,[66] but at this earlier date we can discern the course his thought would take. His critique of phenomenology and the Continental thinkers illustrates to some degree the position he would later develop more fully. Following James, Voegelin's empirical investigation centered on concrete experience, not sense perception. In this regard he distanced himself from the current dogmatic debates that reduced consciousness to an autonomously existing object. A true science of consciousness had to expose the nonscientific motivations of the prevalent reductionist positions. For example, any attempt to reduce experiences of order to the order of the so-called unconscious[67] (Freud, Jung) on one hand or the intersubjective[68] (Husserl, Scheler) on the other, or any other source outside the reality of conscious experience, had to be seen for what it was: a calculated effort to constrict the horizon of reality for nonrational, even ideological, reasons.

From these considerations Voegelin was able to draw the following principles: First, there is no absolute starting point for a philosophy of consciousness. All reflection on consciousness occurs in the middle of an ongoing process of philosophizing and presupposes this process, the movement of the participating consciousness itself, and its structure. Second, consciousness is not "pure" consciousness. It is the consciousness of a human being, which means that consciousness is not constituted by the radically immanent phenomenon of the present moment ever vanishing, but rather is founded in a body, in the physical world, and in the life history of a person whose experience is made present through a process of memory and interpretation. Consciousness as existential can never become an object over against itself. It knows itself as participating in a larger reality that constitutes it. The philosopher always lives in the context of his or her own history, the history of humankind, and the history of the cosmos.[69] Third, a philosopher's reflection is the process of clarification of his or her own formative experiences, that is, all the prereflective experiences that lead one to ask questions about the nature of consciousness and the reality of which it is a part. Such reflection leads to a process of meditation.. Voegelin means this in the traditional Christian sense. Meditation is the process by which a thinker anamnetically penetrates his or her own engendering experiences and reaches the awareness of transcendent being. To use Augustine's language: meditation is the soul turning its *intentio* beyond all earthly things toward God. Or, to quote the author of *The Cloud of Unknowing*: "It is needful for thee to bury in a cloud of forgetting all creatures that ever God made, that you might direct thine intent to God Himself."[70] Meditation engenders as well as recovers experiences of transcendence toward the divine ground of being. It is through these experiences that philosophical clarification of human existence is reached, and an adequate theory of consciousness can be formulated.

This is the breakthrough of 1943. It laid the foundation for Voegelin's philosophy of history which was to follow. It is on the basis of these theoretical results that he embarked upon his "anamnetic experiments" later that same year. These meditative experiments led Voegelin back to the source of his own philosophizing consciousness formed by the engendering experiences of his childhood.[71] Hence, his theory was not a speculative construct; rather, it was anchored in the very concrete and critical rendering of his own personal experiences.

The preceding is an account of Voegelin's theory of consciousness in the shape it took upon his own theoretical breakthrough in 1943. In the 1950s, after abandoning the already advanced "History of Political Ideas," he worked out the historical dimensions of his theory of consciousness. The fruits of his labor in this middle phase of his work are contained in *The New Science of Politics* (1952) and the first three volumes of *Order and History* (1956–57), to which we now turn.

2

THE HISTORICAL DIMENSION: THE MIDDLE WRITINGS, 1951–59

In the years that followed his breakthrough of 1943, Voegelin held fast to his new understanding of the nature of consciousness, its process, and the ground it illuminates. During the ensuing years in his search for the order of the human being and society, he worked through the historical dimension of consciousness by embarking on an extended study of experience and symbolization in history. The first results of his research came to light when he was given the opportunity to present the Walgreen Lectures at the University of Chicago in 1951. Under the title "Truth and Representation," these six lectures were published a year later and given a new title: *The New Science of Politics*.

The New Science of Politics

In the late 1940s, while Voegelin was working on his "History of Political Ideas" he encountered insurmountable problems.[1] These problems arose from the source materials themselves, for what he was actually studying were sources of order wherever they could be found, and he discovered that they could not be constrained under the conventional rubric of "the history of ideas." He was still working within the accepted framework of political science and history textbooks that assumed that history began with the Greeks as if nothing of interest occurred before that. This dominant bias in academic circles began to dissolve when the great advances in understanding Near Eastern civilizations occurred in the 1920s and 1930s. With the work of the Chicago Oriental Institute, for example, a new appreciation of ancient, mythical societies such as Israel, Mesopotamia, and Egypt came to the fore.[2] The transition from myth to rational thought became clearer, and it was evident that the conventional understanding of history had to be changed. What was required was a shift from the history of ideas to the history of experiences and their symbolizations.[3]

During this time Voegelin was also helped by his reading of Schelling. Through Schelling's philosophy of myth and revelation he discovered that the fundamental substance of history could not be reduced to ideas or concepts.[4] What was real in history were the experiences that came to expression in symbols, concepts, and ideas, and a true understanding of history would have to go beyond myth, thought, and philosophy to the experiences that generated them. He came to the conclusion that "the conception of a history of ideas was an ideological distortion of reality."[5] For the myths and rituals that formed political life in ancient societies could clearly not be construed as ideas. To treat them as such would be a gross distortion of how human order is attained. As he put it, "There were no ideas unless there were symbols of immediate experiences."[6] Reflecting back upon this period of his work, Voegelin described the discovery which led to the abandonment of his project in the following terms:

> A history of political ideas was a senseless undertaking, incompatible with the present state of science. Ideas turned out to be a secondary conceptual development, beginning with the Stoics, intensified in the High Middle Ages, and radically unfolding since the eighteenth century. Ideas transform symbols, which express experiences, into concepts—which are assumed to refer to a reality other than the reality experienced. And this reality other than the reality experienced does not exist. Hence, ideas are liable to deform the truth of the experiences and their symbolization.[7]

So the philosophy of consciousness that Voegelin had been working on earlier became all the more critical now as he realized that his "history of political ideas" would have to yield to a study of order in history, and this study would have to focus on the relation between experience and reality, with the emphasis shifting from the symbols to the engendering experiences.

The *New Science of Politics* was Voegelin's first attempt to describe the nature of ordering experiences and their symbolization in history. This book, the first Voegelin published in English and his first to appear in the United States, was to become his most famous, according him a national reputation.[8] The new science referred to in the title was actually and ironically the old science of Aristotle. Voegelin attempted to recover the *episteme politike* of classical political philosophy which was indeed new to the study of political science, where positivism and behaviorism prevailed.[9] In this vein Voegelin characterized the new science as "a restoration" of classical theoretical principles, and so political science, far from being a description of existing institutions, must become "the science of human existence in society and history, as well as of the principles of order in general."[10] Along with his cry for "a return to a consciousness of principles," Voegelin introduced a startlingly simple definition of science: "Science is the search for truth concerning the nature of the various realms of being."[11] He felt that only such a depiction of science, inspired by the classics, could combat the various and pernicious reifications of contemporary social science, whether it be Weberian, neo-Kantian, positivist, or behaviorist.

What distinguished Voegelin's *New Science* from the spate of other approaches in social science was his unique understanding of empiricism and theory. What many of Voegelin's readers shrank from was his insistence that the transcendent was the source of political order, and experiences of transcendence the focus of empirical inquiry. They interpreted this as a retrogression to a theocratic past, with science taking its stance on revelation. Nothing could be more anathema to a social science mired in various forms of secularized scientism. For modern political scientists this connotes a world of specious "spirituality" that has nothing to do with political realism. A science of politics that has reduced itself to the negotiation of power in and between societies, where the chief decision is who gets what, when, why, and how, cannot fathom a philosophy of order whose principles are grounded in experiences of transcendence. Yet Voegelin indeed saw the ordering experiences of revelatory events to be the center of an empirical science from which a study of politics must take its bearings. His emphasis on the revelatory role of the "experiences of the wise" is based on the epistemological premise that the movements of a soul that lovingly turn toward the source of wisdom and truth are not incidental; they reveal reality in its true depth. Such experiences become scientific data. They are the true source of authority that turns everything else into mere opinion. An empirical science of being must reflect these experiences, for without them it deteriorates into an uncontrolled intellectual game that has no connection with reality.

And so, under the influence of Schelling, Voegelin came to see clearly that the substance of history he sought was only "to be found on the level of experience, not on the level of ideas."[12] Such a shift required a retheoretization of theory. The theoretical foundation that underlies Voegelin's study was formulated in two critical passages that few of his readers were able to appreciate and understand. Read together they displayed what Voegelin meant by an empirical study of the human being and history:

> Theory is not just any opining about human existence in society; it rather is an attempt at formulating the meaning of existence by explicating the

content of a definite class of experiences. Its argument is not arbitrary but derives its validity from the aggregate of experiences to which it must permanently refer for empirical control.[13]

A theory of human existence in society must operate within the medium of experiences which have differentiated historically. There is a strict correlation between the theory of human existence and the historical differentiation of experiences in which this existence has gained its self-understanding. Neither is the theorist permitted to disregard any part of this experience for one reason or another; nor can he take his position at an Archimedean point outside the substance of history. Theory is bound by history in the sense of the differentiating experiences. Since the maximum of differentiation was achieved through Greek philosophy and Christianity, this means concretely that theory is bound to move within the historical horizon of classic and Christian experiences. To recede from the maximum of differentiation is theoretical retrogression; it will result in the various types of derailment which Plato has characterized as *doxa*.[14]

This view of history, as differentiating experiences of human self-understanding, was clearly a foreshadowing of what was to come. As such, it stands as a proem to the first three volumes of *Order and History*.

As already indicated, *The New Science of Politics* had two primary functions: to critique the deformations of contemporary social science and to recover the classical symbolisms of political representation (introduction and chapters 1 and 2). To this end Voegelin amassed a great amount of historical material in which he conducted an empirical investigation of how political societies represent the truth of their existence through language symbols. As a special case study he concentrated on the struggle of Christianity for representation in the Roman Empire (chapter 3). The second half of the book took up the problem of gnosticism as the modern deformation of political society (chapters 4–6). Because *The New Science* was a prolegomenous work much of this material was carried over into *Order and History*,[15] which will be investigated shortly. So an analysis of this rich historical material here is unnecessary for our purposes; however, a brief statement summarizing the intent of the book will be useful at this juncture.[16]

Although Voegelin deals with a variety of societies that represent themselves symbolically in order to establish themselves in history, his main concern is with the self-interpretation of Western civilization that took place through Christianity. The subsequent distortion of the symbols that expressed the original Christian experiences Voegelin identified as gnosticism. Gnosticism in the modern era presented itself as a dangerous threat to the truths revealed in Christianity. The real motive of Voegelin's study, then, can be seen in the way in which he shows how the symbolization of order can break down once the experiences that ground its truth are no longer present in the consciousness of the political, ecclesial, and intellectual rulers who interpret the original symbols. Through the gnostic deformation of Christianity, he analyzed the process by which the Christian symbols of salvation beyond history were transformed into immanentist ideologies that promised an imminent perfection of the human being and society within history. The revolutionary mass movements that these ideological reinterpretations helped catapult led to the riotous destruction of order in our time. In fact, it was in direct opposition to the Marxist and national socialist attempts to "immanentize the eschaton" that *The New Science of Politics* was written. So, as previously indicated, Voegelin's interest in righting the disorder of contemporary society, which he sought in his retheoretization of political science, was motivated by very concrete concerns.

The enterprise of retheoretization begun with this work required preparatory studies that would once again put an interpretation of Western history on solid footing in opposition to the deformed interpretation of the modern rationalists and positivists. Given the centuries-long encrustation of the deformation, Voegelin's "new" science would indeed be revolutionary. The hallmark of this restored science would prove to be a general diagnosis of the underlying religious experiences of the mystic philosophers as emitting the highest degree of rationality over against the modern philodoxers (Comte, Marx, et al.) whose denial of the religious ground of rationality subjected them to the lowest rank of irrationalism.[17] A renewed study of Greek philosophy would make this possible, something Voegelin did not satisfactorily achieve until volumes II and III of *Order and History*. But these studies also had to discern critically the characteristic differences between Greek and Christian "metaphysics." Without a satisfactory analysis of the relation between the two pillars of Western civilization a theoretically intelligible order to history, into which the various religious phenomena could be organized, would be impossible.

Based on these preparatory studies what emerged was Voegelin's formulation of three different types of experience of order and their symbolization in history. It was a formulation in development, as a comparison to his later formulation of these same types in *Order and History* will soon reveal. In *The New Science of Politics* Voegelin distinguished three types of truth: (1) cosmological truth, represented by the ancient empires, whereby society is conceived as a microcosm of cosmic order, principally through a king who represents divine order to the people;[18]

(2) anthropological truth, represented by Greek philosophy, whereby the order of a society is based on the order of its citizens' souls, with the philosopher providing the standard of measure;[19] and (3) soteriological truth, represented by Christianity, whereby the revelation of grace in history through the incarnation of Christ opens the soul and society to a process of redemption.[20] This typology was carried over into *Order and History* with certain modifications. Cosmological truth was studied in terms of the cosmological myth. Anthropological truth was studied under the symbolic form, philosophy, which emerged in the Greek polis and reached its fullest differentiation in Plato. Soteriological truth was not explicitly discussed. It was generally included in the discussion of revelation in Israel, but usually only in oblique references to what Christianity, with its experience of incarnation and redemption, added to Israelite revelation. Not until volume IV, *The Ecumenic Age*, where Voegelin discussed the meaning of transfiguration in Paul, did this symbolism reemerge and become articulate in a revised form.

However, through this threefold typology for articulating the fundamental forms of truth, Voegelin was able to speak of the clear breakthrough that occurred with Christianity. He explained this in terms of how the human–divine relationship was uniquely understood in Christianity which marked a decisive enlargement over Greek philosophy. In Aristotle the love or spiritual bond between men created by their common participation in the *nous* was the foundation for political order. This *philia politike*, or political friendship, was possible only because of the equality established between men through the mutual love of their noetic selves. Between unequals the social bond would at best be weak if not altogether nonexistent. For this reason, Aristotle believed that friendship between the human being and God was impossible because of their radical inequality. Voegelin claimed that this impossibility of *philia* between God and humans was symptomatic of the whole style of anthropological truth. The accent of the mystic philosophers was placed on the human side in which the soul moves toward divinity, a one-sided movement in which God in God's utter transcendence does not respond in an equal movement toward humans from the beyond.[21]

Christianity marked a distinct advance in the experience of the divine–human relation through what Voegelin called

> the bending of God in grace toward the soul. . . . The experience of mutuality in the relation with God, of the *amicitia* in the Thomistic sense, of the grace which imposes a supernatural form on the nature of man, is the specific difference of Christian truth. The revelation of this grace in history, through the incarnation of the Logos in Christ, intelligibly fulfilled the adventitious movement of the spirit in the mystic philosophers.[22]

The incarnation marked a pivotal period in history because the human self-understanding reached in Christianity achieved a new "critical authority over the older truth of society."[23] However, in Voegelin's analysis, Christianity never adequately confronted the truth of philosophy because Christianity developed in a predominantly Roman, not Greek, civilization. Athens had little impact on Roman political theology.[24] As a result, the truth of existence represented by Athens and Jerusalem has remained in conflict to this day. A synthesis of sorts was attempted by the Christian fathers, especially Augustine, and later by the medieval scholastics, especially Aquinas, but an adequate understanding of these maximal differentiations of truth on the level of experience has never (before Voegelin, I would dare say) been fully achieved.

Although *The New Science of Politics* represented a great achievement in Voegelin's developing thought, it was not without its weaknesses. The limitation of this work is that the theory of consciousness that stood behind it was not made articulate, a limitation that hampered some misguided reviewers. Voegelin's best reviewer was his dialogue partner, Alfred Schutz, the person who helped Voegelin sharpen his developing theory of consciousness a decade earlier. It was through continuing correspondence with Schutz that the essential matter of Voegelin's work came to light.[25] Schutz criticized Voegelin for making truth claims in the name of social science that could only be grounded in the author's personal Christian faith.[26] He also claimed that these experiences do not prove a supernatural reality by which individuals and societies must take their bearings. Although Schutz was basically ignorant of Voegelin's "metaphysical position," he could not be faulted for misconstruing the text. For Voegelin's answers to Schutz's criticism were not to be found in his book. His position was made clear only later, when his theory of consciousness was made thematic. But in his letter to Schutz he indicated the outline of such a philosophy.

"Philosophizing," said Voegelin, "seems to me to be in essence the interpretation of experiences of transcendence."[27] These experiences cannot be proved any more than sense experience can be proved. Yet there is nothing esoteric about such experiences. Insofar as everyone experiences reality, everyone has experiences of transcendence, at least on a limited level. A philosopher who experiences his or her consciousness as transcending discovers the ground of philosophizing, and no special belief is required to substantiate it, for it is self-evident. To deny the self-transcending nature of one's consciousness would be to deny one's own experience. Such a denial is certainly possible, but then one would not be operating rationally; one would be closed to the reality one is trying to investigate. One may arrive at a number of different conclusions but one cannot in good faith deny the nature of transcending consciousness.

With Christianity a decisive differentiation of experience that cannot be ignored has occurred in history. With the emergence of what Voegelin called "essential Christianity," contained in the doctrines of Christology, Trinity, and Mariology,[28] there were illuminated aspects of transcendent truth which even Plato had not grasped. In Plato's parable of the cave there is something missing. One of the shadow watchers is "forced" to turn around and is dragged up to the entrance where he now sees the sun. But the question is, who forces the cave-dweller to undergo this conversion? Thus, the problem of divine grace is posed rudimentarily on the Platonic level but it is not made thematic. Plato's compulsory force symbolized by the *periagoge* is experienced by Christianity as the revelation of divine grace. This discovery of "the intervention of transcendence in human life" is new; it superseded the Platonic conception.[29] In philosophical matters this meant that no one could adequately deal with transcendence with pre-Christian conceptions. By no means identical with "the Catholic main line," Voegelin saw in "essential Christianity" the pinnacle of metaphysical truth in the human being's experience of transcendence.[30] That this position was foreign to Schutz's understanding of science and empiricism should not be surprising, for Schutz did not share Voegelin's metaphysical convictions. But as an historian and political theorist, Voegelin believed he had to confront the questions raised by the historical materials themselves, just as a natural scientist would have to deal with his or her object of inquiry in an open and unbiased fashion.[31] This was so because the fundamental principle of Voegelin's historical investigation was that "the order of history emerges from the history of order."[32] The stage was now set for the great work which was to follow.

Order and History

The great strength of the body of writing that became *Order and History* was the dialectical movement between the empirical data of history and the theory of consciousness which Voegelin had developed. The empirical materials, which presented themselves as the symbolic self-understanding of human experience in history, anchored his theory of consciousness, while his theory of consciousness illuminated the empirical materials. The thrust of Voegelin's search was always back to the origins of consciousness wherever consciousness first manifested a new awareness of being. A science of politics has to trace the order of humankind and society back to its roots. This source of order lies in that mysterious dimension of experience where humans encounter the ground of their being, an experience that occurs not in world-time but in the time of the *distentio animi*. It follows, then, that an *episteme politike* must become a philosophy of history and consciousness. The essence of Voegelin's endeavor during this period of his work is his anamnetic recovery and analysis of the historical symbols of human consciousness and the engendering experiences that ground them, through the hermeneutic process of "experiential exegesis."

Before examining the substance of Voegelin's historical study, a review of the basic principles upon which *Order and History* is predicated will be helpful. These principles are the building blocks in Voegelin's entire analysis of reality. They can be summarized by the following list:[33]

1. Consciousness is a process that is aware of itself being a part in a comprehensive reality that embraces it. Our fundamental experience is one of participation in this larger reality that transcends us.
2. Knowledge of this reality is not the knowledge we have of an object (i.e., Husserl's intentionality which is a substructure of our participation in this larger reality). Because consciousness is part of the process of reality in which it partakes, there cannot be a separation of subject and object, of the knower and the known. The human being's participation in the drama of being is as an actor, not a spectator.
3. The structure of consciousness is always concrete, and it is constituted by the knowledge which consciousness has of itself. A consciousness that is attuned to itself is more in tune with the reality of which it partakes than one that is not. This "attunement" is the process by which the comprehensive reality becomes luminous for its truth as consciousness becomes present to itself.
4. The historical dimension of this process consists in the various records of our human forebears who have expressed their experiences of reality in language symbols. The differentiation of this historical dimension is an integral part of the self-articulation of consciousness and the reality of which it partakes. In fact, the process of reality is discerned in the historical record of human experience and its symbolization.
5. The knowledge of consciousness that is luminous is the experience and symbolization of the tension toward the divine ground of being. The study of the symbolizations of experience toward the divine ground in their historical sequence provides the key to understanding the meaning of history and its order; for it is through these symbols that societies express their own limited

understanding of transcendent reality, thereby making the order of being transparent.

6. The order of being is composed of the primordial community of God and humankind, world and society. This community of being and its quarternarian structure is known to a human being only through the participation of his or her existence in its mystery. Human participation in the drama of being makes the human being consubstantial with being. Nevertheless, the meaning of the drama remains unknowable.

7. The totality of human experience and its symbolization in history does not constitute the whole of reality. That totality is the record of participation in the whole which itself remains beyond all human experience. The balance of consciousness is maintained when this relation between part and whole is not disturbed, that is, when the tension of existence toward the divine ground is emphatically understood to be the ineluctable context in which all humans experience the mystery of being.

These were the fundamental principles concerning consciousness and reality that guided Voegelin's study of history. Although they later underwent considerable refinement and amplification, they withstood the test of critical scholarship when he applied them to the historical materials. In fact, it was the amplification of these principles that led Voegelin to the great discovery of his philosophy of history.

In the sequence of symbolizations in history, Voegelin discovered the development of consciousness from compact to differentiated forms. The primary form of symbolization of reality is the cosmological myth. The myth is the compact symbolization of the experience of order, and the overriding experience for the ancients is the consubstantiality of being. It is what Voegelin calls "primary experience of the cosmos," where primary refers to its position in the long history of human consciousness. This primary experience, Voegelin stresses, is a "compact" experience in the sense that it contains within itself all the reality which will ever be experienced. The development of consciousness from ancient to modern is not a process in which new realities are added to the stock of human experience. Reality in its fullness is always present, but aspects of the whole (i.e., the cosmos) previously experienced in a vague or indistinct manner become, under certain conditions, illuminated. They are distinguished from the whole and articulated through language symbols. This is the process Voegelin calls "differentiation."

And so in the process of history other forms of symbolization have arisen which express a higher and more adequate (or more differentiated) understanding of reality than the earlier myths. The sudden emergence of these new symbolizations Voegelin has variously called "leaps in being," "spiritual outbursts," "theophanic events," and "revelations." He distinguished three great leaps in history which completely broke with the older cosmological myths in their symbolization of human and divine order; they are: Israelite revelation, Greek philosophy, and Christianity.

According to Voegelin, the inherent weakness of the cosmological myth is to be seen in how it attempts to symbolize the two essentially different modes of reality (immanence and transcendence) through a structurally homogeneous symbolism. The poles in the tension of reality (between world-immanent being and the transcendent ground of being), experienced as one in the cosmological style of truth, break apart under the impact of the leap in being. The cosmological symbolism is thus inadequate for expressing human experience in its differentiated mode. A more adequate representation of human and divine being is required. This is accomplished through various processes of "desacralization," "dedivinization," or "disenchantment," whereby the God beyond the intracosmic gods appears as the one transcendent reality shorn of intraworldly countenances. Both the transcendent and immanent poles of the experienced tension in reality are present in the cosmological myth, but they are left indistinct and thus have a limited adequacy for expressing the true order of existence.

This discovery of a revolutionary change in the human experience of order led Voegelin to articulate another set of principles which govern the structure of consciousness in history. These three principles which emerged in the course of his study were formulated as follows:

1. The nature of the human being is constant.
2. The range of human experience is always present in the fullness of its dimensions.
3. The structure of the range varies from compactness to differentiation.[34]

These terms "compact" and "differentiated" refer not only to the different types of symbolization, but also to the accompanying form of consciousness that produced them. They are not so much the possession of an individual consciousness, though individuals can certainly be formed by one or the other or both, as they are a social and historical movement that constitutes the intellectual and spiritual horizon of individuals existing in a particular time. The significance of these changing symbolizations of reality can be appreciated when one realizes that they constitute the movement of reality becoming luminous to itself. Therefore, they cannot be ignored by any philosopher who reflects on the nature of consciousness and reality. Voegelin is emphatic on this point:

> There are degrees in the differentiation of experiences. I would take it as a principle of philosophizing that the philosopher must include in his interpretation the maximally differentiated experiences and that, so long as he is operating rationally, he therefore does not have a right to base his interpretation on the more compact types of experience while ignoring differentiation, no matter for what reason.[35]

Understanding past symbolizations poses considerable difficulties to the philosopher who must interpret their meaning. These difficulties call to mind further hermeneutical principles that Voegelin invoked in interpreting these symbols: First, since a thinker's abstract statements about consciousness are based on concrete experiences of reality by concrete human beings who must articulate their experience in language-symbols, then all statements concerning consciousness have both an abstract and a concrete dimension. Hence, when an interpreter seeks to understand the meaning of a thinker's statements, the process of interpretation must penetrate to the "engendering experiences" which give rise to the language symbols in the first place. The truth of these experiences can only be ascertained by an experiential response on the part of the interpreter. The philosopher, then, must attempt to recover or reenact the original experience in his or her own consciousness. This process of experiential interpretation Voegelin later came to call "meditative exegesis."

Next, these engendering experiences and the symbols that express them must not be thought of as separate entities. All one has in interpreting a text is an experience as formulated in a certain symbolic language. Experience and its symbolization are not separable objects. Neither in the process of reenactment is there an experiential response that is a separate entity, but again an experience that is articulated in language symbols. Voegelin has exhorted his readers not to reify or hypostatize the language of myth, philosophy, or revelation, that is, not to confuse symbols that communicate experiences for names of objective entities, i.e., ideas, concepts, or propositions. An example of this would be the Greek word *psyche*, or soul, which symbolized the Greek experience of the self as the site of the illumination of transcendent reality. It did not refer to an addendum to the body, a separate part of the self divisible into various components.[36]

To summarize, then, consciousness of the divine ground of being is illuminated when the compact symbols of human participation in being are differentiated. When a dimension of humanity's total experience of reality is rarefied, sharpened, and clarified through some special event, then the symbolization of the compact experience, i.e., the cosmological myth, must yield to the more differentiated understanding and articulation of experience. However, this sharpened consciousness of a dimension of reality does not invalidate the other dimensions of the compact experience. Rather, it provides a clearer lens or a higher viewpoint from which to grasp the whole of human participation in the divine order of being.

Nevertheless, there is a price to be paid for the historical advance of differentiation, for this breakthrough can indeed eclipse something of the compact experience. Though compact, the myth is more comprehensive of reality than differentiated symbolisms. While differentiation is more adequate to the various dimensions of the quaternarian structure of being, it also makes deformation of these dimensions possible. With differentiation there is now more to deform through hypostatizing detachment and a lessening of the enthusiasm meditated by the primary experience of the cosmos—the experience which provides an immediate "spiritual" grasp, however inadequate to the structure of being, of the whole of being. The compact comprehension is valid because it truly orders human existence. In a recently published essay that Voegelin completed around 1968, he states that "order in existence . . . corresponds to a man's actualization of his relation to the ground through ritual, meditation, faith, and prayer but does not correspond to the degree of differentiation."[37] The reason for this is that reason itself is present in the cosmological myth even though it has not yet articulated the dimension of the transcendent Beyond. Reason orders human existence whether it be in a compact or differentiated mode. It is at the core of all symbolizations that relate human existence to its ground. But reason can also lead to the disordering of existence when after differentiation it is not actualized through practices of meditation. Such practices are not idle reflections on what reason knows and articulates in the form of philosophical doctrines. Voegelin means this in the sense of Aristotle, who understood the life of reason (*nous*) as *theoretike energeia*, or contemplative action, which not only characterizes the highest form of life but orders human existence to the point of inducing *eudaimonia* (happiness). These practices are closely parallel to the cosmological form of existence, for as Voegelin explains, "the action of contemplation is the philosophic equivalent of ritual in myth."[38]

There is simply more to human existence than what noetic experience can differentiate. First and foremost is the primary attunement to the ground of being that an undifferentiated faith, ritual, prayer, and myth can mediate. This is especially true of the myth, "for the truth of myth consists in its adequacy as a symbol of the directly given experience of being as not grounded in itself."[39] Voegelin long held the view that when humans attempt to articulate the infinite in the finite such expression must inevitably be translated into myth. The myth is the only proper recourse that an imagination enthused with the divine has for making the divine transparent. As we shall see, the philosophical myths that emerged out of Plato's differentiated consciousness are the paradigmatic illustration of this. Mythic symbols and images cannot be entirely transposed into critical philosophical symbols and concepts, especially for the vast majority of people who are neither philosophers nor mystics. The contemporary world, declares Voegelin, has lost sight of this primary mythic ordering of existence because of "the desensualization of the myth through Western rationalism" which has resulted in masses of people " 'being lost' in a world that has no more fixed points in the myth."[40] From these statements we can draw the conclusion that people of common faith and piety may indeed be existentially more attuned to the divine than philosophers whose differentiated reason puts distance between them and the reality they seek to articulate. Though the truth of philosophy can be judged superior to the truth of myth insofar as philosophy differentiates the realm of the nonexistent ground of existent things that the myth inadequately images as intracosmic, it must in the end assume a humble position because of its inherent limits in making the transcendent reality it illuminates adequately and comprehensively transparent. Moreover, no society has accepted philosophy as its style of truth, as its political constitution so to speak, in the sense of Plato's appeal in the *Republic*. The order of society and history is inevitably dependent on the mediation of meaning by the myths and rituals of political and religious communities. This is obviously the case with the great breakthroughs in ancient history which arose out of cultic communities that were necessary to communicate and preserve the new truth discovered. This was as true in the breakthrough of philosophy, which in Plato's time required the communal life of the Academy to protect it from deformation, as it was in the breakthrough of revelation, which required the cultic life of the chosen people of Israel to keep their society in right order under God.

In the first three volumes of *Order and History*, Voegelin applied the aforementioned principles to his analysis of the human drama that unfolded in ancient Israel and Greece. In these two regions of the world, at approximately the same time in history (what Karl Jaspers called the "axis-time" of history), there occurred two distinct leaps in being. In both the Israelite and Greek cultures the age of the cosmological myth had come to an end and a new symbolization of order arose. In Israel the break with the myth was inspired by revelation. In Greece the myth was subsumed by philosophy.[41]

An adequate explication of the historical materials, which is so richly detailed in Voegelin's study, is beyond the scope of this chapter. The following account attempts only to highlight the most significant elements of the first three volumes of *Order and History*. Thus, I discuss only the major historical events as well as the important theoretical insights which Voegelin advanced in his study of Israelite revelation and Greek philosophy, as these pertain to the unfolding of his theory of consciousness.

Israel and Revelation

Enigmatically, the breakthrough to differentiation occurred almost simultaneously in human history in two adjacent locales. According to Voegelin, when this breakthrough to a new order of existence happened in ancient Israel, there appeared "a new type of man on the world-political scene."[42] This new person who appeared stood forth as an individual creature who lived and acted politically and historically vis-à-vis a world-transcendent God, who was discovered to be the source of all being. This leap in being was for the Israelites an experience of a deity who, unlike the intraworldly gods of the ambient cosmological societies, was a world-transcendent God that called forth a new understanding of men and women as human. The understanding of both the divinity of God and the humanity of the human being must necessarily develop together. As Voegelin states it, "the personal soul as the sensorium of transcendence must develop parallel with the understanding of a transcendent God."[43] The new symbolization of order to which this experience gave rise, Voegelin calls the "historical form."

The emergence of this historical consciousness in Israel can be traced through the following historical events:[44]

1. In the ancient Near East, people lived within a "cosmological civilization." Their and society's participation in divine being was expressed mythically according to the order of the cosmos. This world was experienced as the microcosm of the cosmic divine world. At the sacred center (*omphalos*) of society, heaven and earth met. It was the place where divine being flowed into society and where social order was periodically regenerated. In Mesopotamia, for example, these rituals of regeneration occurred during the New Year celebration when the

king, who represented the deity, led the people in their annual victory over the forces of chaos.[45] Through the recitation of the *Enuma elish*, the cosmogonic epic that compactly told the story of the origins of human and divine being, the people of ancient Babylon were able to constitute themselves in the order of existence that this annual ritual made efficacious. Babylon itself was the sacred *omphalos*, as proclaimed in the preamble of the Code of Hammurabi, where the city is established "in the midst of the world" as an everlasting kingdom. In Egypt this consubstantiality with divine being was symbolized by the pharaoh, who was the mediator between society and the divine Maat. The pharaoh manifested the presence of God and allowed all of his subjects to partake in cosmic order through the sacred authority of his rule. These mythical styles of attunement with divine being created a static but stable civilization that lasted for centuries without any radical change.

2. In these civilizations there were tendencies toward a breakthrough into "the radical transcendence of divine being" over against mundane society. In Egypt these tendencies were especially evident in the theogonic speculation of the Memphite theology, the symbolism of Akhenaton, and the personal piety of the Amon hymns,[46] which contributed to making the cosmological myth transparent for transcendent being. But the movement toward a complete differentiation of compact experience never occurred there. Rather, gods and humans, heaven and earth, the rituals of fertility and politics were all held together in one compact whole. The escape from "the primary experience of the cosmos" into an experience of transcendence that could become the new ordering force of society was held in check.

3. In Israel an irruption did occur from which emerged a new kind of religious personality and a new kind of community. The search for the true order of being was advanced when Moses led an "exodus from cosmological civilization" in the thirteenth century B.C., leaving behind the limits of imperial symbolization and entering a new order of existence under God. The Exodus, Voegelin observed, was not merely an incident in pragmatic history, but a spiritual irruption, an event of divine liberation. Subsequent to this event occurred the revelation on Mount Sinai. Together, these events encapsulated the religious experience of Israel that made her a chosen people of God. These theophanic events Voegelin interpreted as "an irruption of the spirit [which] transfigured the pragmatic event into a drama of the soul and the acts of the drama into symbols of divine liberation."[47]

4. The Exodus symbolized the liberation of Israel from the Sheol (realm of death) of Egypt for the new life in historical form. By way of this differentiation in historical form, the chosen people of Israel attained

a heightened awareness of the gulf that separates immanent existence, where gods and human beings live in the intraworldly "consubstantial community," and the transcendent divinity that is beyond the cosmos. It must not be forgotten however, that this leap in being toward a more perfect attunement with the divine ground primarily occurred as a theophanic event in the soul of Moses. Through Moses, existence in immediacy under God was the leap in being that constitutes existence in historical form. It must not be misinterpreted as a "subjective" experience, because, Voegelin states, as "the entering of the soul into divine reality through the entering of divine reality into the soul, the historical form, far from being a subjective point of view, is an ontologically real event in history."[48] Since consciousness is concrete, the recipient of revelation must be a particular individual who, like Moses on Mount Sinai, may represent all of humanity. Only afterwards may the revelation penetrate into the corporate consciousness of the community. As Voegelin writes: "Revelation and response are not a man's private affair; for the revelation comes to one man for all men, and in his response he is the representative of mankind."[49] Moreover, "the mutual presence of God and Moses in the thornbush dialogue will then have expanded into the mutual presence of God and his people, through the Berith, in history."[50]

5. The decisive threat to the "theopolitical constitution of Israel" came from the establishment of the monarchy.[51] For the king himself tended to become the son of God that Israel already was. Politically this meant that "when Israel found its national existence through the creation of a king as its representative, it also found, in Yahweh, the transcendental representative of the nation."[52] As a result, cosmological symbolism was allowed to reenter the ritual life of the people through the cult that grew up around the monarchy and which left its imprint of ritual formulas on the psalms.[53] This cosmological infestation did not destroy the historical form Israel had attained, but, claimed Voegelin,

> a tension had been created through the introduction of a rival experience and its symbolization that troubled the history of the Kingdom to its end. And for the Davidic and Solomonic period, at least, it is justifiable to speak of a decomposition of the old Yahwist order.[54]

It was this theopolitical problem that undergirded the tension between the prophets and the kings throughout the history of the monarchy.

6. Of course Moses was not the only recipient of the "inrush of divine reality" in Israel. The new order of the soul and the new order of society living in immediacy under God was eminently prefigured in Abraham, who, in trust and fortitude, responded in his own soul to the

word of Yahweh by embarking on Israel's first exodus from the land of Ur in order to found a new community in the land of Canaan that was "pregnant with future."[55] The other "carriers of divine reality" who followed Moses were the prophets. They were the representatives of Yahweh who rejected the establishment of the monarchy and awakened Israel to the universal truth of Yahweh's action in history, first revealed to Abraham and Moses. When Israel appeared to lose the historical mode of existence under God that it had gained from its leap in being, the prophets rose to protest the waywardness of the people. Their mission was to recall the people to a life of righteousness, to the covenantal order of existence under God. To this end they had to oppose both the cult of the empire and the formalism of the law. They admonished the people for their parochialism and externalization of the law and for failing to keep their personal *berith* with Yahweh, a *berith* that should be written on the heart. "The insight," Voegelin remarks, "that existence under God means love, humility, and righteousness of action rather than legality of conduct was the great achievement of the prophets in the history of Israelite order."[56]

7. The climax of Israelite prophecy was Second Isaiah's portrayal of the suffering servant, the human figure who, through a profound faith, entered into the suffering of God. The highlight of the servant's message is "Israel's exodus from itself" which must occur if all humankind was to be penetrated with God's revelation. The servant represents a new spiritual community imbued with an ecumenical consciousness, for God's kingdom not only will reign in Israel but will include anyone whose soul is a "sensorium of transcendence."

With Jeremiah the *omphalos* of divine order in history had contracted from the chosen people into his personal existence. "The Chosen People had been replaced by the chosen man."[57] Through his solitary entrance into the suffering of God, the prophet becomes the son of God. "In Jeremiah," says Voegelin, "the human personality had broken the compactness of collective existence and recognized itself as the authoritative source of order in society."[58] Not Israel, not Torah, but the individual human personality was finally discovered as the divine *omphalos* of order. The universalist potential and eschatological component of Israel's experience, then, came to fruition only in the later prophets. For only through them did the "mortgage" of the historical symbolism of a chosen people dissolve, to be replaced by the realization that the order of God could not be incarnated within a particular society in earthly time. What originates here, Voegelin argues, is the insight that revelation cannot be identified with the laws or customs of a particular ethnic or religious community. The order of the spirit inevitably differentiates from the order of a people's institutions and mores.[59] Nor can revelation be identified with any "religion"[60] or any "book,"[61] for the divine mystery is uncontainable. For Israel this meant that the God that was revealed to Moses, "is now revealed as the God of all mankind."[62]

Even with this amazing elevation of the individual personality as the new center of order, Voegelin adverted frequently in this study to the absence in Israelite thought of a conception of the soul as immortal.[63] The concept of immortality requires the experience of the individual soul and its right orientation toward the invisible God. He explains that "that experience never in Israelite history is clearly differentiated from the compact collectivism of the people's existence."[64] Voegelin tells how this collectivism was an obstacle for the emergence in Israel not only of an immortal soul but of philosophy also:

> With regard to philosophy, one must say that its development in the Hellenic sense was prevented by the irresolution concerning the status of the soul. The *philia* reaching out toward the *sophon* presupposes a personalized soul: the soul must have disengaged itself sufficiently from the substance of particular human groups to experience its community with other men as established through the common participation in the divine Nous. As long as the spiritual life of the soul is so diffuse that its status under God can be experienced only compactly, through the mediation of clans and tribes, the personal love of God cannot become the ordering center of the soul. In Israel the spirit of God, the *ruach* of Yahweh, is present with the community and with individuals in their capacity as representatives of the community, but it is not present as the ordering force in the soul of every man, as the Nous of the mystic-philosophers or the Logos of Christ is present in every member of the Mystical Body, creating by its presence the *homonoia*, the likemindedness of the community. Only when man, while living with his fellow men in the community of the spirit, has a personal destiny in relation to God can the spiritual eroticism of the soul achieve the self-interpretation which Plato called philosophy.[65]

To summarize then, without Israel there would be no history, only the recurring rhythms of cosmological civilization. The end result of existence in historical form is the differentiation of the spiritual realm from the pragmatic one, which were compactly united in primitive societies. In Israel the eternal rhythms of pharaonic order were replaced by the discovery of humankind's relation to divine reality as an ongoing drama of revelation and response. However, this historical form that emerged was precarious; it was not a state of being that could be established once and for all. "The historical form of the people," says Voegelin, "unfolds in time; but it remains historical form only as long as the people, while lasting in time, live in the tension of response to the timeless, eternal revelation of God."⁶⁶ The defection from this covenantal state of historical form is what led to the prophetic uprisings. The retrogression to the secure gods of the fertility cults of Canaan was cast in aspersion by the prophets who attempted to reestablish the unique symbolic form of Israel's founding experience, the Mosaic leap in being which was on the verge of being lost. In this very attempt to reestablish the meaning of the present under God, constituted by the Sinaitic events, "unknown authors elaborated such traditions as were preserved in cult legends, poems, and prose accounts into the paradigmatically heightened dramas."⁶⁷ These dramas have come down to us through what we call the Old Testament. This body of texts does not contain facts of geopolitics, and it cannot be interpreted in terms of pragmatic history. Voegelin never tires of exhorting those who distort the texts through literalizing tendencies. Rather it contains the facts of revelation and response, and thus its primary meaning is spiritual.

As Voegelin reminds us, there were other irruptions of divine reality in history, but only in Israel did there occur "the maximal clarity of divine revelation." From the standpoint of Israel's faithful experience, therefore, the whole history of humankind must be viewed as a drama in which every society struggles for a heightened spiritual consciousness and attunement with divine being.

The Polis and Philosophy

In volumes II and III of *Order and History*, Voegelin turned to the Greek experience concerning the proper mode of human participation in reality. This study is based on a presentation and analysis of those symbols that emerged in the course of Greek civilization which sought to articulate the heightened consciousness of being. The leap in being that occurred in ancient Greece is on an equal par with the Israelite leap in being; however, it took an entirely different form. The primary symbol that evolved from the Greek experience was philosophy.⁶⁸ Although its full elucidation did not occur until the Platonic dialogues, the conditions leading to its irruption can be traced back to a time as early as the Minoan civilization in Crete (ca. 2000–1700 B.C.). Volume II, *The World of the Polis*, details Voegelin's analysis of how philosophy, the new mode of order engendered by the Greek participation in being, developed.⁶⁹ His inquiry traces the principal stages, beginning with the cosmological myths of the Minoan and Mycenaean societies, moving through the Homeric myth and the Hesiodian speculation, to the philosopher's break with the myth. Not until the Hellenic age of the polis did philosophy experience its flowering. During this time, the most important pre-Socratic thinkers who were the carriers of the philosophic differentiation were Xenophanes, Parmenides, and Heraclitus. They set the stage for the culmination of philosophy which was initiated in the soul of Socrates. In volume III, *Plato and Aristotle*, Voegelin presented a brilliant analysis of this culmination of the philosophic quest as embodied in the works of these two great thinkers. His interest in reconstructing the emergence of philosophy in history is based on his theoretical intention of showing how the order of the soul can combat the disorder of the modern age. Echoing the parallel process in Israel, the birth of philosophy in Greece as a form of existence-in-truth discloses the historical process by which the opening of the soul toward transcendence is simultaneously the disclosure of the nature of humanity itself.

Plato and Aristotle lived in a time not unlike our own, a time of social and political crisis. Times like these provide ample opportunity, not only to discover how the disorder in society is a reflection of the disorientation of consciousness, but also to recover, anamnetically, the meaning of authentic humanity. It is Voegelin's hope that his own anamnetic recovery of Greek philosophy will serve as a therapeutic effort to heal the present disorder. This is precisely what Plato attempted to do during the collapse of Athenian society. He devoted his whole life to the struggle of persuading his fellow citizens that only through a loving relationship with the divine, inspired by a process of existential conversion (*periagoge*), could one save one's own soul from psychic disorder and death. Upon this new source of authority depended the salvation of society as well.

Today it is the false consciousness of modern ideologies and their distortion of reality that Voegelin seeks to resist by regaining the truth of philosophy. The ideologies are fueled by the "metastatic faith"[70] that seeks to change the structure of reality, whether it be in the form of utopian dreaming, revolution, or "enlightened" social science. This attempt to reconstruct reality is a "matter of life and death for all of us to understand the phenomenon and to find remedies against it before it destroys us."[71] The spiritual disease of ideology is existence in rebellion against God and humanity. The remedy which Voegelin offers us is philosophical inquiry. In a remarkable passage delineating the intent of his own personal labors, Voegelin describes the nature of philosophy and it's remedial function. Like all his work it reflects in a nutshell the great influence of Plato's own struggles and achievement:

Philosophy is love of being through love of divine Being as the source of its order. The Logos of being is the object proper of philosophical inquiry; and the search for truth concerning the order of being cannot be conducted without diagnosing the modes of existence in untruth. The truth of order has to be gained and regained in the perpetual struggle against the fall from it; and the movement toward truth starts from a man's awareness of his existence in untruth. The diagnostic and therapeutic functions are inseparable in philosophy as a form of existence. And ever since Plato, in the disorder of his time, discovered the connection, philosophical inquiry has been one of the means of establishing islands of order in the disorder of the age.[72]

We can sense here the passion behind Voegelin's own philosophic inquiry (*zetema*), and we can understand more fully now why the task of recovering the historical origins of philosophy was a necessary aspect of his life's work.

A review of philosophy's origins in Hellenic society will further our understanding of how human consciousness has differentiated in history. The roots of philosophy in ancient Greece emerged in the following historical events:

1. Although ancient Greek society lacked any unity on the level of institutional organization, both social and political, its civilizational order was constituted by a continuity of historical consciousness. This historical consciousness was formed out of a body of shared traditions which found their articulation in the representative works of imaginative thinkers. It was these creative minds who constructed and interpreted the meaning of Greek experience. Their symbolic productions were originally handed on through oral traditions until they eventually took written form.

2. The first great emergence of civilizational unity was provided by Homeric epic poetry.[73] These epic poems were the first written attempt to suggest a common meaningful past composed of Minoan and Mycenaean traditions. The Achaeans and Trojans were already associated by their common allegiance to the Olympian gods, but the import of Homer's myths was its claim to insights into an order that extended beyond the political realm of the Achaeans, transcending even Mycenaean civilization itself. Although they refer to events long past and represent societies whose existence had been exhausted, Homer's epics were offered to new societies (Illyrians, Thracians, Dorians) in the hope of providing them with those conditions that foster right order. Homer's diagnosis of Achaean disorder rested on the analysis of how the inordinate passions of human beings (i.e., the wrath of Achilles,

the lust of Paris) thwart the use of right reason which ultimately is the basis for knowing the real and establishing the common good.[74] Of equal importance is how Homer established this new authority. It was specifically noncosmological insofar as he expressed an inchoate understanding of human existence under God, symbolized, for example, by the incantations to the Muses, which suggest a relationship between the poet, Homer, and a divine source of wisdom. Of course the Homeric myth still lacked a concept of radical transcendence, of a God beyond the cosmos, as well as an adequate understanding of the human being characterized by *psyche*, i.e., reflective self-consciousness as the sensorium of transcendence. Homeric *psyche* is merely a life-force that leaves a person at death. It is one of a number of organs (along with thinking and the emotions) that comprise a bundle of forces that constitute humans as decisively mortal.[75] So even though he anticipated Plato in understanding social disorder as a function of individual disorder, Homer's experience of order remained relatively undifferentiated. Nonetheless, Homer's achievement rests in the definite loosening up of the compact structure of the myth and a more adequate understanding of human nature.

3. Homer represents the first phase in "the transition from myth to metaphysics." In the search for true order, begun by him, there emerges the incipient creation of the historical form and the autonomy of rational speculation. Ultimately, this form of rationality will develop into the fullness of noetic experience whereby the symbols of the cosmological myth will be abandoned altogether. In order for this to happen, the immanent order of the world must first be dedivinized. This occurs when the restrictive horizon of the myth slowly yields, by the force of questioning, to the growing awareness of a transcendent ground. This tendency is clearly expressed in the works of Hesiod.[76] His poems, *Theogony* and *Works and Days*, represent the first attempt to provide a Greek philosophy of history. Like Homer, Hesiod retained the form of the myth but speculated on the deep anxiety and destruction of his "time of troubles" in a way that sought universal validity for his interpretation of past events and future possibilities. Hesiod abandoned Homer's cosmology but stopped short of penetrating into the depths of the *psyche* which alone could provide an adequate rendering of human existence. His achievement was limited because for him the soul remained "inextricably interwoven with the fabric of social and cosmic order."[77] It took several centuries before the soul came into its own as the source of order in opposition to society, which occurred in the life and work of Plato. Thus, the Greek science of order was led by Hesiod through a transitional stage, somewhere between myth

and philosophy.[78] This intermediate form is most appropriately called "theology," the term used by Aristotle to designate the Hesiodian form of symbolization.[79]

4. The further differentiation of consciousness required an experience of *psyche* as both self-conscious and transcendently grounded, which was to be more clearly articulated in the following centuries. Yet without Homer and Hesiod, as Voegelin makes clear, the movement from myth to metaphysics in Hellenic civilization would have been impossible:

> The mythopoetic work of the two poets was a spiritual and intellectual revolution; for inasmuch as it established the types of cosmic and ethical forces, as well as the types of their relations and tensions, it created, in the form of the myth, a highly theorized body of knowledge concerning the position of man in his world that could be used by the philosophers as the starting point for metaphysical analysis and differentiation.[80]

Such differentiation was carried forward by the Ionian poets, by Tyrtaeus, and by Solon—as well as by the religious mysticism of Orphism and of Pythagoreanism, both of which maintained the essential divinity of the soul.[81] But the break with the myth and the emerging truth of existence was given its greatest impetus by the pre-Socratic philosophers of the sixth and fifth centuries. Although their writings have survived only in fragments, which has permitted much wider room for interpretation than if their works had been preserved in their entirety, there can clearly be discerned in these thinkers a substantial advance over their poetic predecessors. The break is especially ascertained in the iconoclasm of Xenophanes.[82] It is Xenophanes' concern with the "unseemly gods" that he shared with the earlier poets which led to his discovery of the universality of a transcendent reality, to a more adequate representation of the one, universal God beyond the gods.[83]

Voegelin finds in Xenophanes the basis for judging the inadequacy of modern theories of anthropomorphism which view mythical symbolization as a "projection" of human images onto the gods. It is an interpretation that has gained wide acceptance since the time of Comte and Feuerbach and is a complete misunderstanding of human consciousness in its historical development. An adequate philosophy of symbolic forms would first of all understand that the gods of the Greek myth were never really represented as human beings.[84] In the first place, the gods were endowed with a number of nonhuman characteristics: superior knowledge and strength, invisibility and change in form, and, chief of all, immortality. Secondly, the human characteristics the gods do reflect are the result of the idea that humans have of themselves. When no adequate understanding of humankind exists, the divine *and* human areas of reality will be confused, because *neither* has been properly differentiated.[85] When a more adequate conception of humankind emerges (as it did when Xenophanes criticized Homer's and Hesiod's anthropomorphism), the earlier symbolization will appear "unseemly," because it "corresponds to a past phase in the self-understanding of man."[86] In every present the symbolization of divine reality is in harmony with the degree of differentiation that the human being has achieved. Modern theories of anthropomorphism must be abandoned because they "hide the process in which the idea of man differentiates and correlatively with it the symbolization of transcendence."[87] These theories fail to take account of the consubstantiality and compactness of the early Greek experience of reality which is the perspective of a consciousness less differentiated than the modern.[88]

The problem of representation of divine reality is permanent. Though Xenophanes marks an advance with his criticism of the myth and his postulate of unseemliness, he never reached the extreme of a complete ban on representational activity as in Israel. Voegelin explains that the limit of representation

> reaches its climax when the differentiation of man has advanced to the point where the nucleus of the spiritual soul, the *anima animi* in the Augustinian sense, is discovered. At this ineffable point of openness towards transcendent reality, at this heart of the soul where the infusion of grace is experienced, the divinity becomes ineffable, too. The god of the mystic is nameless, beyond dogmatic symbolization.[89]

At this point anthropomorphism dissolves under the sway of analogical symbols, the approach which St. Thomas perfected in his delineation of the *analogia entis*. Nevertheless, Voegelin sees in Xenophanes "the first conscious, though still primitive, attempt at dealing with the analogy of being."[90]

5. Although the mystery religions of this period expressed belief in the divinity and immortality of the soul, it was not until Parmenides understood the mystical transport of the soul in light of an "intellectual grasp" of being that the philosophical differentiation of consciousness began. Voegelin explains: "Parmenides' philosophy is a speculation of the *Eon*, on Being. The symbol 'Being' appears for the first time; and without exaggeration it can be said that with Parmenides the history of philosophy proper, as the exploration of the constitution of Being, begins."[91] Parmenides called the faculty of the soul that has this vision of being the *nous*. *Nous* is the organ of the soul that brings being into experiential grasp. A further faculty, the *logos*, a term that also appears for the first time with Parmenides, is what articulates the content of being.[92] Together they comprise the "way to truth" which is conceived

as existence-in-tension between the possibility of openness to being and immortality, or closed existence in delusion (*doxai*) and death. This initial differentiation of the soul reveals a something with an "inner dimension" which leads toward the border of transcendence.[93] The light in the soul allows a thinker like Parmenides to speculate about transcendent being because he discovers his soul as a sensorium of transcendence. The human soul is marked, then, not by its possession of truth, but by its movement toward the divine source of truth from the ever-present position of *doxa*.[94] This movement inevitably encounters the experience of immortality which causes a break with the traditional attribution of immortality to the gods alone. With qualifications, the soul is perceived as immortal because it participates in the divine. But this participation is precarious: it may increase or decrease, it may be gained or lost.[95] Hence, the quest for personal order will depend on the "cultivation of the immortal part through occupation of the mind with things immortal and divine."[96] What was required now was an exploration of the inner dimension of the soul that would substantiate the experiential sources of knowledge which alone could authenticate speculation on transcendence beyond the "seemliness" of the myth. This was the work of Heraclitus.

6. The essence of humanity is now conceived to be the movement of the *psyche* toward the divine wisdom (*sophon*).[97] It is Heraclitus's achievement to understand the distinctly human character of this participation in being. He asserted that the agreement of the soul with the *logos*, in the midst of strife and flux, is the condition necessary for human community. Only by following the *logos*, which is common in every soul and which transcends the world of multiplicity and individuality, can a true community come into existence. Presaging St. Paul's pronouncing the Christian theological virtues, Heraclitus also enunciated the orienting forces in the soul that make this attunement possible: faith, hope, and love.[98] These are the orienting forces in the soul. Voegelin believes that the parallel should be given its full weight particularly in viewing the long preparation for the irruption of revelation in Christianity. Yet there is no touch of revelation in Heraclitus. As Voegelin says, "the divine is hidden indeed and does not reveal itself clearly in the soul."[99]

Heraclitus also specified a distinction between the "Alone Wise" of divinity and the human "love of wisdom," thereby anticipating Plato's insistence that "the soul of man is a source of truth only when it is oriented toward god through the love of wisdom."[100] Voegelin declares that it is this "philosophical orientation of the soul [that] becomes the essential criterion of 'true' humanity."[101]

In the fifh century B.C. the stage was set for the full philosophical differentiation which was to follow. It was this quest for the true order of the soul that forced the mystic-philosophers into direct confrontation with the political order of the polis. Similar to Israel's "exodus from itself," the separation of the spiritual realm of the soul from the political realm of society (the fundamental differentiation that Plato developed as the principle of his political philosophy) was already prefigured by these pre-Socratic thinkers. Above all, this is seen in Heraclitus who, Voegelin points out, was more estranged from his society than any previous philosopher. He claimed that though the *logos* was common to all, few if any ever come to know it. The philosopher who is attuned to the divine becomes an outsider, a lonely critic of his society that has turned away from the source of its being.[102] This was the political problem *par excellence* as seen by Plato. It would be up to Plato to unite the new source of authority in society—the charismatic and wise soul in love with the divine ground of being—with socially effective power. This new order was symbolized by the philosopher-king. In lieu of that, however, Plato realized that institutions of law and education would have to be created for continuing and transmitting the spiritual insights. As we mentioned previously these institutions would have to take on a religious, even cultic, character.

7. The Platonic experience and symbolization of reality, which marks the culmination of the philosophic breakthrough, sprang out of a cultural context formed by three social and spiritual developments which arose in Athens in the fifth century B.C.: the rise and fall of tragedy; the emergence of the Sophists; and the growth and decline of Athens as a political power.[103]

7:1. If the mystic-philosophers turned from mythic stories to a more discursive form of symbolism, the tragedians returned to the form of the tale as their medium of expression. The tragedy continues the search for truth through the device of a play, a contrived drama, which borrows heavily from the stock of traditional myths. Tragedy was a state cult in ancient Athens. Its rituals were held every year in conjunction with the spring festival in honor of the god Dionysus. More than just a "religious" observance, tragedy was the official political cult of Greek democracy in the time of Aeschylus. Also, Voegelin tells us that through its effects on the spectators, it had "become something like a psychological therapy."[104] Elsewhere Voegelin remarked that "the tragedy in its great period is a liturgy which re-enacts the great decision for Dike."[105]

The truth of the tragedy lies in the action of the drama itself which occurs on the new differentiated level of the soul's movement culminating in the decision of a mature, responsible woman or man.[106] The tragedians like Aeschylus and Euripides experiment with the manifold of decisions and crises that occur when a fully self-conscious soul is forced into action. As Voegelin states in his analysis of Aeschylus's *Suppliants*, "the Heraclitean dimension of the soul in depth is dramatized by Aeschylus into the actual descent of a soul in a concrete situation that requires a decision."[107] Such decisions surround the order of *dike* (justice), whereby the searching of the soul must find its resolution without the counsel of the gods, as in Homer, or divine commandments, as in Israelite revelation. Only the Dionysiac descent into the divine depth of the soul where recourse to *dike* constitutes a real decision and real action is what distinguishes the fate of the hero in Greek tragedy. The drama displays "the binding of the soul to its own fate through representative suffering."[108] And the heroic soul-searching and suffering of consequences which comprise the fate of the hero is paradigmatic; it serves to arouse the shudder of their own fate in the souls of the spectators. Even though the tragedy reveals a divine force in humanity that can ally itself with the order of *dike*, this incarnation of divine order is precarious because the forces of disorder (such as the demonic drive toward self-assertion and self-aggrandizement represented by Prometheus) are ever present. The warring forces in the soul yielding to the order of *dike* through the efforts of tragic action reflect the struggle for social order in the midst of demonic disorder. Thus, the course of human affairs becomes the course of history and because of this, says Voegelin, "history was born from tragedy in Hellas."[109] However, the Hellenic experience of history mediated by the tragedians remained more compact than that achieved by Israel because "the Dionysiac component in tragic existence precludes the irruption of a divine revelation from above."[110] Only in Israel did the radical break with the cosmological myth occur, creating a chosen people in the present under God. Yet the foundations for a philosophy of history were secured by Aeschylus because even though he was not a Moses, "he nevertheless discovered for [his people] the psyche as the source of meaningful order for the polis in history."[111] But here lay its limit. Even though Greek society broke from the cosmological myth, it carried the "mortgage of the polis," just as Israel carried its "mortgage of the Chosen People." The breakthrough to a universal humanity under God had to await the appearance of Christ.

7:2. If the search for order entered a unique phase with the rise of tragedy, speculation on order entered its decline with the advent of sophism. The sophists as they came to be known were the Hellenic "foreigners" who came to Athens to instruct the leisure class with their great learning. These migratory teachers were skilled debaters, persuasive rhetoricians, and scholars who perfected the art of political discourse.[112] The sophists debated the right principles of social order: In ethics the debate concerned the unity or plurality of the virtues; in politics they appealed to law as the ultimate educational authority in the polis. In either domain, the teachings of the sophists were markedly different from that of the philosophers. "In sophistic thought," says Voegelin, "there was missing the link between the well-observed and classified phenomena of ethics and politics and the 'invisible measure' that radiates order into the soul."[113] The most celebrated example of this "flight from transcendence" was Protagoras's formula "man is the measure" to which Plato opposed his "God is the measure" as the correct counterformula.[114] The experiences of transcendence in which philosophy had originated were forgotten or abandoned and the symbols of these experiences were separated from the experiences they expressed, made into separate objects of investigation, and generally treated like "things" in the world.[115] This new "enlightened" rationality was actually antiphilosophical in nature because it denied the very core of philosophy, which by definition is located in experiences of transcendence. It was this destruction of philosophy by the sophists that led Plato to emphasize the divine measure, thereby reconstructing philosophy into "a type of theology."[116] In its classical origin, then, theology was actually the new philosophy that had to appear in order to regain its experiential roots. Like the phoenix that emerged out of the embers of its own consumption, theology arose from the remnants of a dead philosophy.[117]

The sophistic destruction had numerous advocates, most of whom we encounter in Plato's dialogues. Anaxagoras, for example, transformed the Parmenidean *nous* from the sensorium of transcendent being into a part of being, into *a* being.[118] The meaning of *nous* and being was torn from its experiential ground and immanentized in metaphysical constructions.[119] Protagoras opposed an immanent *physis* to the divine *nomos* of Heraclitus and declared the human being the measure of all things.[120] In fact the substitution of *physis* (physical nature) as a criterion of order for *nomos* (transcendent law) lay at the very heart of sophism. Hippias represents the replacement of the search that penetrates the depth of the *psyche* with encyclopedic knowledge. His teaching is reduced to information about things, which destroys the spiritual substance that alone can build the order of the soul and society.[121] The moral decline represented by sophism continued till the time of Plato. But already in the last third of the fifth century, under the

impact of the Peloponnesian War, Voegelin tells us, the spiritual substance of Athens had disintegrated and along with it the very idea of
the *nomos*.[122]

7:3. Finally, the upheavals that moved the age also moved Herodotus
and Thucydides to write their historical inquiries. In their work Greek
historiography reached its climax. In the midst of the struggle for civilizational power appears the historian, who surveys the various peoples
with their different *nomoi* and different gods but similar concupiscential
forces, such as greed and fear. From the perspective of the early fourth
century, the rise and fall of national states, with their attendant destruction and misery, all without discernible meaning, could be discerned.
Although Thucydides' historical insight virtually "created" the reality of
the Peloponnesian War out of a manifold of regional conflicts and battles
over a period of twenty-seven years, a true philosophical analysis escaped
him.[123] He could write only the anatomy of disordered passion because
"he could not see that the sphere of power and pragmatic rationalism is
not autonomous but part of human existence which as a whole includes
the rationality of spiritual and moral order."[124] He was unable to admit
that a corrupt society prevents the emergence of rational leadership or
that a wise man of spiritual substance would decline a leadership position
in such a society. Voegelin perceives in Thucydides' inability to even
imagine a spiritual reformer, on top of Athens' inability to create one,
the irrevocable demise of a political culture. An age had come to its
end. The time of the polis was withering, and only with the emergence
of Socrates and Plato did a new epoch of order appear.[125]

Platonic philosophy developed in reaction to these three cultural
forces (i.e., tragedy, sophism, and the decline of Athens), but also
in continuity with the tradition formed by Xenophanes, Parmenides,
and Heraclitus. In the world of the polis a revolutionary change was
fomenting which marked an epoch in the history of humankind. It was
based on an insight emanating from these pre-Socratic thinkers. The
insight is that "the order of the polis cannot remain the unquestioned,
ultimate order of society when an idea of man is in formation that
identifies humanity with the life of the common Logos in every soul."[126]
The problem seen by Plato was how to make this new hierarchical order
of the spirit effective in social practice. It was the question of how to
mediate institutionally the authoritative truth envisioned by a charismatic soul. His symbol of the philosopher-king was his first attempt to
link the order of the spirit with power, but it necessitated a program
of education by which the spiritual insights could be transmitted to
successive generations in society at large.

Plato and Aristotle

The second half of Voegelin's two-volume study of Greek philosophy deals with its two greatest representatives: Plato and Aristotle. It is particularly in Plato that Voegelin discovers the climax of the Greek experience of order, because in Plato is found the new order of the soul in relation to transcendent reality that is articulated on the most philosophically differentiated level.[127]

Plato was born during the great civilizational crises that afflicted Athens in the Greek fifth century. In his youth he experienced the disruptions of the Peloponnesian War and the reign of the Thirty Tyrants. But his most formative experience was "the paradigmatic life and death of the most just man, Socrates."[128] Although Socrates left behind no writings of his own, thus making the task of an historical reconstruction impossible, we are presented a reliable account through Plato's dialogues. To know Plato is to know Socrates. On the level of mind and spirit they are inseparably linked because, as Voegelin puts it, "the divine, regenerative force of order [was] transmitted by Socrates to Plato."[129] The corrupt polis that put Socrates to death made Plato despair of seeking a solution to social disorder through pragmatic politics, and so he turned away from a political career. Although he did involve himself briefly in pragmatic politics by way of his Sicilian expeditions, he became convinced that only the life of philosophy held out any hope for the regeneration of the polis, that the delicate merging of philosophy with political power could alone save society. And since he deemed this union of philosophy and politics, symbolized by the philosopher-king in the *Republic*, as an implausible eventuality, he committed himself to (1) the lifelong pursuit of philosophical truth, the experiences and symbols of which are mediated to us in the form of his dialogues, and (2) the education (*paideia*) of the souls of his followers in the life of the Academy which he founded, the task of educating others in the life of virtue as he had been educated by Socrates. Plato believed that true personal and social order could be attained only through creating an existential community that would form a person's true humanity by itself being formed around the erotic love of divine being. "For the young Plato," Voegelin tells us,

> philosophy consisted of an ordering of the soul by the three forces of Thanatos, Eros, and Dike; and, corresponding to the three forces, philosophy was the practice of dying, the erotic reaching out of the soul toward the Agathon, and the right ordering of the soul through participation in the Idea.[130]

As we can apprehend from Plato's *Seventh Letter*, the erotic relationship has an intimacy beyond words, and thus the wisdom that ensues
from it cannot be put down on paper as a teachable doctrine.[131] Such
an act would be a desecration of a mystery, for it would expose the
revelation to contempt and ridicule from those who do not understand
it.[132] Far from being some esoteric knowledge available only to the
privileged, the revelation is open to anyone who enters the life of
philosophy through the communion of *philia*. This was the experience
that led to the full differentiation of the soul and which formed the
heart of Plato's political philosophy. It is expressed in his anthropological
principle: society is the human being writ large. In any given society the
political order reflects the collective spirit of its members. Ultimately
the individual soul and the body politic not only mirror one another
but are mutually formed by one another.

The Platonic dialogues that Voegelin considers with the greatest
circumspection are principally the *Gorgias*, the *Republic*, the *Phaedrus*,
the *Statesman*, the *Timaeus*, and the *Laws*. I shall offer a brief explication
of each dialogue which should help illustrate the progress of Voegelin's
analysis of philosophical thought in Plato's works.

The *Gorgias* is the first dialogue where the order of a spiritually regenerated soul emerges as the true political authority. Socrates' encounter
with the spiritually disordered Callicles reveals that Socrates has virtually
conquered death insofar as he has allowed his soul to be penetrated by
death and is no longer a slave to the passions. Through this "catharsis of
the soul" the meaning of existence is revealed: through the experience
of death Socrates has reached a new life and in doing so reveals corrupt
Athens, represented by Callicles, as spiritually dead. Athens has lost its
soul. Authority, therefore, is transferred from the dead Athens and its
rulers to the new existential order represented by Plato-Socrates. This
transfer is a revolution on the level of the spirit. Its truth is borne out by
the fact that the order of the soul represented by Plato still has authority
today while the order of Athens went down in ignominy.[133]

Through the myth of the judgment of the dead at the end of the
dialogue, Plato reveals the nature of this new authority. In gist, the
myth is the story of a just man who prefers death to a life of injustice,
for it is better to suffer injustice than to commit it, because to die with
an unjust soul is the worst of all evils. True order is judged from the
"beyond." Only those souls, therefore, that have embraced death in life
can be the true judges of the "living."[134] The order of this "reborn"
soul reveals the new order of relation between God and humankind.
The old myths of the poets are superseded by the new myth of the
soul. "On this question," says Voegelin, "hinges the problem of history

as a meaningful order, i.e., as the process of revelation."[135] The *Gorgias*, therefore, emerges as the earliest of the Platonic dialogues that concern a philosophy of order and history, for by its myth of the soul it shows that "the revelation of divinity in history is ontologically real."[136]

The primary message of the *Republic*, Plato's most famous dialogue, amounts to this: "The right order of man and society is . . . an embodiment in historical reality of the idea of the Good, of the Agathon. The embodiment must be undertaken by the man who has seen the Agathon and let his soul be ordered through the vision, by the philosopher."[137] The vision of the *agathon* rests at the very center of the dialogue and is symbolized by the parable of the cave. Socrates, of course, is the philosopher who has ascended the cave to reach the light of truth only to descend back down the cave of Athens (symbolized by Piraeus in the opening of the dialogue) to educate the disordered cave-dwellers on the true order of the *agathon*.[138] The attack against the corrupt society is not against any political policy or particular social ailment; it is against the disease of the soul. The restoration requires a turning around (*periagoge*) of the whole soul, from ignorance to the truth of God, from opinion (*doxa*) about things to knowledge (*episteme*) of being.[139] Plato calls *paideia* "the art of turning around" toward the *agathon*. Though *periagoge* is not conversion in the Christian sense, it does carry the sense of a divine pull from beyond. *Paideia*, *periagoge*, and *agathon*, thus, are intimately connected in Plato's philosophy of order.[140]

Following Xenophanes, Plato believed that the truth of the one true God who is the same for all human beings and in relation to whom human beings discover their universal humanity must divest itself of the "unseemliness" inherent in the symbolizations of the gods. Plato introduces the "types of theology" as the conceptual instrument for clarifying this issue.[141] In this regard, the poets are grouped together with the sophists as causing the source of disorder because of their false stories of the gods, their false theology. A true theology which sets aright the relation between God and humanity is the problem that dominates the *Republic* as a whole.

Philosophy, therefore, has its origin in the resistance of the soul to the corruption all around it (a "true theology" becoming the ensuing form of resistance). It is most importantly an act of salvation because the right order that is established in the new community it creates saves its participants from the surrounding corruption. In this manner, remarks Voegelin, "philosophy is the ascent toward salvation for Everyman. . . . Plato's philosophy, therefore, is not *a* philosophy but *the* symbolic form in which a Dionysiac soul expresses its ascent to God."[142]

The real concern of Plato in this and his later works is the incarnation of the transcendent within the immanent. In the *Republic* this means that the decaying polis can be saved if it embodies the divine Idea. After first establishing the existence of an autonomous, divine–transcendent realm, accessible to *psyche*, over against the existing order of world and society, Plato reveals the manner in which this realm becomes a real, ordering force in human existence. The diseased polis will be replaced by a good polis, not through the manipulation of institutions, "but in the psyche of the founder or ruler who will stamp the pattern of his soul on the institutions."[143]

Up to this point, following Voegelin, "Plato plays back and forth in the *Republic* between the order of the polis and the order of the soul, illuminating the one through the other."[144] The anthropological principle viewed the soul as a micropolis and society as a macroanthropos. But the disengagement of the soul from society, first theorized in the *Gorgias*, is developed in a new direction toward the end of the *Republic*. At the end of book 9, where Plato makes a contrast between the government (*politeia*) within the soul and the government of existing states, a shift has occurred. The *politeia* within oneself is not employed as a metaphor for the soul as a micropolis; rather, Plato uses it to reflect the great distance between the well-ordered soul and the order of any existing polis.[145] The *politeia* within was previously spoken of as the true aim of education that would realize within the polis the paradigm of true order. Now a new insight emerges in the dialogue between Glaukon and Socrates. To Glaukon's suggestion that a wise man would not willingly take part in politics, this surprising answer follows:

> *Socrates:* By the dog, indeed he will; in his own polis he certainly will, though not in the city of his birth, unless a divine fortune lets that come to pass.
>
> *Glaukon:* I understand, you mean in the polis that we have now gone through as founders, and set up in our discourse, for I think that it exists nowhere on earth.
>
> *Socrates:* Well, there is perhaps a paradigm of it set up in heaven for him who desires to behold and beholding to settle in it. It makes no difference whether it exists concretely now or ever; that polis and none other is the one with which he is concerned. (592a–b)

Voegelin calls this brief exchange an artistic miracle: "Without change of terminology, through a slight switch from metaphor to reality, the inquiry into the paradigm of a good polis is revealed as an inquiry into man's existence in a community that lies, not only beyond the polis, but beyond any political order in history."[146] Later ages, he remarks, have seen correctly in this passage a prefiguration of Augustine's conception of the *civitas Dei*.[147] The paradigm of the best polis which the *Republic* sought to construct is now revealed as a model drawn from a reality beyond history and society. Even though this model ever seeks its realization in society, the transpolitical end of the human being emerges as the ultimate motif of human and divine order. It is this more fully differentiated movement toward the transcendent source of order that judges the leap in being in Plato as real.[148]

Nevertheless, because of his devotion to the polis as the fundamental form of political existence, Plato could not make world history the subject of his theoretical reflections. Parallel to Israel's identity as the chosen people, Voegelin spoke of this limitation in Plato as "the mortgage of the polis."[149]

The *Phaedrus* takes up the vision of the *agathon* in the polis. However, in this dialogue the isomorphic relation between soul and polis recedes behind the more intense relation between soul and Idea. It now achieves a higher degree of participation in erotic madness, in the *mania* of the lover.[150] On this point Voegelin asserts that

> the manic relation between the lover and the loved thus is eminently the *locus* at which the Idea gains its maximum intenseness of reality. In the communion of the manic souls the idea is embodied in reality, whatever may be its status of embodiment in the polis. In the community of the erotically philosophizing companions Plato has found the realm of the Idea; and insofar as, in the Academy, he is the founder of such a company, he has, indeed, embodied the Idea in the reality of a community.[151]

The incarnation of the Idea in the polis is no longer Plato's primary interest. The Idea will be embodied wherever it will, which is most intensely in the souls of erotic lovers. And so the conflict between the decaying polis of history and the best polis constructed in speech, which animated the *Republic*, is now translated into the hierarchy of different types of souls that are ranked in the *Phaedrus*, with the manic soul being the highest. Voegelin claims that after writing the *Republic*, Plato was resigned to the fact that Athens had rejected his appeal. In the *Phaedrus*, he denied the status of ultimate reality to the political realm by choosing to embody the Idea in individuals and small groups who alone would be the carriers of the transcendent in and through their community. In this dialogue, concludes Voegelin, Plato created a new ontology which became the foundation of his late political theory: "The communion is the source of the 'truth' of the mythical poems in which the late Plato symbolizes the life of the Idea."[152] So in a fashion similar to Israel's exodus from itself in the prophets' movement away from the concrete Israel that was symbolized by the suffering servant, the *Phaedrus*, Voegelin believes, "is the manifesto which announces the emigration of the spirit from the polis."[153]

With the acknowledgment of the disintegrated state of the polis as irreparable, Plato began to formulate the problem of politics in a trilogy of dialogues that culminates in the *Statesman*. In that dialogue he employs the myth of the cosmic cycles in which the age of Kronos is superseded by the age of Zeus. With this myth Plato signaled the withdrawal of the mythic gods from the cosmos and attributed the ultimate responsibility for civilizational order to humanity alone. The soul of the polis will not be formed by laws or institutions but by the few who possess the "ruling science" or "art of statesmanship" (*logos basilikos*).[154] The possession of this art determines the true rulers existentially, whether they rule or not. Since law cannot be the true order of human action, it is best that a man endowed with royal wisdom rule.[155] Although law is an inevitable ingredient of social order, in the perfect state the art of the ruler is the law.[156] The royal art is comprised of the weaving of the various virtues in the characters of men into a just fabric of society. Also, by binding the natural characters of men with the divine cord of truth, the true statesman becomes the mediator between the divine reality of the Idea and the people.[157]

The idea of the good polis was never satisfactorily clarified in the *Republic*. Beyond the *politeia* of the well-ordered soul and the paradigm of the best polis laid up in heaven, it left unanswered the question of the order of an actual polis in history. According to Voegelin, this question was answered by Plato in the *Timaeus*. In this dialogue the matter was solved "through the myth which transposes the well-ordered polis of the *Republic* from the status of a story to the status of an order in historical reality."[158] The character of the *Timaeus* is ahistorical; it is a drama within the soul of Plato. This is illustrated in the Egyptian myth of Athenian prehistory wherein Plato discovers Atlantis, not by his own autonomous imagination but through the anamnetic deciphering of the "collective unconscious"[159] living within his own *psyche*. The story symbolizes the dimension of an unconscious depth that is traced through the collective soul of the people to the generic soul of humankind into the primordial life of the cosmos from which springs the human being.[160] Voegelin explains the significance of this new development:

> The *Timaeus* has, indeed, moved beyond the *Republic* with its paradigm set up in heaven and beyond the forces of Thanatos, Eros, and Dike. For the paradigm in heaven now has to be authenticated by the assent of the unconscious; and the forces which orient the individual soul toward the Agathon are now supplemented by the forces of the collective soul which reaches, in its depth, into the life of the cosmos.[161]

The idea of the polis has reached its fullest expression, not because it has been embodied in history, "but because in the life of the soul the solitude of contemplation is now in harmony with the transpersonal rhythms of the people, of the human race, and of the cosmos."[162]

The *Timaeus* marks an epoch in human history because in it Plato develops the classic philosophy of the myth. In this work the *psyche* has reached the critical consciousness of the method by which it symbolizes its own experiences.[163] It marks the rise of spiritual consciousness to new levels. With this elevation to new heights (or depths) Plato has now discovered that "the myth is the ineluctable instrument for communicating the experience of the soul."[164] In contradistinction to the people's popular myths, the philosopher's myth expresses through mythical symbols a more differentiated level of consciousness.

The philosophical use of myth requires great circumspection. It assumes that there exist levels of reality that resist articulation in systematic discourse. It also assumes that the soul reaches beyond the limits of consciousness: "Beyond this area extends the reality of the soul, vast and darkening in depth, whose movements reach into the small area that is organized as the conscious subject."[165] These movements reverberate in consciousness without becoming objectifying entities. These images are not objects, yet they appear to be because "what enters the consciousness has to assume the 'form of an object' even if it is not an object."[166] Thus, the symbols of the myth that express the reverberations in the soul "can be defined as the refraction of the unconscious in the medium of objectifying consciousness."[167]

Although these mythic symbols do not refer to objects, their meaning is intelligible. We cannot apply to myth an epistemology developed on the model of sense experience of external objects. This would presume that the soul has in its totality the structure of "intentionality," that consciousness knows reality solely by intending objects.[168] Voegelin states that this would amount to "the anthropomorphic fallacy of forming man in the image of conscious man."[169] He goes on to say that this separation between the myth which speaks of realities beyond consciousness and knowledge that is constituted by acts of intentional consciousness "corresponds to the Christian distinction between the spheres of faith and reason."[170] Openness to the truth of the myth, which alone expresses the movements of the soul, is tantamount to the insight that found its classic expression in the Anselmian *credo ut intelligam*.[171]

Imitating the work of the Demiurge (Plato's symbol of divine incarnate creativity that represents the process in reality of establishing order out of cosmic disorder), the Statesman creates in the political realm an order analogous to the order of the cosmos. As the Demiurge imposes the paradigmatic order of the beyond on the discordant matter of the cosmos, so the Statesman imposes the form of the Idea on the disorder of recalcitrant historical matter.[172] The basis of political order in the *Republic* went as far as the consubstantial relation between soul and society. The philosophy of order is now expanded in the *Timaeus* by the insight into the consubstantiality of soul, society, and ultimately the cosmos. The evocation of the polis as a cosmic analogue Plato takes up further in the *Laws*.

The *Laws* is Plato's last and longest work. Though it was unfinished at his death it clearly lays out Plato's mature position on political and religious reality. Voegelin's analysis of this dialogue is extensive. For our purposes, however, a few comments will suffice to impart what Voegelin takes as its vital core of meaning.

The *Laws* aspired to an order of the polis that was of less spiritual intensity than that of the *Republic*. In his later years Plato saw that the resources for spiritual reform were nowhere to be found. His earlier appeal fell on deaf ears, he concluded, because people cannot endure the naked reality of the Idea. In the *Laws* the philosopher-savior of the *Republic* becomes the "ecclesiastic statesman" who develops theocratic institutions that will be bearable for people as they are.[173] What is offered now is a good constitution based on laws rather than a direct call for conversion. Accordingly, Plato develops "the second best polis"[174] that "will embody as much of the substance of the first [best polis] as the weaker human vessel can bear."[175] The new order envisaged in the *Laws*

> will consist of persons who can be habituated to the life of Arete under proper guidance, but who are unable to develop the source of order existentially in themselves and, therefore, need the constant persuasion of the prooemia [preamble to the laws] as well as the sanctions of the law, in order to keep them on the narrow path.[176]

The other dominant symbolism of the *Laws* appears in book 4 where Plato retells the myth of the cosmic cycles that first unfolded in the *Statesman* (713a–714b).[177] In the beginning there was the divine age of Kronos where people were ruled not by other people but by divine spirits sent from "the god" to insure peace and mercy, sound law and justice. In the *Statesman* this age was superseded by the age of Zeus marked by the autonomous personality of the philosopher. Redemption from the evils of this age would come about through the agency of the royal ruler who would replace the shepherd-god of the previous age. Now, in the *Laws*, both divine ages are delegated to the past. In book 3 Plato delivered the historical survey that put to a close the age of Zeus and confirmed the necessity for a new start. The new life beyond the age of Zeus will return back to the beginning. The new age will imitate the age of Kronos insofar as its institutions will once again be guided by "the god." The Athenian Stranger speaks accordingly:

> So the story (*logos*), which teaches us truly, is still valid today. It tells us that when a polis is ruled not by God but by man, its members have no escape from evil and misery. Hence we should do our utmost to imitate the Age of Cronos and to order our private and public life in accordance with what partakes of immortality (*athanasia*) within us. And, therefore, we should call by the name of law (*nomos*) the order of *nous*. (713c–714a)

The new god, then, who will rule in place of Zeus is not Kronos. Rather, it will be the new god of the Platonic *kosmos empsychos* (ensouled cosmos), the creative and persuasive *nous*.[178] Because a polis takes the name of its ruling part, it will assume the name of the god who rules over the wise, that is, over those who possess the *nous* (712e–713a). So the new age will be the age of *nous* and the new constitutional order will carry the name laws (*nomoi*). The new divine, ordering principle within the human being is intelligence and wisdom, the basis of laws. Through the *Laws*, Plato meant to transmit the wisdom of the age to future generations.[179] His three wandering interlocutors who seek to create the best constitutional order have "the god" as the goal of their long journey. In the end, as in Plato's end, their goal is inevitably linked to the beginning, for the first word of Plato's dialogue is *theos*: "God or some man, O strangers, who is supposed to have originated the institution of your laws?" (624a). Plato's answer is of course already known and uncompromising: "God is the measure of all things" (716c). This maxim is the hidden creed in all of his written works. In death as in life Plato's faith was likewise unwavering. As his final gesture of faith, Voegelin tells us, Plato helped the Thracian girl playing the flute at his death-bed find the beat of the *nomos* by pointing to the measure.[180]

In the year 367 B.C., over thirty years after the death of Socrates, Aristotle came to Athens and enrolled in the Academy. Plato, who was past sixty, had passed beyond his Socratic phase, which ended with the *Republic*, to embark on a new series of dialogues that elaborated his later theology. Aristotle, thus, entered the Academy at a critical juncture. In his early years he imbibed in the Platonic conception of philosophy as a movement of the soul and it left an indelible impression on him. Although Aristotle was explicit in his later criticism of Platonic theories, he was not as clear on what he took over and developed. But for Voegelin two major influences can be identified: "the young Aristotle was formed both by the Socratic tradition and by the new forces which tended to decompose it into its religious and intellectual components."[181] So although Aristotle certainly entered into the way of life of philosophy, Voegelin contends, he also entered into the debate that arose at this time on the doctrinal symbols that philosophy produced, such as the immortality and right order of the soul, the nature of the Idea, and the relations between God, humanity, world, and society.[182]

The Platonic realm of ideas was one of the symbols that expressed the philosopher's experience of transcendence. Aristotle himself participated in these experiences, but with his concentration on the world of immanent form he rebuked the notion of the Idea in Plato's thought. Aristotle rightly criticized this part of Platonic speculation that treated transcendental being as if it were a datum in the world of immanent experience. But, as Voegelin articulates the problem, Aristotle, while eliminating the confusion about the Platonic realm of ideas with his own clear ontology, "paid the great price of eliminating the problem of transcendental form along with its speculative misuse. . . . The consequence is a curious transformation of the experience of transcendence which can perhaps be described as an intellectual thinning-out."[183]

The political events during Aristotle's life had clearly destined the polis to doom. As a result he interpreted the consciousness of epoch in Plato not as signaling the new age of the regenerated polis but as a new spiritual aeon of the world.[184] Despairing of political renewal, Aristotle in his political philosophy stressed the pragmatic order of the polity. He set himself the task of formulating standards and devising means for their maximum realization under various material conditions. And so a continuity of evolution can be seen from Plato's good polis of the *Republic* through the second-best polis of the *Laws*, to Aristotle's *Politics*. Aristotle's specific aim is not a quest for mystical knowledge or the perfect polis, but a contemplative working out of problems as they present themselves in the world of practical living.

This shift from the transcendental to the pragmatic had repercussions in Aristotle's theory of knowledge and the myth. Compared with the Platonic fullness of experience, Aristotle, according to Voegelin, tended to replace the *psyche*, along with its unconscious depth which assured us of the truth of the myth, with the field of historical studies.[185] Although this was his propensity, in his last years, reflecting perhaps a renewed appreciation of Plato, Aristotle made the statement: "The more I am by myself and alone, the more I have come to love myths."[186]

The contemplative life alluded to above marks the acme of Aristotelian philosophizing. In his anthropology, Aristotle sought to ascertain the highest good in the nature of humanity. He concluded that the life of contemplation (*bios theoretikos*) is the highest good. It is the way of life by which true happiness (*eudaimonia*) can be achieved. This is supported by his analysis of the faculties of the human soul. The rational faculties are the highest because it is through them that humans achieve their greatest excellence. Consequently, the dianoetic virtues (*episteme, phronesis, sophia, nous*) are ranked higher than the ethical ones (justice, courage, temperance), for they alone lead to the *eudaimonia* of the *bios theoretikos*.[187] Ultimately the greatest emphasis falls on the *nous*. As *nous*, the human being achieves immortality by participating in the divine *nous*.[188] Also, the just order of society depends on the noetic order actualized in the human soul. Through this common order human beings enter into *homonoia*, the "political friendship" upon which the just society is based.[189] It must be remembered, however, that Aristotle believes that true happiness can be found only by transcending the life of politics in the practice of the dianoetic virtues.[190] The theoretic life has no purpose beyond itself. As the human being's most perfect excellence its activity is loved for its own sake.

The order of Aristotle's polis would be realized not through the philosopher or ecclesiastic statesman, nor even through a constitution of laws; it would depend most of all on the few, the *spoudaioi*, who, by developing their excellences, would be the only true citizens of the polis. The *spoudaios* is Aristotle's "mature, virtuous person" who seeks the truth in everything and thus is the norm and measure for a society.[191]

In this vein, Voegelin tells us, Aristotle contracted the realm of politics into the institutional means of order. What was held together under the term "political" in Plato is in Aristotle differentiated into "ethics" and "politics": "Ethics is the science of excellences; politics is the science of the institutional means which are apt to produce the excellences in the citizens."[192] As a result, Aristotle was able to articulate the wisdom of the excellences apart from their political actualization. With political history inevitably deteriorating, Aristotle, by this maneuver, elevated the prudential wisdom achieved by Greek philosophy to a standard for all humankind beyond any particular political setting. In this light, Voegelin concludes, "the *Nicomachean Ethics* is the great document in which the authority of the *spoudaios* asserts itself through the ages, beyond the accidents of politics."[193] Unfortunately, this division gave Aristotle's political science a limited horizon since it was conceived as the nomothetic (law-making) art for the polis and nothing but the polis.[194]

Aristotle failed to issue a call for repentance and submission to the incarnate truth. Instead, he concentrated on analyzing the "imperfections" in society (which gave them only ontological legitimacy). By this failure, along with his conception of an immanent fulfillment of the human being in the *bios theoretikos*, Voegelin discerned a problem which he discussed under the title: "the failure of immanentist metaphysics."[195] Aristotle believed that human perfection, though rare, was attainable within the world. Despite parts of the soul participating in the divine *nous*, thereby becoming immortal, the whole soul was not transformed through an experience of transcendence, such as the Platonic vision (*opsis*) or turning around (*periagoge*) toward the *agathon*. In matters of political philosophy, Voegelin opts for the philosophical experience of Socrates-Plato differentiated by "the cathartic experience of Thanatos and the enthusiastic experience of Eros open toward transcendental reality."[196] The human being cannot be described accurately as a world-immanent object. Since the human being exists in openness toward transcendence, Voegelin asserts, "the formation of the soul through invading transcendence is part of that 'nature' that we explore in metaphysics."[197] With the immanentizing of the human being's perfected end, Aristotle neglected to handle properly this complex of experiences that constitutes human nature. In exploring the spiritual order of the soul the philosopher uses language symbols, often mythic, to express the soul's experience of transcendence. Thus, with Aristotle's deficiency in mind, Voegelin declares that "at the border of transcendence the language of philosophical anthropology must become the language of religious symbolization."[198]

With the demise of the Socratic-Platonic impulse, transcendental perfection became transformed into immanent fulfillment. The consequence of this "immanentism" in Aristotle's "metaphysics" became visible in the philosophical schools that followed Aristotle. In Pyrrho of Elis, a younger contemporary of Aristotle, this aspiration produced the suspension of judgment in matters of truth and knowledge. For example, he taught that the nature of things is indiscernible and that we must rest without beliefs, opinions, or inclinations so as to achieve a quietude of mind.[199] The age of skepticism was dawning and the Stoic derailment of philosophy that followed left the originating experiences of the soul in an ever-darkening shadow.

The problem of the Aristotelian aporia, thus, has historical significance, not only in regard to those who immediately followed Aristotle, but also for the subsequent course of Western civilization and its symbolization of order. Voegelin gives this problem the name "the historicity of Truth." It was a problem that would occupy him until he published the next volume of *Order and History* seventeen years later. Voegelin articulated this problem in this way:

Truth is not a body of propositions about a world-immanent object; it is the world-transcendent *summum bonum*, experienced as an orienting force in the soul, about which we can speak only in analogical symbols. Transcendental reality cannot be an object of cognition in the manner of a world-immanent datum because it does not share with man the finiteness and temporality of immanent existence. It is eternal, out-of-time; it is not co-temporal with the experiencing soul. When, through the experiences of the Socratic-Platonic type, eternity enters time, we may say that "Truth" becomes "historical." That means, of course, neither that the flash of eternity into time is the privileged experience of philosophers, nor that now, at a specific date in history, it occurred for the first time. It means that in the critical period under discussion we are advancing, in the Platonic sense, from the symbolizations of the people's myth to the differentiated experiences of the philosophers and to their symbolizations. This advance is part of the historical process in which the older symbolic order of the myth disintegrates in the souls (in the previously described manner) and a new order of the soul in openness to transcendental reality is restored on a more differentiated level. By "historicity of Truth" we mean that transcendental reality, precisely because it is not an object of world-immanent knowledge, has a history of experience and symbolization.[200]

This history of experience and symbolization was to find an even greater differentiation of consciousness beyond that explored in the first three volumes of *Order and History*. The next leap in being emerged with the appearance of Christianity, which Voegelin had planned to analyze in his next volume. Although, as we shall soon discover, he eventually abandoned his proposed study, the outline of what he would have said seemed clear at this juncture. In the first three volumes he sprinkled numerous remarks about the nature of the Christian experience of order which was deemed superior to that achieved by Israel and Greece.[201] For example, he referred to (1) the new revelation of spiritual order through Christ; (2) the existential *philia* between God and humankind; (3) supernatural perfection through Grace in death; (4) the *fides caritate formata* in St. Thomas; (5) the Mystical Body as the new *homonoia*; (6) the *beatitudo* of the soul; and, more cryptically, (7) the incarnation of God in a man. These enticing themes provoked a craving for the long-awaited volume on Christianity. However, Voegelin diverted from his original plan and instead eventually published a volume that was received with some bewilderment, even reproach, by a number of Christian scholars, among them even his own followers.

The analysis of human order in history symbolized through myth, philosophy, and revelation underwent new linguistic articulation in

Voegelin's later work, but not in discontinuity with these first three volumes. The subject matter treated in these volumes required renewed interpretation as a result of Voegelin's extended study of the historical materials and his developing theory of consciousness.

3

THE THEORY REFINED:
THE LATER WRITINGS, 1960–74

A Period of Transition

Between 1960 and 1974, Voegelin published a series of essays that expressed a more refined view of his understanding of consciousness and its experiences of transcendence.[1] The continual development of his philosophy of consciousness was prompted by the incessant theoretical problems that he encountered in the wake of a more careful scrutiny of the historical materials. As a result, these studies reveal a transitional period in Voegelin's work, a period in which he moved away from the further explication of the order of history conceived as a course toward a more foundational analysis of consciousness and history. This shift prefigured the break in the original program of *Order and History* which was to be announced in volume IV, *The Ecumenic Age*.[2] What can be observed in these essays are the characteristics of consciousness that came to light through the prolonged study of the classical texts, certain attributes that were lacking in Voegelin's earlier account of consciousness.[3] Reaffirming his conviction that human consciousness is constituted by its tension toward the divine ground of being, he proposed new concepts (such as *metaxy, noesis, ratio,* pneumatic vision, linguistic indices, dogmatomachy, flowing presence, etc.) which contributed to a more advanced explication of consciousness and its derailment. This revision also carried with it a more developed understanding of reason and revelation. The basic features of Voegelin's refined theory can be outlined as follows:

Human being participates in eternal being. This participation is consciousness itself. The engendering experiences of philosophy reveal the soul as the site where the temporal being of humans and the eternal being beyond the human interpenetrate. The knowledge of this interpenetration is not a form of object knowledge but the awareness of a tension between two poles of being. These poles are not "objects" separable from experience; rather, they denote the reach of experiences of transcendence. From the temporal pole the experience is characterized by seeking, yearning, and receiving; from the eternal pole it is characterized by a pouring forth of grace and love.[4] These are the philosophic experiences that are symbolized by Plato in the allegory of the cave in the *Republic* and by Socrates' speech on love in the *Symposium*. It is the experience of transcendence that Voegelin calls "noetic."

But how does a finite temporal being experience an infinite eternal being? How do these two realities interpenetrate? Since these experiences are beyond any doubt to those who bear them, and whose validity thus is beyond the realm of proof, Voegelin suggests that there is something nontemporal within the human being by which he or she experiences the tension toward the ground. Voegelin overcomes this seeming paradox by interpreting the temporal being of humanity not as an objective property within the human being but as an "index" of experience. "Temporal being" and "eternal being" are both linguistic indices of noetic experience.[5] They are characterizations of experiences of participation which arise out of a philosopher's interpretation. This tension of participation, then, may be described by directional indices of immanent and transcendent poles of being. The immanence of the world is no longer understood as a part of the primary experience of the cosmos, but as a feature of the structure of reality which arises in noetic experience. So the range of human experience is now conceived to contain three dimensions of reality: (1) the world of things known through perception, which lies on the temporal pole in the tension of time and eternity; (2) the divine reality of the ground (*arche*), which lies on the eternal pole of the tension; and (3) the reality of consciousness itself, which participates in both.

If time and eternity are indices and not objects, where then do experiences of transcendence occur? Voegelin, capitalizing on a Platonic term that has been given faint recognition as a symbol of transcendence, says that they occur in the *metaxy*, the in-between reality that is in neither time nor eternity:

> By "in-between" I translate the concept of the *metaxy* developed by Plato in the *Symposium* and the *Philebus*. Man experiences himself as tending beyond his human imperfection toward the perfection of the divine ground that moves him. The spiritual man, the *daimonios aner*, as he is moved in his quest of the ground, moves somewhere between knowledge and ignorance (*metaxy sophias kai amathias*). "The whole realm of the spiritual (*daimonian*) is halfway indeed between (*metaxy*) god and man" (Symp. 202a). Thus, the in-between—the *metaxy*—is not an empty space between the poles of the

tension but the "realm of the spiritual"; it is the reality of "man's converse with the gods" (202–203), the mutual participation (*methexis, metalepsis*) of human in divine, and divine in human, reality.[6]

A difficulty that arises with this new problem of the timeless *metaxy* is that experiences of transcendence are felt as having duration in world-time. Voegelin firmly believes, however, that these experiences do not occur in time but in the *metaxy*, between time and eternity. The appearance of duration in world-time occurs because we can assign dates of world-time to the experiences, and this is possible because the subject who undergoes the experience is a concrete human being with a material body that exists in time. This difficulty Voegelin calls "a fundamental problem of ontology," but it does not justify our placing the *metaxy* in world-time.[7] However, this view does modify the thesis of his 1943 essay that the present in the luminous process of consciousness possesses past and future as inner dimensions. Therefore, the metaphor of Augustine's *distentio animi*, from which this understanding of time was derived, must now be rejected in order to account for the experience of consciousness as the nonobjective reality of the in-between. In order not to confuse the past, present, and future of the external world with the luminosity of consciousness in which immanence and transcendence interpenetrate, Voegelin introduced the term "flowing presence." This temporal flow of experience in which eternity is present "cannot be dissected into past, present, and future of the world's time, for at every point of the flow there is the tension toward the transcending, eternal being."[8]

The upshot of this more refined view is that there are processes in reality that do not occur in world-time. The process of the ground occurs in the *metaxy*. Since experiences in the *metaxy* are encounters between God and human beings, then history consists not in prag-matic happenings in world-time but in the divine–human encounters in the flowing presence. As a consequence, Voegelin asserted that the only constant in human history is the structure of human existence understood as a process in the mode of presence (and not as chronolog-ical progression). Since this process is known only in the engendering experiences, Voegelin was led to formulate his important theory of "equivalence." According to this theory, no matter what symbolic form the participation of the human being in reality assumes, the engendering experiences are equivalent (not the same) insofar as they reveal the metaxic structure of existence. In his major essay on this issue, Voegelin spelled out the contours of the theory:

The sameness which justifies the language of "equivalences" does not lie in the symbols themselves but in the experiences which have engendered them. The language of "equivalences," thus, implies the theoretical insight that not the symbols themselves but the constants of engendering experience are the true subject matter of our studies.

What is permanent in the history of mankind is not the symbols but man himself in search of his humanity and its order.[9]

This theory of equivalence was an attempt to overturn the conventional theory of values which dominates the contemporary intellectual scene. The myriad symbols generated throughout human history can no longer be considered as disparate expressions of various cultural experiences relative to one another, but as the multifaceted manifestation of the one search for the divine ground. And so, for Voegelin, the basis of a comparative study of symbols becomes a search for the constants of experience, one constant being the search itself which has been going on for millennia. As he explains, this shift of viewpoint brought the cosmological myth into a new light:

> Myth is not a primitive symbolic form, peculiar to early societies and progressively to be overcome by positive science, but the language in which the experiences of human-divine participation in the In-Between become articulate. The symbolization of the participating existence, it is true, evolves historically from the more compact form of the cosmological myth to the more differentiated forms of philosophy, prophecy, and the gospel, but the differentiating insight, far from abolishing the *metaxy* of existence, brings it to fully articulate knowledge.[10]

The culmination of these insights would reach their climax in *The Ecumenic Age*, where Voegelin would state flatly that "there is no history other than the history constituted in the Metaxy of differentiating consciousness."[11]

In working through the classic and Christian sources more deeply during this period, Voegelin also had to revise his earlier strict distinction between philosophy and revelation. His reason for doing so was that the conventional pairing of these terms tended to imply a strict contrast, whereas his heightened understanding of theophanic experiences required the articulation of principles which emphasized their fundamental continuity. This rearticulation was perhaps triggered by Voegelin's increasing realization that the cultural contexts of the emergence of philosophy and revelation were in many ways accidents. That philosophy emerged in Greece and revelation in Israel is indubitably true, but we must not conclude from this fact that they represent completely separate forms of differentiation. Breakthroughs in consciousness occur where they will, but the difference between these two primordial styles of differentiation (that *de facto* emerged, not *de jure*) may lie more in the differences of the ethnic societies that carried them than in the breakthroughs themselves. It is an unquestioned premise today that how a person interprets and symbolizes an experience will be determined by the culture that mediates that individual's world of meaning. One's social history is all important, especially in the case of a theophany. A Jeremiah will interpret his experience of God on the order of prophetic preparation beginning with Abraham and Moses, and proceeding through Elijah and Isaiah. A Plato will interpret his experience of God on the order of philosophical preparation beginning with Homer and Hesiod, and advancing through Parmenides and Socrates. Each is concerned with the experience of God but understands the encounter differently due to his cultural, ethnic, and religious context. Both breakthroughs are elicited by revelation, and both employ human reason, though the accent on one or the other is weighted differently depending not just on the nature of the experience itself, which is primary, but also on the cultural preparation of the experiences that guides their interpretation and symbolization.

Nevertheless, there is a structural distinction on the level of experience. Accordingly, Voegelin formulated a new conceptual framework to account for the fact that encounters between God and the human being in the *metaxy* have two distinct modes. In some experiences of transcendence the accent falls on "the human seeking-and-receiving pole"; in other experiences the accent falls on "the divine giving-and-commanding pole." For the first, experience has the character of an illumination of the *metaxy*, and the order of being becomes dominant. These are the philosophic or "noetic" experiences. For the second, experience is condensed to a communication of a divine irruption. Voegelin calls these "pneumatic experiences."[12] The divine ground of being can be experienced either noetically as the actualizing *nous*, or pneumatically as the attracting and drawing God who is both creator and savior. As an example of these dual modes of experience, Voegelin discovered in his research into equivalent symbolizations that the "drawing" (*helkein*) of the divine ground, which is a property of noetic experience portrayed by Plato in the *Republic* and the *Laws*, is equivalent to the pneumatic experience portrayed in the Gospel of John, where identical language is used.[13] Although distinct forces of existential unrest, the divine drawing (*helkein*) or tensional pull, and the human seeking (*zetesis*) or tensional push, are one and the same movement of the soul toward ultimate reality. In other words, every movement of the soul toward a heightened participation in being is actually composed of two distinct forces: the seeking for truth from the side of the human pole and the graced drawing from the side of the divine pole. Depending on which pole is more prominent in the experience, the experience can be designated as either noetic or pneumatic. If the emphasis is on the struggle for truth and reflective illumination, then the experience is under the guise of noetic control and psychic balance will consequently be maintained. If the emphasis is on the *mysterium tremendum et fascinans* and its awesome presence, the transcendent force on the soul, although eliciting a spiritual regeneration, can lead to a disabling enthusiasm and noetic distortion. If it is powerful enough, the immediate experience of divine being can evoke uncritical symbols, whereby the metaxic structure of existence is lost or forgotten.[14]

Voegelin would eventually distinguish the Greek differentiation of consciousness from the Israelite-Christian differentiation by claiming that in both cases "the structure of a theophanic experience reaches from a pneumatic center to a noetic periphery."[15] But in the former there is an emphasis on the noetic control of meaning, whereby the recipient of the revelation is led to analyze the structures in reality revealed by the new insight, while in the latter the recipient is so enthused by the deeper, more encompassing vision of the whole experienced in the theophanic event that he or she is not inclined to understand the new insights in relation to the primary experience of the cosmos but rather to be absorbed by the preeminence of the new transfiguring order. The language that ensues from such a pneumatic experience is thus not philosophical but prophetic, which emphasizes the redemptive order glimpsed by the recipient that is radically different from the order of this world. However equivalent the structural forces are in the theophanic event, Voegelin was adamantly clear that the response of a Plato is not that of a Jeremiah. In a passage reflective of this transitional period, found in his essay "What Is History?" which was completed about 1963, Voegelin reminds us of the unique difference of these two fundamental modes of response to the truth of existence:

> The philosopher is not a prophet. The truth as pronounced by the prophet is as valid for him as for any other man; but when the philosopher himself pronounces on the truth of existence, he is not permitted to use the symbols of Revelation or, for that matter, of Myth. His is the realm of Reason; and in the noetic domain the drama of history is not enacted by the *dramatis personae* of a Jeremiah.[16]

Because of their fundamental continuity, however, noetic philosophy does not stand opposed to pneumatic revelation. The noetic striving of the philosopher is motivated by the same love of God that is central to pneumatic experience. In fact it is this very experience of falling in love with the goal of one's being that instigates the noetic striving toward it. This is why Voegelin speaks of "the constitution of reason through revelation,"[17] for reason was itself a revelation in the *psyche* of the Greek philosophers, and the New Testament was not devoid of noetic articulation. In this light, one must understand symbolizations like Augustine's "the heart is restless until it rests in thee" and Pascal's "the heart has reasons that reason does not know" as indicating the bilateral structure of religious experience, inclusive of both noetic and pneumatic dimensions. However one formulates the relation between reason and revelation, the strict division between these two modes of divine-human mediation, Voegelin eventually urged, must be abandoned altogether:

> This double status of the symbols which express the movement in the *metaxy* had been badly obscured in Western history by Christian theologians who have split the two components of symbolic truth, monopolizing, under the title of "revelation," for Christian symbols the divine component, while assigning, under the title of "natural reason," to philosophical symbols the human component. This theological doctrine is empirically untenable— Plato was just as conscious of the revelatory component in the truth of his *logos* as the prophets of Israel or the authors of the New Testament writings. The differences between prophecy, classic philosophy, and the Gospel must be sought in the degrees of differentiation of existential truth.[18]

In Voegelin's later writings, these differences were to be more clearly spelled out;[19] but before we turn to a consideration of volume IV, *The Ecumenic Age*, it will be helpful to recapitulate the language symbols that express the authentic philosophic experience which is so important to Voegelin's theory of consciousness.[20] I shall then delineate in a preliminary manner the significance of this philosophic experience for Voegelin's mature philosophy of history.

Consciousness is experienced as a process of participation (*methexis*, *metalepsis*) in the in-between (*metaxy*) of the immanent reality of things on one side and the transcendent reality of the divine ground on the other. Consequently, the soul (*psyche*), which is experienced as the site and sensorium of transcendence, is situated between the unbounded source (*apeiron*) of all particular things and the one eternal beyond (*epekeina*) experienced as *nous*. This area of metaleptic reality, between the apeirontic depth and the noetic height, is the proper domain of human knowledge. The process of consciousness occurs in the tension (*tasis*)[21] between these two poles. The existential unrest of the philosopher, compounded by wondering (*thaumazein*), seeking (*zetein*), and questioning (*diaporein*) experienced from within, along with the pull (*helkein*) of the divine ground (*arche, theotes*) from beyond, moves (*kinesis*) him or her to undertake a rational (*noesis*) quest (*zetesis*) for the ground. This quest is an immortalizing (*athanatizein*) process experienced (*pathos*) as a personal conversion (*periagoge*), a turning around from ignorance (*agnoia, amathis*) and opinion (*doxa*) toward the one true reality (*aletheia*), toward real knowledge (*episteme*) and the good (*agathon*). The concrete modes of existence which orient the spiritual person (*daimonios aner*) toward the object of his or her search are faith (*pistis*), hope (*elpis*), and love (*eros, philia*). The name of the dimension of consciousness which participates most fully in transcendent divine being is reason (*nous*). The exegetical account of that participation comprises the philosophy of the human being.

Of course these differentiating insights can be lost, forgotten, or deformed through a process of hypostatization and doctrinalization. Worse, they can be obliterated altogether by "philosophies" which rebel against the ground. These are in fact pseudo-philosophies which express themselves in modern gnostic and apocalyptic symbolisms which Voegelin has analyzed in great detail. They are radically immanentized versions of transcendence, and the ultimate source of these deformations, according to Voegelin, is rooted in human *superbia vitae* or *libido dominandi*.[22]

Turning away from the ground is *the* spiritual disease that grips the modern age. To escape the tension toward the ground is to reject reason and to forsake one's humanity (or in contemporary parlance, one's authentic self). Thus, the modern form of existence is variously expressed in terms of "alienation," "anxiety," or "rebellion."[23] This deformed mode of existence found precise articulation in the *divertissements* of Pascal,[24] which are the substitutes for the real ground of existence, i.e., Augustine's "rest." As world-immanent pseudo-grounds these substitutes cannot alleviate the restlessness of the modern person. Their failure only adds to the desperate search for more substitutes. This frantic and perpetual quest for fulfillment is constricted to the realm of the self which knows no horizon beyond the self. One's eternal destiny and the life of the spirit are absorbed into an egophanic act of self-salvation. And so the symptoms of this disease are chronic self-indulgence and self-aggrandizement which only eclipse reality rather than reveal it.[25] In an important essay devoted to an analysis of this spiritual disease, "The Eclipse of Reality" (recently published in its entirety), Voegelin specified further the symptoms of the person afflicted with disordered existence but who seeks to regain some semblance of the real:

His life may then assume such behavioral forms as libertinism, hedonism, the cult of violence, destructiveness, vandalism, or outright criminality. If even his animal vitality should fail him, he may sink even lower—for instance, into the stupor of television watching—or he may take to drugs in order to "turn on" an existence that has been turned off beyond hope, or he may find the way out into a clinical neurosis. The phenomena adumbrated, common in our time, must be understood as severe forms of existential disintegration under the pressure of a social environment in which the truth of reality has been successfully eclipsed by the authority of ignorance.[26]

Philosophy in its therapeutic mode must, therefore, confront what Schelling called the "pneumapathology" of the age in order to recover the noetic order of human existence.[27] All forms of pneumapathology must ultimately be traced back to some strategy for repressing or denying the inevitable tension of life in the in-between. This metaxic tension is most fully realized in the life of mystics through the experiences of what, as they say, are ineffable—experiences that are universally available to, and ultimately constitutive of, all humans as human, though rarely achieved. But Voegelin's great efforts in overcoming this deformation of the tension has not rested with his own therapeutic recovery of the soul's movement toward the beyond in classical mysticism. His whole project has been directed toward the larger task of restoring the problem of the *metaxy* for society and history.[28] As such it can be categorized as concurrently and without contradiction a philosophical and mystical, as well as, in the ancient meaning of the words, scientific and political, endeavor.

In light of this larger task, finally, some further comments on Voegelin's own development as a philosopher must be noted before we analyze *The Ecumenic Age*. First of all, it should by now be clear that the transitions which Voegelin was forced to undergo in the course of his studies mirror the very nature of philosophy described above. For philosophy is by no means a construing of a field of study; it is a *zetema*, an endless inquiry into the heights and depths of reality via an exegesis of consciousness. As it proceeds it develops particular interpretive models or symbols which by their mythic and analogical character attempt to circumscribe the nature of reality under analysis. The philosophical rendering of reality is never absolute because by definition it is motivated not by the right view of things (which ultimately belongs to God alone) but by "openness" and "existence in truth." The self-interpretation of consciousness is never achieved once and for all; it is a process in the lifetime of a human being. As a result, the definitions, concepts, and symbols of a philosopher achieved at an earlier stage of his or her *zetema* are likely to be superceded by those achieved at a later stage. The *zetema* as an ongoing quest for truth never achieves a final resting point; it comes to a halt only with the death of the philosopher, only then to be taken up by others. Therefore, a philosopher like Voegelin must be read in a way that views the later insights and symbols achieved in the course of his study as qualifying and superseding the earlier ones.[29]

Secondly, as the questing consciousness of the philosopher makes the truth of reality luminous, one can speak of a never-ending *zetema* within history. This larger *zetema* is constituted by the advances achieved by every philosophical and historical inquiry that builds upon past achievements. This *zetema* advancing through history, which is formed and deformed by the forces of order and disorder and which must be captured and recaptured by the philosopher's meditative process, is the truth of reality becoming ever luminous through image, symbol, and word. No image or symbol or word, however, is absolute. Every vision of reality, no matter how comprehensive, finds its imagery corrected by the differentiating process of reason and revelation in history.[30] In his final study, Voegelin expressed the corrective work of imagination in these words:

> The movement toward truth always resists an untruth. Every thinker who is engaged in the quest for truth resists a received symbolism he considers insufficient to express truly the reality of his responsive experience. In order to aim at a truer truth he has to out-imagine the symbols hitherto imagined.[31]

In short, history is the unfolding of the human *psyche*. If philosophy is the meditative analysis of the *psyche* in its apeirontic depth and noetic height—the undertaking that was first identified by Heraclitus—then historiography is the reconstruction of the unfolding of the *psyche* through the *psyche* of the historian. The work of interpretation and reconstruction requires the participation in the great dialogue that proceeds through the centuries among those who partake in the *zetema* of their own nature and destiny. This participation will always look toward the best minds as the authoritative guides on the way to achieving growth in intellectual and spiritual stature. This is why Voegelin always returns to Plato and Aristotle in his own internal dialogue; but he does not simply repeat what they said, for he is a philosopher in his own right, engaged in his own *zetema*.

Hence, we can illustrate Voegelin's unique contribution to a philosophy of history by stressing the following point: Voegelin did not simply baptize Plato and Aristotle. He recognized the need for a "more differentiated language than that of classic philosophy"[32] which he set out to provide. And his advance beyond the classics is further elucidated by recalling that Aristotle did not continue after his *Ethics* and *Politics*, which dealt, respectively, with the individual and society, to write an *Historics*—whereas Voegelin did, and in this endeavor lies his greatest achievement: *Order and History* is not only a great work in ethics and politics, it is also an historics of human existence which may be the authoritative guide in historiography for generations to come.

The Ecumenic Age

In his last major work, *The Ecumenic Age*, Voegelin adds a new dimension to his developing theory. This work, which announces the break in his original program, marks the third stage of his philosophy of history and consciousness.[33] This stage represents the mature thought of a philosopher who after years of study was forced to revise the course of his program in order to accommodate the intractable data of history. In order to overcome the impenetrable problems that arose upon discovering that the historical materials could no longer fit the unfolding of the order of history as he first schematized it, Voegelin had to abandon his original program and adopt a fresh course of analysis.[34] A change in perception was required in order to render intelligible the true order of history. Although there was nothing wrong with the original principle of the study, and his prior analyses "were still valid as far as they went," the project as originally conceived "was untenable because it had not taken proper account of the important lines of meaning in history that did not run along lines of time."[35] In explaining this change, Voegelin outlined two specific problems he encountered: expansion of the spiritual horizon and historiogenesis.

EXPANSION OF THE SPIRITUAL HORIZON

The first problem pertained to the Ecumenic Age itself. This is the critical period in imperialism and empire building, lasting roughly eleven hundred years between the sixth century B.C. and the sixth century A.D. The conquest of a multitude of ethnic societies by vast empires during this epoch laid the foundation for the rise of ecumenic consciousness. It was also a period of great spiritual fecundity, characterized by a great diversity of spiritual experiences. At the beginning of this period a number of different spiritual "outbursts" appeared in both East and West with little apparent connection with one another: In Persia, there was Zoroaster; in China, Confucius and Lao-Tzu;

in India, the Buddha; in Greece, the philosophers; and in Israel, the prophets and Christ. The parallelism of spiritual outbursts could not be explained by cultural diffusion—the nineteenth century view influenced by positivism.[36] Voegelin, who as a philosopher will not engage in either positivist or theological a priorities, had to conclude that the totality of truth in history cannot emanate from one single, spiritual event, that history is constituted by an unconnected plurality of spiritual events. In other words, "the spirit blows where it will" (John 3:8). Furthermore, it is impossible to locate these events on a single line of time or in any scheme of linear progression. Jaspers's conception of an "axis-time," which draws together these theophanic events into one significant "age" of humankind, appeared to be a plausible alternative. But even this formulation Voegelin rejected as empirically unsound, not only because Jaspers's periodization was limited by all it excluded, but also because there was no such common experience in the consciousness of the participants; it was a characterization imposed from the outside.[37] So even though the evolution of modern historiography, advanced by men such as Spengler, Toynbee, and Jaspers, culminated in a retheorization of the philosophy of history, their work did not go far enough. The explosion of empirical materials, freed from ideological constructs only in our century, demanded a still-higher viewpoint that encompasses the truth of existence, universal humanity, eschatology, and experiences of transcendence and their equivalence, as foundational for the new study of order and history.

This expansion of the spiritual horizon, along with the new emphasis on "the equivalences of experience and symbolization in history," led Voegelin to nearly abandon the "leap in being" terminology. This was so chiefly because he wanted to escape the ambiguity inherent in a phrase whose further use could leave his radically universalist stance questionable. The enthusiasm and sense of discovery that accompanied the great spiritual experiences, the so-called leaps in being, did not lead to a sensitive and balanced appraisal of earlier times. For example, in the wake of the Israelite and Hellenic theophanies, symbols appeared that marked the before and after of revelation.[38] This demarcation first appeared in the lives of those who received the revelation (e.g., Moses, Socrates, Plato, Jesus, and Paul). In retrospect the revelation denoted a representational advance in society as a whole, or even for the whole of humankind. But this before/after symbolism is apt to cast a shroud of oblivion on the discoveries which preceded the event. The new person who emerges from the event is not so radically new as the enthusiasm of the event might lead the experiencer to believe, nor is the old person consigned to the past so radically superseded. The historiographic conventions based on this symbolism can distort cultural history and are usually blind to the fact of continuity in the unfolding of revelation in history.[39] In his essay, "The Gospel and Culture," Voegelin gave clear expression to this problem, stating that

> the spectacular breakthroughs in history leave in their wake a sediment of Before-and-After symbols which severely distort reality, when they are used in the interpretation of cultural history: before philosophy there was myth; before Christianity there were pagan idols and the Jewish Law; before monotheism there was polytheism.... This sediment of phenotypes ignores that, as a matter of historical record, the truth of reality is always fully present in man's experience and that what changes are the degrees of differentiation. Cosmological cultures are not a domain of primitive "idolatry," "polytheism," or "paganism," but highly sophisticated fields of mythical imagination, quite capable of finding the proper symbols for the concrete or typical cases of divine presence in a cosmos in which divine reality is omnipresent.[40]

HISTORIOGENESIS

The other problem Voegelin encountered pertained to his understanding of the development of human consciousness. Previously, he understood meaning in history to be constituted by the movement from a "cosmological" mentality to a "differentiated" one, whereby the "leaps in being," represented by Israelite revelation and Greek philosophy, yielded a historical consciousness. Although this view was basically sound it had to be modified when Voegelin discovered evidence of historical consciousness antedating by centuries the Israelites and Greeks. Furthermore, he realized that this historical consciousness was given expression in a symbolic form that was cosmological. By the end of the third millennium B.C., in the ancient Near East, there existed a form of speculation of meaning in history that provided a "unilinear construction of history, from a divine–cosmic origin of order to the author's present."[41] Voegelin gave this newly discovered form the name "historiogenesis."[42] Historiogenetic speculation, which is engendered by the experience of cosmological societies being threatened and preserved, is primarily mythical in its construction incorporating intramundane deities, superhuman rulers, and a fanciful retelling of past events. Nonetheless, this symbolic form must now be recognized as the first appearance, no matter how undifferentiated, of historical consciousness.

Voegelin defined historiogenesis as a "mytho-speculative extrapolation of pragmatic history toward its cosmic-divine point of origin."[43]

As such it is one of a type of symbolism in search of the origin and ground of existence. Along with theogony (myths which account for the origin and cause of the gods), anthropogony (myths which account for the origin and cause of humankind), and cosmogony (myths that account for the origin and cause of the cosmos), historiogenesis is any mythical construct that attempts to account for the origin and cause of society and its order. Since these speculative constructs correspond to the quaternarian structure of being (God, the human being, world, and society), taken together they are equivalent to a philosophy of being on the level of the cosmological myth.[44] But from the standpoint of the Mosaic experience and the philosophic experience, with their understanding of human existence in its immediacy before God, historiogenesis is to be seen as a more compact type of symbolism. History, in the strict sense Voegelin understands it, is a clear advance in differentiation beyond historiogenesis, insofar as the latter, by tying the human relation to God to membership in a society and its past, represents a distinctly mediated form of existence.[45] Historiogenetic constructions are thus found in cultural orbits in which the personal being of the individual in the relation to transcendence has not yet fully disengaged from the compactness of the social collective.

Spengler, Toynbee, and Jaspers (and even Voegelin in his earlier work) failed to unearth historiogenetic symbolisms because they did not penetrate to the experiential forces which motivate the construction of such lines of meaning in history, even though they were obviously incompatible with the empirical evidence. In its origin, historiogenesis is motivated by the anxiety aroused by the vicissitudes of imperial order, the breakdown of empire, and existential alienation. Under the impact of such anxiety the fabrication and manipulation of historical material is easily accounted for. In the age of imperial conquests the historiogenetic symbolists legitimize the new rule by letting it descend from the mythical beginning in an unbroken line. At the price of violating historical reality the new order is sublimated to "the emergence of order in the cosmos, so that the events would have a meaning that made them worthy of transmission to posterity."[46] Through this historical reconstruction that exacted only one line of descent, the imperial conquerors appropriated not only new territory but also the ancestry of the conquered.

Accordingly, Voegelin came to view any historical construction as a historiogenetic enterprise whenever it attempts to contain historical elements on a single line of meaning while excluding others that do not fit. So even Jaspers's "axis-time" became a historiogenetic symbolism because it attempted to impose a reality upon the historical participants who had no consciousness of any axis of history. The fact that there are parallel spiritual movements, both Eastern and Western, that know nothing of one another can only lead one to conclude that there are meaningful structures in history, not that there is a unilinear history with a single progression of events, however disparate. If there is a structure in history it is found not on the level of events; one discovers it only by penetrating the structure of experiencing consciousness. In Voegelin's oft-quoted remark, "History is not a stream of human beings and their actions in time, but the process of man's participation in a flux of divine presence that has eschatological direction."[47]

In fact, Voegelin began to realize that this mixing of history and cosmology was a "millennial constant" which does not disappear as consciousness differentiates. Indeed, it persists even in our own time. Almost all philosophy of history is historiogenetic, including even the Pauline and Augustinian versions, to the degree that they engage in "techniques of selecting and omitting materials, as well as of rearranging their time sequence, so as to let one line of meaning emerge from a field that in fact contains several such lines."[48] This kind of "interpretation" of history is a form of cosmological speculation with imperialist overtones that unites, on a level of equivalence, Hegel's *Philosophy of History* with the Sumerian King List.[49] What distinguishes these two particular historiogenetic symbolisms is that the "pre-historic" Sumerian symbolism is inspired by the primary experience of the cosmos, while the modern, Hegelian construction occurs at a time when the differentiating disengagement of the soul from society (the truth of existence discovered by the prophets of Israel and the philosophers of Hellas) has already been achieved, and thus represents a "retrogressive retreat" into a more compact mode of order.[50] Hegel does not stand alone, for historiogenesis appears in all the modern speculations on the origin and end of history that have imperialist overtones, whether they be progressivist, idealist, materialist, or positivist.

Voegelin came to view this type of manipulation of history as a gnostic enterprise (vestiges of which were present even in his own historiography) which had to be abandoned at all cost. The actual history of consciousness is much too complex and nonlinear to conform to a historian's chronological scheme. In rejecting the unacceptable symbolism of linear history and axis-time, Voegelin argues that, in principle, there can be no solution on the level of phenomena or events in history. One must ultimately return to the structure of consciousness itself.

So the emphasis of Voegelin's study now lies much more on the permanent and recurring features of human experience. He turned away from reconstructing the history of order *per se* so as to analyze the "constants of consciousness" which appear in culturally distinct, but structurally similar, "equivalents." As a result, he entered deeper

and deeper into the philosophical foundations of his own theory of
history and consciousness. This shift in emphasis has the following
traits: (1) Whereas history was originally conceived as a process which
was made intelligible as a "struggle for true order," the structure of
which could be "discerned retrospectively in a flow of events that
extends . . . indefinitely into the future,"[51] the struggle is now for an
increasing differentiation of consciousness and its participation in the
metaxy. (2) The process of reality, which is intelligible in the flow
of events, is now placed in "the stratification of man's consciousness
through the process of differentiation."[52] (3) What was the original
intelligible structure of history has now become the "process of history,"
which is "a mystery in process of revelation."[53] The focus shifted from
the structure of history, with its flow of political-social events on a linear
time-scale, to the movement of consciousness toward emergent truth.

It appears now that Voegelin, while stressing the mystery of being,
takes his stand on Plato's vision of permanence in order to protect
against the misunderstandings of history which are omnipresent. Therefore, the order of history is now grounded in the order of existence
conceived ontologically. This makes sense given his process theory of
being which figures so heavily in the argument of *The Ecumenic Age*.
What, if anything, is permanent in this endless process of history? For
Voegelin, there are three fundamental dynamics in human experience
which remain constant.

First, there is the primary experience of reality which can be expressed as follows: Whatever comes into being must perish; nothing
that exists is its own ground of existence; existence is an intermediate
movement between being and nonbeing; pure being and pure nothing
are the same, and their truth is the movement from one to the other, i.e.,
becoming.[54] This primal experience was given its classic formulation by
Anaximander's dictum: "The origin (*arche*) of things is the Apeiron. . . .
It is necessary for things to perish into that from which they were born;
for they pay one another penalty for their injustice (*adikia*) according
to the ordinance of time."[55]

Second, there arises the etiological question of the ground: "What is
this mysterious ground the existent things don't carry within themselves
but nevertheless carry with them as a sort of matrix of existence?"[56]
Whatever the ground is, it must be something—not a thing among
other existent things, but the nonexistent origin of all things.

Third, there are various answers promulgated by the questioning
consciousness. History has provided a plethora of examples, all structurally equivalent: Plato's divine *nous*; Aristotle's *prote arche*; the Amon-
Re of Egypt; the Israelite creator-God; the pre- and transmundane

God of Christianity; the Neoplatonic world-soul; Hegel's immanent *Geist*; Bergson's *élan vital*; Heidegger's epigonic Being; etc. Voegelin explains that these various answers to the question of the ground are not simply relative to one another on a scale of truth.[57] They are, however, indicative of the ontic constants and equivalent symbolizations of human consciousness:

> For the answers make sense only in relation to the questions they answer; the questions, furthermore, make sense only in relation to the concrete experiences of reality from which they have arisen; and the concrete experiences, together with their linguistic articulation, finally, make sense only in the cultural context which sets limits to both the direction and range of intelligible differentiation. Only the complex of experience-question-answer as a whole is a constant of consciousness. . . . No answer, thus, is the ultimate truth in whose possession mankind could live happily forever after, because no answer can abolish the historical process of consciousness from which it has emerged.[58]

In modern philosophy, this constant complex of experience-question-answer was given its archetypal formulation by Leibniz's two metaphysical questions: Why is there something, why not nothing? and Why do things have to be as they are and not different? Leibniz's answer was simple: "This ultimate reason of things is called God."[59]

THE ECUMENIC AGE

Having established the preceding premises, Voegelin proceeded to explore the meaning of the Ecumenic Age and its importance to his theory of history and consciousness. This is the age defined as "a period in the history of mankind which roughly extends from the rise of the Persian to the fall of the Roman Empire."[60] It is the age that succeeds the cosmological empires of the preceding millennium and precedes the orthodox empires of the Middle Ages and beyond. The three major empires whose imperial drives constitute the Ecumenic Age are the Persian Empire that arose in the sixth century B.C. and had its center in Persepolis; the Macedonian Empire that arose in the fourth century B.C. and had its center in Alexandria; and the Roman Empire that appeared in the third century B.C., had its center in Rome, and survived the longest.

According to Voegelin, the distinguishing feature of the Ecumenic Age is the fundamental division that emerged during this time between the temporal and the spiritual poles of existence. Under the pressures of imperial conquest the compact society of the cosmological empires differentiated into a society ordered by pragmatic and spiritual domains. With the attempt to encompass human reality under one umbrella— the imperial drive which marked the political aspirations of Cyrus, Alexander, and the Caesars—the essence of humanity is called into question by those who reflect on the new events. The emphasis of the question of order shifts from the political realm to the spiritual realm. This is so because "the carriers of spiritual order tend to separate from the societies of their origin because they sense the unsuitability of the concrete society as a vessel for the universality of the spirit."[61] The new events require a new interpretation of the meaning of order and the meaning of the human being. From the disintegration of whole societies, explains Voegelin, "new experiences of order, new symbolisms for their articulation, and new enterprises for their institutionalization were developed."[62] In inchoate form, church and state began to emerge.

The term *ecumene*, which refers to the humanly inhabited globe, signals an important breakthrough in the self-understanding of people living in this time. The term appears in two separate contexts. It means, first of all, the pragmatic *ecumene* which refers to the unification of all people, actual or potential, by imperial conquest, as in Polybius. It also can refer to the spiritual *ecumene* which means the desired unification of all humankind under one spiritual force.[63] For example, spreading the gospel throughout the world was for Paul the spiritual equivalent of the pragmatic expansion of empires effected by their conquering armies. It led to the rise of Christianity as a new ecumenic religion in the West. In the third century in the East, Mani attempted to found another ecumenic religion based on his eclectic teachings which would have no regional limitations. And in the seventh century Mohammed attempted to combine religion with imperialism in the quest for the true ecumenic religion. The struggle for ecumenic truth, both spiritual and political, began its long course of human affliction on the battlefields of imperial expansion.

So the pragmatic and the spiritual *ecumenes*, though distinct, were closely intertwined. The process by which these two ecumenic orders arose can be more clearly depicted in the following developments:

1. There was the rise and fall of successive empires through indiscriminate imperial conquests. These empires transformed the political landscape of the ethnic societies they overran into a sea of "senseless misery." The expansion of the multicivilizational empire toward some mythical horizon left not only a mass of destruction in its wake but also a power vacuum, an organizational shell bound together by little more than a conqueror's will to power. Furthermore, there was a dearth of spiritual substance to unify the new social form because of the absence of a coherent cultural base.

2. The result of this continual upheaval was a sense of pointlessness. Pragmatic history was a series of events that led nowhere. The spiritual life was cast into a void. With the collapse of political and religious order, anxiety and meaninglessness were the rule of the day. Out of this groundswell of turmoil a new realm emerged in which order was experienced. Since it could no longer be found in society, spiritual order was pursued independently from the political realm in personal existence. This contraction provided the fertile soil for the spiritual outbursts and the growth of religions. The one feature these spiritual outbursts held in common was the symbol of a universal humankind, conceived initially by prophets, mystics, and philosophers. This spiritual insight emerged to meet the senselessness of the expanding organizational shells of power of the various empires.

3. This bifurcation of the pragmatic and the spiritual realms also promoted the alienation of consciousness from reality, as exemplified by gnosticism and apocalypticism. Given the meaninglessness and misery of history, it was easy to conclude that history itself is evil and needs to be overcome by escaping into another world away from this world. Such a "loss of balance," however, was not inevitable, and gradually devices were developed to protect against it. Of course the main protection was the truth of existence itself, experienced in the revelatory events. To make this truth socially effective and to keep it uncontaminated, there resulted the creation of scriptures as a fixed canon of literature embodying the sacred truth, as well as the codification of truth into doctrine—the authoritative vessel of the spiritual insights. A similar process occurred in philosophy as the Stoics demythologized the teaching of Plato and Aristotle and converted it into literal, propositional form.

4. As ecumenic self-understanding developed, there emerged a missionary impulse among the philosophers and religious leaders who saw themselves as representatives of a truth valid for all humankind. What followed was a convergence of their aspirations with the pragmatic aspirations of the empire builders. The coincidence seemed providential. The purpose of an empire was to facilitate the spread of philosophical and religious truth to humankind. This is seen in the Stoic and Christian attitude toward the Roman Empire, which eventually reciprocated the embrace by adopting Stoicism as its philosophy and Christianity as its ecumenic religion. However, as already intimated, this reconciliation between pragmatic and spiritual order, which once again gave history a meaning, was won at a price. Because scripture and doctrine tended toward the objectification of truth they were liable to sever it from its experiential ground. For now the resulting dangers need only be recalled by name: hypostatization, dogmatization, relativization, secularization, egophanic revolt.

These dangers have been fully realized in modern history. In fact
Voegelin suggests that modernity in large part consists in a revolt against
symbols inherited from the Ecumenic Age, symbols whose meanings
were deformed through metaphysical and theological "dogmatomachy."[64] The modern revolt, however, only succeeded in compounding
the problem by adding more doctrine. So modern errors were added to
medieval ones, resulting in a "massive block of accumulated symbols"
which only served to eclipse reality.[65] The problems of our time, therefore, are directly linked to the events of the Ecumenic Age. Voegelin's
implication is that we need to view with great skepticism how the truths
discovered long ago have been handed down to us. Only by a process
of experiential regeneration and anamnetic recovery can the truth of
existence be regained.

History has its origin in the differentiation of consciousness which
occurred in the Ecumenic Age. Although on the "empirical" level history during this period appears to be a meaningless succession of empires
competing to represent all humankind as its source of authority, only
on the "philosophical" level, through the "leap in being," can a proper
understanding of history be obtained. Plato, Aristotle, the prophets of
Israel, and the early Christians were conscious that something fundamentally new was happening in reality in the theophanies they experienced. Thus, they distinguished the before and after of revelation.
History, then, became the peculiar mode of human existence in time,
to be differentiated from the cyclical time of nature. The human mode
was clearly distinct because it involved human consciousness. There is
meaning in history, therefore, because consciousness has a history.

This emanation of the truth of existence as historical has ontological
significance. Through the differentiation of human consciousness reality
itself was becoming self-conscious and luminous for its meaning. Reality
was experienced as being in motion, as having a processive character
and a particular direction to the process. Moreover, this direction was
discovered to be eschatological. In both the Greek and Christian milieu,
there was experienced, through the movement of the soul, a process
of "immortalization" (Aristotle) or "transfiguration" (St. Paul). In these
experiences reality as a whole was interpreted as moving in the direction,
beyond the cosmos, beyond the disorder of finitude, toward the one
transcendent reality. Because there occurred alongside the experience
of theophany the equally significant experience of the lasting of the cosmos, which is not eliminated by transfiguring experiences, the structure
of reality revealed itself to be paradoxical. Reality was headed beyond
itself. As Voegelin phrased it, the structure of reality was the movement
beyond its own structure in the direction of emergent truth.

As a result of this insight human existence came to be seen as both mortal and immortal. Because this "paradox becomes intelligible as the very structure of existence itself,"[66] it must be respected if consciousness is not to lose its "balance." Given the overwhelming power of the spiritual experience the tendency toward unbalancing is very likely. One can be swept away by visions of transfigured reality, and only the greatest care will prevent this from derailing into apocalypticism. This is precisely the inclination that Voegelin found in St. Paul.

THE PAULINE VISION OF TRANSFIGURATION

A new context emerged in humanity's search for order when the outburst of a more differentiated experience of reality came to light in the Judeo-Christian revelation. For Voegelin, this pneumatic revelation was the source of new insights but also new errors. The locus of this new theophany was St. Paul's experience of the resurrected Christ. Paul's experience was principally a pneumatic vision. It was the experience of the *pneuma* of Christ that was so overwhelming that Paul's life was radically transformed by it. Such a conversion experience led him from persecuting the followers of Christ to being their chief emissary. Indeed, without Paul and his spiritual force, Christianity would probably have failed as a religious movement within the Roman Empire. And so it is upon the writings of Paul that Voegelin focuses his inquiry.[67]

Voegelin locates the crux of Paul's vision in 1 Corinthians 15. He begins his analysis by noting the similarities between the Christian and philosophic revelations.[68] He says that the critical difference lies in their treatment of *phthora* (perishing). In the noetic theophany of the philosophers, the *athanatizein* (immortalization) of the *psyche* is kept in balance with the rhythm of *genesis* and *phthora* in the cosmos. In Paul's pneumatic theophany the *athanasia* of the human being is accomplished alongside the abolition of *phthora* in the cosmos. Plato maintains the balance of consciousness by leaning toward the Anaximandrian mystery of *apeiron* and time in his unfolding of the paradox in reality. His grasp of a reality beyond the *nous* is harnessed by the primary experience of the cosmos that perceives the insurmountable cycle of birth and death, that knows that all things that come into being must go out of being. On the contrary, Paul, who is fascinated by the transfiguring effects of his theophany, allows his imagery of a *genesis* without *phthora* to interfere with the primary experience of the cosmos. The *aphtharsia* (imperishing) is an event to be expected in the lifetime of his readers (1 Cor. 15:51–52). This daring claim, Voegelin professes, is a metastatic expectation of the Second Coming.[69] Although Paul was not a philosopher this kind of articulation must be recognized for what it is: an error. It is motivated by the turbulence of his spiritual experience. What is inherent in Paul's experience is the explicit differentiation of the directions that were implicit in the philosopher's experience. The difference lies in Paul's peculiar interpretation of his fervent theophany.

In Paul's case, the interaction of divine presence and human response was perceived in regard to the problems of the social context. Although Paul's analysis of existential order closely parallels that of Plato and Aristotle, "the accent, however, has decisively shifted from the divinely noetic order incarnate in the world to the divinely pneumatic salvation from its disorder, from the paradox of reality to the abolition of the paradox, from the experience of the directional movement to its consummation."[70] Philosophy emphasizes the structure of human existence in the cosmos and articulates the structure through language symbols. Christianity emphasizes the radical change one undergoes in a particular experience which is elaborated in terms of the ultimate transfiguration of history and reality beyond the transfiguration of an individual soul. One experience does not exclude the other, for the Platonic emphasis on structure hesitantly apprehends a further unrest, and the Pauline exodus from reality through transfiguration does not abolish the cosmos, its structure, or the problems that arise while living within it. But Voegelin claims that Paul believed it did precisely this. With his expectation of an imminent transfiguration in history there resulted the loss of balance. The crux of Paul's interpretation, says Voegelin, is his "inclination to abolish the tension between the eschatological *telos* of reality and the mystery of the transfiguration that is actually going on within historical reality."[71] After Paul, the postponement of the *parousia* was inevitable when it failed to appear. Not until Augustine's *Civitas Dei* was an adequate symbolization of this paradox in reality achieved.

The problem of unbalancing is further complicated by the secondary symbolisms and doctrines that appear in the wake of a theophany. Voegelin attributes the origin of this phenomenon to the crises of the Ecumenic Age in which the miseries of ecumenic expansion, where whole societies were destroyed, motivated the attempt to preserve the spiritual outbursts. A tangible form was needed, one suitable to the new emerging societies that would safeguard the precarious insights once gained. Unfortunately, the task was done by those who did not have the spiritual depth to recover and invigorate the meaning of the original experiences that had real consequence for the order of a universal humanity. Stoic philosophers deformed the symbols, and Jewish and Christian thinkers, after canonizing certain texts as scriptures, misinterpreted the symbols by treating them as doctrinal formulas or objects in the external world. Objective propositions absorbed noetic and pneumatic meanings. In the Roman Empire such a move had a preservative function that was not wrong, but it inevitably compromised the heart of the theophanies and led to their spiritual dissolution in time. In modern Western civilization the symbolic distortion has become deleterious because the spiritual awareness is almost entirely lost. Recovering the life of the spirit is especially taxing because "the deforming doctrinalization has become socially stronger than the experiential insights it was originally meant to protect."[72] In spite of the difficulty, recovering the originating truth of experience underneath the baggage of secondary symbols and doctrines is the dauntless task of the philosopher today.

An example of the recovery of spiritual insight can be gleaned from Voegelin's brief treatment of the Christian doctrine of incarnation. Voegelin accepts the symbolism of the God-man (incarnation not divinization)[73] particularly in its "open," developing, pre-Nicene formulations (such as found in Origen's *theanthropos*), but he criticizes the Chalcedonian formula (which he says is hampered by "the conditions of philosophical culture in the fifth century A.D.")[74] for being a dogmatic construction "couched in the philosophically secondary, semihypostatic language of 'natures' "[75] which "has become inadequate in the light of what we know today about both classic philosophy and theophanic events."[76] Voegelin's basic argument is that "there can be no question of 'accepting' or 'rejecting' a theological doctrine" because the vision of the resurrected Christ is not a dogma but "an event in metaleptic reality."[77] The vision occurs in the *metaxy*. Therefore, there can be no splitting up of a subject and an object of the vision. The only "object" is the experience as received; the only "subject" is the response to the divine presence in one's soul.[78] Whether one accepts or rejects any doctrine as formulated is irrelevant compared to the unquestionable reality of the theophanic event itself, which the doctrine may or may not adequately convey. The point is that truth lies not in any doctrine but in the reality experienced by a differentiating consciousness, which differentiates in accord with the revelatory experiences as experienced and interpreted. The function of doctrine is to preserve and protect the revelatory insights, not to replace them by translating their meaning into a fixed dogmatic proposition. The meaning is mediated through the originating experiences themselves or, lacking that, through the imaginative and meditative reconstruction of their symbolic expressions. The hermeneutical method for this reconstruction, which is a highly personal task, Voegelin calls in some places "experiential analysis" and in others "meditative exegesis." In any case, it is the attempt to recover the experience behind the linguistic articulation being interpreted, for it is the experience which alone provides the proper ground for understanding symbols, texts, and doctrines.

Furthermore, the notion of a "human nature" is problematic. A definitional explanation of humanity and its essence (such as Aristotle's *zoon noun echon* or *zoon noetikon*) can derail into a definition in the nominalist sense, whereby a "human nature" will become a fixed concept in the history of philosophy.[79] This connotes a structuralist bias which orients the truth of existence toward the primary experience of the cosmos and the unchanging structure of consciousness. On the other hand, the disordering bias can emphasize only the turbulent events in which consciousness experiences itself as moving beyond its own structure. It is a transfiguring experience which sees reality as moving beyond its own structure too; and the human being, who participates in the process, is also seen to have a structure that changes. The true order of existence can be maintained only by apprehending the paradox of reality which understands the nature of the human being (in contemporary terms, the structure of consciousness) as both changing and unchanging. In other words, as dynamic, human nature is structured in a way that it moves in a direction beyond its own structure.

For Voegelin, this dependence on the language of nature can disturb the balance between the constant, and yet transfiguring, process of reality in history by hypostatizing the dynamic movement of the soul into a thing or essence to be looked at or conceptualized. The paradox of reality maintains the balance. It is the discovery (by the classical philosophers) of the structure of reality moving beyond itself. The tension between the two reaches its limit in Plato's vision of the *hyperouranion* (the place beyond the heavens) in the *Timaeus* where he constructs a theogonal myth to articulate the divine creative action in the cosmos. In his noetic theophany he senses his *psyche* moving beyond the intracosmic gods, toward the divine ground of all being, and in this movement even senses "the truly Tremendum, the ultimate, nonpresent Beyond of all divine presence."[80] The uncertainties in the myth suggest to Voegelin that Plato's "revelatory experience had indeed moved toward the divine abyss beyond the Demiurge and his Nous."[81] In other words, Plato had indeed reached the divine depth beyond all manifestation: the Unknown God that was revealed to Moses as the ineffable "I am." Although the thornbush symbolism was of a different, essentially pneumatic, type of revelation, Voegelin uncovered the parallel noetic revelation in Plato's work, which was tempered by his reluctance to pursue the differentiation of the divine beyond. Although he was aware that revelation had a dimension beyond the *nous*, Plato's uncertainties were due to his fear that any elaboration of it would disturb the balance of consciousness.[82] Plato believed that this revelation was unstable, exceeding the reaches of noetic ordering. Because he wanted to protect the core of his experience, that is, the revelation of the *nous* as the source of order in human beings and the cosmos, he stopped short of a full differentiation of spiritual experience. The flooding of consciousness with the divine beyond could destroy the insight into the tensional structure of reality, with the subsequent temptation of bringing it under human control. This is the closest Plato comes to a pneumatic, transfiguring vision in his noetic consciousness. He knows there is a divine reality beyond the divine presence that is revealed to his philosophical *psyche*, but it lies in the ineffable beyond. For example, in the *Phaedrus* (247c) he has Socrates say that no poet has worthily praised the *hyperouranion* or ever will. The philosopher's myth, the *alethinos logos* or "true story," is the only form that can express this revelation, which at best can only point to the pneumatic beyond. Plato remains within the noetic sphere of self-transcending consciousness.

Plato maintains the balance by keeping the accent on the structure itself, which is ordered by the primary experience of the cosmos. But Paul's accent (motivated by the turbulence of his pneumatic experience) falls on the eschatological direction of the theophanic event, on the "Exodus" within reality. Thus, his emphasis on the transfiguring movement in history is acquired at the expense of the personal and political dimension of existence. In other words, with the expectation of an imminent *parousia*, the truth of existence became unbalanced. Life in the *metaxy* was dispensed with by the eschatological hope of fulfillment beyond the *metaxy*. Paul's differentiation of pneumatic consciousness, although superior to that achieved by the classical philosophers, was not counterbalanced by the requisite noetic control of meaning, which would have preserved not only the balance of consciousness but also the unfathomable mystery of history as well. The mystery of history constituted by theophanic events was replaced by the meaning of history in which theophanic events occur. With the hope in an imminent Second Coming, the meaning of history was finally known: the End was near.[83]

Voegelin argues that the modern egophanic revolt which attempted to bring about the day of perfection itself (through self-bestowing grace) in the near future, is a deformation of the Pauline experiential symbolism. The representatives of the revolt, in effect, capitalized on, and deformed, Paul's unbalancing expectation of the *parousia*.[84] No longer just expected, the fulfillment of history was actually sought through revolutionary mass movements and immanentized by gnostic philosophies of history. For Voegelin, Paul's myth of transfiguration indeed tipped the balance with its metastatic expectations. His prophetic vision lacked the philosopher's control of meaning, a control that could harness the turbulence of a pneumatic revelation. Although for Voegelin the roots of the modern egophanic revolt can be traced to the Pauline symbolism,[85] Paul is not to be faulted for the subsequent dogmatic deformation in Western history. Bad was the doctrinization of derivative symbols and pseudo-philosophical terms which buried the originating experiences; worse were the egophanic constructions which reinterpreted the accretion of hypostatized symbols and turned them into grist for the ideological manipulators' mill (e.g., Hegel, Comte); worst of all were the twentieth-century messiahs who turned the speculative philosophers' ideological ruminations of a century before into cannon fodder for their murderous escapades. For Voegelin, the meaning of reality revealed in the theophanic events, both noetic and pneumatic, philosophical and prophetic, which came to the surface in the Ecumenic Age, became lost in the modern egophanic deformation of history.

Whatever one wants to make of Voegelin's assessment of the writings of St. Paul, we must agree with him when he admonishes those who attempt to control the process of history or to proclaim its meaning once and for all. The mystery of the historical process must remain open. Anything less should be viewed as another ideological attempt to stop history. That fantastic venture must always be rejected.

THE UNITY OF HUMANKIND

The consciousness of universal humanity was the major insight that emerged from the Ecumenic Age. The attempt to encompass all of humanity under one *ecumene* was the adventurous goal of both the burgeoning empires as well as the new religions. Some further comments on the meaning, origin, and limits of the term *ecumene* will help flesh out Voegelin's mature philosophy of history.

The term *ecumene* is a cosmological symbol which was redefined due to the differentiating events. The original term *oikoumene*, meaning the inhabited world upon which all people dwell, is found in Homer's epics. Its kindred symbol *okeanos* referred to the "horizon" which marked the boundary between this world and the mysterious world of the gods beyond.[86] When the presuppositions of this compact symbolism were abolished, the idea of *ecumene* was retained, although its meaning was altered. In Polybius, for example, the *ecumene* was reduced to a pragmatic conception. It meant the known territory upon which an imperial conquest advanced. It was simply a geographical expanse without the connotation of mystery. However, the ecumenic religions also adopted the term and reinvested it with a spiritual meaning. The spiritual *ecumene* was the potential range of all living converts to the one universal truth. It assumed that conversion of individuals would unify the *ecumene* regardless of other differences.

Both concepts were deficient, Voegelin claims, particularly the pragmatic *ecumene*. The unity provided by conquest was no real unity at all, and it never succeeded in attaining its goal. With every conquest the *ecumene* grew larger, making it harder to organize, until it eventually collapsed under its own weight. The ecumenic religions solved this problem by establishing an order of humanity that transcended the empire; but they too were frustrated by their limited range of influence. Besides this, they encountered the weightier problem that, as Voegelin puts it, ecumenicity is not identical with universality. Those human beings who inhabit the earth at any one time do not constitute the whole of humanity; their predecessors and successors must also be included as part of universal humanity.

The problem of ecumenicity became more complex as historical knowledge expanded. Voegelin discovered that an ecumenical consciousness developed simultaneously in China during its age of imperial unification. The Chinese symbol to denote the resulting society, *t'ien-hsia* (all-under-heaven), is the exact equivalent of the Greek *oikoumene*.[87] This coincidence cannot be attributed to cultural diffusion since no evidence exists to suggest any contact between the East and the West during this period. The question one must ask is how these two *ecumenes* are to be related. Is it appropriate to speak of two humankinds? If not, what justifies speaking of one humankind? And what about societies that are not included in either the Eastern or the Western Ecumenic Age? If there is a plurality of humankinds, is there a plurality of histories?

Voegelin's answer to these questions is that humankind is in fact one, but this unity must be understood as an eschatological symbol. Though it never received articulate expression during the Ecumenic Age, the recognition gradually developed that the unity of humankind does not have its basis in the structure of society, but rather in the eschatological movement of reality. Universal humankind is not a society existing anywhere in the world, nor is it a biological species. It is, rather, the community formed by the movement of divine presence in the soul. The order that is discovered in such experiences is universally valid for all people, and this order is the basis of their humanity. The symbol of universal humankind was given articulate evocation by Christianity in the communal bond of the spirit that was experienced through the *homonoia* of its members. Because the spirit is transcendentally eternal it is universally present at all times, dwelling in every person equally in whatever age or place one happens to exist. Thus it creates a spiritual bond among all people past, present, and future.[88]

This symbolization of the spiritual *ecumene* ultimately converges with historical consciousness. History takes the place of the mysterious *okeanos*. The process of history becomes the horizon of mystery without which the idea of the *ecumene* remains incomplete. Together, universal humanity and the process of reality in history form a symbolic equivalent to the archaic *oikoumeme/okeanos*.

With the expansion of ecumenic consciousness during the Ecumenic Age and the concomitant insight into the paradoxical structure of reality, we must now finally ask: what is meant by history? Though no definitive answer can be given, since history is essentially an unfolding mystery, the best answer lies in Voegelin's notable words: "History is not a stream of human beings and their actions in time, but the process of man's participation in the flux of divine presence that has eschatological direction."[89] Furthermore, the truth of order emerges from the midst of disorder and in its fullest differentiation it all amounts to this: "Meaning in history is constituted through man's response to the immortalizing movement of the divine pneuma in his soul."[90] This is the substance of Paul's vision. Plato and Aristotle's immortalizing response to the theophany of the *nous* did not fully unfold into the one God that Plato sensed as the God beyond the gods.[91] It did not extend to the structure of divine reality in its pneumatic depth of creation and salvation. The third age of the *nous* had to await the epiphany of Christ for the eschatological structure of history to be ordered under the one God of all ages. Only with Paul did history appear as the horizon of divine mystery where the process of differentiation became a process of transfiguration.[92]

Nonetheless, Voegelin tells us that "the truth of existence . . . does not emerge from one single spiritual event."[93] The one truth of existence is spread across a spectrum of spiritual eruptions which bear the mark of the ethnic cultures where they occur. So human responses to divine being "tend to accentuate different aspects of the one truth of man's existence under God, such as the Greek noetic or the Israelite-Jewish pneumatic revelations of divine reality."[94] The consequence of this is that no theophanic event and its exegesis could develop into a fully balanced symbolization of order that would cover the whole area of human existence. One revelation does not abolish another. A full account of order would have to encompass all the spiritual peaks in the total drama of human history. And if it is truly open to all reality, it must include those events in the future that have yet to be experienced, for the revelation of Mystery has no end in time and the search for order is likewise never-ending.

Because of this vast expansion of the spiritual horizon, history can no longer be periodized into distinct ages or epochs, such as beginning, middle, and end. As Voegelin contends, "the process of history, and such order as can be discerned in it, is not a story to be told from the beginning to its happy, or unhappy end; it is a mystery in process of revelation."[95] For this reason Voegelin would now repudiate the consciousness of epoch if it is exclusively determined by any particular spiritual event. As a result, he is more and more reluctant in these later writings to use the term "leap in being," preferring instead "theophany" or "spiritual outburst" to describe the breakthroughs to differentiated insights that give history its substance.

Voegelin provides us with a final summation of the insights into the structure of history that emerged from the Ecumenic Age:

(1) Through the differentiation of consciousness, history becomes visible as the process in which differentiations occur.

(2) Since the differentiations advance man's insight into the constitution of his humanity, history becomes visible as a dimension of humanity beyond man's personal existence in society.

(3) Since the differentiating events are experienced as immortalizing movements, history is discovered as the process in which reality becomes luminous for the movement beyond its own structure; the structure of history is eschatological.

(4) Since the events are experienced as movements of human response to a movement of divine presence, history is not a merely human but a divine-human process. Though historical events are founded in the external world and have calendar dates, they also partake of the divine lasting out-of-time. The historical dimension of humanity is neither world-time nor eternity but the flux of presence in the Metaxy.

(5) The mankind whose humanity unfolds in the flux of presence is universal mankind. The universality of mankind is constituted by the divine presence in the Metaxy.[96]

THE BALANCE OF CONSCIOUSNESS

As we have seen, Voegelin's philosophical analysis of history ascertains a paradox in reality which can never be alleviated. It is "the paradox of a recognizably structured process that is recognizably moving beyond its

own structure."[97] In other words, the study of history reveals that reality
is dynamically alive with theophanic events that point toward an ultimate
transfiguration.[98] In the exegesis of reality this paradox can easily derail
into misconstructions. Of the two paradoxically linked experiences, the
lastingness of the cosmos and the transfiguring theophany, an exegete
can favor one at the expense of the other. The result, depending on
which experience is made superior, can lead to either apocalypticism
or the pseudo-psychologies of projection of the nineteenth century. As
Voegelin explains, the task of the philosopher today is to maintain the
tension of consciousness in the face of such surrounding deformations:

> The philosopher must be on guard against such distortions of reality. It
> becomes his task to preserve the balance between the experienced lastingness
> and the theophanic events in such a manner that the paradox becomes
> intelligible as the very structure of existence itself. This task incumbent on
> the philosopher I shall call the postulate of balance.[99]

The deformation of reality occurs when the balance of consciousness
is lost. The loss of balance, for Voegelin, inevitably leads to some form
of gnostic derailment. The third great theme of The Ecumenic Age has
to do with how the balance of consciousness is lost in regard to the two
modes in which the divine reality is experienced. Reflecting the paradox
of reality explained earlier, the two directions in which consciousness
can apprehend the divine ground of being are toward the beginning
and the beyond. As Voegelin describes it:

> Though the divine reality is one, its presence is experienced in the two
> modes of the Beyond and the Beginning. The Beyond is present in the
> immediate experience of movements in the psyche; while the presence of
> the divine Beginning is mediated through the experience of the existence
> and intelligible structure of things in the cosmos.[100]

These two modes of experience require two different types of language for their adequate expression. The unknown God of the beyond,
whose immanent presence is experienced in the movement of the soul,
requires the revelatory language of consciousness. This is the language
of seeking, searching, questioning, of ignorance and knowledge, of
being drawn toward the ground, of turning around, of illumination
and rebirth. The God of the beginning, whose mediated presence is
experienced through the existence and order of things in the cosmos,
requires the mythical language of a creator-god or Demiurge, a divine
force that creates, sustains, and preserves the order of things. In fact,
the cosmogonic myth is the only symbolic form that can adequately
render the experience of the cosmic–divine beginning.[101] It requires a

great linguistic sensitivity to maintain the distinction between these two modes of divine presence, and to uphold the mystery of "a cosmos that moves from its divine Beginning toward a divine Beyond of itself."[102] If this movement is "torn out of the context of reality in which it arises" and made the autonomous basis of human action, then the mystery is abolished and the experiencing consciousness will be deformed. This is the gnostic derailment. Instead of maintaining its foothold in reality, the gnostic expands and inverts the relation between the beginning and the beyond:

> The fallacy at the core of the Gnostic answers to the question is the expansion of consciousness from the Beyond to the Beginning. In the construction of Gnostic systems, the immediate experience of divine presence in the mode of the Beyond is speculatively expanded to comprehend a knowledge of the Beginning that is accessible only in the mode of mediated experience.[103]

This is the origin of the great gnostic psychodramas which use the imagery of its expansive speculation to explain the beginning, the fall of the divinity into the cosmos, and the cosmic imprisonment of the *pneuma* in humans by the saving *gnosis*. Voegelin goes on to state that this

> imaginative game of liberation derives its momentum from an intensely experienced alienation and an equally intense revolt against it; Gnostic thinkers, both ancient and modern, are the great psychologists of alienation, carriers of the Promethean revolt.[104]

In his last writings, Voegelin developed the necessity for "reflective distance" that would prevent the revelatory outburst of the beyond from expanding through identification with the process of the whole. He finally interprets it as a problem of maintaining a balance between *noesis* and vision, as exemplified in *Laws* 713b–716b.[105] As we shall see in the next chapter, where we take up Voegelin's final works, the noetic vision within the balance of the *metaxy* has become the basis of his new vision of order. As a consequence, the accent falls heavily on the mystery of the process.

The mystery of the process is rooted in a number of unanswerable questions: If history is a process in which the truth manifests itself more and more clearly, why is this truth not given to everyone? Why must there be epochs of advancing insights in the first place? Why must the insights once gained be restricted, deformed, and rejected? Why must they be recovered and renewed again and again? These questions are so fundamental to understanding the process of reality that Voegelin calls them "the Question."[106] Since the Question concerns the existence of evil in the world, it evokes the further question of why existence should have a structure from which humanity must be saved.

Voegelin's response to the Question is the same as Plato's. In the *Laws*, Plato tells the "true story" (*alethinos logos*) of the human being as a puppet of the gods. It is a cosmogonic myth that raises the perturbing question of why the gods pull humans not only by the golden cord of truth but also by the steely cords of untruth. Yet one pull is just as divine as another. Do the gods will evil? And why would they make the human being a puppet? As Voegelin tells us, "Plato's answer is uncompromising: 'Regarding this matter we can know nothing at all' (*Laws* 644d–e)."[107] The mystery of reality remains: "There is no answer to the Question other than the Mystery as it becomes luminous in the acts of questioning."[108] Further on he states that

> the horizon of the Mystery in time that opens with the ecumenic expansion in space is still the Question that presents itself to the presently living; and what will be worth remembering about the present, will be the mode of consciousness in our response to the Question.[109]

The mode of Eric Voegelin's consciousness has undoubtedly been one of reason in search of truth. But his has been a reason based on a profound faith. This fact is demonstrated throughout his work. It is most keenly expressed in his frequent citations of Hebrews 11:1, such as this passage from near the end of *The Ecumenic Age*: "To face the Mystery of Reality means to live in the faith that is the substance of things hoped for and the proof of things unseen."[110] The nature of faith enables a human being to maintain the balance of consciousness. It gives the serenity needed to preserve one's grasp of reality in good times as well as in bad. This view of faith was beautifully expressed by Voegelin over two decades earlier in *The New Science of Politics*:

> Ontologically, the substance of things hoped for is nowhere to be found but in faith itself; and, epistemologically, there is no proof for things unseen but again this very faith. The bond is tenuous, indeed, and it may snap easily. The life of the soul in openness toward God, the waiting, the periods of aridity and dulness, guilt and despondency, contrition and repentance, forsakenness and hope against hope, the silent stirrings of love and grace, trembling on the verge of a certainty which if gained is loss—the very lightness of this fabric may prove too heavy a burden for men who lust for massively possessive experience.[111]

Only a person of faith in love with divine wisdom could undertake in our time the kind of study that Voegelin has bequeathed to us. As a conclusive word indicative of his faith, a sentence that appears on the penultimate page of *The Ecumenic Age* will serve as this chapter's crowning stroke: "Things do not happen in the astrophysical universe; the universe, together with all things founded in it, happens in God."[112]

This expression of faith, however, was not to be Voegelin's final word. The search for transcendent order is never ending, and the structure of the *fides* that instigates the search appears to the philosopher as having central importance. Voegelin's last writings, although left unfinished, continued the development of thought where *The Ecumenic Age* ended. This final stage of his life's work includes a few essays he wrote since 1975 and ended with his crowning achievement in *In Search of Order*. These writings reflect yet a further development of Voegelin's study of consciousness, a philosophical analysis that is more explicitly meditative and even mystical in its import.

4

THE THEORY ACHIEVED: THE LAST WRITINGS, 1975–85

The last of Voegelin's major writings include the recently published essay "The Beginning and the Beyond: A Meditation on Truth," "Wisdom and the Magic of the Extreme: A Meditation," the valedictory essay "Quod Deus Dicitur," and the final volume of *Order and History: In Search of Order.*[1] As their titles suggest, these writings assume the form of meditations. As we shall explore in this chapter, these works alone would ascribe to Voegelin the epithet of philosophical mystic.

In Search of Order, which was left incomplete at the time of his death, is Voegelin's most fully refined analysis of consciousness and transcendence. As such, it must be viewed as the key to all his other works. Although it is characteristically abstruse, it may someday achieve the reputation of being among the finest philosophical writings of our time. In my opinion, it is destined to attain the stature of a great meditative analysis of divine mystery alongside such classical works as Plato's *Timaeus,* Augustine's *Confessions,* Anselm's *Proslogion,* Bonaventure's *The Mind's Journey to God,* and Descartes's "Third Meditation." Indeed, the last twenty pages of *In Search of Order,* on Plato's *Timaeus,* is perhaps the most exacting piece of Voegelin's whole corpus. It treats the most sublime of topics in a philosophically recondite, yet penetrating, fashion.

The three essays mentioned above belong to the same meditative horizon as *In Search of Order,* and so they are investigated together in this chapter. Beginning with *In Search of Order,* then, I examine these final works by highlighting the climactic insights which refine Voegelin's philosophy of consciousness. But before we discuss the content of this last phase of Voegelin's output, some remarks on his writing style will bring into greater relief the import of these last writings.

In the course of his later philosophical studies Voegelin explored a literary form which is virtually unique today. Given the deformed state of language in our time, which Voegelin spent a lifetime combatting, a new emancipation was called for, where philosophy could again regain its evocative power to make transparent the experiential ground of reality. Because the prevailing concepts and speculative results of past attempts had smothered consciousness with opaque symbols, Voegelin found it necessary to undertake a new exegesis of consciousness. Since any such attempt must be done in opposition to the prevalent dogmatisms (the initial tenet of Platonic philosophizing), Voegelin's work took on the form of meditative essays which recover or remember (hence the title of his work during his transitional phase: *Anamnesis*) the human condition revealing itself in consciousness, and which at the same time analyze the current obstacles to human self-understanding. For this task Voegelin chose as a literary form neither the aphorism employed by Heraclitus, Pascal, or Nietzsche, which is essentially the expression of autobiographical moments of illumination; nor the *via negativa* of Christian mysticism; nor the form of a Platonic dialogue; nor the discursive treatise of Aristotle; and certainly not the *questio disputatae* of the medieval *summa*. Voegelin selected instead the philosophical meditation that yields a kataphatic rendering of the structures of consciousness and reality. It is also a style that affords great sensitivity to the limits of language and its deforming tendency. In this vein, his symbolic expressions keep as close as possible to the engendering experiences; and the works are deliberately composed in such a way as to guard against libidinous abuse and doctrinalization.[2] Consequently, inasmuch as he is resisting these deforming tendencies, Voegelin's style also employs apophatic elements. It is a literary form that is uncommon today but has affinities with the works of Plotinus, Augustine, Pseudo-Dionysius, and the author of *The Cloud of Unknowing*. Perhaps it is the form that for our time is most conducive for engaging in what could be called "philosophical mysticism" (an endeavor which Voegelin, alone among his contemporaries, has mastered in these later writings), the form that alone carries the persuasive power to recapture the meaning of life in the *metaxy*.

Again, with this peculiar style in mind and in order to avoid as much as possible any distortion in discussing these demanding works, I stay as close to Voegelin's own language as elucidation permits. On this point I only wish to heed Voegelin's own warning not to violate "the elementary rule that a thinker's language takes precedence of the interpreter's."[3] Still, I must invite the reader to work through meditatively these imposing texts on his or her own, for no explication by an interpreter can substitute.

This chapter, then, analyzes *In Search of Order*. It incorporates some of the important supporting material from the other major essays, but the thrust of these writings is discussed directly only in the final sections where I examine the Christian context of Voegelin's analysis of faith and vision.[4]

The Meditative Search for
Transcendent Order

In Search of Order continues Voegelin's search for transcendent order in history. Accordingly, the first thing to say about this final work is that it is perhaps fitting that Voegelin died before completing it; otherwise it may have given the false impression to some readers that the quest for order is something that could possibly come to completion. As Voegelin underscored so often, the *zetema* of any philosopher is an unfinished story within the larger unfinished story of history which remains a prevailing mystery. Both the philosopher's quest and the process of history are structured by the same unknown divine mystery that pulls all participants in the cosmos to its unknown end. *Order and History*, as the story of the revelatory presence of this mystery in the course of human experience, reveals itself in the end as a philosophical paean to this unknown mystery. We can recognize this now in the fact that the first and last words of Voegelin's multivolume story invoke the name of this unknown mystery with the symbols "God" and "divine." The aim throughout *Order and History* has been resolute and unwavering, and the end is now linked to the beginning. Between the beginning and the end there has been a long but steady ascent, a search for the divine that began with faith in the divine. But also contained throughout these volumes has been the constant proviso that the essence of this mysterious beyond is unknowable and unnameable. This truth is exhibited in the following passages from *The Ecumenic Age*:

> Once the psyche has begun to move beyond the intracosmic gods toward the divine ground of all being, it will not cease moving before it has sensed the truly Tremendum, the ultimate, non-present Beyond of all divine presence. In the case of the noetic theophany, the experience of a God who embodies his Nous in the cosmos, limited by Ananke, cannot but point, by implication, toward the non-incarnate, acosmic abyss of the divine beyond the Demiurgic action.[5]

> Whether it is Plato or Paul, whether the noetic or the pneumatic theophany, whether God reveals himself as the Demiurge of structure or as the Redeemer from structure, revelation is experienced, not as identification with, but as participation in, divine reality. Beyond the theophanic presence experienced there lies, in the language of Aquinas, the tetragrammatic depth of the unfathomable divine reality that has not even the proper name "God."[6]

And in his last volume, Voegelin frequently employs the paradoxical phrase "the experience of the non-experientiable reality," to denote

"the tetragrammatic depth" of this ineffable mystery beyond all revelation. Here again we can perceive Voegelin's mind struggling against
the ultimate limits of language to form new linguistic constructions that
attempt to make ever-more transparent the ineffable divine.

Based on this final work we can conclude that, along with Plato, the
core question animating all of Voegelin's writing up to the very end
is "Who is this God?" (*Laws* 713a).[7] Voegelin of course can provide
no final answer to this question, but his meditative *zetema*, devoted to
an analysis of the revelatory experiences and symbols which have given
substance to this question throughout history, has gone further perhaps
than anyone today in bringing to clarity the critical parameters of the
problem. The acme of his noetic analysis lies in his discernment of
the structure of beyond in consciousness, revealed in peak moments
in history, whereby the ensuing history of revelation is seen to reveal the beyond of history and revelation.[8] This beyond is discerned
in the historical advance of differentiating insights that emerge from
revelatory experiences. Moreover, as Voegelin often reminds us, "the
fact of revelation is its content," meaning that revelation is not a piece
of information or an object to be possessed, but "the movement of
response to an irruption of the divine in the psyche."[9]

The thrust of Voegelin's final work must be seen as a significant event
in the history of reason and revelation that advances in our time the
human search for transcendence. It accomplishes this by articulating in
precise philosophical language the existential and historical horizons of
consciousness from which the fundamental question of human existence
arises: Who is this Unknown God that draws all humans to itself? So
to circumscribe Voegelin's final response to this question the content
of *In Search of Order* will be treated in the next six sections, beginning
with a discussion of the paradox of consciousness and ending with the
return to the Platonic myth.

The Paradox of Consciousness

Voegelin speaks of consciousness now as having a paradoxical structure.[10] It is structured according to its two modes of intentionality
and luminosity. Intentionality is the form of knowing reality in the
form of being-things, of phenomenal objects. Because consciousness is
concretely located in a concrete body, the reality it intends invariably
assumes the status of external thingness. Luminosity is the mode of
knowing reality as a nonthing. Consciousness as luminous is consciousness experienced as an event of participatory illumination in the reality

that comprehends it. As such, it is not a subject that intends objects but is itself a predicate of the subject "reality" as it becomes luminous for its truth. For Voegelin, then, generally speaking, intentionality employs concepts and ideas in its imaging of reality, while luminosity images reality by way of analogous symbols.

Because of this dual structure, consciousness inevitably yields a symbolization of reality in the conceptual form of being-things, when in fact what it knows in the mode of luminosity is the nonthing beyond of things. The beyond can only be experienced through its *parousia*, its presence. This presence of the beyond is a formative presence that pervades the whole of reality in the form of things. In itself this beyond is nonexperientiable, but since experience somehow reveals the beyond of experience mysteriously present in experience, this beyond needs to be evoked. But in conjuring this beyond, consciousness must inevitably image it in the ambiguous and limited form of being-things, that is, "objectively" through symbols and concepts, even though these symbols and concepts refer to no object.

Reality itself is structured by the being-things of the cosmos and the beyond of things beyond the cosmos.[11] The comprehending reality that includes the thing-reality of the cosmos and its nonthing ground, Voegelin calls the "It-reality."[12] The It-reality denotes the reality that comprehends the partners in the community of being: God and the human being, world and society. And so the It-reality is a subject that takes as a predicate the bodily located consciousness called "the human being" that is a participatory event in the comprehending It-reality. This is not a far-fetched notion if one stops to consider how the mysterious It occurs in our everyday speech when we use such phrases as "It is raining."

This structure of things and their beyond is what constitutes the tensional structure in human existence. Indeed, this dual isomorphism of consciousness and reality must lead one to say that reality is constituted by consciousness while consciousness is constituted by reality, with the provision of course that the primacy always lies with the prior-forming reality. Reality precedes and outlasts any embodied consciousness that participates in its mystery in the mode of existence; and in this formative reality, consciousness always finds itself moving, but only in consciousness can reality "appear."[13]

It is within this formative reality that the concrete consciousness called Eric Voegelin found itself moving in two directions: toward the beginning and toward the beyond. In his *zetemic* search for order in history he discovered that divine presence is experienced in these two directions and these two only, for no other direction is possible.

The great historical representations of these two modes of presence of the one divine mystery are found in the Book of Genesis and Plato's *Republic*. The cosmogony of Genesis, dated about the sixth century B.C., tells the story of the heavens and the earth created by God in the beginning. In the fourth century B.C. Plato tells how the existence and essence of all things, including their knowability, originate in the beyond of the knower and the known, in the *agathon*. The *bereshit* of Genesis and the *epekeina* of the *Republic* are the representative symbols of the two experiential modes of divine reality.[14]

However, we must not forget that Voegelin's anamnetic meditations cover millennia of divine presence, as *Order and History* confirms in its story of God's presence throughout human history. He is quite aware that these differentiated expressions of the beginning and the beyond have a long prior history of compact articulation. Indeed, he even came to recognize the presence of divine mystery experienced and symbolized in Paleolithic petroglyphs, circa 20,000 B.C. Nevertheless, true to his hermeneutic principles, the texts which represent the greatest differentiations must be the authoritative guides for contemporary exegesis of consciousness.

Every search for truth in existence is structured by the tensional poles of the beginning and the beyond of existence. This is the metaxic structure common to everyone, including the authors of Genesis 1 who in their attempt to address the problems of beginning composed in mythic symbols the classic story of the beginning of everything:

> The authors of Genesis I . . . were human beings of the same kind as we are; they had to face the same kind of reality, with the same kind of consciousness, as we do; and when, in their pursuit of truth, they put down their words on whatever material, they had to raise, and to cope with, the same questions we confront when we put down our words. In the situation created by the question: what is that kind of reality where the spoken word evokes the structures of which it speaks? they had to find the language symbols that would adequately express the experience and structure of what I have called the It-reality.[15]

This passage clearly spells out the fundamental message that Voegelin has been saying throughout his work: that what occurs in the great-souled men and women throughout history who have given expression to their visions of divine presence in symbols, stories, and myths is what occurs in all people who are given to reflect on what moves their own souls. In other words, no matter how diverse and pluralistic the symbolizations of theophany in history may be, everyone's existential consciousness is constituted by the same movement of the soul in the *metaxy*, whether he or she is explicitly or only inchoately aware of this structured movement. No matter what culture or religious tradition contextualizes one's consciousness, reflection on what moves one will yield the same basic structure. And the response to this experience is also everywhere the same: either formative ascent or deformative resistance. It is this common movement we share with the great poets, prophets, and philosophers who have come before us, that not only brings us into *homonoia* with them, but that also helps us to know, through their guidance, the one divine mystery that draws all beings unto itself.

The great souls that preceded us teach us another lesson. In whatever time or place humans find themselves, the starting point of their various quests for truth is always and everywhere the same: the middle.[16] The story of the beginning and the beyond must always begin in the middle, for one's quest has nowhere else to begin. No one was present at the beginning and no one will be present at the end. Since consciousness always finds itself in the middle, it must tell its story from its own vantage point, from the limited perspective of a particular concrete historical existence. Temporally, the quest for truth is always located in an intermediate position bound by the past stories that precede it and the future stories that will succeed it. We recall that, given the metaxic structure of existence, consciousness always finds itself situated in the in-between of past and future, the temporal and eternal, things and nonthings, birth and death, beginning and beyond, etc. So every quest for truth, whether it takes the form of philosophical analysis, or mythic story, or both, must begin where it finds itself: in the bodily located consciousness of the questioning human being. There is no Archimedean point outside any middle that could serve as an "objective" footing for the quest.

Given a plurality of stories there must then be a plurality of middles, validating a plurality of quests, each telling valid stories about the one beginning and the one beyond.[17] As Voegelin points out, this inherent pluralism in the various stories of truth was recognized as a phenomenon in history as far back as the written records go, to the third millennium B.C.[18] There have been various responses to this problem, ranging from tolerance to imperial violence, from benign indifference to dogmatic conflict, from historical relativism to radical nihilism.[19] The only resolution to this historical and theological problem lies in the recognition that there is a beginning and an end beyond the beginning and end of every quest and every story, a fact of which all reflective storytellers are aware, including the storyteller Voegelin, who tells the story of a plurality of stories with a plurality of middles. The meditative storyteller recognizes that history is a plurality of episodes all occurring in the same comprehending story, and the It-reality that tells this comprehending story is the divine beyond that is formatively present in all things, including every authentic quest for truth. Put simply, history is the enigmatic, unfinished story being told by God. Human beings are the characters in this ongoing drama, this play of human and divine forces where the history of truth emerges from the quest for truth. And given the historical conditions of formation and deformation that every serious quest is subject to, this drama could be more aptly considered a divine comedy.[20]

The Symbolic Ambiguities of
Divine Presence

Voegelin has now set the stage for his analysis of the inherent ambiguities which lie at the heart of the problem. Because the paradoxic structure of consciousness in its dual modes of intentionality and luminosity, along with their corresponding objects of thing-reality and It-reality, includes within its complex the very language we use to describe these realities, Voegelin speaks of the complex "consciousness-reality-language" to refer to the tensional nature of existence in which humans move toward order. Words and meanings are as much a part of reality as the things to which they refer. As Voegelin states it,

> language participates in the paradox of a quest that lets reality become luminous for its truth by pursuing truth as a thing intended. This paradoxic structure of language has caused certain questions, controversies, and terminological difficulties to become constants in the philosophers' discourse since antiquity without approaching satisfactory conclusions.[21]

In the second half of *In Search of Order* Voegelin analyzes these difficulties as they have arisen in history. There he is quick to affirm that the struggle of the human imagination to symbolize adequately the differentiating experiences is a constant in history. The terminological difficulties arising from the differentiating process of experience and symbolization of the cosmos and its beyond in history have led to the deformation of the symbols in the modern context. Thus, the therapeutic recovery of the engendering experiences, made transparent by the meditative exegesis of their symbols in their original emergence, must become the critical task of philosophy today. Voegelin has engaged in this task not to achieve some final end of analysis but to raise to full consciousness the unending quest for truth which, wherever it occurs, is an event in an unfinished story being told by the comprehending reality in which the philosopher by his or her substory, seeking ever greater adequacy, participates.[22]

Before partaking in an interpretative analysis of the historical ambiguities that led to the modern deformation, Voegelin introduces a dimension of consciousness which has been present throughout his work but that he only now develops explicitly. In addition to the paradox of intentionality and luminosity there is a third dimension of consciousness that is aware of this paradox which he characterizes as a "reflectively distancing remembrance."[23] It is the dimension of noetic consciousness that Plato in a more compact language called *anamnesis*. Voegelin has cultivated this aspect of consciousness into a philosophical discipline. He calls it simply "reflective distance."

This third dimension of consciousness is not an automatic formative force, for although it is an inherent structure in existential consciousness that cannot be abolished, a philosopher can indeed forget this distancing remembrance in his or her own consciousness. As a result, the metaleptic character of the quest for truth can be cast into "imaginative oblivion."[24] This occurs most often when philosophers in their symbolic representation of reality assert their power of imagination in a way that becomes a quest for power, a deformed quest that is manifested in the egophanic pursuit of absolute knowledge. The role of the philosopher as a participant in being gets initially short-circuited by the attempt to control reality through the hypostatization of emergent symbols. When these symbols assume the form of separate entities they can then be manipulated in a possessive fashion that forgets their experiential origin. In other words the symbolic language that emerges in anamnetic meditation is transformed into propositions about things. When the experiential complex of consciousness-reality-language is fragmented, that is, when the part of the complex that produces imaginative symbols is separated from the complex as a whole, there will inevitably arise "definitional concepts referring to definable things."[25] Accordingly, Voegelin argues, a reflective distance that remembers the structure of consciousness symbolized by the complex of consciousness-reality-language and the paradox of intentionality and luminosity, of thing-reality and It-reality, is the only means to prevent this perversion and to preserve the aura of mystery in the original illuminative event of reason/revelation.

What Voegelin is up to at this point of his analysis is working out a viable theory of imagination, a theme he did not pay direct attention to in his earlier work. At center stage in his theory of consciousness now is the mediating role of imagination to form and deform, illuminate and obscure, the reality it images. With this new emphasis Voegelin is once again underscoring the personal sources of insight and knowledge over against the mediating role of social, political, and ecclesial institutions and traditions, for these traditions are often the harbingers more of deformative untruth than of formative truth. But the problem lies not just in dogmatized symbols and hypostatized insights mediated by the collective; the problem lies in human imagination itself, in the personal mediation of reality to individual consciousness and its expression in image and symbol. When a creative person tries to delineate a vision of reality through an inner image, the product is invariably far from the original experience and insight. This is why Plato said that in the last analysis truth is inexpressible (*The Seventh Letter*, 341b–345a). Truth is indeed ineffable, but this does not deter Voegelin from speaking the truth out of his vision of the truth, however ultimately incommunicable the truth is, given the limits of image, symbol, and language as carriers of the truth imagined. As a philosopher Voegelin is not one to enter a Wittgensteinian silence. But the philosopher knows that to put one's vision of reality into words inevitably betrays the inner experience. This is a humbling affirmation, for a philosopher who is in quest of objective truth knows that at the most profound level there is no such thing as objective truth communicable in its essence. Humans not only do not know how to express mystery very well, they could not do it even if they tried. Imagination is inherently flawed; no vocabulary is up to the task of penetrating the essence of things, no set of images and symbols can ultimately do the job.

Voegelin "defines" imagination as the "ability to find the way from the metaleptic experiences to the imagery of expressive symbols."[26] In attempting to avoid an immanentized psychology, he suggests that imagination is less a faculty to create symbols as it is a participatory event by an existent consciousness that reveals reality itself as internally imaginative. A thinker who imagines the comprehending reality comprehends the comprehending reality as the subject endowed with imagination.[27] The truth of reality is dependent on an individual's imaginative response to reality's appeal. This response is above all constituted not just by the soul's movement within the height and depth structure of reality, but by the soul's imaginative articulation of that movement. Invariably this movement is governed by the corrupting escapes from reality through the imagination's deformative force. The worse corruption is the libidinous power play, when imagination is used to escape from the participatory movement in, to dominating control of, reality. The ability to create images can give the imager a sense of power over reality. As Voegelin elaborates, "the image of the world becomes the world itself. By his imagination, we may say, man can out-imagine himself and out-comprehend the comprehending reality."[28] A constant in history, this perversion is not an intellectual error or oversight in cognition so much as an ever-present potential in the play of forces in reality itself, rooted in the paradox of consciousness, in the tension between truth and untruth where every philosopher finds himself or herself. It must always be resisted and overcome by the calling into question of all received symbolisms. No symbolism can match the responsive experience of a person who is in quest of the truth. The truth always calls a seeker to out-imagine all preceding images of truth, short of the hubris of believing one is a creator of a world through creating images of it. The seeker is caught between defending the truth of reality as it is revealed to him or her and resisting the means of that defense, that is, the symbols and images that, however inadequately they express it, are nonetheless necessary to articulate the revelation imaginatively. In other words, no symbol, image, or word is final; the vision of reality always outdistances its expression. The truth of reality is always more than the truth of experience beheld, and the truth of experience beheld is always more than what imagination can render transparent. It is in this paradoxic complex of consciousness-reality-language that we can locate Voegelin's own imaginative mind living in the erotic tension of existence, for he is a philosopher caught between mysticism and skepticism. He seeks to experience and make transparent the height and depth of reality while resisting all received symbolisms of that reality as inadequate to his own vision. Since symbols arise in the *metaxy* they can never be made absolute as if they were outside the flux of reality. This goes even for symbols that explain the *metaxy* itself. Imagination participates in the movement of reality between immanence and transcendence while participating in both and being located in neither.

Two examples of the perversion of consciousness will help illustrate the meaning of Voegelin's critique. Perhaps the most persistent perversion we can cite is the familiar literalist and fundamentalist deformation of language which warps a large segment of modern society. There is simply no such thing as a preexistent and inerrant language of divine revelation bestowed on humans from above. In the complex of consciousness-reality-language that constitutes our life in the *metaxy* the only language that arises in the revelatory process is the language that emerges in consciousness symbolizing the divine appeal and human response. The hypostasis of language contradicts the constitutive role language plays in the metaleptic dynamic of spiritual experience. Both the consciousness of reality and its emergent language are constituted in such historical events as the prophet's theophany and the philosopher's vision. Voegelin underscores this insight when he states that "the men whose utterances emerge from the divine-human encounter are well aware that the language erupting in them is as much divine as it is human."[29] The "word of God" that emerges in the encounter must not be misunderstood in a literalist fashion as an auditory experience of the prophet who "hears" God's voice, nor as an ocular experience of a prophet or philosopher who "sees" God only to speak God's word emanating from the vision. The divine/human word is not an utterance of immanent humanity; it cannot be reduced to an intentionalist, propositional language "about" reality. The word of God *is* the word of the human being and the word of the human being *is* the word of God when the word that emanates from the divine–human encounter speaks the truth of the event. The prophetic insight into the illumination of consciousness that emanates in "the Word" is that the universal presence of divine reality is the source of illumination in every person. In the personal encounter with God the inner word of illumination is seen as the same word as the outer word of the prophet. To hear the word of the prophet, then, does not mean one merely repeats the prophet's utterances; it requires an attentiveness to the stirrings of one's own soul. The function of scripture as a protective device is distorted when fundamentalist prognosticators lose the experiences and insights it is trying to protect to their own possessive and ideological claims to truth.[30]

Another example of this perversion, which still governs contemporary philosophy and theology, is the medieval separation of "natural reason" from revelation. This perversion of Plato's *nous* deteriorated even further when, under the impact of Enlightenment rationalism, the nonrevelatory "reason" became an antirevelatory "reason" in revolt against the Church.[31] The doctrines of the Church, which had originally preserved the truth of revelation, became hardened into a possessive and inflexible monopoly of revelation when the ecclesial resisters revolted against the Enlightened resisters. Subsequently, in the modern ideological revolt, the possessors of truth arrogated for themselves the authority of revelation, and in this usurpation distorted the nature of reason even further. The truth of reality becomes opaque under the shroud of resistance to noetic truth whether the resisters are ecclesial, Enlightened, or ideological.[32]

A reflective distance from the immediate engendering experience/ vision that is sufficiently noetically detached but nevertheless erotically moved by the experience of divine appeal/human response is the necessary dynamic in a remembering consciousness that seeks to make explicit the parousiaic mystery that draws the philosopher toward the beyond of his or her own quest for truth. In this manner the quest is a salvational, immortalizing venture of divine–human participation in the metaxic structure of existence.

After having illuminated the above principles in the first chapter of *In Search of Order*, Voegelin tackled the terminological difficulties that inevitably arise in the quest for truth. He accomplished this by analyzing certain significant texts in representative figures, i.e., Homer, Hesiod, Parmenides, Bonaventure, and Leibniz, which contain ambiguous symbols of divine reality in various stages of emergent differentiation. However, before he could embark on an evaluation of these generally positive, but ambiguous, symbolists, he had to tackle the modern context which is rife with deformative language, oftentimes used for ideological purposes. In this endeavor, Voegelin was forced to address the "revolution of consciousness" that occurred in the German context, where idealistic philosophers attempted to differentiate the anamnetic structure of consciousness but ended up only distorting reality. In his own quest for truth Voegelin found himself resisting these practitioners of "imaginative oblivion." In order to make the opaque symbols of divine mystery speak once more with the authority of revelation, he had to return once again to the modern sources so as to extirpate their dominant deforming tendencies.

"Imaginative Oblivion" in the German Context

In Voegelin's analysis of the German sources, Hegel, as expected, receives the greatest opprobrium. Given Hegel's systematized attempt to establish a "science of the experience of consciousness," he suffers the brunt of Voegelin's critique. In his analysis Voegelin brings to light the "imaginative oblivion" and "public unconscious" that contributed to a deformed understanding of reality and its structure in the German context. A review of this critique will further illuminate Voegelin's own exegesis of consciousness.

In essence, the goal of the German thinkers was a worthy one: to recover the experiential basis of consciousness which had been burdened by the incrustations of doctrinal systematizations of thought. According to Voegelin, by the eighteenth century consciousness had become deformed by a long tradition of "metaphysics, ontology, and theology that had made the intentionalist method of dealing with the structures of consciousness convincingly unconvincing."[33] The intentionalist thinking that viewed reality in the mode of subject-object could not serve as a foundation for the recovery of consciousness. However, the valiant attempts by Kant, Hegel, and others to restore consciousness to its predogmatic reality was marred by the incorrigible habit of thinking in terms of thing-reality which the prestige of the natural sciences of the day, particularly Newtonian physics, only reinforced. As the model of experience in Kant's *Critique of Pure Reason*, this intentionalist form of thinking became further legitimated. Moreover, the role of "natural reason" in Kant could not adequately lay bare the area of the It-reality which Kant had actually recognized as the numinous dimension beyond the realm of the natural sciences. His symbol *Ding-an-sich* indeed refers to this dimension of reality, but for Voegelin, the "in-itself" of a thing cannot itself be a thing; it can only evoke the structure of the It-reality in consciousness, leaving Kant's formulation of the problem wholly inadequate.[34]

As a result, the dominance of the thing-reality in the imagination of philosophers determined the course of problems as they were to emerge in the German context. Without recounting the whole of Voegelin's analysis of this development, we can say in brief that it inevitably led to the splitting of consciousness into two separate acts of consciousness: the consciousness of a reflective subject who explores the objective facts of his or her own consciousness, and the resulting objectivized consciousness whose exploration becomes a further fact to explore. This intentionalist form of consciousness reduces existential consciousness to an infinite series of subjective acts of reflection. To maintain the integrality of consciousness, consciousness in this manner of formulation would become a person's *Ich* seeking identity with the *Ich* of existential consciousness. This self-identical *Ich* then became not another fact of consciousness but the transcendental form of consciousness that became immediately evident not in experience but in "intellectual intuition."[35] Thus arose the "idealism" in the German strain of philosophy in its various Kantian and Hegelian versions.

The authority of participatory consciousness that allows reality to become illuminative through the "reflective distance" that is a part of its structure is reduced to the nonparticipatory intentionalism that perceives the task of philosophical consciousness as achieving the "reflective identity" of the *Ich* with itself. This new type of consciousness was designated by the symbol "speculation," and the project of conforming reality to the speculator's system of science, which achieved its full flowering in Hegel, was underway.[36]

What was deformed in the project of reflective identity was the equivalent symbolizations of the mutual participation of consciousness in reality that emerged in history. Hegel's predecessors formulated this relation variously: In Parmenides there is the insight that being and thinking are the same; in Heraclitus the insight that the *logos* of his discourse is the *logos* of reality; the symbols of participatory consciousness, of *methexis* and *metalepsis*, appear in both classic and scholastic philosophers; and *Aletheia,* with its double meaning of truth and reality, is a symbol employed by both Plato and Aristotle.[37] These various ways of symbolizing the identity and nonidentity of the knower and the known find their equivalence in Hegel's "absolute knowledge" and "absolute reality," where there is achieved the paradoxic identity of identity and nonidentity.

However, in these definitional formulations, Hegel actually impedes an analysis of the structure of consciousness and lapses into the construction of a system to end all systems. The truth is there can never be any symbolism that is exempt from being one more historically equivalent truth. Nor is there an absolute experience that can found such an absolute system. There are only equivalent symbols that refer to experiences that are themselves equivalent. The constants lie on a level deeper than the level of equivalent experiences and their equivalent symbols. To symbolize these constants is not to engage in system building, for the constants lie on the level of "depth" which is discerned by philosophers examining the process of differentiation in their own consciousness. The new truth of reality discovered in the process of differentiation emerges from the depth but cannot be hypostatized into an absolute truth or an ideal system, for this depth is beyond articulate experience. It has no substantive content outside of the experiences of participatory tension, i.e., outside the primordial field of God and the human being, world and society. It is not a separate realm to be explored by so-called depth psychologists who are somehow not bound by the limits of conscious experience. The content of the unconscious depth cannot be experienced outside of its entering consciousness. The unconscious area beyond consciousness is indeed a dimension of the *psyche* but this psychic depth has no unconscious content apart from what is yielded in consciousness exploring the emergent process of differentiation. In other words, as Voegelin articulated it in his 1970 essay "Equivalences of Experience and Symbolization in History," the analysis of consciousness cannot go beyond the limits of its metaxic structure,

> for the depth is neither an "object" to be described as a content; nor a conveniently vacant area to be used as dumping ground for the psychoanalytic unconscious; nor a seat of authority to be occupied by a thinker who wants to fulminate a system; nor the kind of murkiness that will endow thought with the quality of "deep" or "profound" in the vulgarian sense.[38]

In order to avoid these reifications, the height and the depth must be understood not as separate definable entities, but as the two poles of a reality in which the movement of one's soul is symbolized by "ascent" and "descent."[39] A further discussion of the depth and constants of reality will be deferred until we take up Voegelin's final reflections on the philosopher's myth in the *Timaeus*.

In the generations after Hegel, the task of symbolic imagination had to carry the mortgage of the second realities produced by his system. The new symbols this system produced derailed into the will to dominate the reality symbolized. Consequently, Voegelin declares, Hegel's solution, instead of overcoming the deformation of philosophy, actually necessitates the abolition of philosophy:

> The love of wisdom, the erotic tension toward the divine Beyond, a love that never seems to reach its object, this indefinite process that never comes to an end will have to be brought to its End by wisdom possessed in the shape of absolute knowledge, by a conclusive *Wissenschaft* beyond the inconclusive love. We are at the heart of the ambiguity. The program of a philosophy that makes an End of philosophy is the most glaring symptom of the intellectual confusion dominant at the time. Critically we have to say: The program excludes the experience of existential consciousness, of existence in the tension of the metaxy, from the "experience of consciousness."[40]

And so the new Hegelian symbolism imposed itself on the contemporary scene in the same imperial fashion that instigated the revolt against the older symbols.[41] It is a curious turn of events that, in Voegelin's judgment, can be attributed to the level of "unconscious consciousness"[42] in the intellectual debates of the time. He asserted: "The state of philosophy around 1800 was miserable, legitimizing the revolt of the best minds, even if the revolt culminated in its own deformation."[43]

Voegelin contends that the crux of the Hegelian deformation originates in Hegel's inversion of the *periagoge* in Plato. In the allegory of the cave Plato has the prisoner "turn around" from the shadows on the wall and ascend to the light coming from beyond the cave. Hegel employs the identical symbol; but Hegel, who is a prisoner in the cave of his own age, conceives the "turning around" (*Umkehrung*) of consciousness to turn not toward the divine light of truth but to his own speculative system. His *Umkehrung* is not a loving response to divine grace but a self-assertive act of deformed consciousness. Thus, there transpires in Hegel the inversion of formation-deformation as understood by Plato. In Hegel's "science of the experience of consciousness" he eliminates from consciousness the experience of being drawn into the quest for truth by the divine reality from the beyond. The consequence, as Voegelin describes at length, is devastating:

Plato's work of a lifetime in exploring the experience of the quest, of its human-divine movements and countermovements, of the ascent to the height of the Beyond and the descent into the cosmic depth of the soul, the anamnetic meditations, the analysis of existence in the tensions between life and death, between Nous and passions, between truth and opinionated dreams, the Vision (in the *Laws*) of the divine formative force—this overwhelmingly conscious drama of the quest, this reality of consciousness and its luminous symbolization in a philosopher's existence, is excluded from the "experience of consciousness" and relegated to an unconscious "necessity" behind Plato's back. Together with the consciousness of noetic existence and its symbolization, there is thrown out of consciousness Plato's reflective distance to his work, his consciousness of his work as an event that marks a Before and After in the history of truth without putting an end to the quest for truth. What remains for "consciousness" is a body of literary work, to be understood in a fundamentalist manner as a set of propositions in the subject-object mode, with Hegel conveniently forgetting Plato's energetic declarations that anybody who understood him in this manner had not understood what he was doing.[44]

Hegel, according to Voegelin, inverted Plato's noetic consciousness into a state of unconsciousness; and rejected the myth as "scientifically worthless" but kept the critical symbols of the myth, such as the Platonic *periagoge*. Voegelin concludes that the noetic structure of the myth is present in Hegel's consciousness but that he consciously wills to forget it. Here lies the principal act of what Voegelin calls "imaginative oblivion," the act of willfully forgetting the structure of existence in tension toward the beyond. It is the direct contrary of the anamnetic recovery of consciousness which Hegel set out to accomplish; instead he ended up deforming the *nous*.[45]

It is in Hegel's *Logik* that Voegelin finds the apex of philosophical deformation. In opposing the symbol *Geist* to the Platonic *nous*, Hegel makes the fantastic claim in this work to have reached the mind of the eternal God. When the realm of the *Geist* comes into its truth, says Hegel, "it is without veil in and for itself. One can express oneself therefore in this manner: its content is the presentation of God as he is in his eternal Being before the creation of nature and a finite *Geist*."[46] Voegelin's reproach of this philosophical hubris is unrelenting:

The passage transmogrifies the Gospel of Saint John 1:1. According to the Gospel, the Logos was in the Beginning with God; now the Beginning turns out to be no more than a beginning in time that comes to its full revelation, to its true modern End, in the *Geist* of Hegel's *Logik*. . . .

. . . The symbol *Geist* remains a paracletic eschatology, the vision of
a descent of the Spirit that will achieve what the Petrine and Pauline
Christianities have not achieved—*i.e.*, the ultimately salvational Parousia
of the Beyond in this world.[47]

Under the veil of this further deformation in the German context, the
original symbols that had emerged from existential consciousness could
not yet recover their lost meaning. An adequate exegesis of consciousness had to go back behind and beyond these speculative constructions
to the original experiences from which the emerging symbols derive
their meaning. It had to return to the sources that symbolized the
participatory movement of consciousness in reality. On this occasion
Voegelin chose to return to Hesiod who was the first to symbolize,
within the limits of compact language, the remembering distance to
the experience of reality as a whole, particularly the experience of the
nonexperientiable divine beyond whose *parousia* is symbolized by the
gods. The divine–human Mnemosyne is Hesiod's evocative symbol that
first differentiated the experience of reflective distance, thereby availing
consciousness of the paradoxic structure of reality, a reality whose
process is an unfinished story. In this regard, Hesiod is the perfect foil
to Hegel who knew very well the constitutive role of remembrance in
historical consciousness but who also wanted to finish the story, to bring
the mysterious process of reality to its end in his system of science.[48]

Hesiod and Remembrance

The significant text of Hesiod is the beginning of the *Theogony*
where in the invocations of the Muses he develops the symbolism
of Mnemosyne. (The *Theogony*, we recall, after Homer's two great
epic poems, the *Iliad* and the *Odyssey*, is the principal source for
our knowledge of classical Greek mythology. It contains the myth
that describes the origin and history of the Olympian gods.) In an
extraordinary interpretation of the opening verses of Hesiod's text,
Voegelin examines the breakthrough to a differentiated expression of
divine truth that they represent.[49] The Muses are the daughters of
Mnemosyne, of Remembrance, who in union with Zeus begets these
offspring of highest divinity. The Muses are mediations of divine reality
in the form of gods but are begotten in a Jovian beyond, a realm beyond
the Olympian gods. In Hesiod's vision of reality this Remembrance is
internal to the divine beyond. By invoking the Muses that mediate
this Remembrance, Hesiod's poem suggests the need to remember the

divine presence that lives presently whenever divine order is victorious over the disorder of the older gods. Such an event occurred when the Olympian gods under the reign of Zeus were victorious over their predecessors, the Titans, under the reign of Kronus. More importantly, in the present of Hesiod, the divine ordering event repeats itself when the God beyond the Olympian gods emerges as the true representative of divine order. Voegelin explains this emerging differentiation:

> In his compact language of the myth, Hesiod expresses his insight into Remembrance as the reflective distance to the existentially ordering event in the metaxy. The reflectively distancing Mnemosyne is the dimension of consciousness in which the presence of the Beyond, experienced as the ordering force in the event, gains the reality of its Parousia in the language of the gods. The "existence" of the gods is the presence of the divine Beyond in the language symbols that express its moving Parousia in the experience of the not-experientiable ordering force in the existential event. With Hesiod, we are touching the limits of symbolization in the language of the gods: there are no gods without a Beyond of the gods.[50]

In Hesiod, even though the Jovian beyond differentiates a realm of divinity beyond the Olympian gods, Zeus is no longer representative of the ultimate beyond. And although the gods are superseded by the force of noetic pressure, they will not die. The advantage of this ambiguity, for Voegelin, is that this intermediate stage of differentiation stops short of projecting a beyond in the form of an intentionalist entity, thus averting the need to resist a hypostatized *parousia*. The disadvantage is that it does not imaginatively advance to a noetic beyond.[51] The language remains too compact to be free of problems of symbolization. Hesiod's experience is more differentiated than the symbols at his disposal allow him to articulate. But the value of his symbolism lies in his making intrinsic the act of remembering when the story of participation in the It-reality is told. What is remembered is the participatory character of consciousness in the struggle of the *metaxy*, whose genesis is part of the comprehending story told in reflective distance.[52] The past symbolizations of divinity, even though outmoded, are as much a part of the comprehending story as the differentiated ones: "The past of experience will not die with differentiation; it is part of the Whole of reality, of 'things that are, that shall be, and that were before.'"[53] The gods participate in the unfinished story of the one reality, a reality that is engaged in a movement toward its one true order. The disorder of the present is experienced as part of the endless struggle toward perfection. According to Voegelin, the vision of the whole that encapsulates this tension toward order, the tension between a divine beyond of time and its temporal *parousia*, was surely experienced by Hesiod. But his vision did not generate the corresponding noetic symbols. As a result, his symbolism remained ambiguous. It could not sufficiently make transparent the differentiating event of his vision. Because of this discrepancy between experience and symbolization, the problem of an ever-more adequate rendering of divine reality remained. Indeed, this was the problem that has required millennia of experiential and linguistic exegesis. This endless labor has left in its trail a question that persists even in our own time. It is the incessant question that Plato encountered throughout his life and which became the formidable question of his last work: "Who is this God?" this God beyond the gods of the poets? this god who does not speak from Olympus but from somewhere beyond the cosmos? this god beyond the realm of human imagination?[54]

This revelation of the divine beyond in the vision of the poet Hesiod, and later in the vision of Plato, has the form of an "indelible present" that occurs not in the past or future, but in the eternal now.[55] With Parmenides, one must say that eternal being "is," not "was" or "shall be."[56] It is an ever-present comprehending reality that participates in its timeless presence in the time-full moments of existing beings. This experienced *parousia* of the beyond in time is what Voegelin once again calls the "flux of divine presence" which endows all phases of time— past, present, and future. This flux of presence is what philosophers of every age seek to articulate when they experience their souls moving toward their transcendent *telos*, which they recognize as the same movement in others who express in imaginative symbols their experience of the same divine mystery.

The Ambiguities of
Bonaventure and Leibniz

In the movement of Voegelin's soul we find him ever striving for the proper linguistic tools to meet the analytic demands of his meditations. He is in habitual conversation with the achievements of past thinkers, struggling with the same difficulties they experienced in adequately symbolizing divine reality. This is illustrated in his brief reflections on the symbolisms of Bonaventure and Leibniz who represent medieval and modern attempts to resolve the problems of divine symbolization that first appeared in Hesiod's mythospeculation. What distinguishes these thinkers is that they manifest the same structurally equivalent vision of reality that is found in Hesiod's compact language.[57] Their reflections are also implicitly motivated by the question "Who is this god?" However, in interpreting their works, Voegelin concludes that in the Christian meditations of Bonaventure the ambiguities that arose from his mystical vision were only potentially deformative, while in the Enlightenment context of Leibniz's thought the vision of divine reality was symbolized in such a way as to be both formative and deformative.[58] A brief examination of Voegelin's reflections on these figures will specify further the intractable problems of symbolic imagination.[59]

The significant text of the medieval Franciscan Bonaventure is the *Itinerarium mentis in Deum*, section five.[60] Voegelin contends that in his attempt to ward off deformation, Bonaventure's "empiricist inclination" to identify thing-reality with being was overcompensated by his according the monopoly of being to the comprehending reality. So in attempting to prevent the potential transformation of thing-reality into being and, correspondingly, of being into nonbeing, Bonaventure did not clearly maintain the paradoxic structure of reality. The interaction and inseparable tension between It-reality and thing-reality could not be preserved by Bonaventure's ambiguous language which, in Voegelin's language, carried "a defensive touch."[61]

In Leibniz the significant texts are *Les principes de la nature et de la grâce fondés en raison* (esp. § 7–8) and the *Monadologie* (esp. § 32, 38), both written about 1713, shortly before his death.[62] For Voegelin, Leibniz's late writings are inspired by a meditative vision that is equivalent to Bonaventure's. His meditations are rooted in an attempt to preserve the unity of reality, since in his time the poles of the tension had been practically split and reduced to autonomous and unrelated things: the God of the theologians with its formative and deformative construction, and the spatiotemporal things of the mathematized sciences. Leibniz's *grand principe* that nothing happens without sufficient reason, eventually yields the two ultimate questions: Why is there something rather than nothing? Why do things exist as they are and not otherwise? Applying his great principle, Leibniz concludes that "this ultimate reason of things is called God."

In an otherwise positive analysis, Voegelin argues that the ambiguous results of Leibniz actually lean in the direction of deformation. The divine reality that is symbolized by the language of the gods in Hesiod becomes in Leibniz a language of things. "God" becomes the "sufficient reason" of a human mind in quest of a causal explanation of the spatiotemporal order.[63] In Leibniz's words:

> This sufficient reason of the existence of the universe cannot be found in the series of contingent things. . . . The sufficient reason which needs no further reason, must be outside this series of contingent things, and must

lie in a substance which is the cause of this series, or which is a being that bears the reason of its existence within itself.[64]

In Voegelin's perceptive analysis, the great mystery of Plato's *nous* has become the great principle of Leibniz's enlightened mind: "a piece of information well known to a metaphysician who knows his business, to a connoisseur of *les choses*, to an expert in all of the 'things' of whom God is one."[65] In conclusion, says Voegelin, "by the time of Leibniz, the practice of what may be called conceptually systematizing metaphysics had indeed widely diverged from noetic analysis and its recognition of the mysteries of reality."[66] When compared to Bonaventure, Leibniz's remarks have transformed the problem of ambiguity into the problem of imaginative oblivion.

As these reflections of Voegelin demonstrate once again, the search for transcendent order is a ceaseless enterprise. With his return to Plato's *Timaeus*, in the final section of *In Search of Order,* Voegelin sought to advance further the symbolization of existential consciousness and divine being which Plato had advanced so very far himself beyond the initial breakthroughs of Hesiod and Parmenides. The question: "Who is this God?" remains as real and as stirring for Voegelin as it was for Plato twenty-four centuries ago.

The Return to the Platonic Myth

In the end, Voegelin returns to Plato for guidance. Why, we must ask, does Voegelin end his meditations with a further analysis of the *Timaeus*? This appears perplexing after he had stated so clearly in *The Ecumenic Age* that the Pauline myth was, in his judgment, distinguished by "its superior degree of differentiation." As Voegelin asserted on that occasion, once the pneumatic depth beyond the *nous* had been articulated, the Platonic type was no longer suitable for expressing the ultimate truth about God and the human being.[67] The symbol of a human being redeemed by the loving grace of God, Voegelin told us, differentiated the truth of existence that became visible in the philosopher's experience of *athanatizein*.[68] The pneumatic theophany experienced through the epiphany of Christ in Paul's vision was a fuller, pleromatic differentiation of consciousness in the *metaxy*. This was essentially the same view that Voegelin had taken as early as 1943 in his letters to Schutz where he affirmed that the Christian experience of grace surpassed the similar experience of transcendence expressed by Plato.[69] Also, we must not forget his discussion of "soteriological truth" versus "anthropological truth" in *The New Science of Politics* where he once again professed the decisive enlargement of the mystic experience of the Greek philosophers by Christianity. Why, then, did Voegelin return to the Platonic myth instead of expounding on the superior achievement manifested by Christianity? And why did he choose the *Timaeus*, which he had already treated at great length in volume III of *Order and History* as well as in his article on "Equivalences"?

Some possible reasons come to mind. First, as a philosopher, Voegelin sought maximal clarity in the symbolization of divine reality. This symbolization must be articulated in such a way that it would preclude the derailment of the balance of consciousness. Such a task requires the meditative procedure of noetic analysis that only a philosopher who is aware of the critical issues can undertake. The *Timaeus* is the great representation of the critical issues surrounding the beginning and the beyond by the greatest philosopher. To analyze its symbols in light of the various deformed analyses of modernity would be to participate in the "advance" of the story of reality becoming luminous. In other words, noetic analysis of mythical symbols is, to use the Christian symbol of St. Anselm, the philosopher's *fides quaerens intellectum*. In fact, for Voegelin, the *fides* seeking its *intellectum* through meditative reflective distance is the critical operation of philosophy and theology at all times—in the time of Plato, in the time of Anselm, and in our time today. It is the decisive method for laying bare the content of consciousness in the modes of both intentionality and luminosity. This is as true for a philosopher like Plato, who in the *Timaeus* directs his *fides* toward the cosmos and the divine mystery that penetrates the cosmos, as it is for a Christian theologian, whose *fides* is directed toward the divine presence incarnate in Jesus the Christ.[70] In his generalized version of the *fides quaerens intellectum* we see manifested Voegelin's turn toward the Augustinian/Anselmian meditative faith that he essentially took in the 1943 letters to Schutz when he first surpassed the limitations of the Cartesian and Husserlian forms of meditative analysis of consciousness.

Secondly, in addition to its being the expression of Plato's *fides*, the importance of the *Timaeus* is unquestioned due to its pervasive influence on philosophical and religious thought since antiquity. In his first treatment of this portentous dialogue of Plato some thirty years before, Voegelin spoke of its significance in the following way:

> The *Timaeus* marks an epoch in the history of mankind in so far as in this work the psyche has reached the critical consciousness of the methods by which it symbolizes its own experiences. As a consequence, no philosophy of order and symbols can be adequate unless the Platonic philosophy of the myth has been substantially absorbed into its own principles.[71]

Noetically, then, the *Timaeus* represents the height of spiritual consciousness in that, through the medium of the myth, there is symbolized in this dialogue the movement of a *fides* seeking to understand its object, which for Plato is the cosmos and its divine ground. Voegelin even stated that on some crucial points Plato's tentative formulations "are analytically more successful than the later attempts of the Christian theologians to find the *intellectus* of their *fides*."[72] For this reason alone we can comprehend why he returned to it. In short, we can say that Voegelin regards the *Timaeus* as the quintessence of Platonic theology to which Christian theology must continually return for noetic guidance.

Thirdly, we must consider the possibility that Voegelin was not satisfied with his prior treatment of the Platonic myth, particularly as he had analyzed it vis-à-vis the Pauline myth. Perhaps he discovered more there than what he was able to articulate previously. We must presume that Voegelin, without retracting any of his earlier assertions, saw in his last years a surplus of meaning in the Platonic myth that he had failed to see earlier. Indeed, a studied reading of his final analysis of the *Timaeus* shows this to be so. What, then, were the new insights that he uncovered?

To help answer this question it will help to recall the former insights that Voegelin had articulated in the 1966 foreword to *Anamnesis*. There he discussed the importance the *Timaeus* had for his own philosophy of consciousness. On that occasion he said that in the *Timaeus*,

> remembrance raises the comprehending knowledge of human-social existence attuned to the order of history and the cosmos from the unconscious into consciousness. The remembrance expands into a philosophy of consciousness in its tensions of conscious and unconscious, of latency and presence of knowledge, of knowing and forgetting, of order and disorder in personal, social and historical existence, as well as to a philosophy of symbols in which these tensions find their linguistic expression.... When remembrance reaches articulation in the linguistic expression of knowledge it falls to the conditions of the world; in the external world the symbol can separate from remembering consciousness, it can become opaque for the experience expressed; and the remembering knowledge can again sink from the presence of consciousness into latency of oblivion. In times of social disorder, like our present time, we are surrounded by the detritus of symbols expressing past remembrance, as well as by the symbols of revolt against the state of oblivion; hence the work of remembrance must be started again.[73]

This passage illustrates once again how in fact all of *Order and History* must be viewed as a work of remembrance, a work which culminates with a remembering meditation on Plato's great meditation on remembrance. But what is remembered in the *Timaeus*? What purpose did the *Timaeus* serve for Plato? And what purpose does it now serve for Voegelin? Is there a more differentiated insight that emerged in Voegelin's final reading of this dialogue that is explicitly theological?

Towards an initial approximation in answering these questions, we must first of all realize that the myth of the cosmos in *Timaeus* is not a cosmological myth. It is a philosophical myth representing the exposition of a philosopher's *fides*. Briefly stated, the *Timaeus* is Plato's *fides quaerens intellectum* in action. (This articulation of the meaning of the dialogue is new. Indeed, the attribution of a *fides quaerens intellectum* to Plato is the result of Voegelin's interpretative genius, and as far as I know, solely his discovery.[74] Its theological consequences will be drawn out in the next section when we discuss the Christian context of faith and vision.) What kind of tale is being told in this mythic exposition of a philosopher's *fides*? Plato equivocated between calling this new truth an *alethinos logos* or the more doubtful *eikos mythos*, that is, between a true story or a likely myth (26e, 29c–d). The equivocation arises from the fact that Timaeus's account of the cosmos can only be an image, a story. The truth (*aletheia*) of the story belongs to God, while the faith (*pistis*) that spins the images and symbols of the storied account is humanity's. But "according to the likely story" the cosmos is "in very truth a living creature endowed with soul and intelligence by the providence of God" (30b–c). Thus, we must conclude that the *eikos mythos*, the likely story, renders something more than likeliness. It renders the very truth (*aletheia*) of the cosmos as this truth is incarnated in the cosmos; and yet this account cannot penetrate beyond the incarnate truth to the paradigmatic beyond.[75]

Ostensibly the myth concerns the origins of Hellenic society and its order as this order relates to the cosmic order. Included in this tale is the story of the origin of all of Hellas that is now lost. Yet Voegelin's final analysis of the *Timaeus*, just like his earlier treatment of the *Theogony*, recalls none of the conspicuous details of the myth, for his primary interest lies in penetrating to its experiential basis in order to reveal the divine presence behind the symbols of Plato's imagination. The social and historical elements become irrelevant. Among these, we recall, is the lost paradisal island of Atlantis, Plato's anamnetic symbol for the origins of the collective soul of Hellas, a symbol which emerged in the exploration of his own soul in its unconscious depth.

Another approximation in our quest to understand why Voegelin returned to the *Timaeus* rests in the fact that, for Voegelin, the *Timaeus* developed the differentiated context in which the prior ambiguous symbols of reality found their resolution. Borrowing the symbol *ta eonta* (being-things) of Homer, Hesiod had discerned the divine presence formatively moving in all things of the cosmos. To further articulate this differentiating beyond, Parmenides advanced the symbolism of reality beyond the ambiguities of the poets. The beyond could no longer be symbolized as one of the "things" in which it was formatively present. All being-things (*ta eonta*) must therefore partake of the singular being (*to eon*) which at no time came into being but is eternally. What began to emerge in Parmenides is the It-reality. But in his self-assured discovery of this "new" being, Parmenides slips into his own ambiguity with his problematic identification of thought and being when he says, "For the same is thinking and being" (B 3).[76] The balance of consciousness is potentially disturbed when the identity of thinking and being tends to overlook their nonidentity.

Only with Plato was the tension between thought and being preserved. It was preserved when he articulated the experience of reality with the dominant symbol *to pan*, the all. In this shift of symbols, from *to eon* to *to pan*, Plato was able to appeal to a comprehensive reality that comprehends the *ta eonta* that come into being, including the gods, as well as the one being that never becomes. In addition to these two kinds of being Plato adds a third kind, the *psyche*, a composite kind of being that partakes of, and exists between, the other two. The all which is both being and not-being, and yet neither, is the cosmos. And this cosmos in turn discovers its order in the meditative movement of the *psyche* which mediates between the opposite poles of the structured cosmos.[77]

Plato's analysis of the cosmos presupposes the compact language of the gods. As a quest for divine order it is a search for the beginning. This search was equivalently expressed in the biblical account of the beginning in Genesis chapter 1, an account which manifests a pneumatic irruption in consciousness. However, in his noetic quest of divinity, Plato is searching for a balanced language of reality that will adequately express his *fides quaerens intellectum*. He is struggling with the traditional *fides* in the intracosmic gods who are present in all things from the beginning.[78] His vision of reality forces him to move beyond this inadequate representation. The object of Plato's *fides* is the cosmos, the all, which has absorbed Parmenides' *to eon*, which in turn absorbed the poets' *ta eonta*.

The difficulty for Plato arises when he asks if the cosmos truly has a beginning or whether it is eternal. Since the comprehending whole that is the cosmos comprises both being-things and nonthing being, is its beginning genetic or not? Plato's paradoxic answer is both Yes and No. Insofar as the cosmos has a *soma*, a body, composed of finite things, it is indeed generated, it has a beginning. But insofar as the cosmos has an intelligible, everlasting structure and is the comprehending whole of all things, its beginning cannot be expressed in terms of a cause, in the sense of causality in the external world. Its "cause" (*aition*) is found only in the paradigmatic order designed by a divine Demiurge. The visible cosmos, then, is an *eikon*, an image of this eternal paradigm.[79] This *eikon* of eternity is called "time." Time, thus, is the moving image of eternity; there was no time before time was generated as this moving image. But the eternity which it images cannot be spoken of in the language of time, as in the terms it "was" or "shall be." Therefore, being that is eternal can never truly "become."

Voegelin is quite aware of the literal inconsistencies in the *Timaeus* along with the controversies it has generated due to its seeming illogic. But these well-known problems are of little concern to him because he is trying to show how Plato, in attempting to advance the symbolization of existential consciousness within the limits of a *fides* of the cosmos, is struggling with a language that is inherently insufficient for the task.[80] What emerges from the *Timaeus* is not an absolute rendering of reality in unequivocal speech but, rather, a complex of symbols which are the constants in the movement of noetic consciousness trying to understand its comprehending structure. In reflective distance Plato is aware not only of the paradoxic structure of reality, of thing-reality and It-reality, but also of the limits of language that is governed by this paradox. Unlike Hegel, who attempted to out-comprehend the comprehending reality, Plato knows that one cannot create a language beyond reality and its paradox.[81]

In order to avoid the temptation to turn the poles of the tension into metaphysical entities, a second level of language must be forged out of the paradox, a language that locates the truth of reality in the tensional complex rather than in the poles taken singly. In Voegelin's analysis, this second level is the constants of experience and symbolization, of the movements and countermovements, of the various complexes and their relations. But are these constants really constant? Because they seem to point beyond themselves, Voegelin saw in Plato the need for a higher reflectively distancing language that would reflect the superconstant encompassing the structure of tensions and poles.[82] He claimed that Plato, in his attempt to resolve this problem of the various constants, created a third level of language. In his symbolism of the *to pan*, the all that is the cosmos, "or whatever it prefers to be called" (28b), he invoked the one "super-constant" that governed the constants.

However one assesses this peculiar development of constants and superconstant in Voegelin's analysis, it cannot fail to strike one as a particularly new and insightful understanding of Plato, an understanding that calls for a reevaluation of the substance of Plato's noetic myth. Through Voegelin's perceptive interpretation we can begin to discount much of what has been made of Plato's so-called doctrine of creation in the *Timaeus* as it has been read and commented upon by centuries of Christian theologians.[83] A further reading of Voegelin's discussion of the *Timaeus* will bear out this view.

In his experienced tension of reality, Plato asked the question whether the cosmos is one, and if so, why? His answer is paradoxic but not ambivalent. Though the cosmos is accessible to sense perception, it is not a thing. It is experienced as the image of the paradigmatic *to pan*, the divinely ordered comprehending reality of all things. The symbol "comprehending" (*periechon*) does not mean that the cosmos contains a lot of reality. It means that it is comprehending of all reality. In other words, the cosmos is one. If there were more than one cosmos there would have to be another comprehending reality that included the multiple worlds. But this very notion of multiple worlds is incompatible with the experience of the It-reality. The oneness of the one cosmos is not meant numerically. Plato wished to make explicit, rather, the one-ness of tensional reality that embraced everything including the beyond of every thing. For this he invented a new symbol: *monogenes* (31b). Usually translated as "only-begotten," *monogenes* also means unique or one-of-a-kind, minus the numerical connotation. It refers to the one existential tension that embraces all things and the intelligible whole that comprehends all things. This *monogenes*, thus, is not a thing but the visible god generated in the image of the intelligible god—the intelligible god being not the Demiurge but the paradigmatic divine beyond, beyond the reach of the *nous*.[84] The linguistic difficulties that arose when Plato tried to symbolize adequately this tensional oneness forced him to coin yet another new symbol: *monosis*. As Voegelin explains, "the Cosmos has been generated *monogenes* in order to make it image most perfectly the *monosis* of the divine *paradigm* (31b). Monogenesis as the image of Monosis thus parallels the symbolization of Time as the image of Eternity."[85]

The symbol *monosis* was not preserved in the history of philosophy. According to Voegelin it faded away under the impact of existential alienation and spiritual revolt that accompanied the imperial expansions of the Ecumenic Age. Still, while the *monosis* disappeared, its genetic image, the symbol *monogenes,* survived. In fact, it reappeared in the Gospel of John where it is made an attribute of the Son of God (John 1:14, 18; 3:16, 18). For Voegelin, this transferring of the symbol *monogenes* from the cosmos to the Christ reveals the experiential shift in emphasis from the God who creates the order of the cosmos to the God who saves humanity from its disorder, a shift which implicitly affirms the greater pneumatic differentiation achieved within the Judeo-Christian orbit.[86]

Nevertheless, no matter how significant this symbolic shift may be, the problem of symbolizing divine reality remains. The symbolizing imagination cannot make the mystery of the beyond and its *parousia* any less mysterious. No matter how the *parousia* of the divine beyond is symbolized, whether in the compact language of the gods, or in an intermediate differentiating language of a representative god beyond the lower gods, or in the fully differentiated language of a God beyond all gods, the divine beyond remains the unrevealed reality beyond its revelation. All reflective symbolizations illuminate on some level this stratification of divine mystery that reveals itself in the process of history as the ineffable divine reality beyond its presence.

For our purposes, the significant insight that surfaces in Voegelin's exegesis of this Platonic text is this very oneness of divine reality. In our age of religious and theological pluralism we overlook the fact that Plato essentially confronted the fundamental problem of "multiple revelations" of divine mystery long ago. In Plato's *fides* of the cosmos the divine ordering force reveals itself as one. However manifold and diverse the experienced presence of God in history is, Plato's experience of a cosmos that is the *periechon* of all things, revealing a oneness to divine reality as its ground, is in principle the prototype of all symbolizations of mystical experiences of divine/cosmic unity, for this symbolization essentially cannot be surpassed. If we view this breakthrough in Plato's noetic analysis as one that confronts head-on the problems of imaginative symbolization, we cannot help but see in it the philosophical resolution to current debates that rage over the issue of religious pluralism. When Christianity appears in history as one revelation among other revelations, as one religion among other religions, or as one ultimate claim to truth among other competing claims, the noetic insights that would maintain the balance of existential structure tend to get lost in the ensuing dogmatic debates.

The problem does not lie in the Christian shifting of the focus of the *fides* from the cosmos to Jesus the Christ,[87] for by all historical standards this shift was clearly necessitated by the more differentiated truth revealed (i.e., the epiphany of God's pleromatic presence in a human being who reveals the salvific force of divine grace). The problem lies in the theologically libidinous attempts to possess the whole truth, isolating one revelation from the total history of revelation and thereby losing the existential tension of life in the *metaxy*. The essential problem today is not that "faith" and "understanding," whatever their content may be, are in themselves misguided. The problem is forgetting that the movement from one to the other requires a seeking, a quest in which truth is never possessed, only more or less adequately, and ultimately deficiently, grasped. No matter what may comprise the specific content of one's faith, and no matter what arises in the understanding of that faith, the critical matter that would unite people of various "faiths" and various understandings is the middle term of the *fides quaerens intellectum*: the seeking, the being drawn, the movement toward a more and more adequate rendering of divine reality. This is the movement of the soul that all people share as the basis of their common humanity.

From these reflections we would have to infer from Voegelin the following: If theology is to remain the science of "faith seeking understanding" then it must enter a horizon beyond the parameters of Christian faith which, however sound within its own orbit, must today be open to other non-Christian *fides* that represent God's ubiquitous presence in history. This is possible if theology sees itself not as possessing a faith that contains immutable truths, but as a faithful movement from the givens of revelatory experience to the understanding of this experience in symbolic imagination via the existential quest for truth. The quest cannot dismiss any authoritative experience of transcendence, whosesoever it may be. Consequently, theology must take as its guide a noetic philosophy which is able to handle the various problems that arise in the quest, including the problem of multiple, and seemingly disparate, quests. It would be a philosophy informed by a theory of consciousness that Voegelin, following Plato's noetic analysis, has done the most to articulate.

Plato essentially confronted the fundamental problems of theological analysis and symbolization long ago, but he could not foresee what would follow in the centuries after his death when the theophanic events peaked with Christianity and when the noetic instruments that could guide the newly differentiated experiences toward a balanced understanding became deformed. Today we have inherited the legacy of confusion produced by these age-old problems. Only by returning to the sources (as Voegelin found himself forced to return to the Platonic myth of divine creation) can we eliminate the burden of false and inadequate theologies and ascend once again to the light of the one truth that embraces us all. By recovering the tetragrammatic God beyond the personal God of the Jewish, Christian, and Islamic successors of Plato—the ineffable God that they knew in their mystical quests but oftentimes forgot in their dogmatic theologies and imperial, missionary expansions—can we begin to move toward a resolution of the fundamental theological problems that plague us today. Recognition of this divine mysterious beyond, this ineffable reality we call "God" who embraces all of its multiple symbolizations in history (including the Olympian Zeus, the Platonic Father-god, the Israelite Yahweh, the one Jesus called "Abba," and the Allah of Mohammed), would greatly serve our contemporary search for global religious harmony.

It was Plato who first encountered the problem of pluralism. Technically, he resolved the problem on the level of noetic analysis. He discovered that the quest for the one God of his *fides* moves all symbols of divinity into a reflective distance which realizes that the awe inspired by the experience of the *mysterium tremendum* inevitably blends with its all-too-human symbolizations, rendering it less than the truly one of the experienced revelation beyond its revelation. The differentiating experiences never seem to escape fully the inevitably compact symbols that emerge to express them. Reflective distance discerns this "tensional pressure" as an intractable problem. With this insight, Voegelin introduces something new into the analysis:

> This tensional pressure appears to be a constant in the history of revelation. Neither will the gods disappear, nor will the Beyond let them die in peace. Compactness and differentiation, then, would not be simply historical stages of consciousness, the one succeeding the other in time, but poles of a tensional process in which the revelation of the Beyond has to overcome progressively a hard core of compact resistance without ever dissolving it completely. Plato was conscious of this hard core and tried to find its experiential source in the structure of existence.[88]

The quest for truth within the *metaxy* is now discerned to be structured by the tensional poles of compactness and differentiation which are no longer just historical stages in the quest. In all his earlier work Voegelin would go no further than to say that the "differentiation of a segment [of reality] does not abolish the truth of reality experienced compactly; there is no simple succession in which a historically later truth makes an earlier one obsolete."[89] Now the tension between compactness and differentiation emerges as a constant of consciousness requiring a further nuance in how the structure of consciousness is formulated. The structure must now account for the differentiating movement of consciousness which can never fully dissolve the inexorably compact symbolization of transcendent mystery. There is always the inevitable residue of "the-all-too-human-image" which pervades the expression of even the most sublime mystical experience. Simply put, the human mind inevitably thinks in terms of things even when it struggles to articulate what is not a thing. The struggle within this tension is an added feature of the arduous search for transcendent order.

Voegelin professes that Plato encountered this "compact resistance" to differentiation and tried to find its source in the structure of existence.[90] He discerned that there is something in the structure of consciousness-reality-language that forces us to think in terms of things. Plato called this something the *chora*, or space (52b). The *chora* is not itself a thing that can be sensed but a "kind of being" that is an "unsensed something" we behold as in a dream, behind all formed thingness.[91] This *chora* seems to impose on all reality, and all thought on reality, the mode of thingness. We cannot think of anything that is, without thinking of it as occupying some place. It is as if the incarnate cosmos, which is the "space" where the paradigmatic beyond is embodied, has to submit to a thingness which by its nature is a disorder from which there is no escape. Since true order lies in the beyond of things, no matter how mystical one's consciousness may be, the search for order is limited by its inability to reach beyond the mode of thingness. Disorder, in other words, appears to be our inexorable lot.

This is of course only a conjecture, and although Plato may have proposed it as such, it must be rejected in light of the dialectical movement of his whole analysis. For as Voegelin remarks, this assumption would lead to the transformation of the luminous symbols that emerge from tensional experiences into intentionalist concepts, thus destroying the paradoxic structure of reality, consciousness, and language. Although the quest for truth seems to get bogged down in the mode of thingness, the illuminative use of symbols avoids just that. The meditative process of the quest, through reflective distance, is the procedure by which the paradoxic tensions are upheld and the deforming fragmentation and doctrinalization of nonthing reality into thingness is averted. Once again the meditative, anamnetic procedure is the singular method for maintaining the balance. This of course must not be construed to deny the intentionality of consciousness which, with its language of "reference," is very real. This intentional mode, which inexorably thinks of reality in terms of subject-object, is the pervasive, but not comprehensive, mode of consciousness. When consciousness "intends" the nonintentional beyond, it cannot be adequately described in terms of subject and object. It can only be described as a process within a reality that comprehends both the cosmos in its divine mystery and the human being in whose mind the mystery becomes cognitively luminous. This is why Voegelin speaks of the luminosity of consciousness which experiences the It-reality as a subject which has us as its predicate. Intentionality is absorbed into luminosity when consciousness intends the nonintentional.

Through his use of symbols which mutually illuminate one another, Plato preserves the balance; for we recall that he speaks of the cosmos as the *periechon* of all things, as the *to pan*, or "whatever it prefers to be called." Although the cosmos appears to be one of the "things," or a peculiar sort of thing, or even a nonthing thing, it is certainly not an object in space. Rather, Plato concludes, the cosmos *has* space. He carefully symbolizes the experience of the cosmos as a nonthing through the *monosis* of its paradigm and through the *monogenes* of its image. It is the It-reality comprehending all "things."[92]

. . . This is the point at which Voegelin's analysis of Plato's analysis of divine creation in the *Timaeus* becomes very exacting and wholly complicated. For precisely here emerge further questions that have to be handled, and the new complexes of symbols that arise to answer these questions have to be penetrated. In the course of his argument Plato's complex symbols keep revealing further facets, as do Voegelin's, which only reinforces the idea that the surplus of meaning these illuminative symbols carry gives them a revelatory force. The reader is faced with this hermeneutical experience: Plato's meditative analysis and symbolization is being penetrated by Voegelin's meditative analysis and symbolization, which in turn must be penetrated by the reader's own meditative analysis. Reading an authoritative text that interprets another authoritative text (which one must read alongside) draws one meditatively into the self-same quest for truth that both texts exemplify. True to the paradoxic realities under investigation, it is an enlightening, but oftentimes befuddling, experience. However exacting the text may be, a concentrative reading at least assures one that one is engaging in the genuine, pivotal problems of philosophy and theology, if not also the truly transforming experience of reason/revelation; for the meditative reading moves one's soul in the same direction as that of the text's questing movement. Again, I can only invite the reader to ponder these pages by himself or herself . . .

The new complex of symbols that designates the internal structure of the cosmos is that of being-becoming-space. This complex is structurally equivalent to the complex of *nous*-in-*psyche*-in-*soma*. Taken together, these complexes further illuminate the isomorphism between consciousness and reality. As being becomes "ensouled" through space, so *nous* becomes "ensouled" in a body. The structure of human existence is aligned with the structure of reality. According to Voegelin, the inevitable question that now arises about whether this space is a preexistent material in which being somehow becomes (which *nous* understands as the paradigmatic beyond becoming incarnated in its *monogenes* image) must, under Plato's advice, return to the original, questioning experience of the beginning. In other words, it must search for the *aition* of the cosmos from which these symbols emerged in the first place.[93]

What would then emerge in this search for the beginning is the comprehending reality of the beyond. The beginning of all things points to their beyond. And this search for the true order of the cosmos reveals the quest itself as the "place," the bodily located event, when and where reality becomes luminous for its truth. The consciousness of the human being is the site of incarnated truth. It is moving toward the unflawed order beyond the disorder of thingliness. It tells the story of this movement in the flawed language of things. The final upshot of all this is that the quest for truth is ultimately penultimate, for there is always the greater truth whose story needs to be told but can never fully and finally be told. The story of the quest, no matter how luminous, can never put an end to Mystery; it can only deepen the insight into its paradoxic penultimacy.[94]

In full awareness of this state of things, Plato devised the symbol of the Demiurge to denote that divine creative "force" which is neither a thing in the cosmos nor a nonthing like the cosmos. It is the nonthing "something" that only submits to the thingness of space when it finds it "necessary" to create "things" (47e–48a). What are we to make of this creative force that resists any imaging in the realm of things? On this Plato can only offer the quip: "To find the Maker and Father of this *to pan* would be a job indeed; and even if found, to tell of him to all men would be impossible" (28c).[95]

Hence, as Voegelin asserts, we are brought back to the impossible task of piling beyond on beyond which the limits of language first forced upon Hesiod. In the experience of the nonexperientiable the seeker of truth becomes conscious of the paradox of a language which, through reflective distance, makes the ineffable effable.[96]

To say it all differently, the silence of God breaks forth in the creative word of visionary illumination only to return once again to the silence. The ultimate Word of God is spoken through the penultimate word of human beings. The Mystery of reality moves from ineffable silence through the cosmos, through humanity, back to the ineffable silence. Plato stresses that this divine mystery cannot be known outside of its incarnate presence in the things of the cosmos. The divine cannot be discerned by itself alone, but only through participating in the things in which it is formatively present (69a). It seems that God had no other way than to create a cosmos that was tensionally structured, subjecting humans to the tensional experience of divine presence, and forever restricting them to the flawed, finite knowledge of divine being. But as a consolation, who, we must ask, in their heart of hearts, could resist the blessing of divine illumination that can be experienced by meditatively wandering through the various authoritative stories of God?

Of course none of these reflections answers the inscrutable question. Why was the Cosmos created in the first place? Why did the order of divine being create a less than perfect order of cosmic being? and Why was it created with the structure it has? One might ask Plato, Why didn't the Demiurge leave "things" well enough alone? Why wasn't being left to its eternal existence free of all tensions, instead of assuming the ordering/disordering form of becoming in the mode of thingness? This question is of course the unanswerable Question. Not even Plato can answer it, except to speculate that the Demiurge out of its "goodness" found it "necessary" to create (29d–30b). In other words, to use the biblical language more familiar to Christians, one can only say that God is good and out of God's goodness God created the world in God's likeness. And the human being too was created in God's image; male and female created God them.

The "stuff" that this demiurgic God created has a structure that Plato finally formulates in the following way. Through the spaced cosmos, being participates in becoming and becoming participates in being. Thus, the poles of the mysterious tension of reality participate in each other. Being, in order to become, goes beyond itself into the tension of the spaced cosmos, and this spaced cosmos which is beyond things goes beyond itself into the tensional reality of material thingness in order to partake of being. Space, which lies at the lower pole of the complex, is metaphorically symbolized as a mother or nurse who receives the noetic order. This "receptacle" lies at the thing-pole of reality but is not itself a thing. It is a mysterious reality, itself tensional, that gives birth to the visibly formed cosmos by partaking of the noetic beyond, which is also tensional in its divinely formative character. For Plato it seems as if this mutually "partaking" reality is the one, ultimate mysterious reality. To symbolize this ultimately ultimate reality, his crowning metaphor in the *Timaeus* is the complex Father-Mother-Offspring. Plato likens the formative source of being to the Father-god from which becoming comes, and he likens the receptive wherein of becoming to the Mother-god. The tensional reality suspended between them must then be conceived as their Offspring (50b–d).[97]

Voegelin "concludes" his meditation on the *Timaeus* by declaring that any expectation of an ultimate symbolism can only be disappointing. Even the Offspring cannot be explained in any way other than as the cosmic reality that is tensionally alive between order and disorder. And the human being as a creature of this Offspring, located in the

metaxic middle, participates in this structured reality by the experiences
of existential movement. Here Voegelin recalls the metaphor of the
"pulls" (from the *Laws*) toward either pole: the thingly beyond of the
chora or the divine beyond of the *nous*. The pull is either a movement
toward a state of existence where God is absent or is an immortalizing
movement toward "likeness" with God.[98]

"Is the God of the Beginning the same as the God of the End?"
asks Voegelin. Is the God who creates the same as the God who saves?
Indeed, the mystery of the divine reality that creates the order of the
cosmos is experienced as in tension with the mystery of the divine reality
that saves us from its disorder. Beyond this impenetrable mystery the
philosopher's *fides quaerens intellectum* cannot go. In the end the experienced ultimacy of the nonexperientiable reality in its paradoxic tension
of revelation can only be illuminated with the symbol "divine."[99]

The last word on the lesson of the *Timaeus* belongs to Voegelin:

> The *fides* of the Cosmos becomes transparent for a drama of the Beyond
> enacted, through the tensional process of the Cosmos, from a demiurgic
> Beginning to a Salvational End. No "principles," or "absolutes," or "doc-
> trines" can be extracted from this tensional complex; the quest for truth,
> as an event of participation in the process, can do no more than explore
> the structures in the divine mystery of the complex reality and, through the
> analysis of the experienced responses to the tensional pulls, arrive at some
> clarity about its own function in the drama in which it participates.[100]

Faith and Vision in the
Christian Context

This Voegelinian analysis of the *Timaeus* now needs to be placed into
the context of this study. The ultimate implications of Voegelin's contribution and challenge to theology, however, wait till the final chapter.
Here I wish to discuss the significance of Voegelin's understanding of
the *fides quaerens intellectum*, particularly as it relates to the experience
of faith and vision within a Christian context. What then, we must
ask, is the relation between faith and vision? And what relevance can
we draw from Voegelin's analysis of these ageless symbols in regard to
theological method?

To answer these questions, we must refer to the two important
essays of Voegelin's later career, which we have yet to discuss directly:
"The Beginning and the Beyond: A Meditation on Truth" (1977) and
"Wisdom and the Magic of the Extreme: A Meditation" (1981). The

first essay, just recently published, contains very significant reflections on St. Anselm and St. Thomas which need to be examined. It also contains Voegelin's most explicit account of his "theological" method. The wisdom essay ends with some extraordinary elucidations of philosophical and Christian truth in regard to the experience of vision. These essays are especially important meditations for theologians to ponder.

VOEGELIN'S THEOLOGICAL METHOD

At the beginning of the second section in his essay "The Beginning and the Beyond," Voegelin queries about the nature of his lifelong inquiry into the history of experience and symbolization from which the problems of truth and language arise. He asks, "What is this inquiry itself? Is it an historiographic study? or is it an act of philosophizing? or perhaps of theologizing?"[101] Since there is no generally accepted language or literary form for handling these problems today, he claims that one must commence on a reflection on the inquiry itself "in order to establish the legitimacy of its method and the criteria of its truth."[102] Whatever reflection this kind of inquiry is, Voegelin asserts, it is neither a "history of ideas" nor an exercise in "comparative religion," for it has nothing to do with the amassing and comparing of information or data. The reflection itself must enter into the "In–Between reality," which is Voegelin's translation of the Platonic *metaxy*, the rich symbol denoting the spiritual field of human experience that is structured by divine being at one end and the human subject at the other. Thus the inquiry must be led by the movements of divine appeal and human response.[103] No other "method" will make the language symbols in history transparent for their truth. No analytical conceptualization by an external "subject of cognition" or "transcendental I," leading to some metaphysical system that claims absolute finality, will do. One must enter the reality itself as a metaleptic participant. Consequently, it must be a radically personal reflection. No matter how "abstrusely abstract" the reflection may become,[104] one's position must be oriented to the concrete reality of one's own consciousness as that consciousness seeks to understand the mystery of divine presence in reality.

Consequently, Voegelin believes that the proper method of this inquiry must be something like the *fides quaerens intellectum* and the correlative *credo ut intelligam* that was first formulated by St. Anselm in the eleventh century. The only significant difference is that Voegelin's inquiry, following the exigencies of the contemporary world, expands beyond the Christian horizon of Anselm's *fides* in order to include the manifold of pre-Christian and non-Christian theophanic events.[105] The historical horizon of today's philosopher and theologian is larger than what was available to a thinker in medieval Europe. Indeed, the concepts that arose within the spatially and temporally limited horizons of the past are no longer adequate to apply to the diverse and expanded horizons of our century. Today the demands of adequacy require a language that can reach a higher abstraction and a higher universality, for we live in a time when the ecumenic horizon has spiritually expanded to globality. Nevertheless, Voegelin argues, the formulation of the inquiry bestowed on us by Anselm remains durable and sound. It only needs to be generalized so as to include all the manifestations of divine presence in history. In short, the firm tie to the Christian creed that the *fides quaerens intellectum* has traditionally borne must today be broken. In this time-honored theological phrase, Voegelin argues, is contained the potential for a profound analysis of historical reality beyond the confines of its inception. "Faith seeking understanding" can be structurally applied not only to the creedal faith of Christians but also to the questing symbolizations of a Taoist speculation, a Platonic dialogue, an Egyptian Amon hymn, or a prehistoric petroglyph. Furthermore, Voegelin claims, if one is to take seriously Jesus' statement that "Before Abraham was, I am," then a philosopher must make intelligible the ubiquitous presence of Christ in these symbolizations just as much as in a Gospel.[106]

Of course this kind of expansion of a Christian symbol will undoubtedly meet much resistance, so Voegelin has to devise its generalized formulation carefully. To do so he returns to the source: Anselm's *Proslogion*.[107] The intent of Anselm's meditation in the *Proslogion*, he states, has been seriously clouded under centuries of interpretation which found in it the so-called ontological proof for the existence of God. The identification of Anselm's argument with this anachronistic phrase effectively assured that the *fides* behind the quest would become lost.[108] Voegelin argues that the centuries of distortion spawned by the critics of Anselm who associated his text with the so-called ontological proof (i.e., Gaunilo, Thomas, Descartes, Spinoza, Locke, Leibniz, Kant, and Hegel) mutilated Anselm's true insight. Only in our century, he believes, has the experiential content of Anselm's *fides* been recovered by studies such as Barth's *Fides Quaerens Intellectum* in 1931, and Gilson's *The Spirit of Medieval Philosophy*, the Gifford Lectures of the same year.[109]

Anselm's argument was distorted because it was hampered by the unsatisfactory philosophical concepts in which it was framed, and also because it lacked the stratum of reflection on reflection that Voegelin has now made essential in the quest for truth.[110] The critical, reflective distance between the philosopher's reason and the symbolism it explored was absent: for Anselm the Christian creed is final. Nevertheless, as a quest for divine transcendence, it illuminates in classical fashion the metaxic structure of the divine–human encounter. This is made clear in the fact that the *Proslogion* is written in the form of a prayer. It is a prayer of love beseeching the creator to grant to the creature a more perfect vision of divine being by way of the questing mind. The prayer is a movement that begins with faith and moves toward a greater understanding of this faith. The understanding is surely limited, for even when understood, faith is still not the vision of God. The quest gives to faith a limited understanding that is so much more than unreflective faith, but still limited compared to what is granted in the beatific vision. Indeed, in another context, Anselm speaks of the understanding possible in this life as "a medium between faith and vision";[111] the more we understand, the closer we come to the final vision granted through grace in death. Hence, with these words, claims Voegelin, Anselm perceptively acknowledges the metaxic structure of existence.

However, the meaning of the in-between is here confined to a Christian *fides* moving by reason in the direction of the beyond. This restriction must not be construed as an attempt by Anselm to establish reason as an independent source of knowledge of divine reality, which Voegelin claims is a misunderstanding that has led some to classify Anselm as a "rationalist."[112] It is not Anselm's reason that is in quest of understanding but his faith. The mind cannot arrive at an understanding of anything that is not already present to it. The *fides* functions as what presents to the mind the "content" of the quest. Reason cannot penetrate reality any more than faith. It does not add anything to faith except an understanding of it, an understanding which can never equal or supersede faith itself. For Anselm this means that when his quest has found the creator of the creed to be indeed the God of his quest, he must admit that the God found by his reason is not yet the God experienced as the formative reality of his existence. He prays: "Speak to my desirous soul what you are other than what it has seen, that it may clearly see what it desires." And then the insight of his reason is surmounted by the further insight: "Oh Lord, you are not only that which a greater cannot be thought, but you are also greater than what can be thought."[113]

We can now see that behind Anselm's *fides* and behind his quest lies the desire of his soul to move toward the divine light. His quest which is also a prayer is in essence the human response to the divine appeal. It is the movement of his soul through the elements of the creed: from the creator to the Christ to the Spirit, from the mortal imperfection of earthly vision to the immortal perfection of the beatific vision, from creaturely existence to the eternal existence in the beyond.

More than just a doctrine for notional assent, the creed is a living appeal, a true symbolization of a reality that moves from creation to salvation. St. Anselm thus evokes the eschatological direction of a *fides* seeking its intelligibility through reason, a reason which is the proper human response to any and every *fides*.[114]

Reason and faith, therefore, cannot be separated. To isolate one from the other and treat it as an autonomous source of knowledge distorts its true reciprocating function in the quest for truth. This is as true for philosophy as it is for theology. Without faith, reason is an oblivious groping in the dark; without reason, faith is a blind fideism that knows nothing. Either state thwarts the quest for truth and confines the seeker to a position of folly.

In fact it is this idea of "folly" that draws out the true purpose of the *Proslogion*. The application of the term "proof" to Anselm's meditation obscures the aim of his noetic quest. First, contends Voegelin, the word proof (*probatio*) does not occur in the *Proslogion*, but only in Anselm's reply to his critic Gaunilo.[115] Secondly, Anselm uses this term only because of the "folly" of the impious who deny God's existence, such as the Hebrew *nabal* in Psalm 13 (14) who says in his heart "there is no God." Since in the *Proslogion* the existence of God is not in question there is no need to call the search for the rational structure of faith a "proof." Only in reply to Gaunilo, who plays the role of the fool (*insipiens*) and who assumes that Anselm is trying to prove the assertion that God exists, does Anselm need to invoke the term. If the fool did not exist there would be no need to talk about "proving" God's existence. In fact the noetic quest can easily derail into an argument about proof or nonproof of a proposition when the fool enters the conversation. And indeed the fool does exist and so cannot simply be dismissed. Folly is a potentiality in everyone's soul, even a believer's, and in such disorderly times as ours it can become a mass movement.[116] The alternative is always the same: the response to the divine appeal can be either hardened resistance or formative and transformative assent.

The response of hardened resistance had its infamous precedent, as Voegelin points out, for in Plato's time the contempt for the gods in the sophistic schools led to the general loss of experiential contact with cosmic-divine reality. In the *Republic* (365b–e) and the *Laws* Plato formulated the negative propositions of the sophistic fools: "(1) It seems that no gods exist; (2) Even if they do exist, they do not care about men; (3) Even if they care, they can be propitiated by gifts."[117] Like Anselm's "proof" Plato countered these negative propositions with positive ones, such as those throughout book 10 of the *Laws* that culminate with the statement "there are gods, they are mindful of us, and they are never to be seduced from the path of right" (907b).

The argument for divine reality of course, whether Platonic or Anselmian, can never be a reasoning in the sense of syllogistic logic. Quite simply reality cannot be proved; one can only point to it and invite the doubter to look. For Plato, the sophistic folly, the *anoia*, is a disease of the soul, a *nosos*, requiring many years of psychological therapy. This is the spiritual disorder that Cicero keenly developed in the *Tusculan Disputations* that Voegelin is fond of citing, calling it the *morbus animi* (disease of the soul) that involves an *aspernatio rationis* (rejection of reason). In the modern context this same spiritual disease was diagnosed by Schelling as the "pneumapathology" that afflicted the positivist fantasizers and gnostic activists of his age.

In his analysis of this disease, Voegelin tells us, Plato created a neologism of great consequence. In the *Republic* (379a) Plato invented the term "theology" to describe both the positive and negative types of propositions about the gods. They describe one of the two possible responses to the divine appeal. The truth or falsity of the *typoi peri theologias*, the types of theology, lie not in the propositions as such but in the existential state of the one who utters them. The truth of the positive propositions is neither self-evident nor provable. They are as empty as the negative propositions if they are not supported in experience by the actual reality of human assent to the divine appeal. But more than simply a symbolization or verbal mimesis of divine truth, the positive propositions (or doctrinal statements, if you will) act as a defense against the negative ones.[118] In its origin, in Plato's discussion of "theology," this was the primary function of true propositional statements: to counter the false ones. If these "doctrines" are taken as embodying the truth in themselves, or if the role played by the fool in their formulation is forgotten, they will derail into the foolishness of believing that their truth is ultimate.[119] The human word that struggles to express God's word is ultimately penultimate.[120] To believe otherwise is to rank among the fools that both Plato and Anselm found themselves resisting.

What makes Anselm's situation unique is that he does not have to invent philosophy as the proper means for subverting sophistic ignorance. Philosophy as a valid search for truth is already alive in the early theologizing of the Christian fathers. In the *Proslogion*, and certainly the *Monologion*, St. Anselm is not writing against the fool; he is writing for his Benedictine brothers who, like himself, are believers but want to know the reason why. Citing the authority of Scripture will not do; nor is the truth of the Creed self-evident. Only reason will supply the necessary fulfillment of their faith. In other words, tradition itself cannot supply the truth behind the inherited symbols. Only the divine–human movement of the personal quest that in the name of reason

continually goes back to the test of the encounter can provide the
necessary assent/ascent. This is the only means for confirming whether
the God of the Creed is indeed the same God as the one we search
for with our reason. And it is this purpose that underlies Anselm's
meditative "proof" for the existence of God. Like Plato before him, he
does not set out to prove the existence of God; this would make him
as guilty of foolishness as the fools he attacks. His purpose, rather, is to
discover and understand the *ratio* in the symbols of his faith.[121]

What I hear Voegelin saying throughout this treatment of St. Anselm
is that, given the structure of human consciousness as the metaleptic
process of human–divine encounter, the only legitimate method for
attaining truth is the meditative ascent that occurs in a generalized and
unrestricted *fides quaerens intellectum*. No other method, phenomenological, transcendental, idealist, etc., can properly render the truth of
divine mystery. This is the very method that Voegelin has now explicitly
adopted in describing his own work.

This does not mean of course that Anselm's formulation of the
method is without problems. Voegelin perceives in it the intellectual
weakness in the philosophical tradition that goes all the way back to
classic philosophy.[122] Specifically, he says, "it suffers from the inherited
lack of clarity about intentionality as a structure in consciousness."[123]
The use of terms like *esse* and *existere*, of being and existence, reflects
an ambiguity that plagued Anselm in his debate with Gaunilo, and that
touches on the problems of philosophizing to this day. These problems
have to do with the paradox of consciousness that Voegelin brilliantly
analyzes in *In Search of Order*. In short, it centers on the intentionalist
reduction which a thinker is liable to commit when he or she forgets
the divine-cosmic whole in which consciousness, including intentional
consciousness, participates. Metaleptic reality will be reduced to the
intentionalist sector of knowledge about objects, making language a
referent for items in reality. This, warns Voegelin, is what causes the formerly discussed tendency to hypostatize the poles of existential tension
into autonomous entities.[124] Under this intentionalist reduction, when
the term "being" is used its plurality of meaning can easily degenerate
into a thing, making opaque the nonthing being in which the being-
things, which are a particular form of being, participate. The divine
mode of being is not the same as the physical mode of being, and if
the language used to denote these realities is not carefully constructed,
it will wreak havoc on the search for truth as well as on the tradition
in which the search finds itself. The language will assume the status
of *doxa* and reduce God to a reality that can appear or not appear in
the mode of thingness. Theological discourse, Voegelin concludes, will

hence devolve into debates about God in which one could arrive at the conclusion that God, who does not exist in the mode of thingness, does "not exist."[125] This is the very same problem Plato meticulously dealt with in the *Parmenides*.[126]

This was the problem that Anselm was not able to resolve completely, given the ambiguity in the philosophical language of his time. The surplus of meaning in the term "being" must not be fragmented. The paradoxic structure of reality must be maintained so as to uphold the being that is the nonobject beyond of being of the questing *nous*, as well as the being-things that participate in the same beyond of being. The ambiguity inherent in the compact use of language can only be resolved in the differentiated language of a thinker who, in noetically exploring the content of his or her faith, is reflectively aware of the paradoxic structure of consciousness-reality-language.

Voegelin sees a similar problem in St. Thomas. Following the work of Gilson,[127] he perceives in Thomas the tendency to splinter the divine and human poles of the quest. Because of Thomas's emphasis on the being-things, whose existence attests to the existence of God, Voegelin claims that his language of being tends to obstruct, rather than facilitate, the soul's movement toward God:

> Gilson is dismayed by an exuberant language of Being that tends to obscure the experience of divine-cosmic reality it is supposed to make intelligible. The dynamics of the human quest threatens to overpower the divine appeal; and the one truth of reality, as it emerges from the Metaxy, is in danger of dissociating into the two verities of Faith and Reason. One can sense in the work of Thomas the possibility of the science of Being sliding over, as it did in the modern centuries, into an autonomous source of truth.[128]

Voegelin, again following Gilson, wants to shift the dynamics of the appeal/response back to where it belongs: to the revelatory, theophanic pole of the existential tension. However, he dissociates himself from Gilson's proposed solution because he perceives an overcompensation in his correction of the preponderant conceptualization of being in Thomas. The visions of Plato, and those of Thomas himself, cannot be construed as autonomous revelatory entities divorced from the questing *nous*. The balance between the revelatory appeal and the human quest must be maintained if we are to understand the nature of vision symbolized by these historic thinkers. The flaw in Gilson's solution to the flaw in Thomas is due to its reliance on a conventional language which has become outmoded in our day. The traditional dichotomies between faith and reason, religion and philosophy, theology and metaphysics,

argues Voegelin, must now be deemed obsolete given what we know
about the rich diversification of divine presence in history and its
structural manifestation in human consciousness. "We can no longer
ignore," he says, "that the symbols of 'Faith' express the responsive
quest of man just as much as the revelatory appeal, and that the symbols of 'Philosophy' express the revelatory appeal just as much as the
responsive quest."[129]

With this perspective, Voegelin contends, we can no longer give
to "theology" the monopoly of revelation, nor can the exploration
of being conducted under the aegis of Plato and Aristotle be termed
"philosophy" in the topical sense. The doctrinaire distinction between
"natural reason" and "supernatural revelation" springs from a medieval
misconception of classic philosophy, a misconception which turned
Plato's analytical language into terms of propositional metaphysics.[130]
The Hellenic thinkers are explicit about the divine appeal from the
beyond that they experience in their souls and which guides their
reflection. They too must combat a traditional *fides* (in the intracosmic
gods) that is deemed inadequate. The struggle in classic philosophy
becomes the quest to unite the God of the beginning who creates
an imperfect cosmos with a God of the beyond who orders the human
psyche and saves us from the cosmic disorder. Is the creator-god the same
as the savior-god? This question, says Voegelin, cannot be answered (as
Gilson attempts to do) by posing a Christian cosmos "full of God,"
to replace a Pagan cosmos "full of gods," for the revelation of the
one divine reality that debunks the status of the gods arises within
"Paganism" itself.[131]

The very same dynamic occurred in Israel's history when the one
God of the chosen people conflicted with the "false gods" of the
ambient nations, eventually deposing them as "no gods" at all. In both
Israel and Hellas there occurred the advance of the *cognitio fidei* from an
intracosmic *fides* to the *fides* of the beyond, a fact which was obscured
when the God of the Israelite-Christian *fides* supplanted the God of
the philosopher's *fides* in Christian theology. Plato's reflection is truly a
fides quaerens intellectum, the *fides* under exploration making transparent
the beyond of the cosmos, and the *intellectum*, when achieved, yielding
images which bear the new standard of truth. Whatever "Christian"
answers to these questions may be, remarks Voegelin, the problem is
definitely pre-Christian and even "Pagan."[132] The question of what
images truly symbolize the truly divine is the eminent question that
animates meditative reflection throughout the course of history. It is
the question that every *fides* seeking its own *intellectum* must always

confront. In every age, including our own, this is the critical problem that every searcher for God must face.

No matter how potent the noetic inquiry seems to be—and indeed it is the rational force that yields the insights into the structure of existence—it cannot provide the *cognitio fidei* of the visions in which *noesis* is only a component part. A philosopher's meditation can only operate within the comprehensive vision that is granted in the theophanic event of experience and symbolization.[133] Hence, imaginative vision and *noesis* are not autonomous and rival sources of knowledge and truth but interacting forces in both consciousness and history.[134] The comprehensive vision is the revelatory component that is present in both the cosmological mode of experience and the differentiated experience of the beyond. In tandem with noetic speculation it is what yields all historic symbolisms of the beginning and the beyond, whether it be Genesis 1, Hesiod's *Theogony*, or Plato's *Timaeus*. Whatever level of differentiation is achieved, Voegelin exclaims, revelation and *noesis* are both present in symbolizations of divine reality, even in the mythical speculations of theogony, cosmogony, anthropogony, and historiogenesis.[135]

But only in Plato does the imaginative vision come into its own as a distinct symbolism *sui generis*. In his assorted philosophical myths there is a distinctiveness that cannot be attributed to Homer or Hesiod or the people's myths. The Platonic vision, the *opsis*, is not a subjective fancy. It is, rather, "Plato's technical term for the experiential process in which the order of reality is seen, becomes reflectively known, and finds its appropriate language symbols."[136] This comprehensive vision which includes the noetic vision appears in such key passages as *Timaeus* 47, where it is spoken of as a gift from God revealing the order of the cosmos. Plato leaves no doubt about its revelatory character, for he speaks about the *epirryton*, the "inrush" of divine light that causes this vision of divine reality (*Republic* 508b).

In this graced vision there is imaginatively created a new type of "mythical" symbol. It evokes neither a subject nor an object of cognition. It cannot be spoken of in terms of intentionality. It is neither a Cartesian *cogito* nor a revealed doctrine. It can only be depicted as the event in which reality becomes luminous for its truth. Thus, in Plato's positive type of theology the truth defended against the negative type is not propositional at all, for the positive type has its meaning only in the truth of experience. When the linguistic articulation of truth is severed from its experiential source, all that one has then is an "inrush" of foolishness. Similarly, in Anselm, this means that the *intellectus* achieved in the quest always falls short of the real constitution of truth formed in the soul by the loving presence of the divine. Consequently, the meditative quest does not lead to ultimate "results" in propositional language; it can only lead one to a better understanding of what one "has" already in faith.

In the event of the revelatory vision and its language we enter the realm in which language does not simply refer to reality but is reality itself emerging as the luminous word from the divine–human encounter. Here "word" means the same as "symbol" in the pregnant sense. The truth of the symbol is not informative but evocative. Its meaning can be said to be understood only if it has evoked in the hearer or reader the corresponding movement of participation in the reality it makes luminous, as occurred in the one who produced the symbol in the first place. In other words, it can be understood only by the one who is drawn into the loving quest. So unless we wish to go the way of either the intentionalist reduction or the fundamentalist derailment, we must not restrict language to the realm of intentionality. Simply put, there is no propositional truth beyond the beyond and its *parousia*. It is Voegelin's view that dogmatic theology has violated this principle. The Church has traditionally packaged revelation in a reified, thing-oriented manner in order to harness "the faith" and thus become the source of mediation of its certain propositional truths. This hegemony on truth was quite early politicized by its spreading the Word in an often-imperialistic fashion. In the ensuing nominalist and fideist conception of Christianity of the Middle Ages, the balance was lost leading to the totalitarian ideologies of the modern age. In fact Voegelin believes the balance was lost at the very beginning when Paul went beyond the boundaries of the noetic control of meaning to express his transfiguring vision of the resurrected Christ.

The consequence for theology in this whole discussion of *fides* and vision is elaborated by Voegelin:

> The symbols of the past, whatever their analytical value may have been at the time of their genesis, cannot be used unquestioned as analytical concepts in our present historical situation. Their critical value as instruments of historical interpretation must be reexamined; and since this reexamination extends to our common language of "philosophy," "being," "theology," "religion," "myth," "reason," "revelation," and so forth, a considerable upheaval in the conventional use of these symbols is to be expected. Still, we do not need an entirely new universe of symbols. Emerging as we are from the distortions of history through the dogmatisms of theology, ontology, the methodologies and ideologies, we discover the new language needed

to be for the most part the old language of experiential analysis that has
been buried under the doctrinal deformations. To the old language of the
Beginning and the Beyond, the *fides quaerens intellectum*, the presence of the
divine reality, the divine appeal, and the human response, the divine-human
movement and countermovement, the human quest and the noetic pull from
the Beyond, the Parousia of the Beyond, the existence in the Metaxy, the
existential agon of man in the Metaxy of mortality and immortality, we
now must add the vision as the comprehensive mode of man's cognitive
participation in reality.[137]

Thus, the culminating stroke of Voegelin's philosophical portrait of
reality centers on an analysis of Plato's vision which adds a new dimension to his theory of consciousness and history.[138] It is the historical
process of the vision that reveals the mysterious It-reality, which we
do not have as an object of consciousness but which rather has us as
its predicate. Reality reveals its truth, not all at once, it seems, but
in a process of history. This is the insight that must now lead us to
see that Voegelin's vision of history is a history of visions and that his
philosophical-theological method is a meditative, experiential exegesis
of such visions. It must be restated that this method is an open-ended
quest for truth that never results in an absolute truth or final answer
or perfect order, or permanent values, principals, or doctrines. If such
were so then history would come to its end.

Voegelin's own personal history, like Plato's, was a long anamnetic
exploration of the visions of a lifetime. Plato's vision was what developed
over the course of his lifelong philosophizing, manifested most clearly
in the entire sequence of Platonic myths culminating in the *Laws*. From
the perspective of the *Laws*, then, Voegelin sees the Platonic vision as so
comprehensive and analytically expressive of itself that it illuminates the
structure of visionary truth in general. Every vision is part of an endless
revelatory process, including the vision of the process itself. Plato is quite
aware of the Orphic and Homeric-Hesiodian ancestry of his own vision,
of the prior Hellenic roots of his own philosophizing consciousness.
He is also aware of the noetic breakthrough of his differentiating vision
in relation to the compact symbolization of prior visions. His vision
thus is both continuous and discontinuous with the historical visions
that precede his own. In other words the same divine reality is present
in all visions but the noetic vision differentiates a component in the
experience of divine reality that the earlier visions did not accentuate.
The earlier visions include Plato's own youthful insights for he is also
aware of the growth of his vision throughout his whole existence, a
theme expressed in the *Laws* where the Athenian Stranger remarks that

"a man's vision concerning such matters is dullest when he is young, and at its sharpest when he is old" (715d–e).

From this processive notion of vision Voegelin is now able to propose a conception of truth that is "a growth of luminosity" in the course of historical existence.[139] The visions and insights of the past are not made irrelevant by present visions and insights that are fuller and more clear, for present visions will become past for a future visionary. Indeed, one's view of reality in the course of one's own life is always subject to "correction" by later, more mature views. Reality is beheld not in any one particular vision but in the processive development of all visions, a process that never ends. All particular visions, therefore, are events of participation in a reality that is becoming ever-more luminous for its truth. The process must be understood as a whole for "there is no truth *of* history other than the truth growing *in* history."[140] It is by participating in the course of this whole, with no part separated from any other, that the philosopher's existence derives its truth. It is derived from the comprehensive truth of reality that is not captured in propositional language but evoked by the philosopher's visionary quest and its articulation. The wisdom the philosopher seeks will depend on maintaining the balance of consciousness within the whole structure of truth's unfolding in history. The balance will be disturbed if the seeker presumes to possess the absolute truth, the deformation which has led to the various relativisms, historicisms, and doctrinalisms of history. The requisite reflective distance in the face of pluralistic and seemingly rival symbolisms will secure the integrity of truth itself which always transcends any particular symbolization or imaging of it. The awareness of this potential disturbance is a component of the philosopher's noetic vision of the whole which forces the necessary precautions and hesitations in his imaginative language.[141]

The vision beholds the historical process itself as a dynamic flux of divine presence in which every vision has the structure of a divine–human encounter, a response to an appeal from the beyond of all visions, endowed with its own integrity and filled with a surplus of truth that its expression can never fully reveal. It is this vision of visions that fills every present moment of revelation as a center of meaning in history. This, Voegelin argues, is the great theme of the *Laws*: "the insight into the truth of reality as the unfinished struggle for the truth—a struggle not to be observed from the outside, but to be conducted within the historical process by the men who are granted, by the unknown divinity, the grace of the vision and who respond with its articulation."[142] The articulation takes the form of a literary work that speaks the truth of the word. It is the word that emerges from the developing vision of a meditative thinker's openness and response to the presence of the beyond in this world. As Voegelin's own considerable labors and voluminous writings reveal, it is a vision that requires many words and many works, the work of a lifetime, to elaborate and refine.

THE CHRISTIAN VISION

A discussion of Voegelin's treatment of the parallel texts in the New Testament that illuminate the Christian response to the experience of divine reality in history will further elucidate the theological dimension of his work. Voegelin's purpose in comparing the significant Platonic and Christian texts is to discern the noetic structure in the noetically less-differentiated Christian visions as well as to show how the Christian symbols illustrate the pneumatic limitations of the Platonic vision.[143] The Platonic and Christian visions are not rival truths. Although they are distinct modes of transcendent experience, they have common elements: an exodus from the struggle of this mortal life (*mache athanatos*) toward a life of perfection, an intermediate beyond that is populated by either immortal souls or angels and saints, and a divinely revealed truth of a saving tale that has been saved from its own death.[144] In one context Voegelin suggests the complex "visionary revelation-struggle-salvation" to express this common experience of existence affirmed by both philosophy and Christianity.[145]

One important feature that distinguishes the Christian from the Platonic experience is that the Christian visionaries do not have to ask Plato's question "Who is this God?" since they know very well that their God is the God of Abraham, Isaac, and Jacob, of Sarah, Rebecca, and Rachel, the God of Moses and the prophets. Rather, they have to ask, "Who is this Son of God, this Christ, who is the living word of divine truth?" This question of course did not eliminate Plato's noetic question, as it too had to be inevitably confronted in early Christian theology. It was that the inrush of divine presence through the Christ was so full and so overwhelming that they had to face this new experience of incarnate truth by itself. Given their unique culture of experience and symbolization, the Christian authors had to confront, in a quite different way from Plato, the experience of a savior-god who is revealed as the same God as the creator-god. Though they did not have the philosopher's differentiated language, the Christian visionaries pneumatically experienced the God of all generations as the same divine beyond whose loving presence they experienced in their souls. "What they had to see, and did see," says Voegelin, "was the presence of God in the man whose word spoke the truth of suffering salvation, in the man Jesus; and the content of the revelatory vision inevitably raised questions concerning the criteria of its truth."[146] The divine "dwelling," "drawing," and "revealing," are the Christian symbols of pneumatic vision. In the Gospels they occur in such passages as Matthew 16:17 ("Blessed are you, Simon Bar-Jona! For flesh and blood has not revealed this to you, but my Father who is in heaven") and John 6:44 ("No one can come to me unless the Father who sent me draws him"). Here we are told that the divine presence of the Father in one man reveals the even greater presence of "the living God" in Jesus. What is affirmed in these passages is that the Son of God cannot be recognized unless one "sees" in Jesus the full presence of the true God who is already present in oneself.[147] The revelation of the Unknown God is dependent on the mutual indwelling of the Father and the Son as well as on the mutual indwelling of the Son and his disciples. On this basis it is clear that the Christ cannot be revealed outside of a community of love, which is why Jesus must establish a circle of friends in order to reveal the living God that dwells within him. The revelation of Christ is dependent on the order of love in the hearts of his followers, without which he could not be recognized. This truth is also expressed in the *logion* of Matthew 11:25–27:

> At that time Jesus declared: "I humbly acknowledge, Father, lord of heaven and earth, that you have hidden these things from the wise and the understanding and revealed them to the simple; be it so, Father, for so it seemed good to your sight. All these things are delivered to me by my Father, and no one knows the Son except the Father, and no one knows the Father except the Son and anyone to whom the Son chooses to reveal him."

The Gospel account clearly delineates the structure of revelation as a disciple's response to the drama of the Son of God within the *metaxy* of existence. Any attempt to extract from the Gospel a historical Jesus and a doctrinal Christ would wreak havoc on the symbolism of the Gospel itself which articulates the existential drama of participation in divine reality. Voegelin elaborates the specific nature of this drama:

> The drama of the Unknown God who reveals his kingdom through his presence in a man, and of the man who reveals what has been delivered to him by delivering it to his fellowmen, is continued by the existentially responsive disciple in the Gospel drama by which he carries on the work of delivering these things from God to man. The Gospel itself is an event in the drama of revelation. The historical drama in the *metaxy*, then, is a unit through the common presence of the Unknown God in the men who respond to his "drawing" and to one another.[148]

Jesus' divine sonship, then, is not a piece of information he gives to his disciples. The structure of revelation requires that they experience in themselves, at least inchoately, the presence of the Unknown God that Jesus manifests fully. The truth revealed is not something to be treated lightly. The story of Peter's confession of Jesus as the Christ and the subsequent founding of the Church in Matthew 16:13–20, ends with the verse, "Then he strictly charged the disciples to tell no one that he was the Christ." This warning, declares Voegelin, makes explicit the distinction between information and revelation. Matthew continues the warning not to debase the truth of what is divinely revealed by transposing it into a piece of knowledge available to the general public. For example, in the immediately following episode of the transfiguration (17:1–13) Matthew has Jesus command his disciples to "tell no one the vision" (17:9). At his trial before the Sanhedrin the theme of silence continues when Jesus remains noncommittal when asked "Are you the Christ, the Son of God?" (26:63–64). And on the following day when Jesus is interrogated by Pilate the response is the same (27:11–14).[149]

Nevertheless, as Voegelin points out, elsewhere in Matthew's account the secret of Jesus' sonship was freely made known to everyone, even to those who resisted.[150] This should not lead one to think that Matthew was confused in his portrayal of Jesus' communication of his divine mission. The point is that a Gospel is not a historical biography, nor an imaginative piece of literary art, but a symbolization of divine presence that fully penetrated the person of Jesus and through him entered into society and history. The revelatory movement is symbolized on a number of planes: Jesus' vision of God at his baptism, the suffering realization of his own sonship, the revelation to his disciples, the transfiguration, and the final submission on the cross and subsequent resurrection.

Furthermore, the drama of the Son is situated within the larger drama of divine revelation in history which, through the imaginative symbols of Israel's consciousness that preceded the Gospel, prepared the reception of God's saving presence in Jesus. Symbols such as Son of God, Messiah, Son of man, and Kingdom of God, Voegelin tells us, were historically available to the Evangelists through Egyptian pharaonic, Davidic royal, and prophetic/apocalyptic symbolisms, as well as through Iranian traditions and Hellenistic mystery religions. Hence, Voegelin writes,

the "secret" of the Gospel is neither the mystery of divine presence in existence, nor its articulation through new symbols, but the event of its full comprehension and enactment through the life and death of Jesus. The apparent contradictions dissolve into the use of the same symbols at various

levels of comprehension, as well as at the different stages of enactment, until
the Christ is revealed, not in a fullness of doctrine, but in the fullness of
Passion and resurrection.[151]

What is meant by "fullness" seems to be for Voegelin the crux of the
Christian Gospel which distinguishes it from the truth of philosophy.
The process of advancing differentiation of truth in history is microcos-
mically structured in Matthew's Gospel as a movement toward the full
comprehension of the truth of God revealed in Jesus, a truth that moves
from pneumatic vision to noetic understanding. But, for Voegelin, the
nature of this fullness is best symbolized, not in the Gospel accounts, but
by St. Paul who struggled to understand the new truth revealed in Christ
in his own language and in relation to the Unknown God that has been
incipiently revealed to the pagans in their cosmological existence (e.g.,
Romans 1:18ff.). The noetic consciousness of the Christian revelatory
vision, Voegelin believes, is eminently articulated in Colossians 2:9,
where Paul says, "In him, the whole fullness (*pan to pleroma*) of divine
reality (*theotes*) dwells bodily (*somatikos*), and in him your own life has
come to its fullness."[152] The Christ is the mystery of God in reality
in its pleromatic presence. By virtue of this "whole fullness" present
in Christ, Paul says, "he is the image (*eikon*) of the invisible God, the
first-born of all creation" (Colossians 1:15). In his noetic interpretation,
Voegelin suggests the source of this visionary experience to lie in Jesus
himself: "Something about Jesus must have impressed his contemporaries as an existence in the *metaxy* of such intensity that his bodily
presence, the *somatikos* of the passage, appeared to be fully permeated by
divine presence."[153]

Paul employs the noetic symbol of the *theotes* (his neologism) to
signify the anonymous immortal beyond that saves human beings from
the struggles of mortal existence (*mache athanatos*), the undying struggle
with death. With this symbol, argues Voegelin, Paul intends to denote
the nonpersonal divine reality beyond the *metaxy* of existence that
nevertheless enters the *metaxy* and allows for degrees of participation
in its fullness.[154] The *theotes* is an experiential symbol of such a high
generality that it can be applied not only to the experience of divine
reality that is incarnate in Christ in its fullness but also to every instance
of *theotes* that is experienced as present in the human being. For this
reason Voegelin much prefers this symbol over the God of the Creed
in formulating his exegesis of experiences of divine reality. Its analytical
force is much greater for it allows Voegelin to " 'identify'. . . the God
who reveals himself, not only in the Prophets, in Christ, and in the
Apostles, but wherever his reality is experienced as present in the cosmos
and in the soul of man."[155] It is indeed, however, a Christian symbol,

one that brings into focus Paul's attempt to understand his vision of Christ in relation to non-Christian experiences of God and thus to render intelligible the meaning of divine incarnation.

Nevertheless, this noetic symbol notwithstanding, the dominant symbolism in Paul's vision is not the *nous* of classical philosophy; it is rather the *pneuma tou theou*, the spirit of God whose maximal presence is experienced in Christ. The *pneuma* symbolizes a dimension in the appeal/response of the divine–human encounter that was not sufficiently differentiated in the noetic visions. In other words, Plato did not "see" the full meaning of the divine saving presence in existence. Plato's *fides* is based in the beyond of the cosmos that has its *parousia* in the cosmos. In the Gospel movement, this cosmic *fides* is radicalized by the *parousia* of the beyond in a human being, in the Christ. This new understanding of divine presence, however, does not invalidate the insights gained through noetic vision. Rather, in the experiential complex of revelation-struggle-salvation the dynamics of the experience alter the meaning of revelation so as to stress the aspect of salvation rather than the struggle.[156] With the vision of God's suffering participation in our life, our ultimate end is deemed victorious. The story of human existence is now wonderfully enriched by the vision of the eschatological fulfillment that comes with the fullest incarnate *parousia* of the divine in the *metaxy*. It is the fullest because nothing more radical could be imagined than the saving presence of God experienced in one man's life, death, and resurrection.

For the one who does not have a bodily experience of the Christ in Jesus himself, such as St. Paul, the same experience is granted in the pneumatic vision, which is forceful enough to require the conversion of the recipient. Voegelin explains the source and content of Paul's vision in the following passage:

> There is, first, the God who, as the pleromatic partner in the encounter, sends the vision to him, the man Paul, who by his responsiveness to the pleromatic irruption becomes the Apostle; and there is, second, the vision itself of the man who by the maximal presence of the *pleroma* has become the Resurrected, who by his visionary appearance as the Resurrected assures that reality is engaged in the immortalizing process of transfiguration, and who by his visionary appearance in the historical event of the Pauline encounter with God is revealed as the Christ. The vision is for Saint Paul the source of the insight into the immortalizing presence of the word, not in Scripture but in man.[157]

A summary of the differences between the visions of philosophy and Christianity that Voegelin highlights brings into greater relief the diverse movement of vision in history:

In the noetic vision the stress falls on the structure of the immortal-izing movement of the soul toward the beyond. It focuses on the person who becomes immortal by his or her response to the divine appeal in the *metaxy*.[158] The *fides* of the quest falls on the cosmic whole and the permeation of the divine beyond in this whole. The cosmos is the great *monogenes* image of the eternal beyond in time.

In the pneumatic vision the stress falls on the transfiguring move-ment within the structure. It is fundamentally oriented toward the imperishable beyond and is thus an eschatological experience. Here the accent shifts from the human participation in divine immortality to God's participation in human mortality.[159] The *fides* is shifted toward the incarnate presence of this divine saving grace in a human being, the Christ. This Christ, the Son of God, is the new *monogenes* image of the divine beyond in time, the beyond that was present at the beginning.

From this pneumatic vision there arises the question: "Who is this Christ?" This is the central question behind the various visions exhibited in the New Testament, including Jesus' own visions, such as reported in Matthew 3:16–17. This Christ is neither a man like other men struggling for his immortality in the *metaxy*, nor is he the divine reality beyond the *metaxy*:

> The visions see in Christ the historical event of God's pleromatic presence in a man, revealing the suffering presence of the God in every man as the transfiguring force that will let mortal reality rise with the God to his immortality. The pleromatic *metaxy* seen in the Christ reveals mortal suffering as participation in the divine suffering.[160]

Voegelin warns that this language of "pleromatic *metaxy*" should not be shocking, for it is exactly what is symbolized in the Chalcedonian Creed. In the philosophical language of the fifth century, which is not as rich or as subtle as what is found in either Plato or the New Testament, the Christ is conceived as one person with two natures, divine and human. These two natures are not annulled by their joining but are uniquely preserved in their hypostatic union. In this definition of the Creed, Voegelin claims, there is rendered "the visionary truth of the Christ's existence in a *metaxy* that is distinguished from the noetic *metaxy* by the pleromatic presence of divine reality."[161]

The vision of pleromatic presence in Christ creates problems in the interpretation of history that Plato had begun to recognize in his vision. The noetic revelation of divine presence is deemed incommensurable with all previous revelations. The vision is experienced as an event (which may not be the last one) in the continuous flux of divine presence in history that creates the consciousness of epoch.[162] The event is epochal because it demarcates a moment in history in which the visionary, by his experience of the vision of immortalizing transfiguration, is transfigured. For Plato it inaugurates the age of the *nous* whose story is told in the saving tale of the philosopher's myth. The saving tale is not just a story of salvation but is a tale that really saves. Reality is really moving toward the immortal *eschaton* of reality. In the Christian context the same problem appears. The overwhelming revelation of pleromatic presence in Christ transfigures the course of history by revealing history as a course of transfiguration with a before and after of the revelatory event. What ensues is the Gospel, the saving tale of love that really saves by drawing those into the saving love of divine presence. Of course this vision of transfiguration can be deformed by those who expect the imminent transfiguration of reality in worldly time, often by their own intramundane images and actions that actually call for the abolition of history. As a result, the structure of past history, warns Voegelin, must not be deformed by relegating it to an "age" that has now come to its end only to be superseded by a "new age."[163] This kind of deformation smacks of the various millennialisms and apocalypticisms that leave a trail of perverse symbols, and often violent death, in their wake. The balance of consciousness requires that even the transfiguring vision of transfiguration be located within a flux of divine presence in history, an "indelible presence" that continually reveals the mystery of the ever-unknowable and incommensurable beyond.

Eric Voegelin's late writings contain his consummate theory of consciousness and history. His quest for truth was a labor of love inspired by the visionary faith in the incarnate and saving love in history. Always resisting the deformations of experience and symbolization in contemporary thought and society, Voegelin began with the inchoate ruminations of an anamnetic philosopher, studiously struggling with the manifestations of consciousness in history. He ended with a thoroughly developed meditative analysis of noetic and pneumatic visions of divine presence in the process of reality, the revelations that constitute human consciousness. His lifelong remembering search has unfolded into a spiritual history of humankind that faithfully tells the unfinished story of God's millennial process of incarnation in time. In his last years Voegelin's meditative adventure, as we have seen, employed most profoundly the classical theological method of "faith seeking understanding." It is a spiritual and intellectual adventure that continues whenever others take up the same quest for truth in their own personal reflections. It is a method by which one appropriates the structure of one's own being, a spiritual self whose stirrings lead one to the silent presence which draws one beyond oneself. Voegelin's response to this divine drawing of himself resulted not only in the formation of a truly gifted *daimonios aner* of our time but also in an intellectual work of the highest order that may well serve as a guide for true order for generations to come. In this light, if his work can be said to serve any single purpose, it would be to restore the *metaxy* to each of his readers' personal consciousness, and through them to society and history as well.

Voegelin worked tirelessly on his imaging of divine reality up until the very end, even correcting a manuscript with all the strength he could muster on the day before he died.[164] His death ended the life of a mystic-philosopher who returned from the middle of this life to the ultimate silence—ended indeed his own *mache athanatos* in a state of faith, hope, and most assuredly, love.

5

LONERGAN'S
FOUNDATIONAL THEOLOGY

Much of the theology written today has developed out of the fundamental principles of contemporary philosophical movements. These include phenomenology, existentialism, hermeneutics, neo-Thomism, pragmatism, process philosophy, and linguistic analysis. The quest for philosophical foundations in theology, however, is certainly not limited to these popular schools of twentieth-century thought. For example, Eric Voegelin's work, as we have seen, offers a philosophical foundation for theology that is every bit as promising as these contemporary schools of thought and is quite distinct from all of them. The work of another contemporary thinker stands out as a monumental contribution to theology today. This achievement is to be found in the seminal work of Bernard Lonergan, who is a more familiar figure in theological circles. His contribution to foundational philosophy and theology we explore in this chapter.

Although in many ways Voegelin and Lonergan are very different thinkers, they are united in viewing the analysis of consciousness as central to philosophy and theology. Indeed, no contemporary thinker has been more concerned with consciousness than these two giants. However divergent their views may be on some fundamental issues, such as their assessment of doctrine, they share a common endeavor. They both depart from the current ethos of relativism by taking their stand on the classical viewpoint which affirms the unity and universality of truth. Lonergan is a foundational thinker interested in formulating a viable "method" for doing theology in today's world. For these reasons his work provides us with a fertile ground on which to compare Voegelin's contribution to theological science. And so the twofold task of this chapter: to highlight the substance of Lonergan's philosophy of consciousness and the foundational and methodical theology that springs from it; and to compare his thought with Voegelin's.

A wealth of secondary literature on Lonergan analyzes and criticizes his work from a variety of angles and traces the evolution of his thought

over the years. This literature would provide the reader with the necessary tools for understanding Lonergan's rather difficult corpus.[1] My
intention is simply to furnish an overview of his foundational thought
insofar as it is relevant to the goal of this study; however, we must allow
Lonergan's thought to speak for itself, in an integral excursus, before
engaging, in the final section, in a dialectical comparison of the basic
principles of Voegelin's and Lonergan's works.

The Anthropological Turn

Lonergan's work grows out of a different orientation from the phenomenological or hermeneutical philosophies that are popular today
and that stress the role of language. But it is not in opposition to these
schools of thought. Those who characterize Lonergan as a neo-Kantian
neo-Thomist are not wrong, but such a facile classification can easily
distort his achievement. His entire effort has been directed toward a
transformation of theology, an attempt to "bring St. Thomas Aquinas
up to date" in accord with the valid methodical procedures of modern
science.[2] All along he has urged "that so great a transformation needs
a renewed foundation, and that the needed renewal is the introduction
of a new type of foundation. It is to consist not in objective statement,
but in subjective reality."[3]

To this end of a transformed theology Lonergan had to face the philosophical exigencies of contemporary thought; he had to confront head-
on the very pressing epistemological problems in modern philosophy. In
doing so he did not at all deviate from the celebrated "anthropological
turn" in modern thought that had been inaugurated by Descartes and
solidified by Kant. In fact, one could say that Lonergan places this
turn to the subject on a more radical foundation in order to overcome
the inadequate developments of modern philosophy, be it rationalism,
empiricism, positivism, or idealism. In this vein he accepts the critical
problematic in Kant's epistemology but radically diverts from the post-
Cartesian view of consciousness as perception, as well as the idealist
notion of consciousness which views the subject as the most important
of all objects (the objectivist conception of human consciousness).

Briefly stated, in answering the problems of subjectivism Lonergan
turns to the subject. In locating the basis of objectivity, Lonergan adverts
to subjectivity. For the *a priori*, constitutive ground of human existence,
second to none in its primordiality and comprehensiveness, Lonergan
directs us to the invariant structure of our own consciousness. However, Lonergan's view of subjective consciousness upholds neither the

subjectivity of psychologism nor the objective self-consciousness of the *cogito*. Lonergan knows no *tabula rasa*, libido, or transcendental ego. He discovers the criteria of objectivity in authentic subjectivity. Rather than beginning with either metaphysics (such as the classical Thomists do with their emphasis on first principles, the human soul, substance, logic, act, potency, etc.) or epistemology (such as the presupposed model of knowing of the neo-Kantians), Lonergan grounds both metaphysics and epistemology in a cognitional theory based on the prevenient, invariant structure of human knowing. Stated differently, Lonergan's philosophy takes its bearings on neither metaphysics nor epistemology but on the normative structure of cognitional consciousness in which the eros of the human mind finds its differentiated operations. In grounding metaphysics and epistemology in cognitional theory, Lonergan attempts to avoid the doctrinaire disputes that arise when philosophy begins from the traditional starting points. Metaphysical positions on reality must be in accord with basic positions on knowing, objectivity, and truth derived from cognitional theory. Metaphysical positions that are not consonant with the basic positions on knowing are false. These "counterpositions," as he calls them, are usually based, implicitly or explicitly, on some erroneous cognitional theory, be it empiricism, idealism, or abstract deductivism. Only a cognitional theory in which the process, structure, and norms of human inquiry are given full play is legitimate and capable of critically grounding a metaphysics. For Lonergan, this cognitional theory is called "critical realism."

Lonergan's cognitional theory is more fully differentiated in accordance with the actual operations of human consciousness than one can discover in any other contemporary thinker. With Lonergan there is no getting beyond consciousness to a transcendental ego or pure apperception, for beyond consciousness one cannot go. He claims that the whole realm of human knowing and meaning has its source in the four phases of consciousness that constitute our being-in-the-world: experiencing, understanding, judging, and deciding. These are the operations that phenomenologically ground his cognitional theory. He advises us to appropriate personally this immanent structure, this primordial pattern of knowing, so as to "own" a method of knowing and meaning to ground all other methods. This personal task of owning one's consciousness is the phenomenological verification for his cognitional theory. It is what gives credence to his oft-repeated statement that objectivity is authentic subjectivity.

Given our current awareness of the historically conditioned nature of all human horizons, and the proliferation of diverse theories of understanding, scientific and otherwise, Lonergan believes that if any norms are to be found for the truth of meaning and the ordering of reality, they can only be found in the subject as subject. He claims that "the prior reality that both grounds horizons and the critique of horizons and the determination of the field (of all human activity) is the reality of the subject as subject."[4] What is prior is not object as object, or subject as object, but subject as subject. The subject as subject is real and discoverable through consciousness. Lonergan's turn to the self as knower is uncompromising: "The argument does not prove that in the subject as subject we shall find the evidence, norms, invariants, and principles for a critique of horizons; it proves that unless we find it there, we shall not find it at all."[5] The subject as subject is the concrete experience of self-presence. It is the awareness of one's own consciousness, commonly taken for granted, but experienced by all people who are not in a dreamless sleep.

Historicism for Lonergan is overcome, not by renouncing the claims of scientific method and objectivity,[6] but by relating them to the dynamic structure of human interiority. What is normative is to be found in the operations of interiority as experienced and appropriated by the knowing subject. This is the only philosophic avenue for overcoming the Kantian bifurcation between the noumenal and the phenomenal. Lonergan holds that this is achieved by attending to oneself as a knowing subject which, when successfully accomplished, can critically ground a foundational method.

Self-appropriation is the heightening of one's consciousness. It is becoming conscious of one's own consciousness not as object but as subject. This self-appropriation occurs not in the realms of common sense or theory but in the realm of interiority. Interiority, for Lonergan, reveals the immanent method for knowing meaning and truth. As such it goes beyond what Gadamer means by "method" (i.e., scientific objectivism), but it also includes the realm of scientific theory which Gadamer disdains. Interiority discloses the proper method critical of all "methods" because it grounds itself in the very foundation of understanding: consciousness. Lonergan explains in another oft-repeated remark why interiority must be primary in any true philosophy:

> If there is to be any general science, its data will have to be the data of consciousness. So there is effected the turn to interiority. The general science is first, cognitional theory (what are you doing when you are knowing?), secondly, epistemology (why is doing that knowing?), and thirdly metaphysics (what do you know when you do it?).[7]

So Lonergan has announced that the exigence of our time is the need for the differentiation and appropriation of human interiority:

"Thoroughly understand what it is to understand and not only will you understand the broad lines of all there is to be understood but also you will possess a fixed base, an invariant pattern, opening upon all further developments of understanding."[8] In other words, "to say it all with the greatest brevity: one has not only to read *Insight* but also to discover oneself in oneself."[9] Lonergan may sound neo-Kantian in his return to subjective consciousness, but he has significantly moved beyond all Kantian presuppositions in his defense of critical realism. The fact is that Lonergan's thought has not at all developed in the same philosophic vein as continental (especially German) philosophy. Lonergan has essentially recovered and augmented the thought of St. Thomas Aquinas. Lonergan's philosophy of consciousness is fundamentally derived from the metaphysics of Thomas, whose monumental achievement, according to Lonergan, was lost after his death because of the bitter controversy between Aristotelians and Augustinians.[10] Thomas's metaphysics, based on the understanding of the human intellect derived from Aristotle, was further buried by the perceptualist, conceptualist, and abstract deductivist biases of decadent scholasticism, which were inherited by modern philosophy. This deformation was the general bias Heidegger termed *Vorhandenheit*.[11]

We can better grasp the development of Lonergan's thought if we know its background. Initially, we would have to locate Lonergan, who is popularly considered a "transcendental Thomist," within the circle of philosophers and theologians who in the first half of this century were busy reappropriating the thought of St. Thomas Aquinas, particularly Thomas's philosophy of knowledge.[12] The great Catholic thinkers who spearheaded the recovery of Thomism in the twentieth century were all united in their belief that truth is found in the judgment. In Thomas's theory of knowing, *esse* is grasped through the *est* of the judgment, its intentional correlate. Principally, this meant that the mind knows being through the abstraction from phantasm (or what Lonergan later came to call the data of sense) in the concept. In the concept the data of sense achieved its universal form; thus, in conceptualization, the mind was able to unite matter and form in a composite whole. How the relation between concept and judgment was conceived and what exactly constituted the act of a true affirmation in knowing were the issues at the center of debate among the neo-Thomists.[13]

It was in his attempt to appropriate personally Thomas's own mind, and not in his fidelity to any school of Thomism or neo-Thomism, that Lonergan staked his advance in the development of a Thomistic philosophy of knowledge. The most significant achievement resulting from his study of the Angelic Doctor lay in his recovery of the act of insight. Lonergan showed that for Thomas the act of understanding is conceived as prior to all explanatory concepts.[14] (The human act of understanding for Thomas is also conceived as corresponding to the greater understanding of the divine mind. As a corollary, the world order is conceived not as an arbitrary act of divine omnipotence but as the intelligibility caused by the perfect understanding of God. Indeed, the intelligibility of the cosmos is grounded in God's unrestricted understanding. Human finite understanding first grasped in the insight is the correlate of God's perfect understanding.) This preconceptual act of understanding mediates the data of sense to the intellect. Beginning in the phantasm, insight finds its abstracted essence in the concept. This mediating act of insight at the heart of Thomas's own thought was overlooked by the neo-Thomists.[15] They took for granted that abstraction for Thomas was an automatic process in which understanding followed as a matter of course. Lonergan showed how a careful study of Thomas's epistemological texts yielded something quite different: not an automatic process but an activity that Lonergan called "insight into phantasm."[16] The mind's grasp of the relevant data presented in experience through an act of insight was the equivalent of Aristotle's constitutive principle of form. In this operative act of "grasping the point" Lonergan defiantly illustrated how understanding (*intelligere*), not conceptual abstraction, was at the heart of Thomas's theory of knowledge. Indeed, Lonergan even discerned a second, distinct, reflective insight in Thomas which was equally neglected. This second insight occurred between the formulation of the universal concept and the act of judgment by which the subject affirms the truth of what is understood in the first insight.

In his *Verbum* articles, Lonergan showed how Thomas's theory of knowledge was at heart an intelligent grasp of intelligible form whereby the prior question, *quid est?* directed to the data of experience presented in the phantasm, is answered by the act of insight. This act in turn yields the subsequent question, *an est?* which is answered in the second act of reflective insight directed to the concepts that emanate from the original act of insight. When no further relevant questions remain after the synthesis has been made, then the subject can answer "Yes, it is so," with self-assurance. When this second question is answered in the affirmative, the conditions for making a true judgment and knowing the real are fulfilled.

Consequently, being is identified neither with what the senses experience (the "already out there now real" of the empiricists), nor with the intelligible essence of the concept (the "in here now real" of the idealists). Being, for Lonergan, became the object of the pure desire to know; it was what could be intelligently grasped and reasonably affirmed. The act from which the notion of being arises is neither sensing nor conceptualizing nor affirming; it is questioning. In the mind's quest for the intelligible and the true, the spirit of inquiry, driven by its intentional finality, is what allows being to emerge. Therefore, the first principles of Lonergan's theory of cognition lie in the *a priori* facticity of questioning consciousness. Between empiricism and idealism, then, Lonergan proposed a critical realism that finds its test in the personal appropriation of human subjectivity, in the *de facto* operations of an inquiring mind.

It was this twofold act of insight, in which the process of knowing moves from the data of sense in experience to conceptualization to reflective judgment, that formed the heart of Lonergan's cognitional theory. He discovered it not so much from reading Thomas's works as by studying how Thomas's mind was actually working in the development of his thought, that is, by appropriating Thomas's own mind. This was possible only because Lonergan was simultaneously appropriating his own mind, by attending to his own internal questions and cognitional acts.[17]

It was this intelligible movement from potency to act in the operation of intellect that Lonergan set out to explore in his great work *Insight*. What was required was to articulate these progressive acts of intelligence clearly in terms of transcendental acts of consciousness that one could discover in oneself, not in terms of metaphysical categories. The anthropological turn in Lonergan, thus, is grounded in the turn to one's own interiority. It is founded not in a metaphysics of knowledge but in one's own process of asking questions and finding answers. It is a turn that achieved a profound expression in the great exegesis of consciousness that is *Insight*.

The fundamental point that this seminal work makes is that essentially words do not mean, persons mean. The truth of a concept, statement, or proposition is not to be found in a person's words or sentences but primarily in his or her insight which finds its expression in words and sentences. What determines meaning is the preverbal, preconceptual act of understanding from which concepts, words, and propositions flow. The concept, or "inner word," is the product of understanding, not its efficient cause. Insight, thus, is prior to language, for it "includes the apprehension of meaning, and insight into insight includes the apprehension of the meaning of meaning."[18]

On this basis Lonergan's work steadily progressed from cognitional theory to intentionality analysis to transcendental method. Consequently, he was able to provide theology with a solid anthropological

starting point. He has given the anthropological turn initiated by the Enlightenment a solid foundation without the errors of the Enlightenment.
One of his statements on Karl Rahner is especially apt for describing his
own work: "He is committed to the anthropological turn and, on that
view, nature gives way to spirit, the supernatural at its root is divine
self-communication in love, and the obediential potency of a formal
ontology has to be translated into terms of consciousness."[19] In his
later work on theological method, the anthropological foundation also
enabled Lonergan to locate theology's normative base in the praxis of
the subject, that is, within the process of religious experience and present
religious living. Thus, for Lonergan, theology became inexorably rooted
in the consciousness of a converted, religious, self-transcending person
in love. Theological method begins with the thematization of transcendent intentional consciousness, and theological foundations derive their
content from the subject's religiously differentiated consciousness.

Having examined Lonergan's essential thought based on his contribution to the anthropological turn, we now turn to a fuller exposition
of the major themes in his work that are pertinent to our study of
Voegelin's foundational theology. These themes are (1) transcendental
method, (2) freedom and the human good, (3) conversion, (4) theological method and foundations, and (5) doctrines.

Transcendental Method

I hope to show that Lonergan's thematization of consciousness offers
an exceptional account of the essential aspects of human being within
the phenomenological realm, or more accurately, the "transcendental
field."[20] For unlike pure phenomenology, Lonergan's transcendental field encompasses intentionality, interiority, intersubjectivity, self-
transcendence, and conversion. These are the constitutive dynamics of
consciousness that the phenomenological and linguistic foci of most
hermeneutical thinkers fail to illuminate. They lie at the heart of Lonergan's "hermeneutical method."

Hermeneutical method for Lonergan is transcendental. Transcendental method is not defined in the Kantian or Husserlian sense, but in the
sense of authentic subjectivity, in the sense of the self going beyond
the self by asking questions and seeking answers. What essentially is
transcendental method? What is this process of knowing that Lonergan asks each of us to appropriate for ourselves? Where exactly does
Lonergan begin?

Lonergan begins not from a proposition, nor an *a priori* category, nor a self-evident truth. Nor does he begin with *Dasein*, nor "language as the source of being," nor eidetic reduction, nor a transcendental ego. Lonergan begins with a performance—the *de facto* performance of consciousness, immanent and invariant in all subjects. It is first discovered as the asking of questions, as primordial wonder, which begins in childhood and never ceases.[21] Such a beginning is rock solid and can warrant no doubt, for "to doubt questioning is to ask whether questions occur, the condition of the possibility of doubting is the occurrence of questioning."[22] One always starts from some question. For Lonergan, questioning itself is the clearly visible, universal, indubitable occurrence of a subject's consciousness. It is the first illumination of the structure of consciousness which reflects the inherent and primordial openness to being. All questions begin with some awareness, some experience, some wonder, that provokes the need to inquire. It is this movement of questioning, beginning in experience, provoking wonder, and inciting inquiry, that reveals the unlimited drive to understand which is at the root of human cognition. As Lonergan states, "This primordial drive, then, is the pure question. It is prior to any insights, any concepts, any words, for insights, concepts, words, have to do with answers; and before we look for answers, we want them; such wanting is the pure question."[23]

The unrestricted desire to understand is a fact. It occurs all the time everywhere in everyone (with the caveat mentioned in note 21). We become aware of it in the mediation of reflection. It is presupposed in all questions. The only thing that can overcome the tension created by the question is the occurrence of an insight. Insight is getting the point, hitting the solution, "seeing" the matter for the first time. Insights are a joyful discovery. They are the apprehension of meaning and the mark of one's intelligence at work. Insights issue in concepts that unify the data of experience in a coherent whole. Such insights and concepts, then, become material for reflection. So if experience denotes the first phase of consciousness which provides the data for questioning, insight denotes the second phase of consciousness which understands the data.

The third phase of consciousness asks whether what has just been understood is in fact so. Insights come a dime a dozen, but now one must ask: Are they true? So the third level of consciousness is rational. It involves critical reason, marshaling and weighing the evidence, and culminates in a judgment. What has been experienced and understood has now become knowledge because the conditions for knowing, first offered by the operations of experience and understanding, have met the criteria for an affirmative judgment. Knowledge is objective because it is virtually unconditioned, that is, it has met the conditions for judging something true. Human knowing, then, consists in this movement from empirical consciousness (experience) to intelligent consciousness (understanding) to rational consciousness (judgment). The unrestricted desire to know always moves through these three levels of consciousness.[24] What Lonergan has discovered in this process is a basic pattern of operations employed in every cognitional act. He speaks of this pattern as transcendental because (1) it is independent of all particular contents, (2) it is invariant over all cultures and all epochs, (3) it brings to light the conditions of the possibility of knowing objective reality insofar as that knowledge is *a priori*, and (4) it is the intentional drive to enter into the fullest relation with being, to acquire self-transcendent knowledge, and to seek a universal horizon.[25]

Hence, human consciousness is inherently oriented toward the concrete totality of the universe and, by the unrestricted desire to know, continues to raise further questions in order to know being ever more fully. Being, however, is not understood in the Heideggerian sense. Lonergan's understanding of being is transcendental: "Being, then, is the objective of the pure desire to know."[26] "Being is what is to be known by the totality of true judgments. . . . It is the complete set of answers to the complete set of questions."[27] The real is not beyond the intelligible or separate from it. The true is not beyond or separate from what can be judged. So the objectivity of human knowing is grounded not in one but in three related operations of consciousness which together comprise the cognitional structure of all persons. It resides in the givenness of the data (experience), in intelligibility (understanding), and in the coherence of a virtually unconditioned (judgment). All three acts are required to reach objectivity.[28] To rely on the first act alone is empiricism; on the second alone, rationalism; on the third alone, idealism. Lonergan claims that these three inadequate theories of knowing are correct for what they include but wrong for what they exclude. Only when all three are taken together in a complete and unified process can a theory of knowing proper to consciousness be established. Reality is known only by verification and most theories of knowledge cannot be verified by sense experience alone, nor by insights alone. Knowledge is achieved only in the culmination of experience and understanding in judgment, or what Lonergan defends as critical realism.[29]

The proper object of mind is attained only when the existence of intelligibility, immanent in the empirically experienced, is apprehended by an insight. Furthermore, only when the insight is subjected to the question, Is it so? and answered affirmatively by the critical reflection of judgment can the reality experienced be identified with being. So intelligibility is intrinsic to reality. If something is unintelligible, it is not real. If something does not meet the conditions for an affirmative judgment, it is not true. If the introduction of new data causes a conflicting insight with one's past insights, and if a new insight causes an incoherence in one's past judgments, then the whole process repeats and corrects itself until the totality of true judgments has been made, or until the complete set of questions has been answered. But the possibility of achieving ultimate finality in knowing is infinitely remote, since as long as there are new experiences there will be new questions, and as long as there are new questions the totality of being will always be out of reach. Therefore, knowing the real in its fullness is only a potentiality, never an actual accomplishment.[30] But this is not to imply that there is in Lonergan a formal separation between knowing and being, as there exists in Kant. If there exists any gap, it is not one of kind but one of degree, for consciousness is the unity of diverse acts that methodically seeks greater attunement with being. Thus, it yields a transcendental method that is "the normative pattern of recurrent and related operations yielding cumulative and progressive results."[31]

With such a view of consciousness and the method immanent in consciousness, Lonergan has been able to conceive of the unlimited increase in one's horizon. The intentionality of consciousness is the unrestricted movement toward an unlimited, transcendent horizon. It is the successive attainment of higher viewpoints reaching toward a universal viewpoint.[32] Lonergan considers one's horizon as the range of questions one can seriously raise. A person's world is constituted not only by what a person knows but also by what a person can seriously question. Lonergan calls this realm the "known unknown."[33] The unknown unknown is the realm about which a person cannot even raise meaningful questions; it is the area that lies outside and beyond one's present horizon.[34] The notion of a transcendent horizon to critique all horizons is legitimate given the unlimited potentiality of the human desire to know. It is a notion that operates in common sense as well as in science. Therefore, from the dynamic structure of conscious intentionality, which constitutes the cyclical, self-correcting process of learning, there emerges a basic and total horizon, which Lonergan has been able to illuminate by a methodical process of self-transcendence.

At this point it is important to clarify the important distinction Lonergan makes between proportionate being and transcendent being.[35] Proportionate being is being proportionate to our knowing. It is being known through "human experience, intelligent grasp and reasonable affirmation."[36] Properly speaking though, being is an unrestricted notion, for it includes not only all that we can know but also all that we cannot know because it transcends the bounds of our human experience. But it is this unrestricted being that our consciousness intends, even though it escapes our limited inner and outer experience. So Lonergan speaks of transcendent being that extends beyond our finite cognitional acts, but which underpins their dynamic structure and conceptual contents. So the basic orientation of human knowledge is beyond the known to the unknown and even the unknowable. Thus a profound connection exists between the heuristic structures immanent in human consciousness and the unrestricted, infinite openness of being. In other words, there exists "an immanent source of transcendence" in the human being which allows human knowing to reach beyond the universe of proportionate being to the realm of transcendent being.[37] This feature penetrates to some degree all human knowing and thus reveals upon inspection the transcendence of being itself. It opens up the possibility of grasping God as the unrestricted act of understanding,[38] as well as the absolute transcendence of God over all created being.

In *Insight* Lonergan maintained that the emergence of the question of God does not strictly arise out of religious experience. The question of God emanates from the natural process of human inquiry. In *Method in Theology* he modified but never refuted this position. There he explained the relation between a transcendental method that is wholly natural in its structure and a theological method that incorporates religious experience:

> It remains, however, that transcendental method is only a part of theological method. It supplies the basic anthropological component. It does not supply the specifically religious component. Accordingly, to advance from transcendental to theological method, it is necessary to add a consideration of religion.[39]

It was a consideration of religion that was absent in *Insight* but was given a central place in *Method in Theology*. The immanent source of transcendence in the human being, which provides the anthropological component, was expanded beyond itself to encounter the essence of religious reality: God's self-revelation. We shall address the foundational role that religion and conversion play in Lonergan's later thought in due course. But first we need to discuss the controversial aspects of his transcendental method as it was first formulated in order to show why Lonergan needed to broaden it.

A common criticism aimed at Lonergan has surrounded his dependence on the intellectual pattern of experience. In grounding philosophical foundations in cognitional theory, Lonergan opens himself to the charge of intellectualism. This criticism needs to be addressed before I proceed.

In *Insight*, Lonergan delineated six different patterns of experience that are indicative of the polymorphism of consciousness: biological, aesthetic, dramatic, intellectual, moral, and religious.[40] In these different patterns of experience, Lonergan explains, lies the reason for the basic misunderstandings and diverse theories of knowing expounded by philosophy down through the ages. These patterns are distinct but can blend, alternate, and interfere with one another. They also account for the numerous diversifications in the objectification of the human spirit: science, philosophy, art, myth, religion, culture, politics, etc. Lonergan chose the intellectual pattern of experience because it offered the clearest thematization of consciousness and could readily serve as a foundation for all the others. And with Aristotle, Aquinas, and Newman as his intellectual forebears, he could do no other than explicate the pattern of consciousness proper to philosophy, that which deals with the knowing subject as intellect. It was a very fruitful starting point for Lonergan which has served him well.

But in the years since *Insight* was published, Lonergan seemed to have had somewhat of a conversion. In the mid-1960s he began to modify his view to incorporate a "higher viewpoint." As he himself confessed: "I've learned a lot since [writing *Insight*]. It's still a moving viewpoint— after *Insight*. It kept on moving."[41] No longer was he centered on cognitional theory alone; he began to work under the rubric "intentionality analysis."[42] Perhaps it was Lonergan's recognition of the centrality of feeling that caused him to expand his own horizon, as he would later come to say, "Without feelings this experience, understanding, judgment is paper-thin. The whole mass and momentum of living is in feeling."[43] Or perhaps it was the desire to treat all the patterns of experience under transcendental method, especially the religious/mystical pattern of experience that would serve as the foundation for his method in theology. But whatever the reasons, Lonergan began to view the subject's consciousness not as cognitional alone, but as existential. With this transition, he needed to articulate a fourth level of consciousness.[44] It is the level of deliberation, decision, and action; the level of responsibility and willing the good; the level where one determines one's values and is motivated by them. In his later work based on intentionality analysis, Lonergan claims that the fourth level of consciousness, the level of feeling, valuation, responsibility, goodness, decision, action, and love, is primary. This level is the existential plane of everyday activity rooted in the subject's interpersonal life. It is principally the level of conversion.

The explication of a fourth level of consciousness was Lonergan's further attempt to ground his view of the subject as subject even deeper in the truth of the subject's existence. It is now necessary to understand Lonergan's transcendental method not from the viewpoint of cognitional theory alone, but from the viewpoint of the subject's total, existential activity and being-in-the-world, that is, from the viewpoint of praxis. An explication of not three, but four, dimensions of interiority is necessary in order to clarify a process of self-appropriation that involves the achievements of authenticity, conversion, moral and religious transcendence, and love.

Along with this expansion of the cognitive to the existential, Lonergan began to talk about not one, but two, directions in human development. He spoke of these as development from below upwards (i.e., from experience to understanding to reflection, verification, and judgments of fact) and development from above downwards (i.e., from the value-context of one's life formed by experiences of love, grace, conversion, and their concomitant value judgments, to the heightened reasonableness, intelligence, and attentiveness that an existential commitment to these realities intends). With this expansion of a twofold movement of consciousness, Lonergan began to articulate in a more complete way the project of self-appropriation. The "way up" is the path of achievement and creativity. The "way down" is the way of love and gift, which supports us long before we learn to advance in the first way.[45]

Lonergan's method can now be considered a hermeneutics of conscious intentionality that is no longer solely cognitive (the context of *Insight*) but existential (the context of *Method in Theology*). His radical hermeneutics of interiority, *qua* intentionality analysis, brings us into direct contact with the complete, concrete dynamics of self-transcendence. As existential, these dynamics of the self cannot be disassociated from how one lives one's life. The hermeneutics of interiority signifies a return to the question of the meaning of life, to the capacity to will and do the good, or—to use Voegelin's expression—to the truth of existence (as opposed to propositional truth). Objectivity (intellectual, moral, and religious) is now explicitly grounded in authentic, self-transcending subjectivity. But what does it mean to be authentic? What does one do to achieve authenticity? How is the good realized? These questions direct us to Lonergan's understanding of freedom.

Freedom and the Human Good

For Lonergan, authentic living is not a matter of following a situational or a deontological ethic. Authentic living results from following the normative structure of one's own interiority. It demands that a person respond to each situation at hand with a creativity and resoluteness that is at once sensitive, intelligent, reasonable, responsible, and loving. Authenticity is the fruit of self-knowledge. It results from developing and following one's own conscience, for Lonergan says, "the topmost level of consciousness is conscience."[46] It operates on the fourth level of consciousness, the level of responsibility. The guiding principles of conscience are the subject's judgments of meaning and value. These judgments and principles are "objective or merely subjective inasmuch as they proceed from a self-transcending subject. Their truth or falsity, accordingly, has its criterion in the authenticity or lack of authenticity of the subject's being."[47] For Lonergan, the hallmark of authenticity, then, is self-transcendence. The human possibility of knowing and willing is dependent on the unrestricted intention that intends the transcendent. Without the process of self-transcendence, humans can know neither the objectively real nor the objectively good.

The best and clearest example of self-transcendence is, of course, insight itself. A genuine insight is not intrinsically conditioned by space and time (however extrinsically conditioned it may be). It is objective because it transcends one's own act of understanding. A genuine insight is an ecstatic experience. I experience it as an illumination that comes from beyond me, and may respond to its revelation with the cry "Eureka!"[48] So the act of understanding itself has a transcendent character.

But self-transcending authenticity is manifest not only when we understand and judge but also, and especially, when we exercise our freedom, when we will and do the good. It is evident in our responsibility, in our social life, and in our commitment to overcome the sin of bias through the liberation of self-knowledge.[49] Cultural progress and the good of social order depend on the achievement of personal authenticity. And the achievement of authenticity is in turn either fostered or hampered by the social conditions in which one finds oneself. Whenever the flight from attentiveness, intelligence, reasonableness, and responsibility is manifest, historical and cultural decline will follow. When individual and group bias is operative, social as well as personal development is stymied. So the real problem of human liberation consists in being freed from the shackles of individual and group bias by obeying the transcendental precepts: be attentive, be intelligent, be reasonable, be responsible. These precepts are not only the internal laws of full human development; in combating group bias they are also the means for relieving the oppressed social conditions in which humans grow.

The solution Lonergan endorses for overcoming the sin of bias and its concomitant cultural decline is "a still higher integration of human living."[50] Hence, he claims that the real problem of liberation concerns the authentic development of individuals.[51] The problem is essentially grounded in "the failure of self-determination, the schism in the body social, and the schism in the soul that follows from an incapacity for sustained development."[52] The problem of liberation consists in the question whether the inherent limitations on human development, i.e., the facticities of one's existence, lead to resignation or to the actualization of effective freedom. In *Insight*, Lonergan summarized the problem of liberation as follows:

> The elements of the problem are basically simple. Man's intelligence, reasonableness, and willingness
>
> (1) proceed from a detached, disinterested, unrestricted desire to know,
>
> (2) are potentialities in process of developing toward a full, effective freedom,
>
> (3) supply the higher integration for otherwise coincidental manifolds on successively underlying psychic, organic, chemical, and physical levels,
>
> (4) stand in opposition and tension with sensitive and intersubjective attachment, interest, and exclusiveness, and,
>
> (5) suffer from that tension a cumulative bias that increasingly distorts immanent development, its outward products, and the outer conditions under which the immanent development occurs.[53]

What is needed, then, is a "higher integration" that will redeem humankind not by eliminating suffering and death but by revealing a higher meaning and value that is capable of transforming suffering and evil into a redemptive good. This need requires a transcendent solution to the problem of evil. It is what raises the question of God on the fourth level of intentional consciousness, the question that directly ensues from the problem of human liberation.[54]

For Lonergan, nothing outside of God is necessary. God is all that is absolute, noncontingent, unconditioned. If that is so, then that leaves a tremendous context for the action of human liberty. Goodness is not imposed by God but is fundamentally up to us to actualize. We are invited into goodness by the lure of a transcendent, redemptive, loving God, but the process of our becoming human and achieving the good is totally contingent on our freedom. Lonergan repeatedly stresses the critical importance of our responsibility: Are we open to everything in the universe that is unfolding? Are we becoming our authentic selves? Are we seeking the good, the true, and the beautiful?

Some things are not up to us to choose but are given to us, i.e., our bodies, our parents, our environment, etc. But we ourselves, who we are, who we want to be, depends on what we decide to make of ourselves. Besides the transformation of nature, there is the transformation of oneself. It is this self-transformation where the role of meaning is not merely directive but also constitutive. It is in this realm of constitutive meaning where human freedom reaches its highest point. It is here where responsibility is greatest. For here in the midst of human freedom emerges the existential subject. It is where one finds out for oneself that one has to decide for oneself what to make of oneself.[55] This radical decision for self-determination is the exercise of one's vertical freedom.[56] It can effect a movement from one horizon to a broader and deeper horizon. Or the movement can be so total that one experiences a complete turnabout and a new beginning—a change of heart or *metanoia*. It is then that our freedom makes possible a transformation of life. Our lives are redirected and reoriented. We confront the truth of existence most profoundly when we decide to commit ourselves to a transcendent realm of meaning. And the truth of existence has to do with the concrete solution to the problem of living, a solution that challenges us with the rightness or wrongness of our overall orientation. In other words, this is Lonergan's reaffirmation of the Augustinian dictum: "God can make us without us but not save us without us." And in order to be saved one has to be converted.

Conversion

As already stated, Lonergan underwent a significant change in outlook between the writing of *Insight* and *Method in Theology*. However, it would be misleading to assume that his discovery of the fact and significance of conversion occurred during this time. Already in his dissertation on *gratia operans* in St. Thomas, he gave much evidence to his interest in conversion.[57] He did not of course simply adopt his interpretation of Thomas's views on conversion as his own. For one, he rejected in his later work the metaphysical formulation of "entitative and operative habits." He was more inclined to view conversion as a conscious and dynamic event in one's personal life. According to Lonergan's basic method, the starting point for theology can no longer be metaphysical categories, but the data of consciousness. This shift is reflected in *Method in Theology* where Lonergan's account of conversion now identifies sanctifying grace with God's gift of love without the metaphysical categories of his earlier work. He retains the basic position on grace from *Grace and Freedom* but in *Method in Theology* transposes it into the horizon of interiority which *Insight* helped to facilitate.

With the rise of modern philosophy and the demands placed on the proper understanding of the subject brought on especially by existentialism and phenomenology, Lonergan needed to transpose Thomistic metaphysics into a new context. In his words, "intentionality analysis routed faculty psychology," and so conversion needed to be translated into terms of interiority, the third stage of meaning. He enunciates this important transition in a single paragraph:

> This gift we have been describing really is sanctifying grace but notionally differs from it. The notional difference arises from different stages of meaning. To speak of sanctifying grace pertains to the stage of meaning when the world of theory and the world of common sense are distinct but, as yet, have not been explicitly distinguished from and grounded in the world of interiority. To speak of the dynamic state of being in love with God pertains to the stage of meaning when the world of interiority has been made the explicit ground of the worlds of theory and of common sense. It follows that in this stage of meaning the gift of God's love first is described as an experience and only consequently is objectified in theoretical categories.[58]

Under the Aristotelian distinction between *priora quoad nos* and *priora quoad se*, the older theology recognized only two stages of meaning, common sense and theory. Thus, when it spoke of divine grace it was either expressed in the compact symbolic language of common sense or the technical metaphysical language of theory. But with the recognition of a third stage of meaning, Lonergan offers a new starting point: "Because we acknowledge interiority as a distinct realm of meaning, we can begin with a description of religious experience, acknowledge a dynamic state of being in love without restrictions, and later identify this state with the state of sanctifying grace."[59] Though notionally different from the scholastic usage, conversion is nonetheless real. It is real because it is a transforming experience that is self-validating.[60] It is personal but not private because God's grace is universal and granted to everyone. And it is so important theologically as to hold a central place in Lonergan's understanding of theological method.

How, then, does Lonergan conceive conversion? First of all, he sees it not as a part of theology for it is pretheological. Conversion has to do with the heart of religion: religious experience. Since theology is reflection on religion, and the heart of religion is the experience of conversion, the experience which provides theology its subject matter, then conversion is foundational. It is what makes religion alive, because it is what makes people religious in the first place. This is true of all the world's major religions, however differently it may be conceived.

(It is especially true of Christianity and Judaism. In the New Testament conversion is symbolized by the term *metanoia*, a change of heart. In Ezekiel it is expressed as God plucking out the heart of stone and replacing it with a heart of flesh.) Secondly, for Lonergan, there is a universal aspect to it much like Tillich's notion of "ultimate concern." But unlike Tillich, Lonergan's understanding of conversion is far more personal: it is like falling in love where one's whole orientation in life is redirected, given new meaning, transformed. But more than an act or event, conversion, like being in love, is a dynamic state. It becomes the first principle from which one takes one's bearings. The fact that it is individual, psychological, and feeling-oriented does not deter from its importance, for religion is first and foremost a personal appropriation.

The heart of human authenticity, then, is conversion. This experience transforms our horizons and reorients our lives. It is consciousness becoming conscience through the slow process of maturation. Conversion is the experience of discovering that all our knowing and doing involves an intentional self-transcendence. The genesis of such knowledge is not a matter of finding out and assenting to a number of true propositions. One can grasp propositions conceptually but one can only possess truth by the power of a transformed consciousness effected by conversion.

Lonergan claims that there are three kinds of conversion in accordance with the three basic patterns of experience: intellectual, moral, and religious.[61] To undergo intellectual, moral and religious conversion means that one must take the time to discover oneself in oneself, to come to grips with one's own being, to mind one's own mind, to heed one's own heart. The threefold differentiation of conversion can be described as follows:

Intellectual conversion is being liberated from the blunder that knowing is taking a good look and realizing that the world is mediated by meaning and motivated by value. It is discovering in oneself that the world is known by a process of experiencing, understanding, judging, and believing. Intellectual conversion reveals to us that the imagination is not the test for reality, that objectivity is not spontaneous but the result of questioning, discovering, and discerning, that knowing is not the result of ocular vision but critical reflection and judgment, and that meaning is not projected but embodied in decisions and acts. In short, intellectual conversion is becoming a critical realist. It is "a personal philosophic experience, of moving out of a world of sense and of arriving, dazed and disoriented for a while, into a universe of being."[62] One consequence of intellectual conversion is that one escapes the danger of common-sense eclecticism.[63] An intellectual conversion brings the diverse strains of eclectic knowledge (i.e., one's sundry opinions, positions, viewpoints) under a higher viewpoint. Consequently, one comes "into the light," experiences a breakthrough in understanding, and has an insight into one's own insights. Common-sense eclecticism fails to see things whole. Only by desiring with all one's heart and mind to understand things whole will one discover the insight of one's own insight and the meaning of one's own meaning. Also, the discovery may affect how one lives one's life, which leads us to moral conversion.

Moral conversion is a shift in the criterion of our decisions and actions from satisfactions to values. It is the exercise of our freedom in attaining authenticity. In discovering and developing our affective life, it is what grounds our values and motivates our actions. It is deciding for ourselves what we are to make of ourselves. It is discerning one's own bias and correcting it. It is being open to the knowledge and wisdom of others so one can more maturely will and do the good. Moral conversion, then, goes beyond the value of truth to value itself, to what is intrinsically good. The consequence of moral conversion is that one is liberated from bias and inauthenticity. It is taking one's bearings by what transcends one's own wishes, desires, pleasures, needs. It answers the question concerning the right way to live. Furthermore, moral conversion is the basis of the sustained development that reverses social, historical, and cultural decline, which brings us to religious conversion.

Religious conversion is being grasped by ultimate concern. It is other-worldly falling in love. It is the total being-in-love that demands total self-surrender. Religious conversion is the heart of religious experience; indeed, it is the heart of religion itself. It is God's love flooding our hearts and so it is a gift of grace. It is the replacement of a heart of stone with a heart of flesh. As Lonergan puts it, it is "the gradual movement towards a full and complete transformation of the whole of one's living and feeling, one's thoughts, words, deeds, and omissions."[64] It is the call to a life of holiness. Although religious conversion has yielded a variety of symbolizations throughout human history, it can be recognized by a common strain of results: an enduring and all-encompassing love, a greater detachment with the things of this world, a life of inner peace, a willingness to abandon oneself for others, a harmonious resolve with one's death. Although Lonergan does not explicitly mention these particular aspects of religious conversion, he plainly states, "by their fruits you shall know them."[65]

To recapitulate: if intellectual conversion moves us beyond the familiar sights and sounds of common-sense reality to critical realism, where the real is the intelligible and not "the already out there now" (a movement commensurate with the insight into one's own insights); and if moral conversion moves us beyond the security of pleasure and flight from discomfort to what is intrinsically good and valuable, where the good overcomes bias and decline (a movement commensurate with the growth of our freedom): then religious conversion moves us beyond the limitations of the finite world in order to be grasped by ultimate concern, assuring us that our own acts of meaning and value are looked upon with infinite worth and occur in a friendly, understanding universe (a movement commensurate with our experience of love). Lonergan sums it up as follows:

> As intellectual and moral conversion, so also religious conversion is a modality of self-transcendence. Intellectual conversion is to truth attained by cognitional self-transcendence. Moral conversion is to values apprehended, affirmed and realized by a real self-transcendence. Religious conversion is to a total being-in-love as the efficacious ground of all self-transcendence, whether in the pursuit of truth, or in the realization of human values, or in the orientation man adopts to the universe, its ground and its goal.[66]

Since all three conversions can and do occur within a single consciousness, Lonergan understands their relation as one of sublation:

> What sublates goes beyond what is sublated, introduces something new and distinct, puts everything on a new basis, yet so far from interfering with the sublated or destroying it, on the contrary needs it, includes it, preserves all its proper features and properties, and carries them forward to a fuller realization within a richer context.[67]

So the pursuit of truth that is intellectual conversion is sublated by the order of value that is moral conversion, and in turn, the order of value is sublated by the order of love that is religious conversion. Although religious conversion sublates intellectual and moral conversion, Lonergan holds that in practice it is causally prior.[68] What normally comes first is God's gift of love which invites moral and intellectual transformation. Likewise, there is here found the major exception to the Latin saying, *Nihil amatum nisi praecognitum.* Thus, says Lonergan, "there is a realm in which love precedes knowledge."[69] Normally, operations on the fourth level of consciousness presuppose the other three, but love is so radical that it is disproportionate to its causes, conditions, occasions, and antecedents. Love, therefore, is existentially prior to knowledge, for it is out of self-transforming love that we seek to inquire, investigate, and reflect. We seek to integrate it with the rest of our living. In other words, consciousness develops in two ways: the movement from below upwards must be complemented by the movement from above downwards. So now there is not only an exception to the conventional rule, "Nothing is truly loved until it is first known," but Lonergan actually reverses the adage: "Nothing is truly known until it is first loved." As he expresses it: "So it is that in religious matters love precedes knowledge and, as that love is God's gift, the very beginning of faith is due to God's grace."[70]

In his delineation of the nature of consciousness and conversion, Lonergan has discerned an immanent lawfulness in the process of becoming fully human. Human being, for Lonergan, is structured according to the total and basic horizon that is discovered in the dynamic operations of consciousness itself. As long as one lives in accord with the transcendental precepts—be attentive, be intelligent, be reasonable, be responsible, be in love—one transcends oneself and achieves true authenticity. As long as this law is not distorted by bias or error, the *imago Dei* remains intact within each person. This law does not derive from deductive metaphysics but from generalized empirical method in accordance with the given structure of human consciousness. Moreover, transcendence is not a matter of necessity. It is the achievement of personal freedom and responsibility for those who decide whether they will really love, whether their decisions and actions will be responsible, their judgments critical and reasonable, their inquiries intelligent, and their attentions sensitive and open to the world of experience. In this lies the uncovering of what is dormant in most people: the development of a heightened consciousness and the salvation of one's soul via the self-actualization that is intellectual, moral, and religious conversion.

Having said this much, we can begin to assess Lonergan's "hermeneutics of conversion" in relation to his transcendental method. It could be said that Lonergan's greatest contribution to foundational theology has been his unfolding of a total and basic horizon that is achieved by a self-appropriated interiority. This achievement does not depend on the social, cultural, and historical conditionings that are the *de facto* qualifications of a subject's present horizon. His conception of a transcendent horizon provides the necessary hermeneutical key for overcoming the emergence of any historicism or cultural relativism. In fact, strange as it may first appear, Lonergan depends on the role of conversion to counter the extremes of both subjectivism and objectivism. Though conversion is not itself a theological operation, it mediates opposing viewpoints and positions by transforming the horizon of the theologian. In this way it offers the possibility of avoiding a relativistic pluralism. Though Lonergan conceives of a pluralism that is enriching because it is complementary (due primarily to the different differentiations of consciousness),[71] he believes conversion prevents contradictory viewpoints from being final. A divisive pluralism is ultimately rooted not in a lack of data or in a failure of logical reasoning; it lies deeper in the hearts and minds of people, primarily in a lack of conversion. Theological pluralism, then, is not only a matter of theologians working out of different differentiations of consciousness but also out of different horizons that arise due to the fact that some are intellectually, morally, and religiously converted while others are not, in whole or in part. Therefore, the attainment of a total and basic horizon is the distinguishing characteristic and mark of supremacy of a transcendental method that operates within the horizons opened up by a threefold conversion.

Lest the vision of theologians' personal experiences of conversion attenuating the harsh disputes that exist among them seem much too sanguine, if not altogether undesirable, let it be noted that Lonergan ought not to be misinterpreted as a quixotic dreamer before his position is criticized.[72] Given the current state of theological pluralism, he does not advocate a flattening out of the legitimate differences in viewpoint through some kind of dialectical steamroller. Lonergan's position is that pluralism *per se* is attributable to the different differentiations of consciousness and their various combinations.[73] He sees pluralism in principle as an unacceptable weight as it stands by itself, because it undermines the scientific nature of theology. Lonergan, who professes the unity and universality of truth, is indeed advancing a particular, concrete criterion for theology that, though it is difficult to test in public, must not be abandoned before it is tried. Indeed, conversion as a criterion for theology has actually yet to be tried in the theological community, even though it is touted as the heart of Christian experience.[74]

The personal nature of conversion does not make it an illegitimate foundation for theology. Because religion is nothing if it is not personal, theology's foundations must be personal also. There seems to be no other way to discuss foundational matters except in light of one's own authentic experience and understanding. Theology would die the death of a thousand abstractions if its method were founded on anything else. Because it is about religion, theology's foundations must necessarily be concrete and personal if it is to remain an authentic and progressive science. Nevertheless, the verifiability of conversion is a legitimate question to be raised. This question is at the crux of the ongoing debate. Lonergan suggests that the self-authenticating nature of the experience is the only real test of its validity, which if one is able to discover it in oneself, it can be discovered in others also.[75]

This method based on conversion can be described as the ongoing, progressive achievement of a transcendent horizon made possible by (1) the pure, detached, disinterested desire to know; (2) a virtually unconditioned intelligibility; and (3) the unlimited potential of human liberty and responsibility. Such an achievement is not only possible but promoted by the human self-transcending capacity to move from what is true for us to what is true, from satisfactions to values, from self-regard to self-sacrificial love. At this point Lonergan's contribution to theological method could be called a "transcendental hermeneutics of conversion." It is

1. the transcending of one's perspective via higher viewpoints to a universal viewpoint;
2. the subduing of all forms of relativism by reaching for what is transcendent, permanent, and normative in human experience and history;
3. taking one's bearings by what is not intrinsically conditioned by space and time;
4. the self-transcending questioning that attempts to achieve God's eye-view (however infinitely remote);
5. a retrieval of the normative implications of the doctrine of human nature as *imago Dei*;
6. the achievement of a total and basic horizon made possible by the full differentiation of consciousness;
7. the differentiations of consciousness capable of operating in the different realms of meaning promoted by the systematic, critical, and transcendental exigencies;[76]
8. the elevation of a new standard and context from which to live one's life: the mystery of love and awe.

From a discussion of transcendental method and conversion, we can now proceed to a more explicit discussion of theology's method and foundations in Lonergan's thought.

Theological Method and Foundations

What would theology based in Lonergan's transcendental method look like? Where would it begin? How would it proceed? What would be its foundations?

First, we would have to anticipate that, for Lonergan, method in theology would not limit itself to any single religious tradition. If it were truly universal it would be capable of being true to all the exigencies of meaning operative in all religions. By its own definition it would have to be open to all the relevant data of human religiosity. It would be transcultural insofar as it would discern in all religious traditions common unifying factors rarefiable for methodical inquiry. It would be transhistorical in that it would avoid both classicist and modernist presuppositions. It would be transideological in that it would succumb to neither dogmatisms of the right nor dogmatisms of the left. It would be metacontextual in that it would not derive itself from any horizon but serve as the instrument for understanding, judging, and transforming all horizons past, present, and future. Some have claimed that Lonergan has provided us with such a theological method, that he has bestowed upon theology a method that meets the challenges of our time.

Although theology operates within a particular culture, it must have a transcultural base. Even though, as Lonergan defines it, "a theology mediates between a cultural matrix and the significance and role of a religion in that matrix,"[77] religion itself has become transcultural. For example, Christianity, with its roots in the Old Testament, has developed for almost two millennia in various cultures. If it is truly a universal religion, with the mission to reach all nations, its theology must direct itself to universal communication.[78] But Lonergan is not giving us a theology *per se*. He is showing us how theology is to be done, where it begins, how it proceeds, what its terms and their relations should be. Indeed, the results of theology would depend on its cultural matrix, but its method would not. Of course one could contend that Lonergan's method applies only to Western Christianity. It is true that his formulation of theological method has been conceived within, and articulated from, his own horizon, a horizon deeply conditioned by traditional Roman Catholicism. Nevertheless, he repeatedly appeals to all the world's religions in demonstrating the universal application of theological method, a point made clear in the following passage:

> Plainly, a theology that is to reflect on religion and that is to direct its efforts at universal communication must have a transcultural base.
>
> Next, the transcendental method outlined in our first chapter is in a sense, transcultural. Clearly it is not transcultural inasmuch as it is explicitly formulated. But it is transcultural in the realities to which the formulation refers, for these realities are not the product of any culture but, on the contrary, the principles that produce cultures, preserve them, develop them. Moreover, since it is to these realities we refer when we speak of *homo sapiens*, it follows that these realities are transcultural with respect to all truly human cultures.
>
> Similarly, God's gift of love (Rom. 5,5) has a transcultural aspect. For if this gift is offered to all men, if it is manifested more or less authentically in the many and diverse religions of mankind, if it is apprehended in as many different manners as there are different cultures, still the gift itself as distinct from its manifestations is transcultural.[79]

Lonergan derives theological method from transcendental method which in turn he derives from the operations of consciousness. Transcendental method has four phases corresponding to the four levels of consciousness. Theological method has eight functional specialties corresponding to the four phases of transcendental method. Theology's eight functional specialties are research, interpretation, history, dialectic, foundations, doctrines, systematics, and communications. These functional specialties are divided into two basic phases.[80] The first phase attempts to appropriate the past. It gathers the relevant data, interprets its meaning, organizes it into an appropriate narrative, and clarifies the dialectical positions taken in regard to the ensuing history. In other words, this phase is the confrontation and assimilation of a past tradition by scientific and scholarly minds. Lonergan calls this phase "mediating theology".

There is also a second phase which attempts to move theology into the future. This phase takes its bearings on a foundational horizon opened up in present experience by intellectual, moral, and religious conversion. When this orientation confronts the conflicts of dialectic and the historical ambiguities of the first phase, a principle of selection ensues and doctrinal judgment may be rendered. The ultimate meaning and coherence of these judgments are worked out in systematics, which in turn seeks its end in the creative communication of its findings. Lonergan calls this second phase "mediated theology." Although mutually interdependent, the second phase finds a special dependence on the first insofar as the second confronts the present and future only in light of what has been appropriated from the past. So for Lonergan, theology has an upward movement and a downward movement which functions in a scissorslike fashion. The pivot of the whole enterprise is the experience of conversion which brings the past up to date and moves it into the future.[81]

Lonergan believes an adequate theology for today must be divided into specializations that accord with what theologians actually do. Theological specialties, therefore, can be specified according to the distinct acts of consciousness. Theology, then, as a set of unique tasks, should be divided according to functional specializations and no longer according to field or subject specializations, which, although still dominant in contemporary thought, hamper the theological enterprise.[82] This dominant way of doing theology is limited because the division of labor is endless and the relations among the various fields and subjects disjointed. It also produces the specialist "who knows more and more about less and less."[83]

The key terms and their corresponding relations in Lonergan's transcendental and theological method are illustrated below (see tables 1–3). Three areas of his overall methodological scheme reveal close connections in structure and theme: the transcendental levels of consciousness (table 1); the relation between transcendental operations and corresponding functional specialties in theology that are derived from them (table 2); and the two phases of theology which are linked by the nontheological "operation" of intellectual, moral, and religious conversion (table 3).

An explanation of theological method as a system of collaborating specialties can be found in chapter 5 of *Method in Theology*. An

LONERGAN'S METHODOLOGICAL SCHEME

Table 1
TRANSCENDENTAL LEVELS OF CONSCIOUSNESS

LEVELS OF CONSCIOUSNESS	A PRIORI TRANSCENDENTALS	TRANSCENDENTAL PRECEPTS	TRANSCENDENTAL CONCEPTS
the empirical	attentiveness	be attentive	the real
the intellectual	intelligence	be intelligent	the intelligible
the rational	reasonableness	be reasonable	the true
the reasonable	responsibility	be responsible	the good

Table 2
RELATION BETWEEN TRANSCENDENTAL METHOD AND THEOLOGICAL METHOD

TRANSCENDENTAL METHOD: OPERATIONS OF CONSCIOUSNESS	THEOLOGICAL METHOD: FUNCTIONAL SPECIALTIES	
1. experience	1. research	8. communications
2. understanding	2. interpretation	7. systematics
3. judgment	3. history	6. doctrines
4. decision	4. dialectic	5. foundations

Table 3
THEOLOGY'S TWO PHASES

MEDIATING THEOLOGY	MEDIATED THEOLOGY
1. research	8. communications
2. interpretation	7. systematics
3. history	6. doctrines
4. dialectic	5. foundations

conversion
(intellectual, moral, and religious)

explication of each functional specialty can be found in each of the subsequent chapters. It would be beyond the scope of this chapter to discuss each one separately, so I will concentrate here on the specialty that concerns us the most: foundations. This is the functional specialty in theology that, along with dialectic, corresponds to the primary, fourth, level of consciousness. It is the functional specialty that deals with religious experience and conversion. In the next section I briefly treat the sixth specialty: doctrines. As we shall see, Lonergan's understanding of doctrine is a controversial matter and will emerge as a point of contention when we compare his thought with Eric Voegelin's in the final section of the chapter.

The first and most important question to ask is, How does Lonergan conceive foundations in theology? His answer is straight to the point: "Foundational reality, as distinct from its expression, is conversion: religious, moral, and intellectual. Normally it is intellectual conversion as the fruit of both religious and moral conversion; it is moral conversion as the fruit of religious conversion; and it is religious conversion as the fruit of God's gift of his grace."[84] Conversion is the movement from inauthenticity to authenticity. As such, "it is the total surrender to the demand of the human spirit: be attentive, be intelligent, be reasonable, be responsible, be in love."[85] Theology's foundations, then, lie in the objectification of conversion. More specifically, in its religious aspect, foundations is the objectification of the mystery of love and awe.

Foundations does not refer to a "merely subjective" experience, for the transcendental exigence, like other exigencies, is an inherent and normative dynamic in the structure of human consciousness. Foundations in theology, for Lonergan, does not appeal to scriptures, doctrines, councils, or other putative authoritative sources. To locate theology's foundations in these sources would be practicing theological method along classicist lines. Rather, foundations refers to what occurs before any articulation, expression, or symbolization. Foundations in theology is not located in the past; it is found in the present of a converted, religious praxis oriented toward the future. Foundations is the functional speciality that reminds us that theology is not grounded in any "objective" contents or contexts of faith (the premise of objectivism or dogmatism in classicist theology). Foundations insists that there are never any definitive pronouncements to ground or exhaust the reality of faith. Rather, only the empirically verifiable, self-transcending experience of conversion embedded in the consciousness of the existential subject is theology's proper foundations.

The religious foundations for theology are the objectifications of religious conversion. Religious conversion supplies the "data" for theological method in its second phase. Lonergan insists that this experience is highly personal and intimate but not private. Although there is no single uniform account of authentic conversion, it has social verifiability and normativity.[86] There is, however, a general, plausible account of authentic conversion, intelligible to those who have had the experience, no matter how idiosyncratic its concrete particularity. Lonergan notes that the one experience that unites the common features of all the world's religions is the experience of being in love in an unrestricted manner:[87] "To be in love is to be in love with someone. To be in love without qualifications or conditions or reservations or limits is to be in love with someone transcendent. When someone transcendent is my beloved, he is in my heart, real to me from within me."[88]

Therefore, the religious foundation of theology is the universal self-transcending experience of the mystery of love and awe. It is an experience that manifests the deepest longing of the heart, the greatest thirst of the mind, and the profoundest hunger of the human spirit. It is an experience that results not from our searching, willing, or choosing, for it is the pure gift of grace. Once one has received this grace there emerges an insatiable yearning to know and to unite with its source. The source of this love is transcendent, outside us, beyond our control, elusive of our desire; but it looms near and is present in our hearts whenever we meet our neighbor in mutual presence.

All true love is self-surrender, but being-in-love in an unrestricted manner without limits or qualifications or conditions or reservations is the acme of religious experience and therefore the foundational reality of all religions.[89] The transcendent state of being-in-love in an unrestricted fashion is what Lonergan describes as a person's falling in love with God. It is not the product of knowing or choosing; it is a conscious, dynamic state of love that orders one's entire life. It determines one's joys, desires, fears, values, hopes, sufferings, decisions, acts, possibilities. It becomes the conscious center of one's total being, and the "known unknown" of one's longing:

> To say that this dynamic state is conscious is not to say that it is known. For consciousness is just experience, but knowledge is a compound of experience, understanding, and judging. Because the dynamic state is conscious without being known, it is an experience of mystery. Because it is being in love, the mystery is not merely attractive but fascinating; to it one belongs; by it one is possessed. Because it is an unmeasured love, the mystery evokes awe. Of itself, then, inasmuch as it is conscious without being known, the gift of God's love is an experience of the Holy.[90]

Love is God's doing. Love flows from its source not in the human heart but from the eternal grace of God. As it flows from God, so it flows back to God. Our neighbor to whom we render our love is God's own being in human disclosure. Lonergan persistently emphasizes the inseparableness of human love and divine love. God's love fills our hearts through our love of each other, and in our love of each other the mystery of God's love is revealed. Lonergan, then, like the great mystics and saints, understands the love of God from the analogy of human love. Consequently, the object of religious love and belief must discover its ground in one's concrete personal experience.

When human love is a great love, the barriers of all human discriminations fall, particularly the barriers between different religions. Religion itself is centered on love. So love, as we can see, is Lonergan's central religious category.[91] Love proves in its own way that there is a God, for it is in love that God is made visible. The mutual love between persons is nothing less than the manifestation of the mystery of love and awe, the mystery that reveals divine presence. All religions are united by the quest for union with God and the path to God is always conceived as some form of mystical love. The belief that God is love flows from an experience of love that is all-embracing. Hence the way to God is, universally, the way of self-transcending love.

Love is the beginning of a religiously differentiated consciousness. Falling in love is affective self-transcendence. It occurs on the fourth level of consciousness and opens one's heart and mind to a transcendent realm of meaning. No other experience effects such a radical transformation of horizon. Love acquires a transcendent horizon because it orients one to what is transcendent in lovableness. Love alone has the power to actualize our potential for the highest reaches of human fulfillment. Human conscious intentionality fulfills itself through falling in love, and the object of love is neither a question, an idea, nor a doctrine, but a person. Since this fulfillment is explicitly religious, one must be in a state of love before knowledge of religious reality can be authentically possessed.[92]

The world's religions are united by the mystery that transcends them. They are not completely irreconcilable because, as Lonergan claims, behind the diversity of human religious beliefs lies a deeper unity in the knowledge of faith born of religious love, which is the true source of religious belief.[93]

Lonergan characterizes religion as "the realm where love precedes knowledge." It is the realm in which we experience the other-worldly love of God in this world. The inner word of religion is the voice of spirit speaking to spirit. It is prior to any expression in language. For Lonergan, it is love speaking to love. The word is the expression of this inner meaning and value, and language is its primary carrier:

Before it enters the world mediated by meaning, religion is the prior word God speaks to us by flooding our hearts with his love. That prior word pertains, not to the world mediated by meaning, but to the world of immediacy, to the unmediated experience of the mystery of love and awe.[94]

This word is the preeminent "inner word" of immediacy and interiority. To this inner word is joined the "outer word" of the religious tradition, which is essentially the story of past encounters with divine love drawing us into a historical community of faith. The word, then, is personal: love speaks to the beloved; social: love draws all together under the one mystery; and historical: love is outwardly expressed through language.[95] All forms of the word manifest the one transpersonal Word, the common *logos* that underlies all human experience, personal, social, and historical.

The intellectual ground of self-transcendence is the pure desire to know. It is the unlimited raising of further questions. It is the self going beyond the self by the detachment and disinterest of the pure desire. But besides the pure desire to know there is the pure desire to love, the desire for union with the beloved. Besides knowledge, then, there is communion. The base for the desire for communion is not cognitive but affective. It does not follow the intellectual pattern of experience but the religious and mystical pattern of experience. In the religious or mystical realm both desires combine indiscriminately to manifest the whole eros of the human spirit. It is the union of heart and mind where knowing and loving become the same activity.

So there is present in love a desire for unrestricted communion which like our knowing cannot be fully satisfied in this world, this side of death. Nevertheless, Lonergan remarks that such unsatisfied desire "plunges us into the height and depth of love, but it also keeps us aware of how much our loving falls short of its aim."[96] But the eros of the human spirit is indefatigable. It is human nature endlessly seeking its divine ground and being endlessly drawn by divine grace.

The human spirit, for Lonergan, is characterized by a dual élan. Along with the eros of the mind there is the eros of the heart. Along with the unrestricted desire to know there is the unrestricted desire to love. Along with the self-transcendence of cognitional intentionality there is the self-transcendence of affective intentionality. For one who has been converted, these two thrusts immanent in human being converge in a single, unified movement of the human spirit seeking ever fuller relation with Being.

Implicit in this discussion of religion has been the notion of immediacy. In various places Lonergan states that besides the infant's world of immediacy there is the adult's larger world mediated by meaning. He observes that much of our confusion and distortion in theories of knowing have resulted from not recognizing this distinction between the world of immediacy and the world mediated by meaning. But Lonergan also recognizes a third dimension of experience. There is indeed a second immediacy in the world of the adult. It is the world of immediacy mediated by meaning. It is not the world of pure perception (which is impossible); it is the world where we experience the "known unknown" immediately present to our consciousness. It is experienced only by appropriating one's interiority: "Besides the immediate world of the infant and the adult's world mediated by meaning, there is the mediation of immediacy by meaning when one objectifies cognitional process in transcendental method and when one discovers, identifies, accepts, one's submerged feelings in psychotherapy."[97] In its more sublime aspects, second immediacy is effected by love's joyful union and is the mark of religious experience: "Finally, there is a withdrawal from objectification and a mediated return to immediacy in the mating of lovers and in the prayerful mystic's cloud of unknowing."[98]

At this point it should not come as a surprise to anyone to realize that where Lonergan is really locating theology's new foundations is in nothing other than mysticism. His repeated references to mystical experience make this explicit:

> When finally the mystic withdraws into the *ultima solitudo*, he drops the constructs of culture and the whole complicating mass of mediating operations to return to a new, mediated immediacy of his subjectivity reaching for God.[99]

> Religiously differentiated consciousness is approached by the ascetic and reached by the mystic . . . the mystical mode withdrawing from the world mediated by meaning into a silent and all-absorbing self-surrender in response to God's gift of his love.[100]

> Community . . . may be ascetic and mystical, teaching the way to total other-worldly love and warning against pitfalls on the journey.[101]

Having laid the foundations for theology proper, Lonergan next treats theology's new categories. The base for theology's new categories is transcendental method and its new special categories, God's gift of love (or what in traditional, theoretical theology was called sanctifying grace).[102] So theology's foundations "will derive its first set of categories from religious experience."[103] And the only unassailable fact that exists in all religious experience, claims Lonergan, is the existence of love. The second set of categories will be derived by moving from the subject to the community to "the history of the salvation that is rooted in a being-in-love."[104] A third set is derived by moving from our loving to the source of our love. It is making explicit "our future destiny, when we shall know, not as in a glass darkly, but face to face."[105] A fourth set will derive not from authentic or inauthentic humanity but from authentic or inauthentic Christianity. A fifth set will deal with progress and decline generated from authenticity to inauthenticity, and concern itself with redemption: the self-sacrificial love that overcomes evil with good.[106]

With the thematization of a fourth level of consciousness, Lonergan was able to move beyond the notion of consciousness as solely cognitive to consciousness as affective as well. This inclusion followed the exigence of perceiving the subject as existential, as whole. It affords an apt hermeneutical insight: if hermeneutics concerns the problem of understanding, then it is not solely an intellectual problem; it entails the problem of "hardness of heart" as well. What is urgent, then, is the liberation of one's affective life. What is necessary for true understanding is conversion, falling in love, and faith.

What then is faith? For Lonergan, faith is principally the universal view reached by the discernments of meaning and value of a person in love. In other words, "faith is the knowledge born of religious love."[107] It is abiding by the mystery of love and awe operative in the universe. Without faith, the ultimate source of value is only intramundane; without faith, the ultimate source of goodness is only human. With faith, however, the value born of religious love is God's value. With faith the eyes of religious love attain God's eye-view of the universe, for "faith gives more truth than understanding comprehends."[108] Finally, says Lonergan,

> faith places human efforts in a friendly universe; it reveals an ultimate significance in human achievement. . . . Most of all, faith has the power of undoing decline. . . . It is not propaganda and it is not argument but religious faith that will liberate human reasonableness from its ideological prisons.[109]

Furthermore, says Lonergan, faith as the eye of love teaches us that "the limit of human expectation ceases to be the grave."[110]

Doctrines

If Lonergan has been accused of undue stress on subjectivity and interiority in much of his *Method in Theology*, he has also been accused of excessive objectivism in his treatment of doctrine. The difficulty

of uniting the subjective with the objective is a major problem in
contemporary theology. Lonergan's solution is to find and draw out the
intrinsic relation between the operations of subjective consciousness,
which produce and affirm judgments about objective reality, and a
theological method which produces and affirms doctrinal statements in
the course of its functional operations. If conversion makes subjectivity
authentic, then the objective judgments affirmed by such a person (in
this case a theologian) will carry the status of fact. In other words,
certain affirmations made by theologians who have reflected upon and
objectified in their own consciousness their experience of conversion
will be "doctrinally correct." This is the transcendental procedure in
consciousness that is carried over into theology. For Lonergan, the
functional specialty of doctrines produces the concrete truths that ensue
when the positions and counterpositions of dialectic are existentially
discerned and mediated by the foundational reality of intellectual, moral
and religious conversion.[111]

Lonergan's view of doctrine has not always been consistent and even
his thematization of doctrines in *Method in Theology* is not without
ambiguity.[112] But I will attempt to state concisely what this position
is without bringing to bear all the controversies and debates that have
been expressed concerning this important topic in Lonergan's work.

For Lonergan, the renewal of theology which has been so pressing for
so long has resulted from its being a traditionally dogmatic enterprise.
This is so because theology arose in a classicist culture which presumed
that there was only one fixed context for truth. Its philosophy was
permanent; its values, laws, and ideals, universal; its verities, eternal.
This classicist view had survived for over two millennia. Because "the
old dogmatic theology had misconceived history on a classicist model,
that it thought not in terms of evolution and development, but of universality and permanence,"[113] there appeared the need for renewal. With
the advent of modern science at the end of the seventeenth century,
dogmatic theology arose in opposition to medieval scholasticism.

> It replaced the inquiry of the *quaestio* by the pedagogy of the thesis. . . . It
> gave basic and central significance to the certitudes of faith, their presuppo-
> sitions, and their consequences. . . so the new dogmatic theology not only
> proved its theses, but also was supported by the teaching authority and the
> sanctions of the Church.[114]

This development, considered by some a decadent scholasticism, was
in many ways a rear-guard defensive maneuver, fueled by the excesses
of the counter-Reformation. But since in the modern world culture is
perceived empirically, whereby the symbolizations of meaning and truth

are considered diverse, historically minded, and pluralist, theology had to abandon its deductivist approach and shift to an empirical method. It had to shift "from the static to the dynamic, from the abstract to the concrete, from the universal to the historical totality of particulars, from invariable rules to intelligent adjustment and adaptation."[115]

With this exigence for theological renewal (or, to use Pope John's term, *aggiornamento*) Lonergan set out to construct a method in theology that would dismantle the dogmatic premises of past ages. But it would also be normative, that is, it would not abandon what is common and universal in human nature: the open, immanent, and operative structure of the human spirit. Such a spirit has developed in history through certain discernible advancements, certain differentiations of consciousness, or what Lonergan called "the ongoing discovery of mind."[116] Basically, this means that with the discovery of different differentiations of consciousness (myth, common sense, theory, scholarship, interiority, etc.)[117] meaning and its expression were seen in their contexts. So whatever doctrines that were promulgated came to be dealt with in contextual fashion. They had to be understood in light of the cultural development in which they originated. If doctrines were to retain their meaning across different cultures or through different periods of cultural development (the development of mind) they had to be recast within the new context. Lonergan came to the conclusion that what is permanent in doctrines is not their linguistic or propositional form but their meaning.

The clearest example of this, which Lonergan had studied and written on for many years, was the development of doctrine in the early church councils.[118] Although it is much too weighty a matter to expound upon at any length here, we can simply state that Lonergan believed that when the Gospel message encountered numerous and diverse interpretations of its truth-claims, its literary and mythical expression had to be recast into theoretical language. And even though this language was foreign to the Gospel itself, it translated its meaning into precise, univocal, and doctrinal formulation. This process of doctrinal development was stirred on by the patristic debates over the nature of Christ. The Fathers sought to provide theoretical unity to the plurality of views concerning the meaning and nature of Christ in relation to the Father and the Spirit, and so such concepts as *homoousios* (consubstantial) at Nicea and *hypostasis* (person) and *physis* (nature) at Chalcedon were introduced to quell the ongoing controversy over the essence of Christian teaching. New terms were introduced "not to set a precedent, but to meet an emergency."[119] The emergency was created by a shift in context: on the investigation of data an inquiry gives rise to questions, questions to answers, more questions to opposed answers, and more answers to further questions. The quandary persists until an insight appears, a discovery that will allow different views to fit together into a single viewpoint. Thus, there develops a set of interwoven questions and answers, a set of terms and relations that reveal the meaning of a text.[120] The language of common sense yields to the language of theory, and the theories change when new problems are introduced. This in a nutshell is the development of doctrine. Development is almost always dialectical: a truth discovered follows a contrary error (heresy) once asserted as true but found to be inadequate to the matter at hand.

And so for Lonergan, doctrines develop within the discovery of mind. "In other words," as he puts it, "the intelligibility proper to developing doctrines is the intelligibility immanent in historical process."[121] Doctrine never ceases to develop, for every answer must meet the requirement of the context where it finds itself, but once it is found its meaning is permanent. Doctrines are permanent in their meaning because "they are not just data but expressions of truth."[122] Their permanence does not mean immutability for when there is required an even better understanding of a doctrine, its formulation may require alteration or modification, although the meaning of the pronouncement is ever the same. Doctrines are subject to the same historicity as all human thought, meaning, and language. Statements have meaning only within contexts, and since contexts are ongoing and ever-changing through cultural development and interaction, there is needed for the proper understanding of doctrine the employment of research, interpretation, history, and dialectic. To state the meaning of a doctrine for today one must proceed through foundations, doctrines, systematics, and communications. It must be communicated to the various classes, cultures, and differentiations of consciousness that it has for an audience. The classicist insistence on worldwide uniformity is yielding to a plurality of manners in which religious meaning and values are communicated. Dogmatic theology which is classicist is today superseded by doctrinal theology which is historically minded.

This in essence is Lonergan's position on doctrines. What can we say about it? First of all, Lonergan believes that doctrines have a distinct value. In a religious tradition they function as normative judgments of fact and value arrived at in the past and handed down to the present. However, Lonergan's position on doctrine in *Method in Theology* follows directly his transposition of theology from a classicist, dogmatic orientation to a historically minded one. According to this shift he no longer begins in truths as given but in data.[123] He begins with the believing subject rather than with the intellectual objectivism of past revelation or the social objectivism of church dogma. This starting point clearly follows the general trend of Western philosophy for the past three hundred years. It is a distinctly modern disposition.

Secondly, Lonergan's new position on doctrine suggests an appeal to biblical personalism, for the content of faith is now understood as "the knowledge born of religious love" rather than "believing in the word as true." Stated differently, being in love is the ground and context for believing the word as true, for it elicits the religious conversion that is the condition for affirming the truth of any religious doctrine. As such, religious belief is not consequent to a prior judgment of fact; it is a discerned truth within the horizon of sanctifying grace. Only within a horizon established by the "inner word" of grace is it possible to assent to the "outer word" of tradition. Consequently, the theological precept "be in love" is the religious event that is prior to doing theology. This transformative event is not a theological procedure; it takes place, so to speak, *between* dialectic and foundations. Doctrines are established by the addition of foundations to dialectic, and they reach their fullest explication in systematics.

To summarize: Lonergan's genius consists in getting out from under the priority of the question of being (the "metaphysics" of the ancients and medievals) as well as the priority of the question of knowing (the epistemology of modern philosophy) in order to ground philosophy and theology in the *a priori* structure of consciousness. Theology dominated by theoretically differentiated consciousness is at an end; it can no longer turn to metaphysics for its guidance. The new source for theological reflection will be found in the interiority of a religiously differentiated consciousness. The full sweep of its method will entail the systematic collaboration of functional specialists, but the heart of the whole theological endeavor will be its foundations, the objectification of which will depend on the subjectivity and conversion of the theologian's own self. In this light, the transformation of theology will depend not on intellectually discovering a need for faith but on the experiential fulfillment of the drive to self-transcendence that occurs with religious conversion. This is the specific theological principle in *Method in Theology:*

> In this fashion philosophy and the root of theological method would come out of the personal experience of the thinker and it would evoke the personal experience of those to whom he speaks or for whom he writes. . . . More than anywhere it is essential here to be able to speak from the heart

to the heart without introducing elements that, however true in themselves, have the disadvantage of not being given in experience.[124]

The experiential grounding of faith and belief in personal conversion is the foundational reality of authentic theology. The only criterion for responsible theologizing is the conscience and consciousness of theologians who are attentive, intelligent, reasonable, responsible, and in love. Any appeal to an objective "standard" over against the theologian's own subjectivity would be a naive and inauthentic theology. In regard to either facts or values, there is no objectivity except authentic subjectivity. Like Aristotle's treatment of the virtues presupposing virtuous souls in the polis, Lonergan's methodical theology presupposes the existence of authentic theologians whose drive for self-transcendence has been fulfilled by the experience of God's grace.

Also with Lonergan, nature and grace have regained their inseparable unity. Theology can no longer continue to prescind one from the other, nor to reify nature and grace in abstract concepts. By way of his method, Lonergan has shown us that theology must be radically oriented to the graced praxis of the individual. It must reclaim the primacy of the truth of existence, and the truth of existence cannot be taught. It is only acquired by persons being attentive in their experience, intelligent in their understanding, reasonable in their judgments, and responsible in their actions—a transcendental movement that culminates in the getting of wisdom. For those who freely abide by this law of human authenticity, and in the process achieve a religious consciousness, the distinction between nature and grace is not very wide.

The gist of Lonergan's whole contribution can be summarized in his own words:

> The divine secret, kept in silence for long ages but now disclosed (Rom. 16:25), has been conceived as the self-communication of divinity in love. It resides in the sending of the Son, in the gift of the Spirit, in the hope of being united with the Father. Our question has been how to apprehend this economy of grace and salvation in an evolutionary perspective and, more precisely, how it enters into the consciousness of man.[125]

This divine self-communication enters into human consciousness, no doubt, by a person "moving beyond the realms of common sense, theory, and interiority and into the realm in which God is known and loved."[126] I might add that it is precisely here "where God is known and loved," where the primal word is spoken and heard, where the mystery of the universe is disclosed in the cosmic conversation that is human history, that there occurs that dimension of human experience that calls for the kind of understanding that is wise.

In the final section of this chapter I compare the work of Lonergan with that of an exceptionally wise thinker who, better than anyone else in our time, has explored the ubiquitous divine/human word that has emerged in history. As we have already seen, Eric Voegelin offers a very challenging "method" for doing philosophy and theology in today's world, perhaps even more challenging than Bernard Lonergan's.

Lonergan and Voegelin Compared

In regard to general intentions, there is much that unites Voegelin and Lonergan.[127] They both share the basic approach for understanding human existence: God, the human being, history, and society are not objects to be known from the "outside"; they can only be known by participating in what constitutes their order. For Lonergan this is achieved by fulfilling the transcendental precepts of authentic human existence. For Voegelin this means recovering the constitutive experiences and symbols of human self-understanding that have emerged in history. In their own way they are each concerned with the reconstitution of human existence in the order of being. What unites them is their belief in the reality that is basic: human order is achieved in the experiences of self-transcendence that move one toward the order of divine being. Voegelin approaches this basic reality by studying the representative symbolizations of transcendent experiences of order as they emerged historically. Lonergan addresses it by articulating a method that can be implemented in all concrete inquiries into human meaning. It is in resistance to the collapse of constitutive meaning and the rejection of the formative experiences and structures of order in modernity that they both direct their intellectual energies. Accordingly, they are adamant in their repudiation of the relativism and historicism that afflict the modern world. Yet neither embraces the opposite pole of absolutism since each appreciates the cultural and religious plurality of human experience as well as its historicity. Their approach to understanding the normative truth of the whole that is intended in their respective inquiries, thus, is intrinsically hermeneutical.[128]

Without being absolutists both Voegelin and Lonergan are guided by the classical and medieval tenet that upholds the universality of truth. As a result, they seek to articulate universal criteria for knowing reality and living ethically. Being concerned with the foundational realities that unite all humans, they both attempt to articulate a way or method for appropriating universal truth, the truth variously expressed in diverse, but equivalent, symbolizations which all persons come to affirm in their experiences and understand in their reflections. They are united in their attempt to reach the objectively true and the objectively real in contradistinction to the deformed Cartesian modes of subjectivism and objectivism that bifurcate knowing and being, a bias which has informed much of modern thought. As a result, both seek to avoid any suggestion of a primordial subject/object split which can either degenerate into a Sartrean solipsism on one hand or a dogmatic extrinsicism on the other.

For his part, Voegelin emphasizes the in-between structure of human experience as well as the noetic structure of the universe as a polarity-in-tension which together oppose any reification of the human being's relation to God, world, and society. Lonergan, meanwhile, in his thematization of self-transcending subjectivity, shows how being is objectively known. In this endeavor he avoids the pitfalls of both a fantasizing subjectivism as well as the opposite fallacy which he describes as "a conceptualist extrinsicism for which concepts have neither dates nor developments and truth is so objective that it gets along without minds."[129] But in his repudiation of the whole language of modern philosophy, Voegelin goes beyond Lonergan insofar as he has genuinely regained the Anselmian-Augustinian meditative exegesis of experience that has been generally lost in the post-Cartesian "philosophies." With their emphasis on various articulations of "transcendental subjectivity" and its corresponding "object-intentions," Voegelin perceives in these modern schools of thought a truncated explication of human experience. Consequently, from a Voegelinian perspective, Lonergan comes out sounding neo-Kantian in his predominant concern with constructing a critical epistemology that bridges the gap between knowing and being. Voegelin's approach generally disregards modern epistemological problems that flow from Cartesian premises since he takes his philosophical bearings on principles that are premodern. Indeed the roots of his theory of consciousness, and the symbols used to explain it, are ancient, which performatively serves to protect his analysis of consciousness from being tainted by the pseudo-problems which preoccupy much of the philosophizing that begins with Descartes and continues up to the contemporary scene.

Also, in their diagnosis of the intellectual, moral, and spiritual diseases that plague modern people—an analysis which cuts to the core of personal, social, and historical disorder—both of these great thinkers' works can be considered a therapeutic exercise for healing the torn and fragmented fabric of contemporary life. The diagnosis of the various forms of disorder that mar the human community and the study of what constitutes true forms of order is Voegelin's primary task; it is also the objective of Lonergan's method.

But Lonergan does not seem to develop the basic insight into human participation in the order of being as far as Voegelin does. Lonergan's analysis of intentional consciousness and the method that stems from it does not penetrate to the level of transcendent order itself as it has emerged in history. His primary emphasis is on the process of knowing, and thus he tends to relegate existential order to a secondary result of that knowing. In Voegelin, existential order is primary and the "knowledge" that ensues from right order is a welcomed by-product, not an end in itself. Their mutual criticism of positivism illustrates their difference in this respect. Whereas Lonergan critiques positivism as an epistemological fallacy because it views knowing as something like looking, Voegelin rejects it because it is an existentially disordered orientation of the soul in that it attempts to reduce all reality to a thing—God, the human being, world, and society become objects to be perceived by a skeptical observer. Like all ideologies which are closed to the divine ground of being, positivism is for Voegelin a spiritual disease, not simply an intellectual error.

Lonergan's view of history as the ongoing discovery of mind is true as far as it goes, but it must be supplemented by a view of history that is not progressivist in the sense that any differentiation of mind does away with earlier articulations of meaning, as Lonergan's notion of theory superseding common sense, or science eliminating myth, can be interpreted in light of. Also it must include a view of history as essentially eschatological, by which mind serves a greater purpose than the discovery of itself. Intellectual clarity about the order of being is certainly venerable, but it only has value to the degree that humans use it to become attuned to true, transcendent order which alone would establish order in history.[130] Voegelin has analyzed the historical process that tells the story of the human struggle for order in existence, in which mind or reason plays a primary role. Insofar as Voegelin's study of the order of history is derived from the actual history of order, his analysis is more concretely historically minded. The higher viewpoint that he reaches for emanates from specific experiences of order in history. Although his analysis of knowing is not as epistemologically rigorous as Lonergan's, Voegelin seems to be able to yield more concrete categories in his work, principally because he identifies the equivalent experiences of reality that emerge in concrete historical events. For Lonergan, meanings that emerge in history would be methodologically equivalent insofar as they are the result of experiencing, understanding, judging, and deciding—operations of knowing which all humans share. But this notion of equivalence does not really penetrate to the study of historical symbols in their concrete representation, as Voegelin's work does. It still remains to be seen just how successful Lonergan's method can be when it is applied to the task of analytically penetrating comparative historical materials.[131]

Another contrast between Lonergan and Voegelin lies in their dissimilar views of science: Lonergan gives to modern science very high marks, believing that on most all accounts it has superseded classical science; Voegelin has a high regard for classical science, whose tenets he believes have been lost in the mathematized and verifiable empiricism of modern science; with some exceptions, modern science, for all its wonders, is viewed with some disdain because of the immanentized scientism that has flourished in its name. As a corollary to this, each thinker has a different view of classical culture. Lonergan is always wont to stress its limits by speaking of its "classicism," an absolutist view of culture which molded later theology. He defers instead to the modern empirical understanding of culture which has superseded the old view by its historical mindedness. Voegelin stresses the insights and principles of classical philosophy and science, believing that modernity, with its relativizing, historicizing, and secularizing tendencies, has not really improved on them. This contrast, however, should not be drawn too strongly since both would agree about the limitations of both classical and modern science and the strengths of each. The contrast is really a matter of emphasis.

Although they are genuinely concerned with the same problems, their fundamental differences become apparent when we consider the intellectual foundations upon which each of them builds. As one would expect, Lonergan takes his stand in theology, and Catholic theology at that. Voegelin, who has no ecclesial tie, is a philosopher—a philosopher who must be a skeptic in the classical sense of one who calls all formulations of truth into question, that is, one who is in quest of the unformulable truth that transcends all formulated truths. But like any theologian (and unlike most "philosophers" today), he takes his bearings on revelation in history. What sets him apart from most theologians is that he believes that the only means for analyzing the structural aspects of revelation must be philosophical, and in this respect he is greatly informed by Plato's differentiated symbolism. Although he grants that the noetic opening of the soul to transcendence is fulfilled by the revelatory insights reached in the Christian experience of redemptive grace, Voegelin believes that the structural exploration of this new domain must remain noetic. For this exploration he finds the language of transcendental method, which he once used himself, less helpful than the symbolism of the Platonic *metaxy*. For him, the language of philosophy must be used for exploring the truth of revelation, and in this regard he has shown the way for the philosophical reconstruction of theology.

What makes Lonergan's transcendental method inadequate for Voegelin is that in using the language of "intention" it becomes too easily associated with the kind of deficient intentionality that is pervasive in contemporary thought on consciousness, such as Husserl's phenomenology, which for critical reasons Voegelin seeks to avoid.[132] The intention of consciousness present in the perception of external objects invariably becomes the model for understanding the intention toward divine reality. Consciousness understood in this way tends to objectify whatever is the so-called object of consciousness even if the object is no object at all, but instead transcendent mystery. The objectifying intention of consciousness, thus, is always in tension with the consciousness of nonobjective reality. Because the transcendental method takes its stand on the intentional operations of consciousness, it cannot do full justice to the nonintentional opening toward divine reality. Transcendental method is not differentiated enough to distinguish between these two modes of knowing reality. Therefore, as already stated, Voegelin thought that a Lonerganian terminology is not technically precise enough for handling the problems that ensue when one attempts to analyze comparative historical materials, such as a Platonic myth or a Christian vision, a prehistoric cave drawing or a Taoist hymn, an ancient Egyptian meditation or a medieval prayer. It is on the basis of these kinds of symbolic expressions of consciousness that Voegelin, following Plato, believes that levels of reality exist that resist articulation in systematic discourse.

In deference to Lonergan, however, there is a clear distinction between his understanding of intentionality and Husserl's. Lonergan insists that objective reality is not the object of sense perception but of understanding and judgment. Thus, his intentionality takes its cue from questions for inquiry, from wonder and awe, and not from phenomena to be grasped. This means that the "object" intended is not necessarily a thing at all. It is whatever is intended in questions and reached in correct understanding, an intentionality which intends nonthings as well as things. And indeed, insofar as intentional consciousness readily reaches to God in questions about the ground of existence, Lonergan's method attempts to avoid hypostatizing objectification. Nevertheless, even in his conscientious formulations, "God" tends to become reduced to the unknown "object" to be known in intellectual inquiry, rather than the mysterious divine presence from the beyond that forms the soul.[133] Lonergan's transcendental consciousness tends to end up asking about the question of God as an afterthought that succeeds a line of

other questions about objective reality, rather than being fundamentally
constituted by the presence of divine reality from the start or seeing the
tension toward the divine ground of existence as the motivating force
behind all questioning. Admittedly, much of this inadequacy Lonergan
attempted to correct in his later writings, particularly by his adding a
fourth level of consciousness to sublate the first three, his distinction of
development in two directions (from above downwards and from below
upwards), and also through his emphasis on religious conversion as prior
to moral and intellectual conversion. But it remains a valid critique
that Lonergan was not fully able to distinguish clearly and integrate
successfully the two different types of human cognition, i.e., the two
distinct ways of experiencing and knowing reality.

It would seem that Voegelin handled this paradoxic structure in
human knowing much better with his distinction between intentionality
and luminosity, with luminosity being the proper mode for knowing
transcendent reality. Whether a transcendental method such as Lonergan's is sufficiently able to relate these two different modes of consciousness remains yet to be seen.[134] Lonergan's esteemed attempt to do so in
Method in Theology is not entirely successful. The problem that surfaces
when one attempts to understand his position in *Method in Theology*
is whether he locates revelation as experience on the first empirical
level of consciousness, or on the fourth level of self-actualization, or
on both. As an experience to be understood and judged, revelation
would seem to occur on the first level; as a matter of conversion it
would occur on the fourth level. Does the fourth level of decision
and conscience now become a more radical first level that yields new
data to be reflected upon? or as a fourth-level reality does it fulfill the
first three? or does the fourth level of consciousness yield a type of
knowledge inaccessible to the first three? These are questions that have
to be directed to Lonergan when one tries to understand the diverse.
elements of human experience that his unified theory of consciousness
attempts to integrate in his later work.

Voegelin eludes these problems by avoiding the language of "cognitional acts," "operational levels of consciousness," and "transcendental
subjectivity" altogether. His aim is not the precise explication of cognitive consciousness but the existential "balance of consciousness" that
understands reason not as the faculty for making true judgments but as
the meditative process in experience for knowing the ground of one's
existence. Whereas Lonergan understands the differentiation of consciousness on the order of the cognitional process of objective knowing
and valuing, Voegelin sees differentiation as a social and historical development based on a particular soul's movement from compact to noetic

and pneumatic experience, a movement that becomes representative for a whole society. These are the differentiated experiences which not only in themselves provide a true knowing and valuing, but also constitute an epoch in history.[135] Thus, the noetic balance Voegelin aims for has to overcome the "public unconscious" that has forgotten these experiences of true order. This loss is the result of what he calls "the split between the intentionalist desire to know and the consciousness of the mystery of reality."[136] For Voegelin, consciousness which is aware of this mystery is luminosity within which intentionality is a component. Voegelin sees intentionality operating within a larger horizon than what is available to it alone; for Lonergan intentionality, because it intends answers to questions and not objects, eventually enters the transcendent sphere of reality, if not by personal, existential conversion, at least by the apprehension of its intelligibility. In Lonergan's transcendental method the "unrestricted desire to know" is not restricted by the intentionality of consciousness. In fact the "known unknown" that Voegelin would relegate to "luminous apprehension" is within the purview of intentionality. Thus, for Voegelin, in regard to transcendence, luminosity absorbs and sublates intentionality; for Lonergan, intentionality covers knowledge of all reality, even transcendent mystery.

The problem that both Voegelin and Lonergan attempt to solve is this: once the intentionality of consciousness in the direction of revelatory experience is distinguished from the intentionality of consciousness in the direction of objects in the external world, how does one get them back together again as the operations of one human consciousness? Voegelin seems to handle this problem better because he was able to identify the emergence of these two directions in the historical process of differentiating consciousness. Once the divine beyond is distinguished from the intracosmic gods, then reality in its fullness becomes known in these two distinct movements, and the knower becomes cognizant of the distinction in his or her own consciousness. Through the historical process of disenchantment, divine reality was disengaged from the external world. Subsequently, this divine reality emerged in consciousness not as a thing to be perceived but as a presence emanating from the beyond of consciousness. Voegelin, and not Lonergan, studied the historical materials in which these two directions in consciousness became distinct. Consequently, Lonergan did not really come to emphasize fully the dimension of consciousness that Voegelin calls luminosity, though he certainly allows for it in his treatment of religious conversion, falling in love, mysticism, etc. This luminous dimension cannot simply be added on to transcendental method because in paradoxic fashion it is in some tension with the transcendental mode of intentionality. It is a distinct direction in consciousness that is, however, intrinsically related to, and flows out of, intentional knowing.[137] Thus, perhaps due to his Thomistic orientation, Lonergan's thematization of interiority, even in his later work where he gives a more than nominal praise for mysticism, seems to stop short of a full integration of experiences of mystical knowing and visionary illumination.

Of course Voegelin reminds us that any attempt to explicate the paradoxic structure of consciousness is itself caught in the paradoxic structure of language. The analysis of consciousness has an inevitably equivocal nature because

> language participates in the paradox of a quest that lets reality become luminous for its truth by pursuing truth as a thing intended. This paradoxic structure of language has caused certain questions, controversies, and terminological difficulties to become constants in the philosophers' discourse since antiquity without approaching satisfactory conclusion.[138]

Thus we must view the distinctive ways that Lonergan and Voegelin go about analyzing consciousness as ultimately rooted in these ancient controversies and difficulties over the use of language. The paradox is an unresolvable constant that first fully came to consciousness in the contrasting *modus operandi* of Plato's and Aristotle's philosophizing. What we can learn from this debate is that there is no luminosity without intentionality but an intentionality that falls short of the mystical threshold is not philosophically sufficient to render adequately the structure of consciousness. Consciousness has a fundamental unity that in reflective distance yields two basic directions.

Voegelin himself speculated that the unity of these two distinct dimensions of consciousness can be found not on the level of differentiation at all but only in the cosmological myth.[139] Back when humans spun imaginative creation stories of an immanent reality that still included divinity, consciousness abided in a predifferentiated oneness. When the truth of reality became known through differentiated experiences that demanded a more adequate imagination of divine reality, the unity of consciousness was lost, perhaps forever. The problem of getting these two modes of consciousness back together again as functions of one human mind is perhaps the unsolvable problem of philosophy. The problem of combining intentionality with luminosity coincides with the merging of the beginning and the beyond of divine reality into one experiential reality. Once the tension of the *metaxy* is made conscious in history there is no going back to a predifferentiated unity. The structure of metaxic consciousness once again emerges as the existential lot of human beings, this time revealing the paradoxic structure which knows no philosophical solution other than the acute awareness and analysis of its own twofold nature, an awareness that stands in obeisance to the imaginative mythic tale of reality that illuminates the divine, the tale which is ultimately impenetrable.

Voegelin once declared that Lonergan's conception of the transcendental method would require a necessary correction in light of the historical materials that Lonergan himself had not taken into account.[140] Because of this deficiency he most probably believed that any transcendental method was inadequate and at best would have to be totally overhauled or eliminated altogether. As has been pointed out by his critics, it is true that Lonergan does not fully incorporate a historical perspective in his method. He primarily confines himself to the intellectual openness to transcendent being, not existential openness. In *Method in Theology,* where he attempts to compensate for this lacuna by stressing the importance of religious conversion and affectivity, the existential openness tends to be simply tacked on to the intellectual openness of transcendental method. In other words, he simply adds another level of consciousness to his previous three levels without considering how this new existential dimension of consciousness may call for a radical revision of the whole transcendental approach in the first place, at least when it comes to knowing nonobjective reality. And if this religious/mystical mode of consciousness is a wholly unique dimension, then it cannot be simply an addendum to the other intentional modes. Existential openness, thus, really becomes less central in Lonergan than it does in Voegelin. As suggested above, it would be an interesting inquiry to pursue whether Lonergan's transcendental method can adequately penetrate or do justice to historical texts which symbolize mystical visions. In other words, the kind of knowledge achieved in visions of transcendence may not be fully accounted for in terms of Lonergan's three- or fourfold operations of consciousness. The rigorous cognitive demands of objectivity are obviously sidestepped in ecstatic, visionary experiences which certainly yield some kind of knowledge of the real. For example, in his vision of the resurrected Christ, Paul is not at all interested in determining how his knowledge of Christ meets the canons of critical realism. Lonergan would of course retort that Paul was not a philosopher, that he was religiously converted without being intellectually converted. But then the same would have to be said of Parmenides, Heraclitus, Socrates, and Plato, who certainly embody various levels of critical self-reflection but who do not orient this reflection on the model of knowing intentional objects in the external world. Their experience is of a reality that is nonobjective but nonetheless real. The faculty for knowing the really real in Plato and Aristotle was the *nous,* its operation being totally determined by existential openness to transcendent reality. In fact it was spoken of not as a self-generated capability of the mind, but, like Paul's vision, as a gift from the gods.

In light of these many considerations we would have to conclude that the principal differences between Lonergan and Voegelin rest generally in the fact that Lonergan finds his orientation in the Aristotelian/ Thomist tradition, while Voegelin's orientation is more Platonic/ Augustinian.[141] Voegelin takes his bearings on the visionary experience of transcendence. Accordingly, he opts for the Platonic image of seeing rather than the Aristotelian image of the identity of the knower with the known. The experience of vision was prototypically formulated by Plato and later taken up by Christian mystics who inherited the Platonic/Augustinian tradition of the *illuminatio divina*. As a religious thinker Voegelin is situated in this tradition. On the basis of this luminous way to truth, he is generally not interested in the epistemological, transcendental, or phenomenological concerns of modern philosophy which by and large prescind from experiences of transcendence. This is why he generally discounts consciousness understood as intentionality in favor of consciousness understood as luminosity, which for him is the proper, exalted mode for encountering divine truth. Rather than beginning from the Aristotelian/Thomistic agent intellect, Voegelin begins with the interior illumination of divine presence evoked by religious experiences. Compared to Aristotle, Voegelin finds in Plato a greater experiential richness in his treatment of the one that lies beyond the range of human understanding. All knowledge occurs within the light of this oneness and lures human minds toward its truth. Where Aristotle is stronger in defining the various defining forms of the many, Plato is stronger in articulating the experience of relatedness to the unformed one beyond the many. The whole of being in its transcendent mystery is at the center of Plato's philosophy, while Aristotle is generally more concerned with knowing the material forms of immanent being. Accordingly, Voegelin adopts a view of consciousness as relational and participatory and thus is generally keen on Plato's mythopoeic constructions in his discourses on divine being. The divine is the mover of human intelligence and thus becomes the immanent "object" of the noetic search. Lonergan too perceives an immanent source of transcendence in human intelligence, but his neoscholastic heritage makes him formulate it in terms of an agent intellect that knows being by possessing a sufficiency of evidence and reason that is verified in judgment. Voegelin finds in the Platonic *nous* a more helpful articulation of metaleptic consciousness, one that knows being through meditative, anamnetic reflection.

In Voegelin's understanding of human existence the distinction held by Aquinas, Scotus, and other scholastics between the supernatural light of God and the natural light of the created intellect becomes virtually indiscernible. The question surrounding this issue is of course how nature and grace are interwoven in the soul's ascent toward God. The Aristotelian/Thomistic orientation tended to view human nature as an autonomous power of individual substance. Thus, there arises the notion of the idea of God that is innate in the mind, allowing humans to know God through the unaided power of their own natural capacity. This understanding of human nature diverged from the Platonic/Augustinian view of the soul as an opening to the infinite light of God within the very structure of its being.[142] In this view, one would have to say that the nature of humans is openness to transcendent grace—the conclusion being that a nature that is not fulfilled by grace is not living according to its true nature. What follows, therefore, is that there can be no facile division between nature and grace, reason and revelation, or revelation and natural theology. Because of the mutual participation of being and existence in one another, reason and revelation, nature and grace are not dichotomous processes. In the core experience of openness to the mystery of being, they are intimately related. Because the divine reality of being is the moving force or grace behind this openness, the process of differentiation always has a revelatory character, whether its emphasis is, in the case of philosophy, noetic, or, in the case of religion, pneumatic. This is why Voegelin speaks of "the constitution of reason through revelation."[143] To be human is to partake in divine transcendence in each of these modes. Although in experience one mode is inevitably accentuated over the other, it does not operate in exclusion of the other. This paradoxic structure of experience cannot be dissolved by the conventional dichotomies of theological discourse. These dichotomies, which bifurcate reality on the level of reflection, assure the endless unsatisfactory analysis in the topical debates.[144]

This is why Voegelin is suspicious of all theological categories and distinctions, preferring instead to recover the language of noetic and pneumatic experience that existed before the emergence of theology as a dogmatic enterprise. Along with the conventional language of theology, Voegelin even repudiates the word "religion." He determines it to be a Stoic deformation of the truth of existence which became identified with the cultic observance and doctrine that was originally meant to protect it.[145] Religion originated with Cicero who was the first to apply the term *religio* to the "phenomenon of a doctrinally deformed mythopoesis." As a result, "*religion*," Voegelin states baldly, "is not an analytical concept of anything."[146]

Another stark difference between Voegelin and Lonergan appears to be their respective views on doctrine. For Voegelin, the truth of reality cannot become an object of intentionalist consciousness, because to make it so would risk hypostatizing it. Although truth for Lonergan is also primarily a matter of realized experience, a matter of existential openness and conversion, he believes it can be articulated in the form of propositions. Thus, he is far more accepting of the importance of doctrine as an ever-developing and always-penultimate objectification of truth. Because Voegelin wishes to avoid all deformations of truth, especially the historically doctrinalized ones, he is quite averse to giving doctrine an essential role in his philosophy, although he does recognize its original purpose as a preserver of spiritual insights that would otherwise be lost in the vicissitudes of history.[147]

But then again Voegelin is not a theologian who pays allegiance to a particular creedal tradition or ecclesial community. Unlike Lonergan, he has never had to assume the posture of a "defender of the faith." Faith seems to be a broader reality for Voegelin than for Lonergan. His *fides* is not confessionally Christian, for it does not emerge from any church's doctrinal formulations, nor is it formed by liturgical celebration and piety. And yet in Lonergan's notable formulation, Voegelin would probably agree with him that "faith is the knowledge born of religious love," except that Voegelin would not use the word "knowledge" here since he believes faith is always in search of understanding. Faith for Voegelin does not culminate in knowledge, for it is not certainty but a fundamental trust that forms the soul under conditions of uncertainty.[148] The horizon of Voegelin's *fides* appears to be more inclusive in that he has claimed to have generalized Anselm's *fides quaerens intellectum* beyond the doctrines, creeds, and symbols of any one religious tradition. It is a philosopher's *fides* that is, nonetheless, deeply formed by Christianity.

In the end I believe there is no ultimate discord between Voegelin and Lonergan on the issue of doctrine. Both would criticize the conceptualist reductionism of doctrine, the obstructionist tendency of doctrine to derail the experiential quest for truth among the spiritually insensitive, or as Lonergan would put it, to eclipse the mediation of real meaning and value on the level of foundations. Both would affirm the usefulness of doctrine to preserve experiential insights, though this is given more weight by Lonergan.[149] The difference between them is again a matter of emphasis, a difference which corresponds to the greater weight Voegelin gives to luminosity, vision, mystery, and myth. For Voegelin the true myth is a tale told by the human participant in the mystery of reality that participates in the larger tale told by reality itself (God's word). In an analogous sense doctrine can be viewed (more so by Lonergan) as the formulation of a truth discovered by humans and revealed by God. Doctrine, however, given its more conceptualist form, cannot convey the paradoxical status of its truth to the degree that myth can, making it more susceptible to deformation and misuse.

There is a dimension in Lonergan's thought, however, that is markedly absent in Voegelin's. It comes to light due perhaps to the fact that Lonergan is indeed a confessional Christian theologian. Although Voegelin is nonpareil in his analysis of personal and social order and his resistance to disorder, he has not fully grasped the Christian mystery of "the law of the cross" that answers the problem of sin and evil in human existence.[150] The order of self-transcending love that redeems us from the struggles of finitude is only hinted at in Voegelin's "Wisdom" essay, nowhere else.[151] The tale that is a saving tale is true of both Plato's philosopher's tale as well as the Gospel, but the Christian belief that in the cross God's solution to the problem of evil is revealed goes decisively beyond the Platonic vision of human/divine order. Lonergan is much stronger on articulating this dimension of human experience.

Similarly, whereas Voegelin speaks very rarely of the order of human love, Lonergan frequently discusses how interpersonal human love partakes of the larger unrestricted love of God that redeems humans from misery and death. It is the experience Lonergan calls "falling in love" whereby one realizes that what one truly seeks in love lies beyond all finite manifestation. The religious conversion elicited by this experience hinges on the awakening of the self to the source of this love. From this awakening we learn to live our lives out of a gratuity to which we have no claim but which pulls us toward ever-greater perfection, and even saves us from evil and death. We can surmise, however, that this awakening of love is commensurate with what Voegelin intends by pneumatic experience.

Indeed, in this vision of love, it has been argued, one finds the essence of Christianity.[152] In the new commandment given by Christ, which is the foundation of the law and the prophets, humans are to love each other as he loved them (John 13:34–35). And his love was surely an unrestricted human love. In fact only by this self-transcending love for each other will they be recognized as his disciples. This supreme form of love was so special that it was believed to reveal God's very nature, a love that binds persons to Christ as well as to each other. The cross manifests the radical act of love as self-gift in death, too extreme for most of us, but nonetheless paradigmatically symbolic of God's deed of salvation that we all share in our death-defying love for one another. It is this dimension of love at the heart of Christian truth that provides greater understanding to Voegelin's frequent, but rather ambiguous, statements about "grace in death" which he perceives to be the distinct, soteriological truth of Christianity.[153]

Nevertheless, we do find in Voegelin a great emphasis on the role of faith, hope, and love (which Heraclitus had recognized and distinguished as sources of knowledge) as virtues which provide the existential orientation toward transcendent reality. Participatory consciousness goes beyond reason alone, for before and after the development of *noesis*, faith, hope, and love are the constant forces that orient one to transcendent mystery. Without the basic trust in the graciousness of transcendent being that faith provides, one could not risk the openness of heart and the pain of love that the longing for truth demands. Only the movement of love allows us to participate fully in the human/divine drama of reality. We can only enter this love with faith and hope, for without them we could not surrender ourselves to the suffering love of God's grace. This, Voegelin holds, signifies one's exodus out of oneself and into the divine reality beyond the soul and beyond the world. On this note he is fond of quoting St. Augustine, whose Commentary on the Psalms (64:2), he believes, gave precise expression to this experience of exodus:

> He begins to leave who begins to love.
> Many the leaving who know it not,
> for the feet of those leaving are affections of the heart:
> and yet, they are leaving Babylon.[154]

Voegelin also referred on one occasion to a "cathartic" statement of Camus's that captured so well the loving tension of existence toward the divine ground:

> Not morality but fulfillment. And there is no fulfillment other than that of love, meaning the renunciation of self and dying to the world. Going on to the end. Disappear. To dissolve oneself in love. It will be the power of love which then creates, rather than myself. To lose oneself. To dismember oneself. To deny oneself in the fulfillment and the passion of truth.[155]

As I have attempted to show, in many but not all respects it is possible to compare the important themes that Voegelin and Lonergan have in common, and to even judge some of the strengths and weaknesses of one's work by the other's. One should be deterred, however, from attempting to forge any kind of facile synthesis of their ideas into a complete "system." The integrity of each one's thought will be preserved by coming to terms with the separate ideas and viewpoints that each employs, not by absorbing one thinker's language into the other's.

To help identify the contrasting features of their thought more explicitly, I offer below a parallel listing of their complementary "positions" (see table 4). This summary concludes my brief exercise in comparative analysis. I hope that my discussion of their respective works as well as their background influences has incorporated enough nuance for understanding the important terms and relations which each figure employs. The comparative abstract attempts to be not an exhaustive catalog— still less a determining checklist—of all the comparable themes in their works that one could possibly itemize but, rather, a heuristic device that juxtaposes the relevant language that illuminates each thinker's philosophical orientation.

Table 4

COMPARATIVE ABSTRACT

LONERGAN	VOEGELIN
Aristotelian/Thomistic	Platonic/Augustinian
the subject	the soul
transcendental dynamism	tension of existence
transcendental method	*zetema* within the *metaxy*
unrestricted desire to know	*zetesis*
truth apprehended in judgment	truth apprehended in vision
truth expressed in propositional statements	truth expressed in language symbols
objective knowledge found in true judgments aiming toward a higher viewpoint	objective knowledge found in the search for wisdom and the universal
experience as providing data for reflection and interpretation	experience as seamless complex of event, memory, interpretation, and existential attitude
center of orientation: converted or unconverted self	center of orientation: theophany or egophany
conversion: intellectual, moral, and religious	conversion: *periagoge* of Plato
intellectual conversion	noetic differentiation
religious conversion	pneumatic differentiation
authentic subjectivity is following transcendental precepts: be attentive, intelligent, reasonable, and responsible	order of the soul is maintaining the balance of consciousness in the *metaxy*
consciousness structured and illuminated by operational acts of knowing	consciousness constituted and illuminated by symbols of experience in history
consciousness as intentionality leading to the question of God	consciousness as luminosity based on transcendent experience
history of consciousness as movement from common sense/myth to theory/science	history of consciousness as movement from compact to differentiated experience

LONERGAN	VOEGELIN
intentional consciousness discovers the "luminous" data by attending to one's interiority	intentional consciousness is distinct from luminous consciousness
differentiation of consciousness as movement from common sense to theory to interiority to transcendence	differentiation of consciousness as movement from immanent/cosmological to transcendent/philosophical mode of existence
existential consciousness: fourth level of intentional consciousness consisting of decision, conscience, values; the lived context for transcendental consciousness	existential consciousness: reflective self-awareness of existence in the *metaxy*; contrasted with intentional consciousness which is oriented to external things
differentiation of consciousness culminates in realm of transcendence or "mediated immediacy" of the mystic	differentiation of consciousness culminates in realm of transcendence or noetic and pneumatic vision
common sense is prerational apprehension of things as they are "for us" not "in themselves"	common sense is a predifferentiated form of rationality consisting of sound judgment and good conduct
truth: judgments of meaning and value that yield doctrines whose meaning is permanent, though the formulation of meaning can alter in different historical contexts	truth: faithfulness of the soul to its experiences of being which can yield only penultimate articulation in symbols and myths
affirms value of propositional truth which undergoes ongoing development in different contexts	mistrusts propositional truth in favor of symbolic truth which is always ambiguous but seeks ever-greater adequacy
science replaces myth; theory supersedes common sense	myth is fullest expression of differentiated truth since it alone can adequately symbolize divine presence in reality
modern empirical science supersedes classical science	modern science obscures timeless principles of classical science which need to be recovered
reason: Thomistic *ratio* and *intellectus*, which are distinct from revelation	reason: Plato's *nous* founded in revelation
philosophy/theology based in transcendental method grounding a generalized empirical method	philosophy/theology based in generalized *fides quaerens intellectum*
philosophy and theology remain distinct; philosophy basically continues to play the role of theology's handmaiden	once theology abandons its traditional misconstructions it becomes indistinguishable from philosophy
theology mediates between a religion and the cultural matrix in which it is found	philosophy/theology does not recognize "religion" but transcendent reality wherever it is experienced and symbolized

LONERGAN	VOEGELIN
theological doctrines extract the true meaning of the Gospels through theoretical formulations	theology has generally deformed the symbolic truth of the Gospels which cannot be translated into doctrines
the "Athanasian victory" at Nicea fulfilled the original theophany expressed in the Gospels because it theoretically differentiated their commonsense symbolisms (*The Way to Nicea*)	the "Athanasian victory" derailed the original Christian theophany by bringing to an end the earlier "openness of the theophanic field" (*The Ecumenic Age*, p. 259) which led to its later dogmatic deformation
intellectual and spiritual disorder rooted in individual, group, and general "bias"	intellectual and spiritual disorder rooted in "closed existence" of ideology and dogmatomachy
cultural progress dependent on level of authentic subjectivity in society	order of society and history dependent on the right order of the soul and the level of reason operative in society
process of history aiming toward the transcendent paradigm of "cosmopolis" which critiques present living	process of reality in history has an eschatological direction whose paradigm is simply "beyond"
theoretically ecumenical but rooted in Roman Catholic tradition	globally ecumenical but rooted in normativity of Western symbols
attempts to enlarge the exclusivism of his tradition to incorporate the significant aspects of other traditions	rejects any exclusivism but upholds the authority of the historical "leaps in being" wherever they arise

6

THE THEOLOGICAL
IMPLICATIONS OF
VOEGELIN'S PHILOSOPHY
OF CONSCIOUSNESS

In the first four chapters we treated at considerable length the sweep of Voegelin's philosophy of consciousness as he developed it in numerous writings over the course of a lifetime. In the last chapter we offered an exposition of Bernard Lonergan's thought followed by a dialectical comparison with Voegelin's. It will now be our task to draw back and, with some reflective distance of our own, assess Voegelin's contribution and challenge to theology as a whole. This will be accomplished by spelling out Voegelin's implicit reconstruction of theology, particularly by addressing those areas of his work which treat various pertinent issues and doctrines in Christian theology. This final chapter concludes with a recapitulation of Voegelinian principles, suggesting in summary fashion the directions a "Voegelinian theology" would take.

Voegelin's Reconstruction of Christian Theology

What exactly are the theological implications of Voegelin's thought? Much has been suggested already but I now attempt to answer this question by paying special attention to Voegelin's controversial treatment of Christianity. Before we begin, it must be reasserted that Voegelin is not a Christian theologian. However, in certain places he subtly suggests that his work could be deemed a theological enterprise. This becomes apparent when we consider that Voegelin identifies two distinct meanings of theology: the classical and the Christian. In its classical roots, "theology" is the neologism of Plato who uses it to distinguish between the true and false stories of the gods. This usage is developed by Aristotle who regards theology as the compact form of philosophizing such as that associated with Hesiod's myths. Theology in the Christian sense is a much different enterprise. It becomes a problem because it is basically the same as philosophy except its purview is restricted to the *depositum fidei* and it takes for granted the dichotomy between reason and revelation, expropriating the latter for itself.[1] With this in mind Voegelin has stated that "there is no theology in the Christian sense which is not at the same time philosophy, also."[2] Thus, in his work we can surmise that Voegelin is actually attempting to marry theology to philosophy in a way that is beholden to philosophy's classical roots. In his view philosophy is not a handmaiden to anything; it is in itself a theological undertaking.

However one might adjudicate this claim, Voegelin's work has been from the start an indisputable attempt to construct a new Christian philosophy of history apposite the contemporary world, a philosophy which theologians ought to begin to take seriously. What makes his work so challenging to Christian theology is not only its broad scope, intellectual rigor, and outright persuasiveness, but also its independence from any Church authority. The authoritative weight it carries is principally due to the experiences it claims to be founded in. Like philosophy itself, its authority is intrinsically rooted in the truth it alone is beholden to. This posture of an independent philosopher who is free from external constraints, political and ecclesial, goes back at least as far as Socrates, the progenitor of the philosophical life whose love of truth and wisdom sealed his fate, thus giving to philosophy ever after a sense of sacrificial risk when it is practiced among its "cultured despisers." But Voegelin finds the claim to intrinsic authority rooted more in Plato's view that the philosopher, the *daimonios aner*, alone has knowledge of the *agathon*. In the Hellenistic context this meant that the authority in the polis that is the existential source of political and spiritual order must shift from external decrees, forms, laws, customs, institutions, etc., to the philosopher who alone is attuned to the divine measure.

We see in Voegelin a modern-day exemplar of this seizure of philosophical authority. We should not view this appropriation of authority as an arrogant attempt to usurp the traditional sources of authority, for Voegelin would only say that the truth he expounds is found, not in himself, but in the "religious" experiences that are potentially available to everyone. He is only bringing to attention the truth of experience that has been lost.[3] Thus, he is always wont to say that the test of authenticity for any philosophy is its unoriginality.[4] His work calls us back to the original experiences that are the formative forces of order in history and society.

Where, then, is to be found the locus of true authority in society and history that one must always turn to? This question is the concern of everyone, the simple believer as well as the philosopher. We see it arise in the early Voegelin who deplored the failure of the Christian Church to provide spiritual experiences and insights that would properly form the souls of the faithful and give their lives true meaning.[5] In large part this loss of spiritual substance was the result of the process of secularization that, since the beginning of the eighteenth century, arose in response to modern science, historical criticism, and the general suspicion of all things religious by people who wearied of interminable religious wars. The loss of spiritual substance that drove people to a general state of alienation was the fault of the Church which depended on its propositional doctrines based on reified symbols and spiritually empty formulas to bolster its dying authority. Voegelin's lament over this crisis of Christianity, written over forty years ago, was quite direct and contains a thinly veiled autobiographical reaction to the sad state of historical affairs that makes opaque the revelatory dimension of present reality:

> If we formulate the deepest sentiment that causes the spiritual tensions of the West since the Middle Ages somewhat drastically, we might say: that the bearers of Western civilization do not want to be a senseless appendix to the history of antiquity; they want to understand their civilizational existence as meaningful. If the Church is not able to see the hand of God in the history of mankind, men will not remain satisfied but will go out in search of gods who take some interest in their civilizational efforts. The Church has abandoned its spiritual leadership insofar as it has left postmedieval man without guidance in his endeavors to find meaning. . . . In the face of this abandonment of the *magisterium* it is futile when Christian thinkers accuse the *superbia* of modern man who will not submit to the authority of the Church. There is always enough *superbia* in man to bolster the accusation plausibly, but the complaint dodges the real issue: that man in search of authority cannot find it in the Church, through no fault of his own.[6]

The Church lost its authority because it failed to see the unfolding of the revelatory process of the divine ground in history. Voegelin believed that the spiritual privation that ensued was the bane of a Church that in a persecutional manner became more interested in dogmatic subtleties than the substance of faith.[7] Through the secularized disenchantment wrought by the modern world the immediate presence of God was gone from contemporary life. Since the late Middle Ages the Church responded to this crisis with only a doctrinal fossilization of opaque symbols that turned living movements of the soul into a dead abstraction.

As early as the 1940s Voegelin argued that this loss of spiritual substance was due in large measure to the destruction of the myth. When the symbols of Christianity met their rational, historical critique at the beginning of modernity, the integrity of Christian truth was doomed. At the heart of the matter was the fact that the symbolic language of Christianity, stemming from its Hebrew and Hellenistic origins, was mythical. The myth was the specific vehicle "for expressing the truth of transcendent reality, its incarnation and its operation in man."[8] In the early Christian centuries this language was not a myth in the modern pejorative sense. It was the precise way to designate religious reality. It only became a "myth" after Christianity was penetrated by the rationalism and the historicizing sciences of the last three centuries. It was the stunning critique of these intellectual movements that debunked the "first naivete" (to use Paul Ricoeur's term) of popular symbols and dogmas and left the teaching authority of the Church with less and less credence. Voegelin's whole endeavor to reconstruct a Christian philosophy of history is rooted in the very urgent need to recover through a "second naivete"[9] the original meaning of the ancient symbolisms, and thus to restore their authoritative status in a way that prevents their institutionalized perversion. This entails a reappraisal and recovery of the myth. The myth is the permanent guarantee for maintaining consciousness as luminosity. The loss of the myth has meant the loss of the consciousness of the It-reality. For Voegelin, the symbolic form of the myth can alone regenerate the transcending movement of the self toward mystery and the eternal, as well as restrain the immanentizing forces of modern gnosticism.

Voegelin always resisted those who attempted to employ his work for either political or ideological ends, or to buttress a particular theological agenda. But if his work does have a theological significance it would lie in this very attempt at symbolic reinvigoration and spiritual renewal. In Voegelin's language, the symbols dear to theology could come alive once again through "the process of experiential reactivation and linguistic renewal," but only if "precautions of meditative practice are taken" to thwart their doctrinalization. To understand this specific pertinence of his work we must first appreciate the particular problem he was induced to confront from the beginning. Long ago he spoke of what a solution to the contemporary crisis would require. The solution, he said,

> would have to be a new Christian philosophy of history and of mythical symbols that would make intelligible, firstly, the new dimension of meaning which has accrued to the historical existence of Christianity through the fact that the Church has survived two civilizations; and that would make

intelligible, secondly, the myth as an objective language for the expression of a transcendental irruption, more adequate and exact as an instrument of expression than any rational system of symbols, not to be misunderstood in a literalism which results from opacity nor reduced to an experiential level of psychology. Obviously it is a task that would require a new Thomas rather than a neo-Thomist.[10]

It will be up to future scholars to determine whether Voegelin's philosophy of history meets the billing he implicitly gave it in this passage. No one could doubt the magnitude of his efforts, for his painstaking labors have virtually amounted to a new synthesis of Athens and Jerusalem. Indeed, the source of the modern crisis is rooted in the historical failure to unite these two cities, for between them there was created a false dichotomy. His historical study of the Ecumenic Age, from which our inherited symbolisms originated, has led to a reintegration of reason and revelation which should stand the test of analytical penetration and adequate formulation for a long time to come.[11] If in this endeavor Voegelin has done for our time what Thomas had done for his, then maybe future generations will come to recognize in him the "new Thomas" that he himself called for.

In spite of all the accolade that scholars have given his work, it should not go unnoticed that Voegelin has had his critics too. Indeed, many of his own followers have become his worst adversaries. A common complaint that many of them have voiced against his work, strange as it may sound, is that he actually neglected to deal with Christianity, or more precisely, with Christian faith. With the appearance of *The Ecumenic Age* in 1974 and the revision of the initial program that it called for, many of Voegelin's own disciples were disappointed that he was not going to deal systematically with the Christian era of Western civilization.[12] To their dismay, the detailed appraisal of the patristic, medieval, and Protestant centuries, which he had originally planned for his later volumes, was abandoned. Even worse, where he did treat New Testament texts, they accused him of failing to take seriously the historicity and uniqueness of Jesus and of having a curious ambiguity toward "the Christian faith." To the displeasure of many of these critics, it became clear that Voegelin's work was not to be an apologetic for Christian orthodoxy. Instead, in its later materialization, it appeared to be a philosophical critique of traditional Christian thought.

Generally, the demeanor that Voegelin assumed against his critics was polite disregard.[13] He responded briefly on only one occasion to the general "complaint" levied against him.[14] Contrary to the popular judgment, he had already handled at some length the Christian sources as they are to be found in the New Testament texts which represent maximal differentiation. But the primary reason for his not giving a more concerted treatment of subsequent Christian thought than he did was not just because, as he suggested, the relevant historical materials were too voluminous for one man to subject to noetic analysis; one suspects it was more because he believed they essentially obfuscated the essential Gospel symbolism under a cloud of secondary symbols. The cardinal insights of the Gospel texts were either deformed or replaced by hypostatic dogma or gnostic speculation, and thus he probably believed that later Christian thought did not warrant the kind of analysis that people expected from him.[15]

To illustrate this point, Voegelin's theory of consciousness allows him to avoid the deforming confusion wrought by Christian thinkers who draw a distinction between "ontological statements" (which purportedly describe the real truth of things) and "symbolic statements" (which are allegedly "only" evocative and rhetorical). But Voegelin would have none of this. Instead he would say that the truth of Christianity is eminently symbolic and not "ontological," a conclusion made not to destroy Christianity but to free it from a literalist deformation, for in the end one cannot separate "revealed truth" from symbol and myth. Transcendence can only be articulated in an analogical language replete with inevitable ambiguity. Such is the nature of human knowing in the realm of transcendence. Within the orbit of faith one cannot move from *mythos* to *logos* pure and simple, for reason itself cannot provide the ground for affirming transcendent reality. For example, to say "Jesus is the Son of God" is a symbolic, analogical statement whose truth is apprehended in faith; it is not an ontological statement of rational discourse (which often is based in an extrinsic objectivism that, as Lonergan puts it, is so objective as to get along without minds). This view of knowledge and language follows Thomas' *analogia entis*, a principle of theologizing which Voegelin adopts. Ultimately one cannot escape the form of symbol and myth in theology; certitude is simply not available.[16] Faith must tell its story in the penultimate language of inescapably ambiguous symbols seeking ever-greater adequacy. There must be respect for the limits of human thought and language. Besides, what is foundational in Christianity is not knowledge but love. Creedal statements about the Christ are really a "love language" to denote the significant meaning of the content of Christian faith for the believer, calling one to a life of conversion. In the fundamental sense Christian faith is the orientation of the soul to transcendent mystery by way of unrestricted love as this mystery and this love is mediated by Christ, albeit a love that must be guided by knowledge (*noesis* not *gnosis*) if it is not to become a destructive force.

The problem with Voegelin's method of experiential exegesis lies in getting behind the symbols that authors use to describe their experience to the experiences themselves, for truth is discovered in experience. In Voegelin's view, since experience and its interpretation are inseparable, there is no other access to others' experiences save through their expression in language. For example, what would it mean to say (as Voegelin's orthodox critics would claim) that Paul and the early disciples *experienced* Jesus as God's only-begotten Son? Is this an accurate way of speaking of the revelatory dimension in their experience? For Voegelin such a statement is clearly the borrowing of a prior symbol to express the disciples' experience of the Christ. What is revealed in experience is not a doctrine or even a symbol but a mystery that yields symbols, some of which may be inadequate to the truth of the experience. How does one get to the truth of another's experience behind the symbols they leave behind when they are attempting to convey the meaning of a theophanic event? Is this possible?

This is a difficult problem, particularly in Christology that today attempts to wed critically the Christ of faith with the Jesus of history, as the Gospels themselves clearly attempted to do. I believe this fundamental problem can only be assuaged by remembering Voegelin's theory of consciousness, *metaxy*, tensions, pushes and pulls. It is Voegelin's foundational principle that revelation occurs not in the external world of things but in the in-between of divine–human *metalepsis*. The critical focus has to remain on the metaleptic consciousness of divine presence that can be discerned in the original experiences and symbols of theophanic events—Voegelin's first hermeneutical principle being that symbols must not be torn from their engendering experiences. Their meaning is moored to their source of emergence: the persons who experienced, interpreted, and understood the transcendent reality they objectified through their symbolic imagination. This is why, instead of focusing on the historical Jesus, Voegelin concerns himself with the *kerygmata* of a Paul, a John, or a Matthew as providing the privileged, indeed the only, access to Christ. The only "historical Jesus" we can know is the one known by the New Testament authors. The event of the *theotes* coming into revelatory luminosity in Jesus and his disciples is the significant reality behind the symbolic language that expresses the event. There would be no Christ without those who pronounced the Christ and recognized the Christ in Jesus. This event of recognition and the symbolic articulation of it cannot be separated.

This leads us to understand just what Voegelin means when he says "the fact of revelation is its content."[17] He is suggesting that revelation has no information to tender.[18] It is not a miraculous event in the external world; in fact nothing changes externally. The content of revelation cannot be separated from its personal facticity, i.e., the event of its occurrence and interpretation in the soul of the recipient.[19] The "subject" and "object" of a revelatory vision cannot be divided. To treat the content as an object of propositional knowledge would be to abuse the experience of the vision as it arises in the *metaxy*. The only way to get at the "content" of the revelation is through its symbolic expression which ideally would bring one back into the mystery of the divine/human participatory event.

In this regard, meaning and being are not the same and Voegelin does not confuse them. Like Lonergan he is adamant in showing, nonetheless, that being is mediated by meaning. There is no other way to "capture" or "point to" being but through meaning. In other words, revelation is an experience and the only way to get at another's experience is through his or her own mediating language; secondary interpretive symbolisms are more often a hindrance than a help. What is important is the mystery or the Question that underpins the original text.[20]

Revelation is constituted in the in-between structure of reality, a fact that was lost when the symbolically recorded experiences were ossified into a scripture containing a reified word of God. In Greece a similar deformation took place when Stoic philosophy transformed the symbolic exegesis of experience into terms of propositional metaphysics. In later Christian history these tendencies were compounded by the dogmatization that Voegelin so vociferously attacks. When the truth of experience is turned into orthodox doctrine a state of deculturation is the inevitable result. On this point Voegelin eloquently cuts to the heart of the matter:

> It is the guilt of Christian thinkers and Church leaders of having allowed the dogma to separate in the public consciousness of Western civilization from the experience of "the mystery" on which its truth depends. The dogma develops as a socially and culturally necessary protection of insights experientially gained against false propositions; its development is secondary to the truth of experience. If its truth is pretended to be autonomous, its validity will come under attack in any situation of social crisis, when alienation becomes a mass phenomenon; the dogma will then be misunderstood as an "opinion" which one can believe or not, and it will be opposed by counteropinions which dogmatize the experience of alienated existence. The development of a nominalist and fideist conception of Christianity is the cultural disaster, with its origins in the late Middle Ages, that provokes the reaction of alienated existence in the dogmatic form of the ideologies, in the eighteenth and nineteenth centuries. . . . Once truth has degenerated to the level of true doctrine, the return from orthodoxy to "the mystery"

is a process that appears to require as many centuries of effort as have gone into the destruction of intellectual and spiritual culture.[21]

This passage further highlights the principal aim of Voegelin's scholarly output, an aim which remained consistent from his early writings to his mature work. The essential aim behind Voegelin's "reconstructive theology" is simply this: to recover the experience of the "mystery" from underneath the centuries-long process of dogmatizing obfuscation, and to regain its truth for all human beings. A philosophy true to this aim cannot primarily concern itself with later dogmas no matter how well they may seem to explicate or capture the true meaning of the original texts. Under Voegelin's theoretical principles, as he originally formulated them and which grounded his entire study, it should be no surprise that he would view later doctrinal formulations, which originally functioned to preserve the experiential insights, as inevitably lessening, by way of further redactorial objectification, their spiritual essence. A proper analysis of revelatory truth has to penetrate to its experiential core that its interpretative and protective vessels tend to obscure, if not eclipse altogether. In other words it is God (not doctrine, not ideas, not cognitive judgments) that is revealed in history. Accordingly, in Christian thought, debates over conciliar formulations in the development of christological and trinitarian theology, perhaps interesting in themselves, could not essentially offer critical material for a philosophy of history and a philosophy of order.[22] Like the Stoic derailment of classical philosophy, or the reified transformation of the divine word to Scripture in Israel, the diminution of the fullness of experience occurred also in Christian theology in its shift from mythic to ontological language, especially in medieval and postmedieval thought.

It now remains to be seen how Voegelin's hermeneutical principles and theological method apply to the question of Christ and Christology.

THE MEANING OF CHRIST

What specifically is Voegelin's understanding of the meaning and significance of Christ, particularly in relation to theological orthodoxy? First of all, Voegelin's view of the transcendent breakthrough in history that is Christianity seems essentially rooted in a reappraisal of the original spiritual insights symbolized in the biblical texts. However, he believes these very insights have been lost in the consciousness of contemporary Christians under the weight of hypostatized doctrine, lack of spiritual acumen, and demythologization. The problem is not isolated to contemporaries, for the process of deformation is ancient in origin. Indeed,

I would venture to say that Voegelin viewed orthodox Christology as a prototype of the obfuscation of theophanic experience in history. To the degree that Christian theology *identified* the transfiguring incarnation of divine reality in history with the man Jesus (in whom no doubt Voegelin would say divine presence was fully manifest), it began to hypostatize divine transcendence by objectifying the total process of transfiguring incarnation in the cosmos into the object of a subjectivized consciousness—the object being the man Jesus.[23] In other words, to put it simply, the names "Christ" and "Jesus" cannot become interchangeable without massive distortion of the structure of reality. The fact that they have been so identified through a process of doctrinalization and imprudent Christian piety obfuscates the paradoxical "identity in difference" of incarnate divine presence.

How does Voegelin approach this preeminent christological problem? How did he view the essential mystery of incarnation? How did he see Christ in relation to all the other differentiating events of world history? An answer can be found in a number of later essays where Voegelin attempted to regain the living immediacy and experiential truth of the word by engaging in a concerted meditative exegesis of the Gospel.

In his 1971 essay, "The Gospel and Culture," alone among his published writings singularly devoted to an analysis of the Gospel,[24] Voegelin declared that at the center of the Gospel movement is "the revelation of the Unknown God through Christ, in conscious continuity with the millennial process of revelation."[25] This is the Gospel itself: "neither a poet's work of dramatic art, nor an historian's biography of Jesus, but the symbolization of a divine movement that went through the person of Jesus into society and history."[26] Voegelin reminds us that the revelatory drama of the Gospel movement is situated in the larger context of the revelatory drama of Israelite history which in turn partakes in the same word of the Unknown God as does the revelatory drama of philosophy: "The Logos of the gospel is rather the same Word of the same God as the *logos spermatikos* of philosophy, but at a later state of its manifestation in history."[27] They are two parallel stories that contribute eminently to the ever-unfolding comprehensive story of the It-reality, the universal presence of the divine beyond in time. Consequently, we must not dichotomize philosophy and Gospel, or Athens and Jerusalem, but, based on Voegelin's theory of equivalence and differentiation, interpret their respective dramas as unique revelations of the same divine reality in different cultural contexts.[28] The word that emerges in each context belongs to the same human–divine *metaxy*. While each story illuminates more completely one fundamental dimension of the truth over the other, they both eminently participate in the larger untold story of history. Athens and Jerusalem, philosophy and Gospel, while culturally and historically distinct, both join side by side as tensional partners in the transcendent City of God.

The crucial problem in the Christian tradition is that the Unknown God, the tetragrammatic God beyond the gods, the God beyond all images of God, has been eclipsed by centuries of theological incrustations upon the Gospel. From the beginning the word became hardened in the defensive process of scriptural canonization and theological doctrinization.[29] Voegelin's diagnosis of this predicament is comprehensive and scattered throughout his later writings, but a couple passages suffice to convey his meaning:

> In the historical drama of revelation, the Unknown God ultimately becomes the god known through his presence in Christ. This drama, though it has been alive in the consciousness of New Testament writers, is far from alive in the Christianity of the churches today, for the history of Christianity is characterized by what is commonly called the separation of school theology from mystical or experiential theology which formed an apparently inseparable unit still in the work of Origen. The Unknown God whose *theotes* was present in the existence of Jesus has been eclipsed by the revealed God of Christian doctrine. Even today, however, when this unfortunate separation is recognized as one of the great causes of the modern spiritual crisis; when energetic attempts are made to cope with the problem through a variety of crisis and existential theologies; and when there is no lack of historical information about either the revelatory process leading up to the epiphany of Christ, or about the loss of experiential reality through doctrinization; the philosophical analysis of the various issues lags far behind our preanalytical awareness. It will be necessary, therefore, to reflect on the danger that has given the Unknown God a bad name in Christianity and induced certain doctrinal developments as a protective measure, *i.e.*, on the danger of the gospel movement derailing into gnosticism.[30]

Continuing his analysis, Voegelin claims we are still living in a time of Gospel deformation:

> At a time when the reality of the gospel threatens to fall apart into the constructions of an historical Jesus and a doctrinal Christ, one cannot stress strongly enough the status of a gospel as a symbolism engendered in the *metaxy* of existence by a disciple's response to the drama of the Son of God. The drama of the Unknown God who reveals his kingdom through his presence in a man, and of the man who reveals what has been delivered to him by delivering it to his fellowmen, is continued by the existentially responsive disciple in the gospel drama by which he carries on the work

of delivering these things from God to man. The gospel itself is an event in the drama of revelation. The historical drama in the *metaxy*, then, is a unit through the common presence of the Unknown God in the men who respond to his "drawing" and to one another. Through God and men as the dramatis personae, it is true, the presence of the drama partakes of both human time and divine timelessness, but tearing the drama of participation asunder into the biography of a Jesus in the spatiotemporal world and eternal verities showered from beyond would make nonsense of the existential reality that was experienced and symbolized as the drama of the Son of God.[31]

The traditional christological doctrines of creation, incarnation, resurrection, transfiguration, and redemption figure strongly in Voegelin's writings on the New Testament texts though not in the orthodox, doctrinaire way. We focus here only on Voegelin's handling of incarnation and resurrection.

Based on his theory of consciousness as a tension of poles and their expression through symbols, Voegelin's exegetic labors strongly indicate that the essential meaning of Christ must be interpreted as neither a humanized God nor a divinized man but the historic fulfillment of life in the *metaxy* in one man's existence which is salvifically representative of all humankind.[32] In other words, Christ exists in the *metaxy* as much as any human being, and thus is neither a god become human nor a human become god but the full embodiment of the divine *parousia* in one human person manifested in his life, death, and resurrection. For Voegelin the intelligibility of incarnation has less to do with a preexistent divine person that became flesh (the view of the incarnation as an exclusive and extrinsic divine incursion in one moment of history) than the emergence of divine presence in human consciousness, which is a historical process, not a one-time event. Thus, in regard to human existence, creation and incarnation should be seen as two facets of the same historical process. Christ's incarnation must be seen in light of divine incarnation elsewhere. Incarnation is essentially the spiritual fulfillment of the created order of the human being who is created in God's image. Thus, the epiphany of the Christ must be located in a history of revelation bounded by the metaxic structure of human existence. Voegelin's rendering of this insight concerning incarnation is captured in the following passages:

> The mystery of divine presence in existence had grown in the consciousness of the Movement long before the drama of the Gospel started; and the symbols which the evangelist uses for its expression—the son of God, the Messiah, the Son of man, the kingdom of God—were historically at hand

through the Egyptian Pharaonic, the Davidic royal, the prophetic and apocalyptic symbolisms, through Iranian traditions and the Hellenistic mysteries.
Hence, the "secret" of the Gospel is neither the mystery of divine presence
in existence, nor its articulation through new symbols, but the event of its
full comprehension and enactment through the life and death of Jesus. The
apparent contradictions dissolve into the use of the same symbols at various
levels of comprehension, as well as at the different stages of enactment, until
the Christ is revealed, not in a fullness of doctrine, but in the fullness of
Passion and resurrection.[33]

The symbolism of incarnation would express the experience, with a date in
history, of God reaching into man and revealing him as the Presence that
is the flow of presence from the beginning of the world to its end. History
is Christ written large.[34]

The incarnation neither overcomes the mystery of history nor completes
the process of revelation; rather, the historical Christ supremely reveals
the eternal divine in a never-ending continuum of revelation in history.
Elsewhere Voegelin expands on the meaning of this historic presence
in Christ:

In the epiphany of Christ, the formation of humanity in history has become
transparent for its meaning as the process of transformation. In Jesus, the
participation of his humanity in the divine word has reached the intensity
of his absorption into the word. The ambiguous personal pronoun [the
"I" of Jesus] in the Gospel expresses this transfiguring absorption as it was
experienced by the men who had seen the Christ.[35]

This of course is not to suggest that Voegelin wishes to disengage
a "historical Jesus" from a "dogmatic Christ," or vice versa. Such a
ploy would only reduce Jesus to a disincarnate symbol and destroy the
metaleptic consciousness of those disciples who experienced the Christ
in him.[36] As a number of his texts show, Voegelin takes very seriously
the historicity of Jesus as the principal locus of divine incarnation. In
addition to the previous quotation there are other remarks of Voegelin
that affirm this, such as his statement in *Israel and Revelation* that, "with
the appearance of Jesus, God himself entered into the eternal present of
history."[37] But after saying this, he immediately adds that this statement
must be understood in light of the stipulation that

the mystery of the Incarnation itself, of the consubstantiality of God and
man, is impenetrable. And its consequences for the substantive order of
history are not fully realized as long as history lasts. . . . the meaning of
history under the Christian dispensation is as far from satisfactory positive
expression today as it was at the time of Jesus and his generation.[38]

Still, Voegelin has elsewhere expressed more favorably the orthodox formulations, such as his references to Chalcedon that were mentioned at the end of chapter 4.[39] It would be safe for us to conclude, however, that Voegelin believes that the incarnation in Jesus, to borrow White-head's phrasing, is not the grand "metaphysical exception" in history, but the "chief exemplification" of divine incarnate presence in history.

What Christ represents for Voegelin, then, is the acme of the developing Judaic insight that the illumination of pneumatic consciousness which results from the personal encounter between God and the prophet stems from the universal presence of divine reality in every human being, the transcendent reality that illuminates itself in the consciousness of every soul as that soul's ground of existence. Christ, then, is the fullness of the mystery of God in reality representative for all people everywhere, not just for contemporaneous Jews or later-day Christians. Christ is the full incarnate presence of the Unknown God made known to those who respond to the same presence in their own souls, for "the divine Sonship is not revealed through an information tendered by Jesus, but through a man's response to the full presence in Jesus of the same Unknown God by whose presence he is inchoatively moved in his own existence."[40]

In his exegesis of the mystery of this revelation Voegelin, as we have seen, is fond of quoting Colossians 2:9 where Paul says "for in him the whole fullness (*pan to pleroma*) of divine reality (*theotes*) dwells bodily."[41] By responding to the maximal fullness of God's presence in Christ (who images the unseen God most fully) through faith, all can achieve the fullness of their own existence.

Further problems remain with the notion of incarnation as it applies to Jesus. A major difficulty has to do with the lack of clear differentiation in the biblical sources between the God of the beginning and the God of the beyond, between the creator God who creates the cosmos and the savior God who saves humans from its disorder. In Israelite history the accent of the divine–human encounter, Voegelin argues, fell so heavily on the irruption of divine presence that little emotional room was left for the noetic search for the truth of the created order of the cosmos.[42] In the Jewish milieu of first-century Palestine when the Hebrew metaleptic encounter reached its peak in Jesus, this particular word from the beyond became so enthusiastically all-encompassing that it further served to prevent the full differentiation of these two modes of experiencing divine reality in the Christian tradition. This is reflected in the high Christology of John's prologue where the two modes are merged. "Even in the gospel of John," Voegelin explains, "the word that is present in Christ has to be the word of the Beginning that now has become flesh, causing the later difficulties of theological construction that could only partially be overcome by the introduction of philosophy and the development of mysticism."[43] Consequently, the problem of classical Christology for Voegelin is rooted in the doctrinalizing of a suspect symbolism, i.e., the meaning of the word in John's prologue which was formulated under "gnostic influences." For Voegelin it is this contraction of the God of the beyond with the God of the beginning that underlies the hypostasis of the preexistent *logos* in classical Christology.[44]

The noetic search for the divine ground that is the hallmark of philosophy is able to maintain the tension between the two modes without mutual absorption because it maintains the necessary reflective distance in an exegesis of the experience. In other words, "the accent of the experience of transfiguring immortalization falls on the search, not on the assurance of transfiguration through the overwhelming divine presence, as it does in the Israelite-Judaic case."[45] In regard to Jesus, Voegelin surmises, the enthusiasm of Paul and the author of John's Gospel were so swept away by the epiphany of the Unknown savior God of the beyond in Christ that Christ in his bodily existence was identified with God's word for all time, a word that was with the creator God in the beginning only to become flesh in this particular historical moment. This identification led to the later problems and ambiguities of theological debate that have never been clearly analyzed.

Not until Voegelin perhaps. In regard to the early development of the Christian doctrine of incarnation Voegelin saw the "Athanasian victory" at Nicea as derailing the original Christian theophany because it brought to an end the earlier "openness of the theophanic field" and transformed it into dogmatic constructions.[46] On the other hand, the abstract formulas of Nicea and Chalcedon can be interpreted as an attempt by the Fathers to maintain the human–divine tension without saying too much, that is, to understand the Christian *fides* concerning the reality of Christ in a heuristically conceptual way that would move beyond the symbolic Gospel texts in order to "define" their underlying meaning and thereby clarify "the faith."[47] But Voegelin's view was that the way the spiritual insights got codified in the formulas and later dogmatized in a hypostatizing fashion virtually killed the mystery of the human–divine union achieved in Christ, an undefinable mystery that is analytically impenetrable, and thus insusceptible to categorization or conceptualization. The high Christology of John's prologue, where Christ is identified with the word that in turn is identified with the God of the beginning, was a principal source used in the christological debates in such a way as to eclipse the *metaxy* of Jesus' own participation in existence before God, a development that rendered divine incarnation not just fully manifest in Jesus but exclusively so.

The fact that in traditional Christian piety Jesus himself is identified with God (a development authorized by some later, enthusiastic but flawed Church theologizing that overlooked the explicit and implicit nuances of Nicea and Chalcedon, not to mention the Gospel sources themselves), shows how doctrinalization can derail the original spiritual insights that emerged from the engendering experiences symbolized in the scriptural texts.[48] The thrust of Voegelin's viewpoint on this issue becomes clearer in the following passage:

> Because the issues of this type were insufficiently clarified in the gospel movement, the derailment into gnosticism became possible. The strength of the gospel is its concentration on the one point that is all-important: that the truth of reality has its center not in the cosmos at large, not in nature or society or imperial rulership, but in the presence of the Unknown God in a man's existence to his death and life. This very strength, however, can cause a breakdown, if the emphasis on the center of truth becomes so intense that its relations to the reality of which it is the center are neglected or interrupted. Unless the Unknown God is the undifferentiated divine presence in the background of the specific intracosmic gods, he is indeed a god unknown to the primary experience of the cosmos. In that case, however, there is no process of revelation in history, nor a millennial Movement culminating in the epiphany of the Son of God, but only the irruption of an extracosmic god in a cosmos to whose mankind he hitherto had been hidden.[49]

I take these words, along with other passages, to indicate that Voegelin rejects the orthodox interpretation of Christ as the eternally preexistent Son of God incarnated only in Jesus, but rather seeks an understanding of the Christ that transcends the historical existence of Jesus of Nazareth. It is a view that does justice to the Gospel texts themselves, claims Voegelin, "for it is the Christ of the Gospel of John who says of himself: 'Before Abraham was, I am' (8:58)."[50] Here Voegelin is attempting to expand the Christian *fides* to include every *fides*: "In practice this means that one has to recognize, and make intelligible, the presence of Christ in a Babylonian hymn, or a Taoist speculation, or a Platonic dialogue, just as much as in a Gospel."[51] The thrust of his position appears to be plain and simple: the Spirit of God is universal and can incarnate itself in diverse modes throughout history and society.

Consequently, Christ is not discontinuous with God's presence in other souls, but neither is he just the same, as kind of a deep but general consciousness of God in all people. Voegelin indicates that there is a uniqueness to Jesus the Christ, in the sense not of isolated and singular but of special and unparalleled. The question to ask Voegelin is In what sense is God's incarnation in Jesus unique, or normative for understanding all others? Some answer is found in his 1953 letters to Alfred Schutz. There he said one could only answer this question by referring back to the time of Jesus and his impact on others, a necessary maneuver in order to avoid later doctrinal symbolisms. On that occasion he said that Jesus' uniqueness lies in his social status as an incarnated god, and not just any god, but the God that excludes all other gods; and, there is the universality of his mediating function.[52] Jesus is representative of all humans, not just Jews or Christians. In discussing the Trinity he goes further in suggesting that the Son represents "the divine transforming intervention reaching into 'nature,' the superimposition of a *forma supernaturalis* in human nature upon the Aristotelian *forma naturalis*."[53] And more suggestively he says in regard to the mariological dogmas: "Just as Christ marks the end of the gods, Mary marks the end of superhuman vessels of the divine. In both instances the symbolism restores the balance between man's splendor and possibilities and his limitations."[54] These insights are never refuted in his later work; in fact, some are developed more thoroughly.

In later writings Voegelin speaks about Christ in the language of "maximal differentiation," "greatest intensity," and "pleromatic presence." More than this he is reticent. He does not say that such an incarnation could happen only once in history, but he certainly wants to avoid the new Christs of spiritual or ideological deformation (those who spit on their hands and become coredeemers of humankind) of which there are not a few in the modern era. For this reason it is easy to imagine Voegelin approving of the doctrine of the absolute uniqueness of Christ as a protective measure against the folly of self-deification (Hitler is the worse example) for which the churches play a needed role in society.

But did Voegelin himself believe in Christ's unsurpassability? Clearly he wants to avoid the gnostic derailment, on the one hand, as well as Jesus idolatry, on the other. But there is indication in his writings that he believes Jesus represents the fullest personalization of divine presence in history. He would certainly accept the view of Christ as the fullest actualization of humanity, the one person who fully responded to the intrinsic grace of the Holy Spirit given to all. So it is apparent that Voegelin's view is based on the notion of Jesus' union with God as unique in degree but not in kind. Nevertheless, his ambiguity on this matter is provocative, and I believe intentional.

Transfiguring incarnation is as old as the cosmos; it is a process that constitutes the meaning of history before and after Christ. God becomes flesh wherever God's *logos* is embodied in human hearts and minds, but supremely so in Greek philosophers, Hellenic poets, Christian mystics,

Israelite prophets, and maximally in the prophet Jesus. Then is Voegelin an "adoptionist"? Though we should not glibly label Voegelin's views on incarnation or any other theological theme with any dogmatic slogan, his affinities to the thrust of this traditionally heterodox theory is striking and warrants a discerning consideration of its "forgotten" truth. Voegelin's apparent echoes of Arius should not easily be dispelled or glossed over.

Having clarified Voegelin's "position" on incarnation how are we now to understand resurrection? For Christians, Christ's resurrection stands as some kind of proof or definitive signification of his divinity and universal salvific power. But given his analysis of the metaleptic and metaxic structure of existence, Voegelin's understanding of resurrection, a symbol that emerged solely in the framework of ancient Judaic con-sciousness, must coincide with the equivalent symbol, immortalization, that emerged in the context of ancient Greek authors, for they refer to roughly the same equivalent experience in the universal drama of human participation in the It-reality: the eternal perfection of human existence through grace in death. What is fundamentally true of resurrection, which arose from a pneumatic vision of the Christ after his death, is true of immortality, which slowly emerged from the noetic vision of the beyond by the Greek philosophers culminating in Plato's vision: the human quest for God is met by the divine love for humans, culminating in the loving union of the human and the divine that holds the promise of "eternal life."

The difference between these symbols would depend on where they place the accent in the tension of existence, immortality emphasizing the human quest for transfiguring perfection in the beyond, and resurrection emphasizing the divine gift of eternal life through the saving love of God. If Voegelin's theory of equivalences of experience and structures in reality is true then we would have to conclude that what is true about resurrection can be said, *mutatis mutandis*, about immortality and vice versa, that is, that "immortality is experienced by mortals; what has been born in time will die in time; its immortality is gained from its participation in the story of the It-reality."[55] Thus, both symbols emerg-ing out of different cultural contexts are attempts to render adequately the experience of participation in the It-reality, a participation that has an eschatological direction beyond space and time, a participation that is sought by every soul but preeminently fulfilled in Christ. Like every human being Christ is born in time and dies in time (is mortal) but gains immortality (resurrection) through full participation in the story of the It-reality (God's saving love). The Christian vision, then, is essentially the story of divine love revealing itself in history as the creative-saving force in the cosmos. Jesus' pneumatic participation in this divine love, his embodiment of this saving force, is so intense and so complete as to incarnate this very love itself. By the maximal presence of God in him and the visionary experience of his followers he has become known as the resurrected. Nevertheless, Jesus' resurrection is not to be construed as exclusive to his existence alone, as the culminating final event peculiar to him, but rather resurrection is the ultimate fulfillment for all who partake in the immortalizing process of transfiguration. This is the heart of the message of the saving tale that is the Gospel. Jesus is the "first fruits," the one who shows the way to resurrected life. This is why he becomes the focus of the *fides* of his followers.

Contrariwise, Plato's noetic participation in this same divine love is not focused on himself or any immortalizing individual (though Socrates must have surely served as a charismatic model of immortalization for him); the focus of his *fides* remains the cosmos, the totality of all created things in tension with their creator. The *fides* of every believing soul is grounded in the hope of eternal perfection. Albeit conditioned by the particularity of historical existence, such hope can be symbolized in quite disparate fashion. The transfiguring reality experienced by such hope is nevertheless the same.

What further distinguishes the Christian story of the It-reality from the Greek story is the shift of focus from creation to salvation. This for Voegelin is attested to in the Platonic symbol *monogenes*, a symbol that attempts to render adequately Plato's experience of the created cosmos in its oneness, oneness not in the numerical sense but in the sense of the intelligible whole of the comprehensive totality of all things. It is a symbol that also arises in the Gospel of John in reference to the Christ as the "only-begotten" Son of God. On this symbol Voegelin asserts that "the wandering of the symbol *monogenes* from the Cosmos to the Christ reveals the movement of experiential emphasis from the God who creates the order of the Cosmos to the God who saves from its disorder."[56] For Plato the *monogenes* of the Unknown God is not a human being but the cosmos itself. The breakthrough to the complete personalization of the divine *parousia* has not yet occurred in Plato, or as Voegelin puts it, "the decisive step of making the experience of man's tension toward the Unknown God the truth to which all truth of reality must conform was never taken."[57] However, Plato's struggle with language in appropriately imaging this divine presence in his soul seems to indicate a movement in that direction within the noetic plane.[58] Yet it is this noetic control of meaning that Voegelin believes gives Plato the upper hand in philosophical-theological reflection on transcendent experiences. For although Plato could not foresee the movements of language in adequately rendering theophanic experiences beyond his death and beyond his own culture, he was quite conscious of the linguistic problems. Accordingly, says Voegelin, "on some points his formulations are analytically more successful than the later attempts of the Christian theologians to find the *intellectus* of their *fides*."[59]

The great spiritual and intellectual minds of every religious tradition, whether Jewish, Christian, or Islamic, follow Plato in returning to the mystical tetragrammatic God beyond all imaging. For Christians we must conclude that this includes the seemingly perfect image of the Christ, the Christ not only of doctrinal theology but the Christ of devotion and prayer as well.[60] True to his vocation as a philosophical skeptic, Voegelin, echoing Plato, is keen in reminding us that all symbols of divinity, including even that of Christ, must move "into a reflective distance in which the awe inspired by the mystery of divine revelation blends with a skeptical detachment aroused by its all-too-human symbolization."[61]

Every image of God, even our most sacred, remains ultimately penultimate. The quest for truth will never put an end to the quest. Thus the story of the mysterious It-reality, of the revelatory drama of God's creative and saving love, will continuously unfold throughout human history. The question of what images truly symbolize the truly divine is the preeminent question that animates meditative reflection throughout the course of history. It is the question that every *fides* seeking its own *intellectum* must always confront. In every age, including our own, this is the critical problem that, not just theologians and philosophers, and certainly not just Christians, but every searcher for God must face.

Voegelin views the meaning of Christ as that event which reveals the depth of God's presence in our *metaxy*, but this does not by any account reduce the divine to an immanent object, the historical person of Jesus, to be fully comprehended by our consciousness. To the degree that we *objectify* God's presence in Jesus by *identifying* Jesus with God, we lose sight of the transcendent mystery that the man Jesus reveals, indeed the one to whom Jesus himself prayed as Father of us all. Even in the event of pleromatic incarnation, the tension of existence must not be extinguished.[62] In other words, Jesus lived in the *metaxy* as inescapably as the rest of us. His death was as much a passage through a dark door as it must be for every human being. The Gospel texts make clear that Jesus faced his ultimate destiny between the same poles of birth and death, faith and despair, love and loneliness, hope and abandonment, grace and sin, comfort and pain, and through the same immortalizing struggle in this mortal life where we all live and work out our earthly salvation. Because his particular life, suffering, and death revealed the saving love of God so fully and so powerfully his followers reflectively attributed to him the title of savior, of God's incarnate word, of the first fruits of the resurrection, of the one who redeems because he was mysteriously transfigured by the saving love that transfigures all of us for responding completely to that love. It is this divine love, then, that is the source of all human love, the love by which we participate most fully in the eschatological movement of reality in history. It is the transfiguring movement most fully revealed by the pleromatic love of Christ.

Principles of a "Voegelinian Theology"

Working out the implications of Voegelin's thought for Christian theology will require the concerted efforts of numerous theologians for many years to come. It will no doubt entail the thoughtful reconsideration of many of the truth-claims of orthodox Christianity. For many this will appear to be a perilous journey. But the theologically faint-hearted need not worry; if theologians are as committed to the truth and the voice of reason as Voegelin has been, then the philosophical exploration of Christianity that he has embarked on cannot be a destructive enterprise. Indeed, the distinct value of Voegelin's thought is that the framework of inquiry that he has worked out seems to solve many of the traditional dilemmas of theology that the prevailing frameworks make inevitable. The liberating challenge he has set down now needs to be seriously considered and prudently implemented by the theological community. In hope of advancing this task I now offer an inventory of the fundamental principles upon which a "Voegelinian theology" would be founded:[63]

Perhaps the most fundamental principle Voegelin offers theology is his insistence on consciousness as the foundational starting point. It is by our consciousness that we are able to participate in and know reality. To understand the structure and dynamics of our consciousness would serve as a foundation for any theological reflection. For Voegelin, consciousness is the in-between reality of participatory experience. The order of human existence in history and society originates in the order of human consciousness.

Any serious inquiry into reality must be rooted in human experience. This chief canon of contemporary thought should always guide theologians in their foundations and methodology. If theology's foundations are not congruent with, nor grounded in, living human experience then they would be wholly inadequate. Less emphasis would be given to ideas and concepts than to the existential reality of personal experience which grounds all symbolizations of reality. In this regard, Voegelin's method is widely empirical in the best sense. His is an empiricism in the original Greek version of it, not the positivist mode of objectivist perception that is available naively to everyone, but the classical mode of personal appeal, of direct persuasion of those whose inner experience conforms to the symbols, images, and analogies left behind by a seeker of truth, to the virtuous who have been graced by the same experiences illuminated by these symbols and whose souls are ordered by the same reality they point to. This was the method employed by Socrates' dialectical conversations. It has every right to be called science.

With Voegelin's fundamental principle that the full range of experience is present at all times, it is possible to discern the recurring, invariant features of human experience wherever, whenever, and however it is symbolized. That we are finite creatures who long for what lies beyond the finite is the universal fact of our experience. This is the ineradicable tension of human existence that structures all our limited knowing. That the range of experience varies from compactness to differentiation is the other Voegelinian principle that allows a theologian to compare various theophanic experiences on a level of equivalence. Consequently, comparative analyses of religious symbols across a range of cultures and ages become eminently possible. Not only theology but also the comparative study of religion is given a major philosophical grounding in Voegelin's path-breaking work.

The global diversity of revelation can be identified as having two fundamental differentiations: noetic and pneumatic. The balance between these two modes of experience would reject a pneumatism divorced from its noetic structure as well as a *noesis* divorced from its pneumatic roots. Theology must take seriously this dual structure of consciousness, which on the level of experience unites Athens and Jerusalem, philosophy and religion, reason and faith, nature and grace. If theology achieves this balance between the noetic and the pneumatic, then the experiential wholeness of theophany is maintained without introducing debilitating dichotomies that are most always motivated by doctrinaire polemics.

Voegelin's method is based in the living experiences of divine–human encounter that evoke faith. The chief human experiences to be analyzed are the great founding experiences of our traditions, the ones that constitute our consciousness. Accordingly, the interpretation of religious texts must be based on an experiential exegesis. This means that theologians must direct their hermeneutical focus not only on the meaning expressed in the texts they study, but also on the existential meaning of their own present experience. With this dual focus one is led back to the roots of divine revelation, both noetic and pneumatic, in one's present life as well as in past history. The strength of this experiential exegesis is that it would allow the text to stimulate parallel experiences in the reader in order to bring him or her into a greater understanding of the reality being addressed. On this score, theology should shift from a foundational concern with theory and the process of ratiocination to symbolic truth and the process of meditation. An adequate theology of revelation would stress the present context of revelation as God's self-communication in love that occurs in our preconscious and conscious experience. This is the hermeneutical principle at the heart of Voegelin's exegesis of the Gospel texts. The height and depth of reality illuminated by the saving tale of the Gospel can be envisioned only on the basis of one's own spiritual-mystical experience.

Voegelin challenges Christian theology to break from its doxic conception of truth. Such a conception leads inevitably to the problems that arise when one thinks in terms of "the one true faith." Faith is not equivalent to a set of truth claims; it is the graced, transcendent orientation of open existence. Voegelin requires a shift from this doxic understanding of faith to a more liberating, personal, and universal conception that would build, not walls of exclusivism with other religious traditions, but instead bridges of inclusivism, mutual respect, and reciprocal illumination. Faith is not rooted in assent to dogmatic propositions. It is rooted in the actually experienced mystical union with the divine which is the universal goal of all religious people and the experiential ground of all religions. A theologian's first loyalty, then, must be to the true and the good as such, embraced by faith, and only secondarily to particular truths and conceptions of the good. As an inquirer, a theologian's fundamental concern must be one of inquisitive engagement, not defensive polemics. The uncertainty of faith requires an attitude of endless wonder and humble insecurity.

Following the above point, Christian theology ought not to become too comfortable with the purported finality of its doctrines. It must recognize that doctrine at best only gives a propositional expression to a faith that remains substantially indeterminate and open-minded. Faith as "the assurance of things hoped for and the conviction of things not seen" is basically a faith in the unfinished story of reality, in the movement of one's soul toward the divine mystery as its ground. Once theology forfeits its noetic inquiry and becomes complacent with the cognitive conclusions it has achieved, it sets the stage for deformation. To be a preacher or missionary is one thing, to be a theologian is quite another. An ever-questioning consciousness seeking to penetrate the cosmic mystery is the mark of a theological mind.

Voegelin's method is further specified by the reflective distance of meditative consciousness. This distance in consciousness is the herme-neutical device for retrieving the noetic control of meaning in theo-phanic visions and the stories of these visions. Without the necessary distance to the originating, enthusiastic experiences of transfiguration, the balance of consciousness would be lost, with metastatic expectations likely to follow. The revelation of truth must be moored to a quest for truth in which one always begins in the middle, in the midst of one's questioning *fides*. To guard against placing undue attention on the end, which can transfix one who has undergone a conversion experience of new birth, a reflective distance in one's *fides* would recover the presence of divine mystery in every step of the process. In the midst of questioning consciousness one recognizes the pull of the golden cord of divine truth that was present all along, that was the basis of one's quest and one's *fides* from the start.

Voegelin gives due respect to the inherent power of intentional consciousness. But unlike thinkers like Lonergan, he understands the range of intentionality to be restricted to the uncovering of the wonders of thing-reality in the material epiphany of being in the spatiotemporal world. Voegelin would thematize the ground of theology in terms of the luminosity of consciousness, thus avoiding the immanentizing tenden-cies of intentionality that first appeared with Aristotle. Intentionality, thus, implicates and yields to luminosity as the mode of consciousness that theologians today must learn to cultivate in the process of their religious self-appropriation. Therefore, in their personal interiority, the-ologians must learn to strike the proper balance between intentionality and luminosity. The internal mediation between these two modes of theologizing would again be facilitated by reflective distance.

This luminous ground is the realm of the mystical. For Voegelin, mysticism should be the heart of theology. In his writings, he has often insinuated the need to supplant dogmatic theology by mystical theology, its tensional foil in Christian history. Like Lonergan, Voegelin would agree that theology has its true foundations in mysticism. Voegelin's primary challenge to theology, then, would be to make sure that its roots lie not in received doctrinal truth but in mystagogy, for any *fides* in quest of its own intelligibility, whether Platonic or Jewish, Islamic or Christian, must always return in experience to the mystery of the one God beyond the personal God or gods of theology.

The inherited dogmas and dichotomies that many theologians have taken for granted are radically overhauled by Voegelin. Among them: that reason and faith stand in some kind of opposition, that the insights of Greek philosophy arise from self-generated knowing and those of

Israel/Christianity stem from revelation, that history is linear and necessarily progressive, that the true advances arise in the West with no parallel in the East. Other theological dualisms such as "Christology from above or below" and "the Jesus of history vs. the Christ of faith" are rendered inadequate in view of Voegelin's analysis of their misconstruction. Also, the notion that the incarnation can be reduced to a once-and-for-all event in the person of one man in history is likewise rejected. The continuum of incarnation in history does indeed reach a peak in Christ's incarnation in Jesus, but what becomes supremely luminous in this differentiating event is God's incarnate presence in history from beginning to end.

On this controversial matter, theologians will have to reassess what they traditionally mean by the uniqueness of Jesus. Voegelin does not directly and definitively answer this question, but we can surmise that he would reject a notion of uniqueness based on exclusivity. He does affirm that Jesus represents the confirmation and fulfillment of divine presence and transfiguration in history. What this means exactly is not fully worked out in Voegelin's writings, but the theological ramifications are pretty evident. According to Vogelin's metaleptic theory of participation, God participates in humanity just as humanity participates in God. Thus, transcendence and immanence, God and humanity, do not form a dichotomy; they are poles in a singular tension. The movement within this tension is both *zetesis* and *helkein*: without the divine drawing there would be no seeking; without the inner thrust toward what we desire to know there would be no sensitivity to the divine drawing. Only after the experience of the divine–human presence in the in-between has happened can the accent be allocated either to humanity and the noetic search or to divinity and revelation. Voegelin's view of the human self as ontologically related to divine being in this participationist fashion, therefore, would allow a view of Jesus as the human person who most intensely manifests what is true of all of us on a limited or inchoate level. Thus, the "high Christology" of the Johannine "word made flesh" would have to be interpreted in light of the emergence of the ubiquitous divine word in history. Jesus lives in the *metaxy* as much as every other human but is the one historical figure whose prophetic life and transfiguring death illuminates most fully the divine salvific grace and ever-present redemptive love in history that we are all called to embody in our own lives.

Voegelin does not often use the word "God," preferring instead to use symbols like divine ground, transcendent being, the eternal beyond, and divine mystery. We must recognize this as an attempt to avoid hypostatized symbols, which is the bane of much theologizing today.

Theology could benefit from this cautious use of symbolism, especially when evoking the transcendent, so as to avoid as much as possible a reified and thus spiritually dead language, and to recover the presence of Mystery operative in our personal existence.

Accordingly, Voegelin insists that we take seriously the mystery of the beyond which cannot be limited to any image. As a result he would give great approval to an apophatic theology based on the mystical ground of experience. It would be a theology that recovers the tetra-grammatic depth of the ineffable divine beyond, which by its sheer incommensurability is able to ground all the commensurable images of the divine. This also would serve as a basis for Christian theology in its encounter with the world's other religious faiths. Voegelin would always insist that theology in its kataphatic mode employ the analogical use of language. It would be a symbolic language based on the preeminent formulation of the *analogia entis* in Thomas Aquinas. This theological task of linguistically constructing and reconstructing valid images and symbols of the divine would recognize the psychological and spiritual process by which images emerge in our psyches.[64]

As a necessary corrective to the over-zealous inclinations of various theologies of hope, promise, liberation, etc., Voegelin warns us not to immanentize the eschaton. Guarding against gnostic deformations of history, he offers us a profound respect for the lastingness of the cosmos in which the human drama is played out. Accordingly, he views history as the revelatory process that discloses divine mystery in a diversity of revelations, all of which point to the transfiguration of all things within the cosmos. This transfiguration is not the result of human will but of the grace of God, to which humans can either formatively respond as partners in the eschatological drama of history, or deformatively resist in their gnostic, ideological, or pneumapathological escapades.

Voegelin's *fides* is the expanded philosopher's *fides* which theologians should take seriously today as the exigent ground for what they seek to understand, a truly adequate *fides quaerens intellectum*. This requires that theology must take seriously the revelations and truth claims of other religious faiths, for "the Spirit blows where it will" (John 3:8). It also demands that faith be conjoined with reason. Personally and spiritually, reason and faith should develop in proportion to each other.

Lastly, what Voegelin is about is what theologians are or should be fundamentally about: conversion. Conversion is either the slow and sure transformation of the self moving toward greater authenticity and attunement with divine being, the path of most spiritual people, or the sudden, overwhelming experience of being "born again" by a visionary encounter with the *mysterium tremendum* given to a select few. On the whole conversion is, for Lonergan, intellectual, moral, and religious. With Voegelin, it is noetic and pneumatic. Like the existential virtues of faith, hope, and love, conversion cannot be reduced solely to human accomplishment; as a human achievement it is inseparable from grace. However one characterizes this experience, its effects are generally the same. It can result in the redemptive life that comes from committing oneself to the transfiguring love of Christ, or it may entail the turning around of the soul toward the noetic beyond and embarking on the immortalizing journey of philosophy. In either case, the movement of the soul is toward the same divine mystery that St. Augustine addressed as the God for whom "the heart is restless until it rests in thee." Theology that is based on theologians' own experience of conversion will guarantee its proper foundation in personal, lived reality.

What Voegelin has accomplished, I believe, is the recovery of the task of theology as the teller of the true story of the It-reality being revealed in history, a theology whose method is a generalized *fides quaerens intellectum*, and whose goal is to return truth, which has degenerated to the level of true doctrine, to its rightful place as the aim of the experiential and reflective search for God, a theology that must return from orthodoxy to the Mystery. It is a centuries-long process that holds the promise of the spiritual and intellectual renewal of human culture.

In the course of this analysis, some important features of Voegelin's writings were left untreated, such as his early German works on race and the specific development of his political theory and his legal theory. These particular themes, along with his understanding and treatment of gnosticism and ideology, continue to warrant concerted study by scholars.[65] Voegelin's most recent work will especially require a good deal of meditative reflection and scrutiny. These recent writings, which I discussed in chapter 4, contain his consummate analysis of the problems of transcendent order and its symbolization. Like the rest of his corpus, these last works need to be seriously studied by theologians. These writings reflect the turn toward mystagogy as the core of philosophy, a turn that is essentially a mystical theology. Students of Voegelin's thought will no doubt contribute to the task of explicating the work of this great thinker in the years ahead.[66] For my part, I hope that this contribution to that process in no way deflects from the clear presentation and accurate interpretation that such work demands. Perhaps it may even plant the seeds of interest in those who, given the opportunity, would become as enthusiastic of Voegelin's thought as I am.

The study of a great thinker is a monumental task but offers very rich rewards. Such a study of Voegelin requires that one embark on the path of true philosophy. In Socrates' words, it "would be the kind of study that would draw the soul away from the world of becoming to the world of being" (*Republic* 531d), for "no other study turns the soul's gaze upward than that which deals with being and the invisible" (529b). In this light, the true reward of the philosophical quest lies at the unknown end on the path of ascent.

Our common spiritual ascent—personal, social, and historical—toward the renewal of truth, goodness, and love has been greatly enhanced by the light cast by Voegelin's brilliant achievement. Indeed, it would not surprise me if some day future historians trace the source for the spiritual restoration of the West back to the writings of Eric Voegelin.

A final question: Can Voegelin's work be seriously considered a work in theology in the broadest sense? This study has analyzed the obvious importance of Voegelin's entire corpus for theology, a body of writings that contains very studious reflections on theological issues by a thinker who tackles the same problems that theologicans do. And so we may conclude that, Yes, Voegelin's is a theological enterprise insofar as his labors are directed toward the same end as that of the best of theologians going back to Plato. Moreover, his work provides a most valuable contribution to theology, in both form and substance, as well as a guide for doing theology at the end of this century and well into the next. Nevertheless, Voegelin's own description of his lifelong project must remain the true basis on how we are finally to understand and judge his work. True to the metaxic structure of existence, he claims to forge a middle ground between an anthropology that tends to focus on the human pole at the expense of the divine, and a theology that tends to focus on the divine at the expense of the human. The name he gives his exploration of the whole of reality, a reality that reaches from the apeirontic depth to the divine height, which humans faithfully seek to understand from their position in the middle, is, simply, "philosophy."

NOTES

Introduction

1. Friedrich Nietzsche, *The Use and Abuse of History*, trans. Adrian Collins (Indianapolis: Bobbs-Merrill, 1957), p. 7.

2. Ibid., p. 69.

3. The most important of these writings which will be discussed in chap. 4 include the final volume of *Order and History*, *In Search of Order* (Baton Rouge: Louisiana State University Press, 1987); and *What Is History? and Other Late Unpublished Writings*, Collected Works 28, ed. Thomas A. Hollweck and Paul Caringella (Baton Rouge: Louisiana State University Press, 1990), which includes the important essay "The Beginning and the Beyond."

4. Thomas Altizer, in a review of Voegelin's *Anamnesis*, made the perceptive statement that "Voegelin's is a theological mind, and it has become ever more deeply theological as it has evolved. We must also add that, scandal as it is to the theological world, his is the only genuine mind that is now truly engaged in anything that we might call political theology" (*Journal of Religion* 59 [1979]: 375). Voegelin never considered his work an endeavor in theology; he regarded himself first and foremost a philosopher whose primary focus is political reality. But his quest for the order of the soul and society necessarily brought him to confront theological problems. We must rest with his view of himself as a philosopher—but in the deep sense of Plato, whose work he characterized not as *a* philosophy, but as *the* symbolic form of the soul's ascent toward God, the soul being ordered by the love of being through the love of divine Being which is its ground. The theological dimension of Voegelin's work is discussed in two essays by William M. Thompson: "Eric Voegelin: In Retrospect," *Religious Studies Review* 10 (1984): 29–33; "Voegelin and the Religious Scholar: An Introduction," in *Voegelin and the Theologian: Ten Studies in Interpretation*, Toronto Studies in Theology 10, ed. John Kirby and William M. Thompson (New York and Toronto: Edwin Mellen Press, 1983), pp. 1–23. For some of the repercussions of Voegelin's work on Christian theology, see also Eugene Webb, "Faith, Truth and Persuasion in the Thought of Eric Voegelin," in *Voegelin and the Theologian*, pp. 356–69.

5. Voegelin's statement of this problem is contained in his important essay "The Beginning and the Beyond: A Meditation on Truth," in *What Is History?*

and Other Late Unpublished Writings, pp. 173–232, at 197. This major essay of Voegelin's late period has great theological significance and will be discussed in chap. 4.

6. Ibid.

7. In an early article, written as part of his "History of Political Ideas," Voegelin argued that the origins of the modern conflict between faith and reason can be traced back to the thirteenth-century scholastic philosopher, Siger de Brabant. See his "Siger de Brabant," *Philosophy and Phenomenological Research* 4 (1944): 507–23. Voegelin claimed that Siger was the first "enlightened" thinker in the Christian West and thus the first philosopher in the modern sense. In his thought, contained in his commentaries on Aristotle, begins the dissociation of philosophy from theology. The authority of reason is established as a rival to the authority of the revealed faith. Consequently, the tension between faith and reason, maintained by Anselm, devolved into the conflict between critical intellect and Christian doctrine. But the liberation of the sovereign intellect from dogmatic hegemony only created the counter-dogmatism of intramundane reason that runs through William of Ockham and culminates in Kant's *Critique of Pure Reason*. Moreover, Voegelin argues, Siger's work is the first concentrated expression of an immanentized understanding of humankind. In his intramundane system of metaphysics and utilitarian ethics he formulated the nascent principles of much of modern secular thought.

8. *Order and History* V, p. 43. See also *Order and History* IV, *The Ecumenic Age* (Baton Rouge: Louisiana State University Press, 1974), pp. 47–48, where Voegelin attributes to Stoicism the roots of the dichotomy between reason and revelation in Christian theology.

9. In spite of the opprobrium given to doctrine throughout his works, on a few occasions, as we shall later discuss, Voegelin identified the value of doctrine as that linguistic form which serves to preserve the original insights of philosophy and revelation which can easily become lost in the vicissitudes of history.

10. The most fundamental dichotomy that emerges out of Cartesian thought is the dualism between subject and object. Voegelin, echoing Heidegger, overcomes this deeply ingrained epistemological construct in modern thought by his "existential" theory of participatory consciousness, a theme that introduces *Order and History* in its opening pages and that will be the central focus of this book, particularly chap. 1, 2, and 3.

11. According to Thomas B. Heilke, Voegelin first employed the concept of hypostasis in his German work of 1933, *Rasse und Staat*. Hypostasis is a concept that Voegelin borrows from Plato to refer to reified symbols that assume an independent existence apart from the experiences they conceptually analyze. See Heilke's *Voegelin and the Idea of Race* (Baton Rouge: Louisiana State University Press, 1990), p. 52.

12. *Order and History* V, pp. 63–64.

13. Ibid., pp. 43–44.

14. Ibid., p. 67.

15. "The Gospel and Culture," originally published in *Jesus and Man's Hope*, ed. D. G. Miller and D. Y. Hadidian (Pittsburgh: Pittsburgh Theological Seminary, 1971), pp. 59–101; reprinted in *Published Essays, 1966–1985*, Collected Works 12, ed. Ellis Sandoz (Baton Rouge: Louisiana State University Press, 1990), pp. 172–212, at 178–79. Throughout this book all quotations from Voegelin's essays will be cited from the collected works volumes if they are reprinted there.

16. In the early Christian centuries we see this same dynamic operating in the conciliar debates that produced "orthodoxies" in opposition to the prevalent "heresies."

17. This Platonic function of the true propositions is no doubt the source of Voegelin's positive view of doctrine as a protective device to guard against the corruption and dissolution of spiritual insights grounded in experience.

18. "The Beginning and the Beyond," p. 203.

19. This insight is profoundly expressed at the end of *Order and History* V, p. 102. This whole last section of the book on Plato's *Timaeus* is a deeply penetrating philosophical-theological meditation on divine being that, for this reader, has no equal in modern thought. It is the culmination of Voegelin's whole exploration of consciousness and transcendence that will be discussed as a model of philosophical "faith seeking understanding" in chap. 4.

20. See "The Beginning and the Beyond," p. 203.

21. *Metalepsis* is Aristotle's symbol denoting the mutual participation of human and divine being in reality. It is a key concept in Voegelin's theory of consciousness which will be discussed in chap. 3.

22. "The Beginning and the Beyond," p. 211.

23. See, for example, *From Enlightenment to Revolution*, ed. John Hallowell (Durham: Duke University Press, 1975), pp. 22–23.

24. One should recall here Voegelin's "theological" declaration in his last writings that it is faith that is in search of understanding, not reason. See "The Beginning and the Beyond," pp. 194–95.

25. Voegelin's concept of historiogenesis will be discussed in chap. 3.

26. *The New Science of Politics* (Chicago: University of Chicago Press, 1952), p. 120. Voegelin's admonition in this book not to "immanentize the eschaton" became a favorite slogan among conservative thinkers arrogating him for their political agenda. However, Voegelin's scientific erudition is a two-edge sword that falls sharply on both liberals and conservatives who read him with an ideological bias.

27. *Metaxy* is Plato's important symbol denoting the in-between structure of human existence, the concept of which is central to Voegelin's theory of consciousness. It will be elucidated in chap. 3 and 4.

28. *Order and History* IV, p. 243.

29. This judgment is corroborated by Lissy Voegelin in the foreword to the volume, where she states: "He liked his work and often talked about it, and he let me know that he knew very well that these pages are the key to all his other works and that in these pages he has gone as far as he could go in analysis, saying what he wanted to say as clearly as it possibly could be said" (p. xv).

30. Such comparative studies, although interesting, tend to diminish the distinctive thought, background, and language of each thinker. This mutual absorption I wish to avoid. Furthermore, an "analysis by association" has its limits of usefulness, as a review article by the literary critic Marion Montgomery demonstrates. See his "Eric Voegelin and the End of Our Exploring," *Modern Age* 23 (1979): 233–45. Montgomery's more recent interpretation of Voegelin in light of such contemporary literary figures as Erza Pound and Flannery O'Connor fares no better. For that effort, see his "Eric Voegelin as Prophetic Philosopher," *Southern Review* 24 (1988): 115–33.

31. The work cited in n. 4, *Voegelin and the Theologian*, is the only book published to date that reflects Voegelin's influence on theologians. It is a 1983 collection of ten essays by religious scholars on various theological aspects of Voegelin's work.

1. Toward a Philosophy of Consciousness: The Early Writings, 1928–50

1. Eric Voegelin, *Order and History* (Baton Rouge: Louisiana State University Press, 1956–87): vol. I, *Israel and Revelation* (1956); vol. II, *The World of the Polis* (1957); vol. III, *Plato and Aristotle* (1957); vol. IV, *The Ecumenic Age* (1974); vol. V, *In Search of Order* (1987). Hereafter, *Order and History* I, II, III, IV, V.

2. Although I shall forgo any detailed examination of Voegelin's life, the most important sources for the biographical information should be noted. A major source of information about Voegelin's early life and thought is his own autobiographical memoirs now published under the title *Autobiographical Reflections*, ed. Ellis Sandoz (Baton Rouge: Louisiana State University Press, 1989). This text is derived from a series of interviews tape-recorded in 1973 by Ellis Sandoz. The transcript of these recordings, originally entitled "Autobiographical Notes," was edited by Voegelin himself and reads like a personal narrative. A large portion of this text was published in Sandoz's intellectual biography of Voegelin: *The Voegelinian Revolution: A Biographical Introduction* (Baton Rouge: Louisiana State University Press, 1981), where it is named "Autobiographical Memoir." Hereafter, when citing Voegelin's *Autobiographical Reflections*, the corresponding pages in Sandoz's work will also be cited if applicable.

Another very useful and more theoretical work is Eugene Webb's *Eric Voegelin: Philosopher of History* (Seattle: University of Washington Press, 1981). Webb's is the best analytical interpretation of Voegelin's thought to date. Also of importance are Gregor Sebba, "Prelude and Variations on the Theme of Eric Voegelin," in *Eric Voegelin's Thought: A Critical Appraisal*, ed. Ellis Sandoz (Durham: Duke University Press, 1982), original, shorter version in *The Southern Review* 13 (1977): 646–76; William Havard, "Voegelin's Changing Conception of History and Consciousness," in *Eric Voegelin's Search for Order in History*, ed. Stephen A. McKnight (Baton Rouge: Louisiana State University Press, 1978), pp. 1–25, original, shorter version titled "The Changing Pattern of Voegelin's Conception of History and Consciousness," *Southern Review* 7 (1971): 49–67; and Joseph McCarroll, "Man in Search of Divine Order in History," *Philosophical Studies* 10 (1984): 15–45.

3. *Autobiographical Reflections*, p. 93; in Sandoz, p. 28.

4. Eric Voegelin, "Autobiographical Statement at Age Eighty-Two," in *The Beginning and the Beyond: Papers from the Gadamer and Voegelin Conferences*, supplementary issue of *Lonergan Workshop* 4, ed. Fred Lawrence (Chico, Cal.: Scholars Press, 1984), pp. 116–17. In the beginning of this brief autobiography (pp. 111–14), Voegelin relates the political and intellectual context of his early education in Vienna, citing the various factors that instigated his philosophical work.

5. The story of Voegelin's escape from Austria is told in *Autobiographical Reflections*, pp. 42–44, 54–56; in Sandoz, pp. 12–13, 68–70. This personal experience lies at the heart of his somewhat cryptic references to murder in his later work. See, for example, his allusions in his treatment of Plato to the murderous intent of the philosopher's enemies (*Order and History* III, pp. 25, 37, 147), which are obviously autobiographical.

6. These are *Rasse und Staat* (Tübingen: J. C. B. Mohr, 1933); *Die Rassenidee in der Geistesgeschichte von Ray bis Carus* (Berlin: Junker und Dünnhaupt, 1933); *Der Autoritäre Staat* (Vienna: Springer, 1936); and *Die politischen Religionen* (Vienna: Bermann-Fischer, 1938). At this date only the last of these has been translated into English; see Erich Voegelin, *Political Religions*, trans. T. J. DiNapoli and E. S. Easterly, III (Lewiston, N.Y.: Edwin Mellon Press, 1986). Voegelin's German years and his relation to the Nazis are reviewed in the translators' preface to this work, pp. xxix–xliv. An overview of Voegelin's German works can be found in Sandoz, *The Voegelinian Revolution*, pp. 47–68.

7. The substance of these works need not be discussed here. For an excellent treatment of these prewar writings of Voegelin, I refer the reader to the first thorough analysis of these works in Heilke, *Voegelin on the Idea of Race*. After Voegelin's emigration to the United States in 1938, when he began to write in English, he continued to speak out against the Nazis and their racist ideology. His wartime analysis can be found in three articles: "Extended Strategy: A New

Technique of Dynamic Relations," *Journal of Politics* 2 (1940): 189–200; "The Growth of the Race Idea," *Review of Politics* 2 (1940): 283–317; and "Some Problems of German Hegemony," *Journal of Politics* 3 (1941): 154–68.

8. Eric Voegelin, *Anamnesis*, trans. and ed. Gerhart Niemeyer (Notre Dame: University of Notre Dame Press, 1978); paperback ed. (Columbia: University of Missouri Press, 1990), p. 4.

9. Ibid., p. 3.

10. Ibid., p. 4.

11. Ibid., p. 3.

12. An analysis of these deformations in modern political science is aptly provided by Dante Germino, *Beyond Ideology: The Revival of Political Theory* (Chicago: University of Chicago Press, 1967). Germino devotes a full chapter to Voegelin's contribution to the reformation of political theory.

13. *Anamnesis*, p. 5.

14. Ibid., pp. 4–5.

15. Plato *Republic* 368d–e. On Plato's anthropological principle, see Eric Voegelin, *The New Science of Politics* (Chicago: University of Chicago Press, 1952), pp. 61–63. See also *Order and History* III, pp. 69, 86, 98, 108–11, 119, 296.

16. Plato *Republic* 502d–541b.

17. Plato *Laws* 716c. See *Order and History* III, pp. 254, 263; and *The New Science of Politics*, pp. 66–70.

18. The Platonic insight that the sick society is the diseased soul writ large has its parallel in the New Testament. See for example, Mark 7:14–23.

19. The *metaxy* is Plato's symbol representing the experience of human existence as "between" the lower and upper poles of reality: between human and divine, birth and death, ignorance and knowledge, mortality and immortality, etc. As we shall see in chap. 4, Voegelin made much use of this symbol in his later work. For its occurrence in Plato, see *Symposium* 202e and *Philebus* 16d–17a.

20. *Order and History* III, pp. 62–63.

21. This view of the life of reason as the ordering force of society and the political norms that follow was discussed in a little-known article by Voegelin: "Industrial Society in Search of Reason," in *World Technology and Human Destiny*, ed. Raymond Aron (Ann Arbor: University of Michigan Press, 1963), pp. 31–46. Here he mentioned the two general postulates of social order that are the maxims of classical politics: "The 'good society' . . . is one which: (1) is large enough and wealthy enough to make the life of reason possible, at least for the minority capable of putting this human potentiality to work; (2) is organized in such a way that the life of reason becomes a social force in a society's culture, including its political affairs" (pp. 37–38). Voegelin went on to

argue that these postulates, with some refurbishing, are applicable to an analysis of political societies today. The gist of the matter is that the good society will foster the life of reason, through philosophy and education, and reason in turn will become an effective part of social organization, without which a society will fall into political and spiritual decay. The life of reason, not constitutional form, body of laws, standard of living, or technical efficiency, is the measure of the good society. Beyond that, the various institutional forms of the good society ought to follow common sense as the practical arbiter and guide for prudent action.

22. The "philodoxers" are what Plato termed the lovers of opinion (*doxa*) who are the sophistic foil of true philosophers. See *Order and History* III, pp. 65, 75.

23. Plato *Laws* 712e–714a. For the myth of the cosmic cycles, see Plato *Statesman* 269c–274e. See also *Order and History* III, pp. 151–57. On the *nous* initiating a new epoch, see *Order and History* III, pp. 139, 284ff.; and *Anamnesis*, p. 90.

24. *Anamnesis*, p. 90. Voegelin makes clear that Plato and Aristotle, unlike the modern gnostic thinkers who divide history into a series of progressive epochs (reminiscent of Joachim of Fiore's tripartite division of history) and then proclaim the final new age to be inaugurated in their own work (e.g., Hegel, Marx, and Comte), did not derail into apocalyptic or utopic expectations of a final realm to come. Instead, the classic philosophers maintained the balance of consciousness by their openness to unexpected possibilities in the future, especially the possibility of further differentiations of consciousness beyond the *nous*.

25. *Conversations with Eric Voegelin*, ed. Eric O'Connor (Montreal: Thomas More Institute, 1976), p. 138. This text is a transcription of four talks with Voegelin at the Thomas More Institute in Montreal. They are entitled "In Search of the Ground" (1965); "Theology Confronting World Religions?" (1967); "Questions Up" (1970); and "Myth as Environment" (1976). The passage quoted here is from the final talk.

26. *The New Science of Politics*, p. 1.

27. Actually, Voegelin said as much in the pithy locution with which he opened the German edition of *Anamnesis*: "The problems of human order in society and history originate in the order of consciousness. Hence the philosophy of consciousness is the centerpiece of a philosophy of politics" (Voegelin's own translation in *Logos* 4 [1983]: 17).

28. *Order and History* I, p. ix.

29. This principle was modified by his later caveat that history can no longer be conceived according to a straight line of time. See the introduction to *Order and History* IV, pp. 1–56, especially p. 2.

30. It should be noted that the specific years of this tripartite periodization of Voegelin's development follow the publication dates of his writings. Since a scholar's published writings reflect the shifts in his or her thinking, they are legitimate guides for chronicling intellectual development, although such dating can only approximate the actual course of an inquiring mind. Such chronicling may often be tardy in the case of Voegelin, who often composed studies a number of years before they were arranged in an acceptable form for publication.

31. See Voegelin's *Autobiographical Reflections*, pp. 28–33; in Sandoz, pp. 20–22.

32. See *Autobiographical Reflections*, pp. 62–84; in Sandoz, pp. 77–84.

33. The meaning of "historiogenesis" will be discussed in chap. 3. For Voegelin's treatment of this very important concept, see *Order and History* IV, pp. 59–113.

34. On this final shift in Voegelin's thinking, see *Order and History* IV, pp. 1–58.

35. Robert Nisbet, "Eric Voegelin's Vision," *Public Interest* 71 (Spring 1983): 110.

36. Eric Voegelin, *Über die Form des amerikanischen Geistes* (Tübingen: J.C.B. Mohr, 1928), pp. 19–52. See also Anibal A. Bueno, "Consciousness, Time, and Transcendence in Eric Voegelin's Philosophy," in *The Philosophy of Order: Essays on History, Consciousness, and Politics*, ed. Peter J. Opitz and Gregor Sebba (Stuttgart: Klett-Cotta, 1981), pp. 91–109. Bueno's article is an excellent summary of the early development of Voegelin's theory of consciousness which I found to be a useful guide in this section.

37. *Über die Form des amerikanischen Geistes*, pp. 20ff.

38. Ibid., pp. 46–52. See William James, *Essays on Radical Empiricism* [and] *A Pluralistic Universe* (New York: Longmans, Green, and Co., 1947).

39. *Essays on Radical Empiricism* [and] *A Pluralistic Universe*, p. 42. Emphasis in original.

40. *Über die Form des amerikanischen Geistes*, pp. 49–52. James, *Essays in Radical Empiricism* [and] *A Pluralistic Universe*, pp. 30–33.

41. See Henri Bergson, *The Two Sources of Morality and Religion*, trans. R. Audra and C. Brereton (Garden City, N.J.: Doubleday, 1935). For an analysis of Voegelin's political philosophy in light of this theme of Bergson's, see Dante Germino, *Political Philosophy and the Open Society* (Baton Rouge: Louisiana State University Press, 1982).

42. For a treatment of James's thought and its influence on Voegelin, see Sandoz, *The Voegelinian Revolution*, pp. 171–76.

43. Eric Voegelin, *Anamnesis: Zur Theorie der Geschichte und Politik* (Munich: R. Piper, 1966), p. 7. Hereafter, *Anamnesis* (German edition).

44. *Anamnesis*, pp. 36–51. "Anamnetic experiments" is the term Voegelin uses to describe the reflective activity that philosophers must engage in if they are to ground in their personal experience a true understanding of consciousness. These experiments offer a "biography of consciousness" that would furnish the real foundation of philosophical reflection because they would bring to consciousness the first experiences of the awe and excitement of existence before any systematic reflection or interpretive accretions have taken hold.

45. *Anamnesis* (German edition), pp. 21–60. The first letter to Schutz, dated September 17, 1943, critically analyzing Husserl's *Krisis der europäischen Wissenschaften*, is not simply a long, critical book review, lacking any alternative formulation to Husserl's egologically constituted consciousness. The second letter to Schutz contains Voegelin's "anamnetic experiments." These are reflections on twenty childhood experiences which he meditatively recovered during the two-week period between October 25 and November 7, 1943. Along with these meditations he included some prefatory remarks showing their relevance to his alternative theory of consciousness. This theoretical analysis followed immediately afterward in a third letter to Schutz. It is the very important essay entitled "On the Theory of Consciousness" and is published as chap. 2 in the English edition of *Anamnesis*. Most of the following discussion of Voegelin's theory of consciousness during his early period derives from this essay.

46. *Anamnesis* (German edition), p. 7. Voegelin's own translation of this passage which I have used is found in *Logos* 4 (1983): 18.

47. *Anamnesis*, p. 14.

48. Ibid., p. 34.

49. Ibid.

50. Ibid., p. 35.

51. Ibid., p. 34.

52. Ibid., p. 15.

53. Ibid., p. 16.

54. Ibid., p. 19.

55. Ibid., p. 20. Voegelin's understanding of the time dimension of consciousness is derived from Augustine's *distentio animi* (extension of the soul), that is, the process of consciousness does not occur in the clock time of the external world but possesses past, present, and future as a kind of inner luminous space. The idea is best explained by two passages from Augustine's *Confessions*, book 11: "Perhaps it might be said rightly that there are three times: a time present of things past; a time present of things present; and a time present of things future. For these three do coexist somehow in the soul, for otherwise I could not see them. The time present of things past is memory; the time present of things present is direct experience; the time present of things future is expectation" (chap. 20). "From this it appears to me that time is nothing other

than extendedness [*distentionem*]; but extendedness of what I do not know. This is a marvel to me. The extendedness may be of the mind itself" (chap. 26). See *Augustine: Confessions and Enchiridion*, Library of Christian Classics 7, trans. Albert C. Outler (Philadelphia: Westminster Press, 1960), pp. 259, 264.

56. *Anamnesis*, p. 21. As we shall see in chap. 4 the "inexperienceable" symbolizes a dimension of reality that will not become fully thematic for Voegelin until *Order and History* V.

57. Ibid.

58. See ibid., pp. 22–23.

59. Ibid., p. 26. As we shall discuss in the final chapter, on the theological implications of Voegelin's work, the destruction of the myth within Christianity is for Voegelin attributable largely to the Church itself.

60. Ibid., p. 27.

61. Ibid.

62. These two complexes described here are the same as the two directions of consciousness toward the beginning and the beyond which Voegelin carefully developed in his later work so as not to carry the mortgage of metaphysics which he became more and more sensitive to. That development will be discussed in chap. 4; I state it here only to point out the consistency of Voegelin's thought.

63. Ibid., pp. 28–29. As this sentence shows, Voegelin still used the language of intentionality in his early work even when speaking of the nonintentional. He would later abandon it altogether when speaking of consciousness as luminous.

64. However, some have exaggerated Voegelin's relation to Whitehead by referring to his later thought as a "process philosophy." See J. M. Porter, "A Philosophy of History as a Philosophy of Consciousness," *Denver Quarterly* 10 (Fall 1975): 104. James Rhodes also makes much of the connection between Voegelin and Whitehead (I believe too much), referring to this early phase of his work as a "process theology." See James M. Rhodes, "Voegelin and Christian Faith," *Center Journal* 2 (Summer, 1983): 63, 100. No doubt Whitehead had some enduring influence on Voegelin during his time in the United States, but it would be erroneous to conclude that any part of Voegelin's work has any connection with the process theologians who take their bearings from Whitehead.

65. *Anamnesis*, p. 33.

66. This was articulated most thoroughly in his 1966 essay "What is Political Reality?" See *Anamnesis*, pp. 143–213.

67. Voegelin's attack on the psychologists (Freud, Jung, and their followers) is expressed in the following places: *Order and History* IV, p. 197; *Anamnesis*, pp. 108, 169; "Philosophies of History: An Interview with Eric Voegelin," *New Orleans Review* 2 (1973): 135–39, at 138; "Equivalences of Experience

and Symbolization in History," *Philosophical Studies* 28 (1981): 83–103, at 96; this is a corrected version that originally appeared in *Eternità e Storia, I valori permanenti nel divenire storico*, ed. L. Paysan (Florence: Valecchi, 1970), pp. 215–34, and reprinted in *Published Essays (1966–1985)*, pp. 115–33. His most trenchant statement on Jung and the unconscious is found in *Order and History* V, pp. 59–61.

Voegelin's contention is that the depth of the *psyche* cannot be explored psychologically; an analysis of experience and its depth can only be handled by the philosophical sciences. The depth of the soul discerned by noetic philosophers has no substantive content; it is beyond articulate experience because the experienced truth of reality is bound by the limits of consciousness. But a level deeper than consciousness can be discerned by thinkers who carefully attend to the processes by which a more differentiated understanding of reality is arrived at. The depth of the *psyche*, then, is the matrix of experience that surrounds and comprehends the area of conscious experience. Thus, Voegelin argues that "there is a psyche deeper than consciousness, and there is reality deeper than reality experienced, but there is no consciousness deeper than consciousness" ("Equivalences of Experience and Symbolization in History," p. 126).

Since the "unconscious" by definition is not available to consciousness, psychoanalysts who attempt to excavate this dimension of the *psyche* are only projecting into an "unconscious" what pathological patients tend to bury in their "subconscious." Jung's archetypes are fully conscious symbolizations of experiences of reality. A healthy consciousness would not place these symbols in a subterranean "subconscious."

68. Voegelin never published anything explicit on this problem, although in *Anamnesis* he refers to it in two parenthetical statements: "The tension in being is not an object that could be known 'intersubjectively' and thus would present about the same phenomenal image to everyone. Rather, it is indeed a tension that must be experienced personally" (p. 133). "The non-objective character of the experience of order admits of no so-called [intersubjective] knowledge of order; rather, the intangibility of the reality, which is no ineffability, allows room for a variety of experiences that motivate a corresponding number of symbolic expressions of the experience" (p. 147). The English translation omits any correspondence to the German word *intersubjektive* from this sentence which renders its meaning unintelligible. See *Anamnesis* (German edition), p. 287.

The problem of intersubjectivity was hotly debated between Voegelin and Alfred Schutz in their correspondence in the early 1950s, that part of which has never been published. The only available clue to Voegelin's position on this issue is contained in a few passages of this correspondence that have been cited in Helmut Wagner's intellectual biography of Schutz. See chap. 12, "Eric Voegelin: Friend in Philosophical Adversity," in Helmut R. Wagner, *Alfred*

Schutz: An Intellectual Biography (Chicago: University of Chicago Press, 1983), pp. 185–204, at 197–98.

Voegelin and Schutz shared a philosophical friendship that spanned nearly four decades, as well as, after their concurrent emigration to the United States, an extensive correspondence which covered the second half of that period before Schutz's death in 1959. For Voegelin's remarks on this relationship, see his "In Memoriam Alfred Schutz," in *The Philosophy of Order*, ed. Opitz and Sebba, pp. 463–65. For further analysis of their long dialogue, see also Helmut R. Wagner, "Agreement in Discord: Alfred Schutz and Eric Voegelin," in ibid., pp. 74–90.

69. *Anamnesis*, p. 33.
70. Quoted in *Anamnesis* (German edition), p. 33.
71. See *Anamnesis*, chap. 3, "Anamnetic Experiments," pp. 36–51.

2. The Middle Writings, 1951–59

1. The portion of "The History of Political Ideas" that dealt with the eighteenth and nineteenth centuries has been published as *From Enlightenment to Revolution*, ed. John Hallowell (Durham: Duke University Press, 1975). A fine review of this work which examines the problems Voegelin encountered during this period is provided by Barry Cooper, "A Fragment from Eric Voegelin's *History of Western Political Thought*," *Political Science Reviewer* 7 (Fall 1977): 23–52. Louisiana State University Press will soon publish "Studies in the History of Political Ideas" in eight volumes as part of Voegelin's collected works.

2. Voegelin alludes to the influence of the Chicago Oriental Institute in *Autobiographical Reflections*, pp. 63, 95. The findings of this school were summarized and published in 1946: Henri Frankfort et al., *The Intellectual Adventure of Ancient Man* (Chicago: University of Chicago Press, 1946). It was republished since then under the title *Before Philosophy* (Baltimore: Pelican Books, 1949); however, this edition left out the section on "The Hebrews" by William A. Irwin. The two essays by the Frankforts, "Myth and Reality" and "The Emancipation of Thought from Myth," only described the transition from myth to philosophy without explaining why. It required Voegelin to fashion an exegetical account of the experiences behind the historical texts and events in order to give substance to the development of consciousness.

3. According to Eugene Webb, the precise date of Voegelin's shift in conception occurred in the summer of 1945. However, Voegelin continued to work on the "History" because the full implications of the shift did not become clear to him until the late 1940s. See Webb, *Eric Voegelin: Philosopher of History*, p. 6, n. 6.

4. See "Autobiographical Statement at Age Eighty-Two," in *The Beginning and the Beyond: Papers from the Gadamer and Voegelin Conferences*, ed. Lawrence, p. 119; and *Autobiographical Reflections*, pp. 63, 78–80; in Sandoz, pp. 77, 80–81.

5. *Autobiographical Reflections*, p. 63; in Sandoz, p. 77.

6. Ibid. Voegelin's groping with this principle can be surmised from a passage taken from the published portion of his "History." Still working under the influence of the history of ideas, he refers to "sentiments" (not experiences) as the ground of ideas which must be considered by a historian: "The historian of ideas has to do more than to report the doctrines advanced by a thinker.... He has to explore the growth of sentiments which crystallize into ideas, and he has to show the connection between ideas and the matrix of sentiments in which they are rooted. The idea has to be studied, not as a concept, but as a symbol which draws its life from sentiments; the idea grows and dies with the sentiments which engender its formulation" (*From Enlightenment to Revolution*, p. 68). In his later work, Voegelin abandoned interest in ideas altogether and never again mentioned sentiments.

7. *Autobiographical Reflections*, p. 78; in Sandoz, p. 80.

8. *Time* magazine devoted most of the feature story of its thirtieth anniversary issue to the impact of Voegelin's book. See "Journalism and Joachim's Children," *Time* (March 9, 1953): 57–61.

9. An appreciation for the academic *Zeitgeist* in political science at the time can be obtained by reading the ideological reviews of Voegelin's book. See especially Robert Dahl, "The Science of Politics: Old and New," *World Politics* 7 (1955): 479–89.

10. *The New Science of Politics*, p. 2.

11. Ibid., p. 4.

12. Ibid., p. 125.

13. Ibid., p. 64.

14. Ibid., pp. 79–80.

15. In fact, Paul Caringella has brought to my attention that much of the first three volumes of *Order and History* was based on studies Voegelin wrote before *The New Science of Politics*.

16. The impact of *The New Science of Politics* was galvanized by Voegelin's renowned thesis that the essence of modernity lies in gnosticism. Although he modified this view in his later years, it remained a central theme in all of his subsequent work. Voegelin's analysis of gnosticism and modernity is too weighty to treat here at any length. I refer the reader to two excellent studies that examine this theme in Voegelin's thought: Russell Neili, "Eric Voegelin's Evolving Ideas on Gnosticism, Mysticism, and Modern Radical Politics," *Independent Journal of Philosophy* 5/6 (1988): 93–102; a revised version of this essay appeared as "Eric Voegelin: Gnosticism, Mysticism, and Modern Radical Politics," *Southern Review* 23 (1987): 332–48. See also Gregor Sebba,

"History, Modernity and Gnosticism," in *The Philosophy of Order*, ed. Opitz and Sebba, pp. 190–241.

17. *The New Science of Politics*, pp. 24–25.

18. Ibid., pp. 54–58, 76–77.

19. Ibid., pp. 61–63, 76–77.

20. Ibid., pp. 77–79.

21. Ibid., p. 77.

22. Ibid., p. 78.

23. Ibid.

24. See ibid., pp. 82–92.

25. This correspondence has been published in *The Philosophy of Order*, ed. Opitz and Sebba, pp. 434–62. It consists of Schutz's long review of Voegelin's book and Voegelin's response in the form of two essay-length letters on Christianity and gnosticism. Voegelin's discussion of Christianity in his first letter is one of the most trenchant statements he ever published on the matter. For a fine treatment of Schutz's and Voegelin's long correspondence, see Helmut R. Wagner, "Agreement in Discord: Alfred Schutz and Eric Voegelin," in *The Philosophy of Order*, ed. Opitz and Sebba, pp. 74–90. Wagner's intellectual biography of Schutz also contains a revealing chapter on Schutz's relation to Voegelin. See Wagner, *Alfred Schutz: An Intellectual Biography*, chap. 12, "Eric Voegelin: Friend in Philosophical Adversity," pp. 185–204.

26. *The Philosophy of Order*, ed. Opitz and Sebba, p. 443.

27. Ibid., p. 450.

28. Ibid., pp. 453–56.

29. Ibid., p. 450.

30. On this point Voegelin stated that the "trend toward a clear interpretation of the symbols has never been fully realized in the Catholic main line either. There is always a tinge of 'literal,' fundamentalistic understanding of dogmatics in the critical work" (ibid., p. 456). In a revealing passage he goes on to say that "all that I have said about the problem of 'essential Christianity' is therefore untenable from the Catholic standpoint and would have to be classified as a variant of that Modernism which has been condemned as a heresy" (ibid., p. 457). For the theological import of this statement we should take Voegelin at his word.

31. Ibid., p. 451.

32. *Order and History* I, p. ix.

33. These principles are culled from the introductions to *Order and History* I and II (see I, pp. 1–11; II, pp. 1–24).

34. *Order and History* I, p. 60.

35. This exhortation is from a letter to Alfred Schutz on the subject of Christianity dated January 1, 1953. It is published in *The Philosophy of Order*, ed. Opitz and Sebba, pp. 449–57, at p. 450.

36. See, for example, *Anamnesis*, p. 125.

37. "Anxiety and Reason," in *What is History? and Other Late Unpublished Writings*, pp. 52–110, at 92.

38. Ibid., p. 91.

39. *Anamnesis*, p. 87.

40. Ibid., p. 26.

41. These terms, philosophy and revelation, were virtually replaced by the terms noetic and pneumatic differentiation in Voegelin's later work. This substitution was made necessary in order to do justice to the revelatory nature of philosophy and the rational character of revelation, which is overlooked by the conventional distinction between "natural reason" and revelation. As we shall see in our treatment of *The Ecumenic Age*, Voegelin later emphasized the revelatory consciousness that is present in the Greek poets and philosophers. He even added that revelation must be seen far earlier because "the mystery of divine presence in reality is attested as experienced by man, as far back as *ca.* 20,000 B.C., by the petroglyphic symbols of the palaeolithicum" ("Response to Professor Altizer's 'A New History and a New but Ancient God?' " originally published in *Journal of the American Academy of Religion* 43 [1975]: 765–72; reprinted in *Eric Voegelin's Thought: A Critical Appraisal*, ed. Sandoz, pp. 189–97; reprinted in *Published Essays (1966–1985)*, pp. 292–303, at 293). With this enlargement of the horizon of human religious experience Voegelin had to abandon the notion that revelation was a unique monopoly of Israel, a convention of Jewish-Christian orthodoxy.

42. *Order and History* I, p. 222.

43. Ibid., p. 235.

44. For an excellent review article of Voegelin's *Israel and Revelation*, see Bernhard Anderson, "Politics and the Transcendent: Voegelin's Philosophical and Theological Exposition of the Old Testament in the Context of the Ancient Near East," in *Eric Voegelin's Search for Order in History*, ed. Stephen A. McKnight (Baton Rouge: Louisiana State University Press, 1978), pp. 62–100. The following outline of Israel's history partially follows Anderson's summation, pp. 66–72. Another lengthy summary and critical analysis of Voegelin's volume is Lynn Clapham, "Voegelin and Hebrew Scripture," in *Voegelin and the Theologian*, ed. Kirby and Thompson, pp. 104–37. Following Anderson, Clapham expands on the defects of Voegelin's treatment of Israel's history. Whatever deficiencies this book may contain in the eyes of biblical scholars, it must not be overlooked that, as an intellectual history of Israel by a philosopher, it is the first, ground-breaking work of its kind.

45. For the Mesopotamian story, see *Order and History* I, pp. 16–45.

46. For these near breakthroughs in Egypt, see ibid., pp. 82–110.

47. Ibid., p. 113.

48. Ibid., p. 130.

49. *Order and History* II, p. 6.

50. *Order and History* I, p. 407.

51. Ibid., p. 243. Voegelin is referring here to the problems of theocracy. He writes under the influence of Martin Buber's *Moses* (Zurich, 1948) and prefers his term "theopolitical" to "theocratic" to indicate "the peculiar constitution, both existential and transcendental, of Israel as a people under God" (*Order and History* I, p. 243, n. 12). See Martin Buber, *Moses: The Revelation and the Covenant* (New York: Harper and Row, 1958), pp. 101–40 (passim), 158, 186.

52. *Order and History* I, p. 215.

53. See ibid., pp. 282–311.

54. Ibid., p. 309.

55. For the treatment of Abraham, see ibid., pp. 188–99.

56. Ibid., p. 440.

57. Ibid., p. 467.

58. Ibid., p. 485.

59. Ibid., p. 501.

60. Ibid., p. 376.

61. Ibid., pp. 373, 378.

62. Ibid., p. 506.

63. See ibid., pp. 232–40, 439.

64. Ibid., p. 439.

65. Ibid., p. 240.

66. Ibid., p. 429.

67. Ibid., p. 428.

68. For the difference between revelation and philosophy as two distinct differentiations and their historical forms, see *Order and History* II, pp. 51–52.

69. *Order and History* II, *The World of the Polis*, is a reinterpretation of pre-Socratic thought. It is unrivaled in its analysis of the experiential roots of philosophy as it emerged in ancient Greece. Its chief asset lies in Voegelin's unfolding of the development of the soul in Hellenic consciousness.

70. On "metastatic faith," see *Order and History* I, pp. 452–58.

71. Ibid., p. xiii.

72. Ibid., p. xiv.

73. On Homer, see *Order and History* II, pp. 67–110.

74. For Voegelin's analysis of Achilles, Paris, and the role of the gods, see ibid., pp. 83–101.

75. Ibid., p. 103.

76. For Voegelin's discussion of Hesiod, see ibid., pp. 126–64.

77. Ibid., p. 157.

78. The importance of Hesiod as a transitional figure reached new heights for Voegelin in his last years. As we shall discuss in chap. 4, Voegelin returned to a study of Hesiod in his last work, *In Search of Order*. He found the beginning of

the *Theogony* to be the first great struggle to symbolize divine reality adequately within the confines of mythic consciousness, thus bringing into greater relief the long drama of differentiation.

79. Aristotle *Metaphysics* 1000a9. See also *Order and History* II, p. 128.

80. *Order and History* II, pp. 136–37.

81. Pythagoras and the Orphics probably had more to do with the development in Greek society of the notion of an immortal soul than Voegelin's study would allow us to think, based on his very brief treatment of them compared to the other pre-Socratic thinkers he analyzes. However, he alludes to the problem of interpreting the real nature of Pythagoreanism and Orphism when he says that, "unfortunately, however, we know very little about its sources; the extant fragments of these movements are so scanty that the development of symbols cannot be traced in continuity. All we know for certain is that in the mystery religions of this period the essential divinity of the soul was experienced, and the experience was expressed in the belief in the immortality of the soul" (ibid., p. 205). Voegelin also refers to this problem of the scarcity of sources in Orphism later in his work in the essay, "Wisdom and the Magic of the Extreme: A Meditation," originally published in *Southern Review* 17 (1981): 235–87; reprinted in *Eranos Jahrbuch, 1977* 46 (1981): 341–409; and in *Published Essays (1966–1985)*, pp. 315–75, at 358.

82. For Voegelin's discussion of these thinkers and movements and the transitional period from myth to philosophy, see *Order and History* II, chap. 6 and 7, pp. 165–202.

83. Ibid., pp. 178–83.

84. Ibid., p. 175.

85. Ibid.

86. Ibid., p. 176.

87. Ibid.

88. See ibid., p. 102.

89. Ibid., p. 176.

90. Ibid., p. 177.

91. Ibid., p. 208.

92. Ibid., pp. 208–9.

93. Ibid., p. 221.

94. On the meaning of Parmenidean *doxa*, which is often misunderstood, see ibid., pp. 214–17. Voegelin emphasizes here that the *doxai* in Parmenides must not be interpreted as false propositions or untruths, but rather as the ever-inadequate starting point, and periodic resting point, for the search for truth that can never end in true propositions. Within the confines of limited knowing in this world the many *doxai* are true, but compared to the one transcendent truth of being they appear as delusion. Parmenidean *doxa* is equivalent to the *eikos mythos*, the "likely myth" in Plato's late work, whereas in Socrates'

speech *doxa* is often reduced to appearance or mere opinion that is fervently denounced. In chap. 4 when we look at Voegelin's later theological work we shall see that this Parmenidean tension between delusion-truth is related to his understanding of faith-reason. Faith is the fundamental grasp of the whole of reality that reason is always in search of; reason is always attempting to understand what faith beholds. The search for truth in one's *doxa* is equivalent to the *fides quaerens intellectum* of St. Anselm. In Voegelin this tension is also closely related to the noetic-pneumatic structure of experience whereby the intentional direction of consciousness in the world of things yields to the luminous direction of consciousness that envisions nonthing reality. On the role of *doxa* in Greek philosophy and politics, see Hannah Arendt's very perceptive 1954 essay, "Philosophy and Politics," *Social Research* 57 (1990): 73–103.

95. *Order and History* II, pp. 206–7.

96. Ibid.

97. Ibid., p. 227.

98. Ibid., p. 228. Voegelin's attribution of these virtues to Heraclitus is a controversial interpretation. Voegelin discerns in Fragments B 18 (hope), B 35 (love), and B 86 (faith) the source for his assertion. See *Ancilla to the Pre-Socratic Philosophers*, trans. Kathleen Freeman (Cambridge: Harvard University Press, 1957), pp. 26, 27, 30.

99. *Order and History* II, p. 229.

100. Ibid., p. 227.

101. Ibid.

102. See ibid., pp. 231, 236–39.

103. For Voegelin's discussion of these three forces, see ibid., chap. 10, "Tragedy," pp. 242–66; chap. 11, "The Sophists," pp. 267–331; and chap. 12, "Power and History," pp. 332–73.

104. Ibid., p. 246.

105. *The New Science of Politics*, p. 73.

106. *Order and History* II, p. 247.

107. Ibid., p. 249. See also Voegelin's discussion of the *Suppliants* in *The New Science of Politics*, pp. 71–73.

108. *Order and History* II, p. 251.

109. Ibid., p. 263.

110. Ibid., p. 264.

111. Ibid.

112. Ibid., pp. 270–71.

113. Ibid., pp. 273–74.

114. Ibid., p. 273.

115. Ibid., p. 275.

116. Ibid.

117. With this recovery of the classical origin of theology, Voegelin is suggesting that theology is identical with authentic philosophy. As we shall discuss at greater length in the last chapter, this reconstruction of the historical roots of theology in Plato serves Voegelin's veiled attempt to remarry theology with philosophy. In this light, philosophy is not the "handmaiden" of theology as it has been conceived in the Christian tradition; rather, it is more like the parent to the child, or, better, like the phoenix to itself. Indeed, the conclusion we shall have to draw from Voegelin is that in the true sense authentic theology *is* philosophy and authentic philosophy *is* theology.

118. Ibid., pp. 293–94.

119. Ibid., pp. 294–95.

120. On *physis* and *nomos*, see ibid., pp. 281–84, 305–12.

121. Ibid., pp. 283–84.

122. Ibid., p. 319.

123. Ibid., p. 350.

124. Ibid., p. 363.

125. Ibid., p. 365.

126. Ibid., p. 239.

127. Voegelin's love for Plato is seen in the fact that he devotes almost three-quarters of this volume to his works. The significance of this volume should not go unmentioned. It contains, for the first time, a complete analysis of the Platonic myths, with an analysis of the symbolic construction of the *Republic* playing a central role. Moreover, this book contains an elaborate philosophy of revelation and myth, a one-of-a-kind study that has not appeared in modern thought since Schelling.

128. *Order and History* III, p. 5.

129. Ibid., p. 7.

130. Ibid., p. 272.

131. Ibid., pp. 18–19.

132. Ibid., p. 20.

133. Ibid., p. 39. As a later-day Plato resisting the later-day Gorgiases, Voegelin himself embodies this intrinsic authority of philosophy. This issue will be addressed in the last chapter in regard to Voegelin's relation to the institutional Church.

134. Ibid., p. 43.

135. Ibid.

136. Ibid.

137. Ibid., p. 47.

138. Ibid., pp. 52–54.

139. Ibid., p. 68.

140. Ibid., pp. 115–16.

141. Ibid., p. 67.

142. Ibid., p. 70.

143. Ibid., p. 87.

144. Ibid., p. 88.

145. Ibid., p. 91.

146. Ibid., p. 92.

147. Ibid.

148. Ibid.

149. Ibid., p. 90. See also *Order and History* II, pp. 169–70.

150. *Order and History* III, p. 137.

151. Ibid.

152. Ibid., p. 141.

153. Ibid., p. 139. I believe Plato gives the interpersonal dimension of erotic mania more weight than Voegelin allows in his analysis of the *Phaedrus*. Indeed, the concrete embodiment of love between persons as the principal vehicle of divine grace is in my mind is an unfortunate lacuna in Voegelin's work. This point will be taken up in the last chapter of this study.

154. Ibid., p. 160.

155. Ibid., p. 161.

156. Ibid., p. 162.

157. Ibid., pp. 168–69.

158. Ibid., p. 174.

159. Voegelin does not mean this term, "collective unconscious," in the sense given it by Jung.

160. Ibid., p. 178.

161. Ibid.

162. Ibid., p. 179.

163. Ibid., p. 183.

164. Ibid., p. 170.

165. Ibid., p. 192.

166. Ibid.

167. Ibid.

168. Ibid.

169. Ibid., p. 193.

170. Ibid., p. 195.

171. Ibid., p. 186. In the last volume of *Order and History*, Voegelin again takes up this problem of consciousness as both intentional and luminous. On that occasion he was compelled to return to the *Timaeus*. Thus, a more detailed treatment of this important dialogue will await us until we discuss that volume toward the end of chap. 4. On that occasion we shall see that not only will the Anselmian *credo ut intelligam* become the interpretative key for Voegelin's understanding of Plato's theology, but its correlative *fides quaerens intellectum* will emerge as the keystone to Voegelin's culminating philosophical-theological enterprise.

172. Ibid., p. 199.

173. Ibid., p. 227.

174. Ibid., p. 222.

175. Ibid., p. 223.

176. Ibid., pp. 221–22.

177. See ibid., pp. 228–29.

178. Ibid., p. 239.

179. Ibid., p. 229.

180. Ibid., p. 268.

181. Ibid., p. 272.

182. Ibid., p. 273.

183. Ibid., p. 276.

184. Ibid., p. 284.

185. Ibid., pp. 291–92.

186. Quoted in ibid., p. 292. This statement of Aristotle's is from a letter he wrote near the end of his life.

187. Ibid., pp. 296–97.

188. Ibid., p. 306.

189. Ibid., p. 321.

190. Ibid., p. 305.

191. Ibid., pp. 300, 302.

192. Ibid., p. 298.

193. Ibid., p. 303.

194. Ibid., p. 356.

195. Ibid., pp. 362–66.

196. Ibid., p. 362.

197. Ibid., p. 363.

198. Ibid.

199. Ibid., p. 369.

200. Ibid., p. 363.

201. For a long annotated list of Voegelin's references to Christianity in the first volume of *Order and History* alone, see McCarroll, "Man in Search of Divine Order in History," pp. 44–45, n. 95.

3. The Theory Refined:
The Later Writings, 1960–74

1. The most significant essays that appeared during this period which represented Voegelin's perfected theory of consciousness were "Eternal Being in Time" (1964); "What Is Political Reality?" (1966); "Immortality: Experience and Symbol" (1967); "Equivalences of Experience and Symbolization in History" (1970); "The Gospel and Culture" (1971); "On Hegel: A Study in

Sorcery" (1971); and "Reason: The Classic Experience" (1974). The first two and the last essays were published in the English edition of *Anamnesis*. The other three can be found in *Published Essays (1966–1985)*.

2. The time lapse between the publication of *Order and History* III and IV was seventeen years. This delay was caused in large part by the shift in Voegelin's thought that resulted from a further investigation of the historical materials. During this period Voegelin published the interim volume *Anamnesis*, a collection of theoretical essays which explicitly foreshadowed the break in vol. IV. The beginning of Voegelin's period of transition can be traced back to his article "Historiogenesis" that first appeared in *Philosophisches Jahrbuch* 68 (1960): 419–46, and was later reprinted in the German edition of *Anamnesis*. An expanded English version comprised chap. 1 of *The Ecumenic Age*, pp. 59–113.

Another reason for the delay in the publication of vol. IV was due to the fact that Voegelin became the founding director of the Institute for Political Science at the University of Munich in 1958, which position he held until 1969. The laborious chores of organization, administration, and fund-raising, on top of his teaching duties, depleted his available time and energy for scholarly work.

3. Arguably the most important of these essays is "What Is Political Reality?" in *Anamnesis*, pp. 143–213. At seventy pages it is also the longest and clearly represents a significant development in Voegelin's thought. It was the first essay to lay out an expanded theory of consciousness in precise, technical terms, which became the basis of his later writings. With few exceptions, Voegelin's commentators have failed to exploit the importance of this essay in relation to his work as a whole. Among the lengthy reviews of Voegelin's work that appeared in the wake of *The Ecumenic Age*, see, for example, John Corrington, "Order and Consciousness/Consciousness and Order: The New Program of Voegelin," in *Eric Voegelin's Search for Order in History*, ed. McKnight, pp. 155–95; J. M. Porter, "A Philosophy of History as a Philosophy of Consciousness," *Denver Quarterly* 10 (Autumn 1975): 96–104; William C. Havard, "Notes on Voegelin's Contribution to Political Theory," in *Eric Voegelin's Thought: A Critical Appraisal*, ed. Sandoz, pp. 87–114; and Bruce Douglass, "The Break in Voegelin's Program," *Political Science Reviewer* 7 (1977): 1–22.

The fact that these reviewers failed to perceive the significance of "What Is Political Reality?" supports the view that the general interpretation of Voegelin's work has failed to grasp the importance of his theory of consciousness (most fully developed in *Anamnesis*) which is the ground for understanding *Order and History*. An exception to this trend is a dissertation on Voegelin: John Kirby, "The Relation of Eric Voegelin's 'What Is Political Reality?' to His *Order and History*," (unpublished Ph.D. dissertation, St. Michael's College, Toronto, 1980). Kirby has also done a great service in his review of the critical literature on Voegelin, concluding that most of Voegelin's critics have failed to interpret him on his own ground due to the general failure to come to terms with his theory of consciousness. See Kirby's essay, "On Reading Eric Voegelin: A Note on the Critical Literature," in *Voegelin and the Theologian*, ed. Kirby and Thompson, pp. 24–60.

4. *Anamnesis*, p. 126.

5. On linguistic indices, see ibid., pp. 134–36, 175–82. Voegelin enlisted the term "index" to refer to any language symbol used in the exegesis of existence in the *metaxy*, such as "being" and "world," "transcendent" and "immanent," "God" and "man," "truth" and "beyond." An index does not refer to an existing entity; nor is it a concept, idea, or definition. It is a linguistic symbol pointing to the poles of existential tension which must be employed to counter any hypostatizing tendency that would reduce these realities to the status of things. Although we speak of them in terms of objects (since consciousness inevitably intends the form of objects), indices have no meaning apart from the movement of an inquiring consciousness in the realm of metaleptic participation. Thus, they are not descriptive but exegetic terms that indicate the movements of the soul in the *metaxy*, terms that emerge from an exploring consciousness struggling to articulate in language its experience of transcendent reality.

6. Ibid., p. 103. Voegelin first introduced the important symbol of the *metaxy* not with this passage but in an essay he published in 1964 entitled "Eternal Being in Time" (see pp. 116–40, at 128, 132–33). However, the term appears in a parenthetical context somewhat earlier in *Order and History* III, p. 66. For an excellent description of the *metaxy* in Plato's dialogues, see Paul Friedlaender, *Plato: An Introduction*, 2nd ed., trans. Hans Meyerhoff (Princeton: Princeton University Press, 1967), pp. 32–58.

7. *Anamnesis*, p. 132.

8. Ibid., p. 133. In *The Ecumenic Age*, Voegelin replaced the term "flowing presence" with "flux of presence" and "flux of divine presence." See *Order and History* IV, pp. 304–5.

9. "Equivalences of Experience and Symbolization in History," p. 115.

10. "The Gospel and Culture," p. 188.

11. *Order and History* IV, p. 243.

12. *Anamnesis*, pp. 138–39.

13. See Plato *Republic* 515c–e, *Laws* 644e–645a; and John 6:44, 12:32. For this and other equivalences between philosophy and the Gospel, see the ground-breaking essay "The Gospel and Culture." A more recent articulation of these equivalences, contrasting the Platonic and Christian visions, is found in the very important essay, "Wisdom and the Magic of the Extreme," pp. 362–71.

14. As we shall see, Voegelin finds these very unbalancing dynamics of theophany present in the articulation of Paul's pneumatic experience of the

resurrected Christ. See the chapter on "The Pauline Vision of the Resurrected," in *Order and History* IV, pp. 239–71. An excellent study of the distortions inherent in various spiritual movements that complements Voegelin's treatment of them is Ronald A. Knox, *Enthusiasm* (New York: Oxford University Press, 1961).

15. *Order and History* IV, p. 244.

16. "What is History?" in *What is History? and Other Late Unpublished Writings*, pp. 1–51, at 50.

17. *Order and History* IV, p. 228.

18. "The Gospel and Culture," pp. 187–88.

19. See especially the treatment of reason and revelation in *Order and History* IV, pp. 48, 228–38. Here, Voegelin states unequivocally that "revelation [is] the source of reason" (p. 228). The relation between classic philosophy and the Gospel is treated explicitly in the chapter "The Pauline Vision of the Resurrected" (ibid., pp. 239–71). Voegelin's pithiest expression of the differentiation of noetic and pneumatic experience is "Wisdom and the Magic of the Extreme," pp. 369–71.

20. The philosophic experience is the subject of Voegelin's important essay "Reason: The Classic Experience," in *Anamnesis*, pp. 89–115; this article originally appeared in *Southern Review* 10 (1974): 237–64, and is reprinted in *Published Essays (1966–1985)*, pp. 265–91. This article is Voegelin's most concise articulation of the nature of classic philosophy and its deformation.

21. The Greek term *tasis* is not a symbol employed by Plato or Aristotle but a later Stoic addition to the philosophic vocabulary. See *Anamnesis*, p. 97.

22. Voegelin's use of the term *libido dominandi* approximates Nietzsche's "will to power." See for example *Order and History* IV, pp. 20, 28, 254. See also *Anamnesis*, p. 106; and *Science, Politics, and Gnosticism*, trans. William J. Fitzpatrick (Chicago: Henry Regnery, 1968), p. 101, where he likens this term and *superbia* to original sin. The source of deformation could also be filled out by other relevant symbols, such as the Greek "hubris," the Augustinian *amor sui*, and the Hobbesian fear of the *summum malum* of death. See *Science, Politics, and Gnosticism*, pp. 102–4; and *The New Science of Politics*, pp. 179–86. Voegelin lists the various symbols of deformation which express a human vice that is a constant in history in *Order and History* V, p. 39.

23. Voegelin claims that practically the whole of modern philosophy reflects this trend, from Hobbes's "fear of death" to Heidegger's *Angst*. See *Science, Politics, and Gnosticism*, pp. 101–2. Bergson and Camus were the two "enlightened" exceptions to this deformation. Their work represented for Voegelin the paragon of resistance to the "climate of opinion" in early twentieth-century thought. See Henri Bergson, *The Two Sources of Morality and Religion*; Albert Camus, *The Rebel*, trans. Anthony Bower (New York: Random House, 1956).

24. See Pascal's *Pensées*, nos. 131, 137, 139–43, 168, 170, and passim, in *Pascal's Pensées*, trans. W. F. Trotter (New York: E. P. Dutton, 1958), pp. 38–44, 49. For Voegelin's discussion of Pascal, see *The New Science of Politics*, pp. 129, 185; and *From Enlightenment to Revolution*, pp. 53–56.

25. Voegelin is fond of citing Cicero as the author of the classic formulation of this spiritual disease, the symptoms of which, given their timeless ubiquity, sound very modern. See for example, "Wisdom and the Magic of the Extreme," pp. 322–23; and *Order and History* V, p 46. Cicero calls it the *morbus animi*, the "disease of the soul," and characterizes its nature as an *aspernatio rationis*, as a "rejection of reason." See Cicero, *Tusculan Disputations*, book 4, 23–36, in Loeb Classical Library, trans. J. E. King (Cambridge: Harvard University Press, 1945), pp. 350–67.

26. "The Eclipse of Reality," in *What is History? and Other Late Unpublished Writings*, pp. 111–62, at 156.

27. On "pneumapathology," see *Anamnesis*, p. 102; *Science, Politics, and Gnosticism*, p. 101; and *From Enlightenment to Revolution*, p. 117.

28. These are the words Voegelin himself used in a letter to Ellis Sandoz to describe his whole restorative enterprise. See Sandoz's introduction to *Order and History* V, p. 12.

29. An appreciation of the *zetema* in Voegelin's work can be found in his reflections on Toynbee's truncated *zetema* in the multivolume *Study of History* (Voegelin, "Toynbee's *History* as a Search for Truth," in *The Intent of Toynbee's 'History': A Cooperative Appraisal*, ed. Edward T. Gargan [Chicago: Loyola University Press, 1961], pp. 181–98).

30. Voegelin discusses this matter in very rich and concise terms in "Wisdom and the Magic of the Extreme," pp. 371–74.

31. *Order and History* V, p. 39.

32. *Anamnesis*, p. 206.

33. The original program of *Order and History* was to have six volumes. In the preface to vol. I (p. x), Voegelin tells us that the last three volumes of the series, which never appeared, were to bear these titles: vol. IV, Empire and Christianity; vol. V, The Protestant Centuries; vol. VI, The Crisis of Western Civilization.

34. Voegelin first alluded to these problems in his essay "World-Empire and the Unity of Mankind," in *International Affairs* 38 (1962): 170–88. This article could be viewed as a miniversion of *The Ecumenic Age*, for it contains all the major themes and many of the insights of the later work.

35. *Order and History* IV, p. 2.

36. Voegelin argues the case against cultural diffusion in his essay "What is History?" pp. 40–42.

37. On the limitations of Jasper's "axis-time," see *Order and History* IV, pp. 2–6, 309–12; *Order and History* II, pp. 19–23; and *Anamnesis*, p. 119. The thesis

of the axial period is argued by Jaspers in his *The Origin and Goal of History*, trans. Michael Bullock (New Haven: Yale University Press, 1953), pp. 1–21.

38. See *Order and History* I, p. 131; IV, p. 187.

39. Voegelin's previous tendency to see the great spiritual experiences in history as ontological leaps that demarcate existence in history as either mythic or revelatory was probably influenced not only by Jewish-Christian orthodoxy but also by Plato, who in the *Republic* draws a division between the mythic-Homeric age and the new age ordained by Socrates. Thus the Platonic division parallels the Christian distinction B.C./A.D.

An example of Voegelin's correction of this tendency in his own writing can be seen in *The Ecumenic Age* where he acknowledges the Egyptian Amon hymns as the expression of actual differentiating experiences on the same level as those of the Jewish prophets, Greek philosophers, and Hindu mystics (see *Order and History* IV, pp. 7, 147–49; "The Gospel and Culture," pp. 194–95). Previously he had characterized the hymns as a "speculative exploration" that "does not break with polytheism" because "the Egyptian monotheistic development is not motivated by a genuine experience of transcendence" (*Order and History* I, pp. 86–87). In order to show that mystical experiences did not begin with the philosophers or prophets, Voegelin now seems more willing to distinguish between a mystic experience that is valid wherever and whenever divine reality enters the soul, and a mystic experience that is accompanied by a more adequate intellectual understanding and conceptual expression.

40. "The Gospel and Culture," pp. 195–96.

41. *Order and History* IV, p. 7.

42. A helpful treatment of this idea in Voegelin's work is provided by Barry Cooper, "Voegelin's Concept of Historiogenesis: An Introduction," *Historical Reflections/Réflexions historiques* 4 (1977): 231–50. A revised form of this essay appeared as chap. 4 in Barry Cooper, *The Political Theory of Eric Voegelin*, Toronto Studies in Theology 27 (Lewiston, N.Y.: Edwin Mellen Press, 1986), pp. 125–60.

43. *Order and History* IV, p. 101.

44. Ibid., pp. 60–64.

45. Ibid., p. 90ff.

46. Ibid., p. 59.

47. Ibid., p. 6.

48. Ibid., p. 59.

49. Lest Voegelin's comparison between these two symbolisms, which are separated by nearly four thousand years, seem too facile or incongruous, let it be recalled that Voegelin sees human experience as essentially the same regardless of the historical epoch in which people live. In this fourth volume of *Order and History* he is beginning to work more and more with the "constants" of consciousness that appear in culturally different, but structurally similar,

"equivalents." Without this view of consciousness as his premise his theory of equivalence would be vacuous. We recall the cardinal principles which underlie this theory and all of *Order and History*: "(1) the nature of man is constant; (2) the range of human experience is always present (to everyone in every epoch) in the fullness of its dimensions; and (3) the structure of the range varies from compactness to differentiation" (*Order and History* I, p. 60). These principles must be seen as a radical rejection of the progressivist doctrines which attempt to carve the history of consciousness into a series of stages, disconnecting the people of one age from those of another. Whatever the time or place, the basic content of human experience is essentially the same: all humans experience an erotic tension toward the divine ground. This is the fundamental nature of the human being which connects a modern person living in the twentieth century with a myth maker in ancient Sumer. It is also what links people across different religious and cultural boundaries. Human nature, primitive or developed, compact or differentiated, is one. All people are united on the level of concrete humanity: the common experience of the loving pull of divine being. The fear of falling from this ordering truth into nothingness is what motivates the construction of myths of order in the first place. On this point, see *Order and History* IV, p. 73; and the very important statement of fundamental principles in *Order and History* II, pp. 4–7.

50. *Order and History* IV, pp. 7–8, 64–67. See also the material on Hegel in *Order and History* II, pp. 16–19; *Anamnesis*, pp. 120–21; and *Science, Politics, and Gnosticism*, pp. 40–44, 67–80. See as well Voegelin's essay "On Hegel: A Study in Sorcery," originally published in *Studium Generale* 24 (1971): 335–68; reprinted in *Published Essays (1966–1985)*, pp. 213–55.

51. *Order and History* I, p. ix.

52. *Order and History* IV, p. 8.

53. Ibid., p. 6.

54. Ibid., p. 74.

55. Ibid., p. 174. On Anaximander's dictum, see ibid., pp. 174–76.

56. Ibid., p. 74.

57. Ibid., p. 75.

58. Ibid.

59. Ibid., pp. 73–74.

60. Ibid., p. 114.

61. Ibid., p. 117.

62. Ibid., p. 134.

63. On the pragmatic *ecumene*, see ibid., pp. 117–33. On the spiritual *ecumene*, see ibid., pp. 134–44.

64. "Dogmatomachy" carries the dual meaning of the war of dogmas and dogmatic or ideological wars. For Voegelin's usage of this term, see ibid., pp. 48, 57, 330.

65. Ibid., p. 58.

66. Ibid., p. 228.

67. One of the more pronounced criticisms of Voegelin's treatment of Christianity in *The Ecumenic Age* concerned his choice of Paul's experience and writings over that of Jesus and the Gospels. But in light of the fundamental principles of Voegelin's noetic inquiry this choice becomes comprehensible. Voegelin's fundamental hermeneutical method seeks to examine experiences as they can be discerned from extant literary texts. Paul left writings that expressed his own experience; Jesus comes to us only through the mediating interpretations of other writers. Voegelin's exclusion of a major figure for direct treatment has precedent. In *The World of the Polis*, for example, Voegelin gives scant attention to Pythagoras, who is generally considered the most influential pre-Socratic figure in Greece. Xenophanes, Parmenides, and Heraclitus, whom he treats at length, all left behind written works (albeit only in fragments), whereas what is known of Pythagoras (like Socrates and Jesus) comes exclusively from second-hand sources.

Another reason for his focusing on Paul concerns the nature of spiritual reality. Voegelin's basic conception of revelation leads him to explain Paul's "vision of the resurrected" as a symbolic expression of the actual event of Paul's pneumatic experience within Paul himself, rather than as some miraculous event such as an empty tomb or physical appearance. Revelation, Voegelin claims, does not tender information about the world. It is not outside human experience; rather, it is a differentiating movement within experience. Those who seek to locate revelation in miraculous events Voegelin would consider spiritually obtuse. See Eugene Webb's treatment of this problem in "Eric Voegelin's Theory of Revelation," *Thomist* 42 (1978): 95–110; reprinted in *Eric Voegelin's Thought: A Critical Appraisal*, ed. Sandoz, pp. 157–77, at 167–68.

68. *Order and History* IV, p. 241.

69. Ibid.

70. Ibid.

71. Ibid., p. 270.

72. Ibid., p. 58. Voegelin finds the beginning of this tendency in Aristotle; see *Order and History* III, pp. 271–92. On the derailment of philosophy, see ibid., pp. 277–79.

73. *Order and History* IV, pp. 144, 255, 259.

74. Ibid., p. 263.

75. Ibid., p. 267.

76. Ibid., p. 263.

77. Ibid., p. 242.

78. Ibid., pp. 242–43.

79. Ibid., p. 253; see also *Anamnesis*, p. 91.

80. *Order and History* IV, p. 233.

81. Ibid., p. 231.

82. Ibid., p. 232.

83. Ibid., p. 268.

84. Ibid., pp. 268–69.

85. In *Israel and Revelation* Voegelin argued that the roots can be traced back to the metastatic faith of Second Isaiah. See *Order and History* I, pp. xiii, 452–58.

86. On *oikoumene* and *okeanos*, see *Order and History* IV, pp. 201–7.

87. On the Chinese *ecumene*, see ibid., pp. 272–99.

88. On the universality of the Christian *homonoia*, see *From Enlightenment to Revolution*, pp. 95–96.

89. *Order and History* IV, p. 6.

90. Ibid., p. 303.

91. Ibid.

92. Ibid., p. 314.

93. Ibid., p. 301.

94. Ibid.

95. Ibid., p. 6.

96. Ibid., p. 304.

97. Ibid., p. 227.

98. The best overview of Voegelin's understanding of history as a process of transfiguration is Glenn Hughes, "Eric Voegelin's View of History as a Drama of Transfiguration," *International Philosophical Quarterly* 30 (1990): 449–64. A revised version of this essay appears as chap. 3 in Hughes's very fine study: *Mystery and Myth in the Philosophy of Eric Voegelin* (Columbia: University of Missouri Press, 1993).

99. Ibid., p. 228.

100. Ibid., p. 17. In this fourth volume of *Order and History* Voegelin began to use the symbols "beginning" and "beyond" as a substitute for his earlier distinction between "myth" and "revelation," the terms he employed in the first three volumes. He did this perhaps to avoid the connotations that "myth"and "revelation" carry in the topical debates. "Beginning" refers to the primary experience of the cosmos which historically found expression in creation myths, while "beyond" alludes to the revelatory awakening of divine presence in the soul in mystic experience, to the transcendent realm that gives history and the soul an eschatological direction.

101. For Voegelin's revised view of the cosmogonic myth, see ibid., pp. 10–11.

102. Ibid., p. 19.

103. Ibid.

104. Ibid.

105. This new development was first articulated in his essay "Wisdom and the Magic of the Extreme." On reflective distance, see pp. 343–45; on vision and *noesis*, pp. 337–38; and on Plato's vision, pp. 357–71.

106. On "the Question," see *Order and History* IV, pp. 316–30.

107. "Wisdom and the Magic of the Extreme," p. 337.

108. *Order and History* IV, p. 330.

109. Ibid., p. 331.

110. Ibid., p. 329.

111. *The New Science of Politics*, p. 122.

112. *Order and History* IV, p. 334. In ibid., pp. 202–3, Voegelin shows how the idea of an "astrophysical universe" is actually historically rooted in the concupiscential ecumenic expansions which under modern science move toward an astronomical horizon, leading to "the vulgarian belief that man is no longer living in the cosmos but in a 'physical universe'" (p. 203). During this period Voegelin took great interest in the philosophical problems of a "physical universe" and once found time in 1968 to formulate his own analysis in a "thought experiment." See his essay "The Moving Soul," in *What is History? and Other Late Unpublished Writings*, pp. 163–72. This short work is a playful exercise in modern physics and cosmology that argues against the notion that a physical universe can be constructed on the basis of theoretical physics, either Newtonian or Einsteinian. Voegelin concluded that "there is no 'physical universe' independent of the perspectival primary experience of the cosmos" (p. 172), that the symbol "universe" is no more than a demythologized version of the myth of the cosmos, a reality which can only be apprehended by a soul in existential tension toward the ground. For further discussion of this essay see the editors' introduction in ibid., pp. xxiv–xxvii.

4. The Theory Achieved:
The Last Writings, 1975–85

1. "Quod Deus Dicitur," an unfinished essay that Voegelin was working on at the time of his death, incorporates about ten pages from "The Beginning and the Beyond." Originally published in *Journal of the American Academy of Religion* 53 (1985): 569–84, it is reprinted in *Published Essays (1966–1985)*, pp. 376–94. Two other, shorter essays that were written during this period are "Response to Professor Altizer's 'A New History and a New but Ancient God?'" *Journal of the American Academy of Religion* 43 (1975): 765–72, reprinted in *Eric Voegelin's Thought: A Critical Appraisal*, ed. Sandoz, pp. 189–97, and in *Published Essays (1966–1985)*, pp. 292–303; and "The Meditative Origin of the Philosophical Knowledge of Order," in *The Beginning and the Beyond: Papers from the Gadamer and Voegelin Conferences*, ed. Lawrence, pp. 43–51, originally published as "Der

meditative Ursprung philosophischen Ordnungwissens," in *Zeitschrift für Politik* 28 (1981): 130–37. These two shorter essays contain material from the longer essays cited above. Also of note is the introductory essay to the English edition of *Anamnesis*, entitled "Remembrance of Things Past" (pp. 3–13), which was composed in 1977 and reprinted in *Published Essays (1966–1985)*, pp. 304–14.

2. Among many examples, see, for instance, *Order and History* V, pp. 20–23, where, in an analysis of Genesis chap. 1, Voegelin embarks on a precautionary digression to ward off the habitual misunderstandings of the text; and pp. 44–47 where he engages in another digressionary reflection on the timeless spiritual disorders that are the "acts of oblivion" the philosopher must resist in the restoration of the symbols of order.

3. "The Beginning and the Beyond," p. 196.

4. To date the only substantive articles on Voegelin's last writings are Paul Caringella, "Eric Voegelin: Philosopher of Divine Presence," *Modern Age* 33 (Spring 1990): 7–22; expanded version in *Eric Voegelin's Significance for the Modern Mind*, ed. Ellis Sandoz, (Baton Rouge: Louisiana State University Press, 1991), pp. 174–205; Fred Dallmayr, "Voegelin's Search for Order," *Journal of Politics* 51 (May 1989): 411–30; and Gerhart Niemeyer, "God and Man, World and Society: The Last Work of Eric Voegelin," *Review of Politics* 51 (1989): 107–23.

5. *Order and History* IV, p. 233.

6. Ibid., p. 264. See also *Anamnesis*, p. 198, where Voegelin applies Thomas's question whether the "He Who Is" of Exodus chap. 3 is the proper name for God (*Summa Theologiae* I, qu. 12, a. 11) to a discussion of the incomprehensible depth of the divine ground that goes beyond the symbolic language of participation.

7. Voegelin repeats Plato's question at *Order and History* IV, p. 229, and *Order and History* V, pp. 79, 82.

8. *Order and History* IV, p. 233.

9. Ibid., p. 232.

10. On the paradox of consciousness, see *Order and History* V, pp. 15–16.

11. Heidegger formulated this same structure in his pre-Socratic distinction between *das Sein* (which is ultimately the Anaximandrian *apeiron*) and *das Seiende* or *die seienden Dinge*.

12. Ibid., p. 16. Voegelin first introduced the notion of the It-reality in "Wisdom and the Magic of the Extreme," p. 362.

13. Once, in his 1968 essay "Anxiety and Reason," Voegelin used the very Heideggerian-sounding phrase "the clearing in existence" to denote the function of "reason" as that human activity whereby reality appears. See "Anxiety and Reason," pp. 87–88.

14. "The Beginning and the Beyond," p. 176.

15. *Order and History* V, p. 19.

16. On every story beginning in the middle, see ibid., pp. 27–31.

17. Ibid., p. 28.

18. Ibid., p. 29.

19. Ibid.

20. Ibid., p. 68.

21. Ibid., p. 17.

22. In one place Voegelin even becomes self-conscious about whether his own meditative story is truly the substory of the comprehending story it endeavors to be. See ibid., p. 83.

23. Ibid., p. 41.

24. Ibid., pp. 41, 61–62.

25. Ibid., p. 41.

26. Ibid., p. 37.

27. Ibid., p. 38.

28. Ibid., p. 39.

29. "The Beginning and the Beyond," p. 180.

30. See ibid., pp. 181–85.

31. *Order and History* V, p. 43.

32. On existential resistance, see ibid., pp. 35–37.

33. Ibid., p. 48.

34. Ibid., p. 49.

35. Ibid., p. 50.

36. See Voegelin's more compendious discussion of the development of the "Ich" philosophy which led to Hegel's derailment in his "Response to Professor Altizer's 'A New History and a New but Ancient God?'" pp. 295–302.

37. "Equivalences of Experience and Symbolization in History," p. 122.

38. Ibid., p. 128.

39. Ibid., p. 126.

40. *Order and History* V, pp. 54–55.

41. Ibid., p. 53.

42. In a twist on Jung, Voegelin uses "unconscious" to mean "a socially dominant state of consciousness deformed by oblivion that causes personal and public disturbances of order" (ibid., p. 61).

43. Ibid., p. 57.

44. Ibid., pp. 58–59.

45. Ibid., p. 62.

46. Ibid. Also quoted by Voegelin in "Wisdom and the Magic of the Extreme," p. 340.

47. *Order and History* V, pp. 62–63.

48. Ibid., p. 69.

49. For Voegelin's discussion of Hesiod, see ibid., pp. 70–79. This analysis must be read alongside Voegelin's earlier treatment of Hesiod in *Order and*

History II, pp. 73, 126–64.

50. *Order and History* V, p. 72.

51. Ibid., p. 73.

52. Ibid., p. 74.

53. Ibid., p. 78.

54. Ibid., p. 79; "The Beginning and the Beyond," p. 211.

55. *Order and History* V, p. 30.

56. Ibid., p. 93.

57. In addition to his treatment of Leibniz and Bonaventure, Voegelin planned to expand this section on "The Hesiodian Vision of Reality" by including a discussion of the symbol of "God" in Thomas Aquinas and the symbol of "autogenesis" in the Neoplatonists. He never lived to complete it. See ibid., p. 79. The direction Voegelin would go in his treatment of the symbol of "God" in Thomas Aquinas can be ascertained by reading his discussion of Thomas in "Quod Deus Dicitur," pp. 376–79, 394.

58. See *Order and History* V, pp. 80–84.

59. Voegelin's analysis in this volume knows no linear progression. He does not treat historical sources in any chronological order; rather, true to his nonlinear understanding of history, the logical progression of this final work is determined solely by the problems under analysis. This compels him to analyze historical sources in a circuitous manner. Thus, in chap. 2, for example, he begins with the modern German context of Hegel (eighteenth–nineteen century), moves backward to the Greek antiquity of Hesiod (eighth century B.C.), then forward to the medieval context of Bonaventure (thirteenth century), returns to modernity with Leibniz (early eighteenth century), and finally back again to ancient Greece and Plato (fourth century B.C.). Other thinkers are discussed along the way, but this is the rough course of his deliberations in this his final work.

60. See Saint Bonaventure, *The Mind's Journey to God*, trans. Lawrence S. Cunningham (Chicago: Franciscan Herald Press, 1979), pp. 71–77.

61. *Order and History* V, p. 84. Ironically, one cannot help but think that Voegelin's work also carries a defensive touch given the possible deformations of it that he consistently attempts to thwart, not to speak of the actual distortions of his writings already in print.

62. See Gottfried Wilhelm Leibniz, *Philosophical Writings*, trans. Mary Morris, Everyman's Library, no. 905 (New York: E. P. Dutton, 1934), pp. 8–10, 25–26.

63. *Order and History* V, p. 82.

64. Leibniz, *Philosophical Writings*, p. 26.

65. *Order and History* V, p. 82.

66. Ibid., p. 83.

67. *Order and History* IV, p. 250.

68. Ibid., p. 251.

69. See Voegelin's letter to Schutz, entitled "On Christianity," *The Philosophy of Order*, ed. Opitz and Sebba, p. 450. On this occasion Voegelin also mentioned the fuller differentiation in Christianity of a Church beyond secular politics: "The differentiation of the problem of church, the understanding that the orientation toward transcendent perfection is not a political one, is still another achievement of Christianity" (ibid., p. 451).

70. Although the symbol *fides* never occurs in Plato's works and the method of a *fides quaerens intellectum* is Augustinian in origin, I find the application of these symbols to Plato very defensible. Without doubt these symbols are historically Christian, not Platonic, but the charge that Voegelin is thus engaged in a dubious anachronism misses the equivalence of meaning in experience and meditative analysis that the symbols carry. Therefore, to speak of "Plato's *fides*" or "Plato's *fides quaerens intellectum*" should be construed, not as a gratuitous imposition, but as a philosophical discovery. As we shall see, Voegelin finds in these symbols an experiential content that transcends the historical parameters of Christian faith and theology.

71. *Order and History* III, p. 183.

72. *Order and History* V, p. 96.

73. "Consciousness and Order: 'Foreword' to *Anamnesis* (1966)," trans. Eric Voegelin, *Logos* 4 (1983): 22–23.

74. See *Order and History* V, p. 90; "The Beginning and the Beyond," pp. 55–59. Voegelin first made this connection in *Order and History* III, p. 186. Although Voegelin never actually points it out, the equivalent of the Christian *fides quaerens intellectum* in Plato is the statement by Timaeus that "as being is to becoming, so truth is to belief [*pistis*]" (29c). But see *Order and History* III, p. 196, where this matter is taken into account.

75. See ibid., pp. 195–98.

76. *Order and History* V, p. 87. Kathleen Freeman translates this fragment as "For it is the same to think and to be." But with the stress on the *einai*, she thinks the tenor would be better stated as "That which it is possible to think is identical with that which can Be." See her *Ancilla to the Pre-Socratic Philosophers*, p. 42.

77. *Order and History* V, p. 89.

78. "The Beginning and the Beyond," p. 211.

79. *Order and History* V, p. 90. On the concept of the *eikon* in the *Timaeus*, see also "Anxiety and Reason," pp. 39–40.

80. *Order and History* V, p. 91.

81. Ibid., p. 93.

82. Ibid., p. 94.

83. For a contemporary example of the conventional assessment, see Robert Sokolowski, *The God of Faith and Reason: Foundations of Christian Theology*

(Notre Dame: University of Notre Dame Press, 1982). Although very perceptive on the relation between faith and reason, and generally inclined to
break away from traditional theological categories, Sokolowski maintains the
conventional divisions that limit his analysis. For example, he typically uses
terms like "revealed religion" and "natural religion," the "Christian God" and
the "pagan god," subjecting Plato, of course, to the latter categories. And yet
Plato fares better than Aristotle because of his transcendental analysis of the
Whole beyond "substance" but nevertheless remains inferior to the Christian
doctrine of creation with its radical distinction between God and the world,
manifested, for example, in Anselm's *Proslogion* (Sokolowski, *The God of Faith
and Reason*, pp. 49–51). In light of Voegelin's interpretation, this kind of reading
can no longer do justice to Plato's accomplishment. Even though one can certainly argue that Christianity exceeded classic philosophy in its symbolization
of divine reality, without a viable theory of differentiation and equivalence
that gives sense to the process of revelation in history, the historical texts
and events will become distorted. Consequently, the real problems of imaging
divine mystery which no philosophy or religion, including Christianity, can
finally solve, will be mishandled or neglected altogether.

84. *Order and History* V, p. 95.

85. Ibid., p. 96.

86. As suggested earlier, Voegelin sees in the pneumatic experience in
Israelite-Judaic history such a heavy irruption from the beyond that there is left
little or no emotional room for the seeker's noetic ascent toward the beyond,
an ascent that would assuage the unrest of the seeker's soul. As a consequence
there was prevented in Israel the full differentiation of the two modes of the
beginning and the beyond. Thus, in the Prologue of John's Gospel the word
present in Christ was made the same word present in the beginning that has
now become flesh. This identification has caused theological problems that have
yet to be fully resolved. See "The Beginning and the Beyond," pp. 186–87.
This particular problem deriving from the high Christology of John's Prologue
will be taken up in chap. 6.

87. Though the Christian faith has Jesus as its focus, its "content" is still
the cosmos at large. The cosmos is the experiential context of every *fides* and
thus every *fides* has the one cosmos as its spiritual substance. This is true even
with Jesus' *fides,* which is directed toward the creator of the cosmos.

88. *Order and History* V, p. 99.

89. "The Beginning and the Beyond," pp. 180–81. Later in this essay
Voegelin suggests the reason that Plato did not dismiss the intracosmic gods
outright. For one, the beyond, which one would expect to dethrone completely
the Olympian gods, does not exhaust all of divine reality experienced in the
cosmological *fides*. This arises with the question whether the beginning and
the beyond are identical. Although his expansion of the *parousia* of being to

the cosmos seems to point in the direction of identification, Plato equivocates, for example, in the *Timaeus*, where he has the creative Demiurge impose an order of form on a preexistent material. The creativity of the beginning has something to do with the surplus of divine reality that Plato believes is not exhausted by the experience of the beyond.

Secondly, the Olympian gods represent the immortality that is to be achieved by the human *psyche*. Since immortality of mortals does not suggest their transformation into the eminent source of immortality, there must be an intermediate realm of immortality accessible to humanity which participates in the immortal beyond. On this Voegelin claims that the ambiguous "function of the immortal gods in Plato's *fides* is equivalent to that of the visions of the resurrected Christ in the Christian *fides*" (ibid., p. 224).

90. *Order and History* V, p. 99.

91. Ibid., p. 100.

92. Ibid., p. 101.

93. Ibid.

94. Ibid., p. 102.

95. Quoted in ibid.

96. Ibid., p. 103.

97. Ibid., p. 105.

98. Ibid., pp. 105–6.

99. Ibid., p. 107.

100. Ibid., p. 106.

101. "The Beginning and the Beyond," p. 188.

102. Ibid. With these words Voegelin is attempting to establish the "objectivity" of his lifelong quest for truth, though, as should be familiar by now, he avoids the use of that word. As shall be discussed shortly, the reason given in this meditation is because of the baggage of "intentionalist reduction" that the word "objective" carries.

103. Ibid.

104. Ibid., p. 191

105. Ibid., pp. 191–92. However, Voegelin has elsewhere said that "even this expansion of the *fides* . . . to all of the experiences of divine reality in which history constitutes itself, cannot be said to go beyond 'Christianity.' For it is the Christ of the Gospel of John who says of himself: 'Before Abraham was, I am' (8:58); and it is Thomas Aquinas who considers the Christ to be the head of the *corpus mysticum* that embraces, not only Christians, but all mankind from the creation of the world to its end. . . . I cannot admit, therefore, a conflict with 'Christianity'; I can admit only that the Thomasic declaration, included as accepted doctrine in Denzinger's *Enchiridion*, has aroused hardly any response among theologians and philosophers in their work on the process of revelatory experiences in history" ("Response to Professor Altizer's 'A New

History and a New but Ancient God?' " p. 294).

106. "Response to Professor Altizer," p. 294; "The Beginning and the Beyond," p. 192.

107. See St. Anselm, *Basic Writings*, trans. S. N. Deane (La Salle, Ill: Open Court, 1962), pp. 47–80.

108. "The Beginning and the Beyond," pp. 196–98. Voegelin argues that because "ontology" is a neologism of the seventeenth century (first used in Clauberg's *Metaphysica* of 1646) it cannot be facilely applied to Anselm without distortion. "Ontology" was the scientific synonym for "metaphysics," which was introduced into the Western vocabulary by the Arab translators of Aristotle's *meta ta physica* and popularized by St. Thomas in his commentary on that work. This was the Aristotelian "first philosophy" or "theology," which for Aristotle "was no more than a general pointer to the area beyond the categories that apply to physical phenomena" ("The Beginning and the Beyond," p. 197). According to Voegelin, the use of the term "ontology" was an attempt to extricate philosophy from the theological dogmatism that arose in the wake of the Reformation. As the "science of being" that attempted to recover the truth of experience, the effort was short-circuited by its failure to recover the experiential basis of the "metaphysical" or "theological" symbolisms. Along with the degenerative dogmatism of the *fides* there was rejected the *ratio fidei* that was Anselm's main concern. So the true reason of the quest, formulated as the erotic/noetic tension toward the divine ground in Plato and Aristotle, was replaced by an instrumental "rationalism" by post-Reformation philosophers. Anselm's "proof" then is not "ontological." To say so would be a gross anachronism. Voegelin declares that since the motive forces behind Anselm's meditative argument are spirit and reason, the only proper adjectives describing his quest are "pneumatic" and "noetic" (ibid., p. 198).

109. Ibid., p. 192; "Response to Professor Altizer," p. 301. See Karl Barth, *Anselm: Fides Quaerens Intellectum*, trans. Ian W. Robertson (Richmond: John Knox Press, 1960); and Etienne Gilson, *The Spirit of Medieval Philosophy*, trans. A. H. C. Downes (New York: Charles Scribner's Sons, 1936), especially chap. 1 and 2 on "Christian Philosophy," pp. 1–41 (see also pp. 59–63).

110. "The Beginning and the Beyond," p. 193.

111. Ibid., p. 194. Voegelin cites this phrase as being from the preface to Anselm's *De Fide Trinitatis*. Anselm never composed a work with this title. This is not, however, a miscitation on Voegelin's behalf. The explanation lies in the fact that Voegelin was dependent on Gilson's *History of Christian Philosophy in the Middle Ages*, where Gilson paraphrases this statement (p. 617, n. 45) and locates its source as *De fide Trinitatis et de Incarnatione Verbi*, preface, in Migne's *Patrologia Latina* 158, p. 261A. The Migne edition of Anselm's works is not the critical edition but an 1863 reprint of the Gerberon edition published in Paris in 1675. The critical edition belongs to *Anselm's Opera Omnia* by F. S. Schmitt published

in Rome in 1940. It is in five volumes and remains the authoritative edition on which all current translations (including the 1984 Anselm concordance) are based. In the Schmitt edition the sentence which includes the phrase *medium inter fidem et speciem* is actually found in the commendation of *Cur Deus Homo* to Pope Urban II, which precedes the preface to that work. For the complete English rendition, see the translation of *Cur Deus Homo* in Saint Anselm, *Anselm of Canterbury* 3, trans. and ed. Jasper Hopkins and Herbert Richardson (New York: Edwin Mellen Press, 1976), p. 41.

112. "The Beginning and the Beyond," p. 194.

113. Ibid; St. Anselm, *Basic Writings*, pp. 67–68.

114. "The Beginning and the Beyond," pp. 195–96.

115. Ibid., p. 198. Actually, contra Voegelin, Anselm does in fact use the word *probatio* in the preface to the *Proslogion*.

116. Ibid., p. 199. See Voegelin's discussion of the fool in "Quod Deus Dicitur," pp. 385–90. This section was borrowed from "The Beginning and the Beyond," pp. 198–203.

117. Ibid., p. 200; "Quod Deus Dicitur," p. 386.

118. In the early Christian centuries we see this same dynamic operating in the conciliar debates that produced "orthodoxies" in opposition to the prevalent "heresies."

119. "The Beginning and the Beyond," p. 203; "Quod Deus Dicitur," p. 390.

120. This insight is profoundly expressed at the end of *Order and History* V, p. 102. This whole last section of Voegelin's analysis of Plato's *Timaeus* (which we discussed in the previous section) is part of a culminating philosophical/theological meditation on divine being that, for this reader, has no equal in modern thought. It is a preeminent model of faith seeking understanding.

121. "The Beginning and the Beyond," p. 205.

122. Ibid., p. 206.

123. Ibid.

124. Ibid., p. 207.

125. Ibid., p. 208.

126. A sample of the *Parmenides* text reads: "Therefore the one in no sense *is*. It cannot, then, 'be' even to the extent of 'being' one, for then it would be a thing that is and has being. Rather, if we can trust such an argument as this, it appears that the one neither is one nor is at all" (141e).

127. See Etienne Gilson, *The Christian Philosophy of St. Thomas Aquinas*, trans. L. K. Shook (New York: Random House, 1956).

128. "The Beginning and the Beyond," p. 210.

129. Ibid., p. 211.

130. See "Wisdom and the Magic of the Extreme," pp. 339, 348.

131. "The Beginning and the Beyond," pp. 209–10, 212. For Gilson's statement, see *The Christian Philosophy of St. Thomas Aquinas*, p. 101.

132. "The Beginning and the Beyond," p. 212.

133. We should recall here that Voegelin earlier expressed this experience as being structured not only by faith but also by hope and love. These three formative forces on the soul, which Heraclitus first identified as distinguishable sources of knowledge, are really interdependent components in the vision upon which *noesis* works. See *Anamnesis*, p. 184.

134. For further discussion of vision and *noesis* as they relate to the philosopher's *fides quaerens intellectum*, see "Wisdom and the Magic of the Extreme," pp. 337ff.

135. "The Beginning and the Beyond," p. 228.

136. Ibid., p. 229.

137. Ibid., p. 230.

138. For Voegelin's analysis of Plato's vision, see especially "Wisdom and the Magic of the Extreme," pp. 343–71, and "The Beginning and the Beyond," pp. 227–32.

139. "Wisdom and the Magic of the Extreme," p. 343.

140. Ibid.

141. Ibid., pp. 344–45.

142. Ibid., p. 348.

143. The similarities and differences between philosophy and the Gospel are analyzed in Voegelin's important 1971 essay, "The Gospel and Culture." See especially pp. 189–96.

144. Voegelin claims the Gospel is "the saving tale of divine incarnation, death, and resurrection" that answers the question of life and death ("The Gospel and Culture," p. 189). As a form of mythopoesis it is equivalent to Plato's philosophical myth such as the myth of Er at the end of the *Republic*, "the tale that was saved and not lost, and which will save us if we believe it" (621b–c). Paul's story of transfiguration is also a mythopoeic "saving tale." See *Order and History* IV, pp. 248–49.

145. "Wisdom and the Magic of the Extreme," p. 366.

146. Ibid., p. 367.

147. Ibid., p. 368; "The Gospel and Culture," p. 202. Elsewhere Voegelin has stated that these verses in Matthew chap. 16 represent "the perfect analysis of the existential tendency in relation to God . . . [that] is as true today as it was at the time the Gospel was written. But the analysis . . . is so buried at present in secondary doctrine and dogma that few people are now aware how grandiose an existential analysis is there" ("Philosophies of History: An Interview with Eric Voegelin," *New Orleans Review* 2 (1973): 135–39, at 137).

148. "The Gospel and Culture," p. 201.

149. The whole episode of Peter's confession at Caesarea Philippi, along with the other Gospel accounts of revelation followed by the protective charge of silence, has a striking parallel with Plato's statement in his *Seventh Letter* that he has composed no doctrines telling of the revelatory truth of his philosophy, nor can he because of its ineffable nature. True knowledge of the most important matters, Plato says, "must come rather after a long period of attendance on instruction in the subject itself and of close companionship, when, suddenly like a blaze kindled by a leaping spark, it is generated in the soul and at once becomes self-sustaining." Plato explains this in a way that sheds some light on both Jesus' prohibition to tell no one that he is the Christ, as well as his general silence before unbelievers: "I do not, however, think that the attempt to tell mankind these matters is a good thing, except in the case of some few who are capable of discovering the truth for themselves with a little guidance. In the case of the rest, to do so would excite in some an unjustified contempt in a thoroughly offensive fashion, in others certain lofty and vain hopes, as if they had acquired some awesome lore" (341c–342a).

150. "The Gospel and Culture," pp. 202–3.

151. Ibid., p. 204.

152. "Wisdom and the Magic of the Extreme," p. 368. See also the more elaborate analysis of this passage in "The Gospel and Culture," pp. 192–94.

153. Ibid., p. 193.

154. Ibid.

155. "Response to Professor Altizer's 'A New History and a New but Ancient God?'" p. 293.

156. "Wisdom and the Magic of the Extreme," p. 369.

157. "The Beginning and the Beyond," p. 183.

158. "Wisdom and the Magic of the Extreme," p. 369.

159. Ibid.

160. Ibid.

161. Ibid., p. 370.

162. Ibid.

163. Ibid., pp. 370–71.

164. See Ellis Sandoz, "In Memoriam: Eric Voegelin," *The Southern Review* 21 (1985): 375.

5. Lonergan's Foundational Theology

1. The best overviews of Lonergan are Patrick H. Byrne, "The Fabric of Lonergan's Thought," in *Lonergan Workshop* 6, ed. Fred Lawrence (Atlanta: Scholar's Press, 1986), pp. 1–84; and William Mathews, "Lonergan's Quest," *Milltown Studies* (Spring 1986): 3–34.

Two longer works helpful for understanding Lonergan's method are Frederick E. Crowe, *The Lonergan Enterprise* (Cambridge: Cowley Publications: 1980); and Hugo A. Meynell, *The Theology of Bernard Lonergan* (Atlanta: Scholars Press: 1986).

Festschrifts of great value are *Creativity and Method: Essays in Honor of Bernard Lonergan*, ed. Matthew L. Lamb (Milwaukee: Marquette University Press, 1981); and *Religion and Culture: Essays in Honor of Bernard Lonergan*, ed. Philip Boo Riley and Timothy Fallon (Albany: State University of New York Press, 1987).

More recent collections of studies include *Religion in Context: Recent Studies in Lonergan*, ed. Philip Boo Riley and Timothy Fallon, College Theology Society Resources in Religion 4 (Lanham, Md. University Press of America, 1988); and *The Desires of the Human Heart: An Introduction to the Theology of Bernard Lonergan*, ed. Vernon Gregson (New York: Paulist Press, 1988).

Earlier collections of essays on Lonergan include *Spirit as Inquiry: Studies in Honor of Bernard Lonergan*, ed. Frederick E. Crowe, *Continuum* 2 (1964), special issue; *Foundations of Theology: Papers from the International Lonergan Congress 1970*, vol. 1, ed. Philip McShane; and *Language, Truth and Meaning: Papers from the International Lonergan Congress 1970*, vol. 2, ed. Philip McShane (Notre Dame: University of Notre Dame Press, 1972). For a more critical assessment, see the collection in *Looking at Lonergan's Method*, ed. Patrick Corcoran (Dublin: Talbot Press, 1975).

2. Some have misinterpreted Lonergan's use of modern science in constructing his theological method. Although he incorporated a great deal from mathematics and scientific theory, he did not intend *Insight* to be a philosophy of science. Furthermore, his empirical orientation in *Insight*, which was to be his prolegomenon for his later theological method, in no way indicates that he conceives theology on the analogy of natural science. Certainly theology as a science is empirical, but not only that. For Lonergan, it must be "generalized empirical method," which means that the data of sense important to natural science must be expanded to include the data of consciousness important to philosophy; this in order to frame an adequate theological method. In other words, Lonergan's interest lies more in the cognitional activity of scientists, to which they themselves rarely advert, than in the logical scientific method they employ. Because the scholastic attempt to conceive theology on the analogy of Aristotelian science was unsatisfactory, Lonergan's attempt to found theology on interiority is a remedy to the defects of an approach based on any such analogy. On this point, see Lonergan's rebuttal of Langdon Gilkey, in *Foundations of Theology*, pp. 224–25.

3. Bernard Lonergan, *A Second Collection*, ed. W. F. J. Ryan and B. J. Tyrrell (Philadelphia: Westminster Press, 1974), p. 67.

4. Lonergan, "Notes on Existentialism," unpublished manuscript (1957), quoted in Matthew Lamb, *History, Method, and Theology: A Dialectical Comparison of Wilhelm Dilthey's Critique of Historical Reason and Bernard Lonergan's Meta-Methodology* (Missoula: Scholars Press, 1978), p. 358.

5. Ibid, p. 359.

6. This is Hans-Georg Gadamer's proposal. See his *Truth and Method*, 2nd rev. ed., trans. Joel Weinheimer and Donald G. Marshall (New York: Crossroad, 1989).

7. *Method in Theology* (New York: Seabury Press, 1972), p. 316.

8. Bernard Lonergan, *Insight: A Study of Human Understanding* (New York: Harper and Row, 1957), p. xxviii; repeated at p. 748.

9. *Method in Theology*, p. 260.

10. See ibid., p. 297.

11. See Martin Heidegger, *Being and Time*, trans. John Macquarrie and Edward Robinson (New York: Harper and Row, 1962), pp. 95–107. In my estimation, the gist of Heidegger's whole project, which especially inspired his pupil Gadamer, is captured in the movement from the apophantical to the hermeneutical. This movement is the transition from seeing the world as *Vorhandenheit* (present-at-hand) to seeing the world as *Zuhandenheit* (ready-at-hand). For Heidegger, the world and its entities seen as *Vorhandenheit* is simply "there" apart from *Dasein*. It is apophantic science: the attitude of scientistic objectivity, of detachment, of technical thought and language. It is the wish to see things "purely," to gaze upon Kant's "thing-in-itself." Heidegger thought the world as *Vorhandenheit* was a deficient mode of being. He claimed that classical metaphysics as a whole is an ontology of what is *Vorhandenheit* (from which arises his pejorative notion of "onto-theo-logy"—metaphysics forgetful of being) and modern science is its heir. Though one could certainly debate that claim (e.g., contra Heidegger, Lonergan would provide metaphysics a certain legitimacy while holding a positive view of modern science), there is a clear connection between this deformed view of knowing the world and what Lonergan calls "the already out there now real." See *Insight*, pp. 250–54. Lonergan, therefore, would espouse Heidegger's opposition to that criterion of knowledge which is the manipulable, publicly measurable and verifiable immediacy of sense.

12. This reappropriation was largely due to the encyclical of Pope Leo XIII (*Aeterni Patris*) which called for "the restoration of Christian philosophy according to the mind of St. Thomas Aquinas." Lonergan's reconstruction of Thomas, which served as the foundation for his theological method, is to be located more exactly within the exigency of Catholic *aggiornamento* pronounced by Pope John XXIII.

13. For a helpful article on the development of neo-Thomism in contemporary Catholic theology and Lonergan's unique contribution to it, see

Gerald McCool, "History, Insight, and Judgment in Thomism," *International Philosophical Quarterly* 27 (1987): 299–313.

14. See Bernard Lonergan, *Verbum: Word and Idea in Aquinas*, ed. David B. Burrell (Notre Dame: University of Notre Dame Press, 1967), esp. chap. 1, pp. 1–46.

15. McCool, "History, Insight, and Judgment in Thomism," p. 302.

16. See *Verbum*, pp. 25–33.

17. Lonergan was also greatly helped by his early readings of Cardinal Newman's *Grammar of Assent*. Newman's "illative sense" became Lonergan's reflective act of understanding. See *A Second Collection*, p. 263.

18. *Insight*, p. xi. Lonergan devoted a whole chapter to the meaning of meaning in *Method in Theology*, chap. 3, pp. 57–99.

19. *A Third Collection: Papers by Bernard J. F. Lonergan, S.J.*, ed. Frederick E. Crowe (New York: Paulist Press, 1985), p. 23.

20. On the transcendental field, see *Method in Theology*, pp. 23–24.

21. In this context, Lonergan is merely echoing Aristotle's first line of the *Metaphysics*: "All men by nature desire to know." Everyone's existence, not just philosophers', is potentially disturbed by wondering. But wondering and questioning can of course be stifled. To say that the unrestricted desire to know is by nature operative in all human beings is true only in the essential sense. Empirically, it is not so at all, for only few adults maintain the unrestricted wonder and curiosity of childhood. Nonetheless, this characterization of consciousness is true even if most people do not live up to the nature of their own questioning consciousness. Cultural conditioning, egoism, bias, ideology, and scotosis are the usual forces that hinder the free operation of conscious activity. See Lonergan's discussion of general bias in *Insight*, pp. 225–42. On this matter he states that "if everyone has some acquaintance with the spirit of inquiry and reflection, few think of making it the effective centre of their lives; and of that few, still fewer make sufficient progress to be able to withstand other attractions and persevere in their high purpose" (p. 225).

22. *Collection*, p. 315.

23. *Insight*, p. 9.

24. For Lonergan's treatment of the structure of consciousness, see ibid., chap. 11, pp. 319–47, esp. pp. 322–24.

25. See *Method in Theology*, pp. 13–20.

26. *Insight*, p. 348. For the notion of being, see ibid, chap. 12, pp. 348–74.

27. Ibid., p. 350.

28. For the three corresponding notions of objectivity, see ibid., pp. 377–83.

29. The most compendious statement on critical realism is found in Lonergan's essay "Cognitional Structure," in *Collection*, pp. 221–39. For the complete treatment of Lonergan's cognitional theory, one must read the first thirteen chapters of *Insight*.

30. Already we can note that on this point Voegelin's view is that knowing reality in its fullness is not even a potentiality, however remote, because there are sectors of reality that are by nature beyond cognitive reach, specifically, the dimension of mystery that can only be circumscribed by myth.

31. *Method in Theology*, p. 5. The clearest and most concise explanation of transcendental method is the first chapter of this work, pp. 3–25.

32. On higher viewpoints, see *Insight*, pp. 13–19. On universal viewpoints, see ibid., pp. xxiv, 564–68, 738–39.

33. On the known unknown, see ibid., pp. 531–34, 546–49.

34. *Method in Theology*, pp. 236–37.

35. *Insight*, pp. 391–96, 640–44, 651–57.

36. Ibid., p. 392. From this account of proportionate being Lonergan is able to define metaphysics as "the conception, affirmation, and implementation of the integral heuristic structure of proportionate being" (p. 391).

37. See *Method in Theology*, pp. 101–3.

38. *Insight*, p. 684.

39. *Method in Theology*, p. 25. For Lonergan's explanation of transcendental method in relation to theology, see ibid., pp. 23–25.

40. *Insight*, pp. 181–89, 385.

41. *A Second Collection*, p. 220.

42. His point of transition was first explicit in his essay "Theology in a New Context," in *A Second Collection*, pp. 55–68. More precisely, the breakthrough that eventually resulted in *Method in Theology* occurred by Lonergan's own account in February, 1965. See Conn O'Donovan's introduction in Lonergan's *The Way to Nicea*, trans. Conn O'Donovan (Philadelphia: Westminster Press, 1976), p. xxiv.

43. *A Second Collection*, p. 221.

44. A fourth level of consciousness was of course already implied in *Insight*, but it was not fully developed until *Method in Theology* appeared fifteen years later. See *Insight*, chap. 18, on ethics, pp. 595–633.

45. This dual movement of consciousness was made explicit only in Lonergan's late writings. It is implicit in his discussion of the two phases of theological method (*Method in Theology*, chap. 5, esp. p. 142); but in his later writings it applies more and more clearly to life itself (see *A Third Collection*, pp. 32, 76–77, 106, 126, 180–81, 196–97). Frederick Crowe has studied this idea in Lonergan's thought (see *The Lonergan Enterprise*, pp. 72–73). This theme of the way up and the way down also plays heavily in Crowe's *Old Things and New: A Strategy for Education*, Supplementary Issue of *Lonergan Workshop* 5, (Atlanta: Scholar's Press, 1986). Although it appears that this idea originated with Lonergan's discovery of the functional specialties, he himself seems to suggest that its origin can be traced back to his dissertation *Gratia Operans*. See *Caring about Meaning: Patterns in the Life of Bernard Lonergan* (Montreal: Thomas More Institute, 1982), pp. 93–94.

46. *A Second Collection*, p. 168.

47. *Method in Theology*, p. 37.

48. For Lonergan's description of insight, see *Insight*, chap. 1, pp. 3–32. For his dramatic description of Archimedes' famous "insight," see ibid., pp. 3–6.

49. On bias, see ibid., pp. 191–206, 218–42.

50. Ibid., p. 632.

51. For the problem of liberation, see ibid., pp. 630–33.

52. Ibid., p. 632.

53. Ibid., p. 630.

54. Lonergan discusses the divine solution to the problem of evil in terms of special and transcendent knowledge. See the last two chapters of *Insight*, pp. 634–730.

55. *Collection*, p. 255.

56. On vertical freedom, see *Method in Theology*, p. 253.

57. This was published as *Grace and Freedom: Operative Grace in the Thought of St. Thomas Aquinas*, ed. J. Patout Burns (New York: Herder and Herder, 1971). In the third chapter Lonergan speaks of conversion in the Thomistic categories as a *gratia operans* which is a *habitus*. In the final chapter he refers to Thomas's threefold differentiation of conversion: "Three types of conversion are distinguished: the perfect conversion of the beatific vision, the meritorious conversion of habitual grace, and the preparatory conversion that does not involve the infusion of a habit but simply the *operatio Dei ad se animam convertentis*" (p. 122).

58. *Method in Theology*, p. 107.

59. Ibid., p. 120.

60. Ibid., pp. 283–84. Earlier Lonergan states that "the apologist's task is neither to produce in others nor to justify for them God's gift of his love. Only God can give that gift, and the gift itself is self-justifying" (p. 123). In this way it is parallel to the knower's self-affirmation, taken up in chap. 11 of *Insight*.

61. On the three kinds of conversion, see *Method in Theology*, pp. 237–43.

62. *A Second Collection*, p. 79.

63. On common-sense eclecticism, see *Insight*, pp. 416–21.

64. *Method in Theology*, p. 241.

65. Ibid., p. 269.

66. Ibid., p. 241.

67. Ibid.

68. Ibid., pp. 122, 243.

69. Ibid., p. 123.

70. Ibid.

71. See ibid., pp. 302–5, 326–30. See also Bernard Lonergan, *Doctrinal Pluralism* (Milwaukee: Marquette University Press, 1971), pp. 12–39.

72. An example of this kind of criticism can be found in Francis Schüssler Fiorenza, *Foundational Theology: Jesus and the Church* (New York: Crossroad,

1984). Fiorenza critiques Lonergan's foundational theology as following a method of correlation between "Christian doctrine and the thematizations of religious conversion" similar to Tillich's which "does not adequately take into account the pluralism, secularity, and common human experience of the tradition" (p. 282). He also endorses Langdon Gilkey's and David Tracy's criticism of Lonergan's foundational theology as "fideistic" because it is based on conversion, which removes foundational theology from the public defense of the Christian faith (p. 275).

For a good comparative study of Lonergan and Fiorenza, see Peter J. Drilling, "The Pyramid or the Raft: Francis Schüssler Fiorenza and Bernard Lonergan in Dialogue about Foundational Theology," *Horizons* 13 (1986): 275–90. Drilling exposes Fiorenza's misunderstandings of Lonergan on essential points. He affirms some of the valid contributions of Fiorenza's "reconstructive hermeneutics" but basically seems to believe it is rather weak vis-à-vis Lonergan's more nuanced elaboration of functional specialties in theology.

73. To the four basic realms of meaning (common sense, theory, interiority, and transcendence), Lonergan adds two more (the realms of art and scholarship) and comes up with a combined total of thirty-one differentiations of consciousness. See *Method in Theology*, pp. 272, 302–5.

74. For a concise statement on Lonergan's position on this matter, particularly in regard to Christian doctrine, see his address, "Unity and Plurality: The Coherence of Christian Truth," in *A Third Collection*, pp. 239–50.

75. See *Method in Theology*, p. 271. Earlier he states that knowing conversion calls for "a high seriousness and a mature wisdom" (p. 269).

76. This seventh point requires clarification. Lonergan claims that there exist in a fully differentiated consciousness four realms of meaning: common sense, theory, interiority, and transcendence. Each is specified by a certain exigence: (1) the systematic exigence is the world of common sense opening to the world of theory; (2) the critical exigence is the world of theory opening to the world of interiority; (3) the methodical exigence is the grasp of transcendental method which moves one through the worlds of common sense, theory, and interiority; (4) the transcendental exigence is the world of interiority opening to the world of transcendent mystery. All the exigencies operate in complete freedom. They are not externally imposed; they arise out of the demands of consciousness. A fully differentiated consciousness can operate in each realm of meaning. To distinguish, clarify, and promote the operations of a subject's consciousness in each realm of meaning is a further hermeneutical function of transcendental method. On the four realms of meaning and each one's corresponding exigence, see ibid., pp. 81–85, 257.

77. Ibid., p. xi.

78. Ibid., p. 282.

79. Ibid., pp. 282–83.

80. For theology's two phases, see ibid., pp. 133, 142–44.

81. Ibid., pp. 142–44.

82. Ibid., pp. 125–26, 145.

83. Ibid., p. 125.

84. Ibid., pp. 267–68.

85. Ibid., p. 268.

86. Ibid., p. 144.

87. For Lonergan's statement on the universal features of the world's religions, see ibid., p. 109, and *A Second Collection*, pp. 149–51. He borrows from Friedrich Heiler's analysis of the seven common elements in the world's major religions. See Friedrich Heiler, "The History of Religions as a Preparation for the Cooperation of Religions," in *The History of Religions*, ed. M. Eliade and J. Kitagawa (Chicago: University of Chicago Press, 1959), pp. 142–53.

88. *Method in Theology*, p. 109.

89. See ibid., pp. 105–6.

90. Ibid., p. 106.

91. See ibid., chap. 4, "Religion," pp. 101–24. This whole chapter expresses the centrality of love in religion and life.

92. This point is stated differently, but effectively, by one of Lonergan's students: "Just as the cognitional theorist ought to identify his or her own experiences of having insights in order to understand what authors in his field are talking about, so also the theologian ought to identify the experience of the love of God in his or her life in order to grasp the true meaning of religious texts" (William Mathews, "Lonergan's Quest," p. 27).

93. *Method in Theology*, p. 119.

94. Ibid., p. 112.

95. On Lonergan's treatment of the inner word and the outer word, see ibid., pp. 112–15, 119.

96. Ibid., p. 36.

97. Ibid., p. 77. One of Lonergan's students, Robert Doran, has used this passage as Lonergan's key statement implying the necessity of a fourth, "psychic," conversion. Doran's work has been a synthesis of Lonergan's thought, Jung's depth psychology, and Ricoeur's philosophy of symbol. See Doran, *Subject and Psyche* (Washington: University Press of America, 1979), particularly pp. 114–31, on second immediacy; pp. 240–52 on psychic conversion. See also Doran's *Psychic Conversion and Theological Foundations* (Chico: Scholar's Press, 1981). These earlier studies have been incorporated in Doran's latest, massive work, *Theology and the Dialectics of History* (Toronto: University of Toronto Press, 1990).

98. *Method in Theology*, p. 77.

99. Ibid., p. 29.

100. Ibid., p. 273.

101. Ibid., p. 118.

102. For Lonergan's discussion of general and special categories, see ibid., pp. 282–93.

103. Ibid., p. 290.

104. Ibid., p. 291.

105. Ibid.

106. Ibid.

107. Ibid., p. 115.

108. *Insight*, p. 723.

109. *Method in Theology*, p. 117.

110. Ibid., p. 116.

111. Ibid., p. 299.

112. His chapter on doctrines is written in a way that could please both liberals and conservatives, orthodox Catholics and modernists. This is not to say that he has pleased everyone and offended no one, quite the contrary. Lonergan's detractors are as vociferous in attacking him as his ardent supporters are in defending him. For two critiques of his view of doctrine from both sides of the theological fence, see Joseph Stephen O'Leary, "The Hermeneutics of Dogmatism," *Irish Theological Quarterly* 47 (1980): 96–118; and Julian Burt, "Lonergan Doctrine: Is It Orthodox?" *Homiletic and Pastoral Review* 86 (1986): 26–32, 50–53.

113. "Theology in Its New Context," *A Second Collection*, p. 59.

114. Ibid., p. 57.

115. Ibid., pp. 63–64.

116. *Method in Theology*, pp. 90–99, 260, 304–18. This he borrowed from Bruno Snell, *The Discovery of the Mind: The Greek Origins of European Thought*, trans. T. G. Rosenmeyer (New York: Harper, 1960).

117. *Method in Theology*, pp. 302–5.

118. His Latin works treat this subject at great length, the most important being *De Deo Trino*. The first part of the first volume of this work has appeared in English with the title *The Way to Nicea*, trans. Conn O'Donovan (Philadelphia: Westminster, 1976).

119. *Method in Theology*, p. 313.

120. Ibid.

121. Ibid., p. 319.

122. Ibid., p. 325.

123. Lonergan's earlier theological work, particularly his Latin treatises, were written in the traditionally dogmatic vein of pre–Vatican II Catholic theology. See, for example, *On the Way to Nicea* (p. 1), where Lonergan viewed doctrines as truths that are given.

At this time, Lonergan conceived revelation as primarily a cognitive event. He understood revelation as basically superhuman knowledge communicated

by God to the minds of believers. With his working out the pressing methodological question of where cognitive judgments stand in relation to historical
scholarship, and with his new openness to the horizon of experience disclosed
in interiority and conversion, his view of theology's starting point began to
change. He himself stated that "formerly I placed the starting point of theology
in truths while now I place it in data" and "formerly a discipline was specifically theological because it dealt with revealed truths, now it is authentically
theological because the theologian has been converted intellectually, morally,
and religiously" (*Foundations of Theology*, p. 224).

Charles Hefling has contributed an excellent study of the development of
Lonergan's notion of doctrine. See his "On Reading *The Way to Nicea*,"
in *Religion and Culture*, ed. Riley and Fallon, pp. 149–66; and his Ph.D.
dissertation, "Lonergan on Development: *The Way to Nicea* in Light of His
More Recent Methodology" (Boston College, 1982). Hefling has also written
a spirited defense of the value of doctrine in light of Lonergan's thought: *Why
Doctrines?* (Cambridge: Cowley, 1984).

124. *A Second Collection*, p. 204.

125. *A Third Collection*, p. 31.

126. *Method in Theology*, p. 84.

127. Each man read the other's work diligently, but only Lonergan discussed
in print Voegelin's thought: see "Theology and Praxis," and "A Post-Hegelian
Philosophy of Religion," in *A Third Collection*, pp. 188–96, 219–21. In both
essays, which are among his later ones, Lonergan praised Voegelin's "The
Gospel and Culture." The only places where Voegelin mentioned Lonergan
in print was in his essay "What Is Political Reality?" where he borrowed
Lonergan's technical term "scotosis" to refer to the psycho-spiritual disease
of blocking out reality (*Anamnesis*, p. 201), and also in quoting a line from
Lonergan's essay "The Dehellenization of Dogma" in the complete version of
"The Eclipse of Reality" (*What is History? and Other Late Unpublished Writings*,
p. 158).

In a brief correspondence initiated by Voegelin in November, 1967, each
man expressed a fondness for the other's work. Their exchange of letters was
accompanied by an exchange of their recently published articles (Lonergan,
"The Dehellenization of Dogma"; Voegelin, "Immortality: Experience and
Symbol"). On this occasion Voegelin remarked to Lonergan: "though from
very different positions, we are concerned with the same problem" (undated);
and Lonergan replied: "I agree that our differences are compatible with a
fundamental agreement on direction" (November 15, 1967). These letters are
found in the correspondence file of Eric Voegelin's collected papers, box 23,
file 25, Hoover Institution Library Archives, Stanford University.

128. Voegelin would never use this term in describing his own work
because of its connection to the neo-Kantian/Heideggerian strain of German

philosophy that he escaped from. For a discussion of Voegelin's work as a hermeneutical enterprise, with some comparison to Gadamer and Lonergan, see Fred Lawrence, "Voegelin and Theology as Hermeneutical and Political," in *Voegelin and the Theologian*, ed. Kirby and Thompson, pp. 314–54.

129. *A Second Collection*, p. 30. This is the sentence that Voegelin quotes in "The Eclipse of Reality," p. 158, mentioned above.

130. This is not to suggest that such a sense is lacking in Lonergan, for it can be found in his analysis of the biases that contribute to the longer cycle of decline in society and tradition, and in his brief elaboration of "cosmopolis" as the transcendently inspired vision of the good that always serves to critique present living. See chap. 7 of *Insight*, pp. 207–44. Such an analysis is Lonergan's concrete spelling out of the social and historical value of individuals appropriating their conscious interiority and undergoing intellectual, moral, and religious conversion, the personal tasks that his work concretely invites.

131. Voegelin himself expressed these doubts about the viability of Lonergan's transcendental method in a letter to David Walsh dated November 7, 1974 (Eric Voegelin papers, box 40, file 2, Hoover Institution Library Archives, Stanford University). After affirming that he and Lonergan are concerned with the same problems, Voegelin states his preference for the symbolism of the Platonic metaxy and the noetic analysis of structure in reality which he believes is superior to transcendental method. He goes on to question Lonergan's concept of intention because of what he saw to be its complication by Husserlian intentionality (see *Anamnesis*, pp. 9–12) which inevitably "has the result of objectifying whatever is the object of consciousness, even if the object is no 'object,' as in the case of God." In his study "What is Political Reality?" Voegelin identified this dimension as the *Gegenstandsformlichkeit* of consciousness (see *Anamnesis*, pp. 166–68, 172, 181, where the term is poorly translated three different ways; German edition, pp. 307–9, 313, 322). It is the object-forming character of consciousness that is always in conflict with the consciousness of nonobjects. This objectifying intention is equivalent to the "phantasms" of Aquinas which Lonergan employed in his theory of cognitional knowing as the data of sense (remembering of course that for Lonergan objective reality is not the object of sense perception, a naive realism, but of understanding and judgment). However, especially in the presence of transcendent mystery, how consciousness relates itself to experienced reality cannot be reduced to data or objects. Such a nonobjective consciousness is the consciousness of mystery that Voegelin talked about in the "Wisdom" essay in the language of "vision" that is best articulated in the symbols of the myth because the symbols of the myth do not refer to objects. As Voegelin warned in his earlier analysis of the *Timaeus*: "The myth is unintelligible if we apply to it an epistemology which has been developed for the case of our knowledge of the external world." Such an epistemology "would imply the assumption that the

soul has throughout the structure of 'intentionality,' that is, of a consciousness intending its object. We would fall into the anthropomorphic fallacy of forming man in the image of conscious man" (*Order and History*, p. 192–93). For these reasons Voegelin concludes in his letter to Walsh that Lonergan's terminology is "technically not careful enough to accommodate the problems which arise when I deal with comparative material. In this point I see the limitation to the usefulness of Lonergan's analysis."

132. Voegelin's criticisms of Husserl were discussed in chap. 3. Nevertheless, it should be noted that Voegelin had great respect for Husserl in his phenomenological "return to the things themselves." Voegelin believed Husserl, in spite of his limitations, was the first in a line of contemporary thinkers to recover what had been lost, a list which included Heidegger, Jaspers, and Bergson. In his recovery of concrete experience, Husserl instigated the turning away from dogmatism and the opacity of secondary symbols to the experiential fullness of existential consciousness.

133. This tendency to turn God into an object is apparent in chap. 19 of *Insight* where Lonergan regards God as the most meaningful object of thought whose existence can be intelligently grasped and reasonably affirmed in essentially the same manner as one would affirm the existence of things in the world.

134. In his comparison of Lonergan and Voegelin on these matters, Lawrence opts for Lonergan's formulation and argues for his more positive view of the doctrinalization of truth against Voegelin's one-sided resistance to dogmatomachy (see "Voegelin and Theology as Hermeneutical and Political," in *The Beginning and the Beyond: Papers from the Gadamer and Voegelin Conferences*, ed. Lawrence, pp. 336–45; and "On 'The Meditative Origin of the Philosophical Knowledge of Order,'" in ibid., pp. 53–67).

135. Although differentiation begins in the soul of one individual (a Plato or Moses) it need not penetrate to society at large, a historical phenomenon exemplified by Zoroaster who was a prophet before his time. See Voegelin's essay, "What is History?" p. 23.

136. "Wisdom and the Magic of the Extreme," p. 373.

137. For the historical emergence of differentiating consciousness, Lonergan is dependent on such studies as Bruno Snell's *The Discovery of Mind*, which does not incorporate the revelatory dimension of consciousness. Because of his orientation toward the development of theory as dominant, Lonergan was unable to appreciate the real meaning and value of myth in his work. For example, in *Insight*, pp. 536–46, he identified mythic consciousness with the counterpositions, with the merely descriptive, and therefore truncated, knowledge of being. Myth, the "untutored" desire to understand which lacked any self-knowledge, was to be overcome by metaphysics which alone can understand things as they are in themselves. In his later writings Lonergan

had to correct this outdated tendency to regard myth as a primitive form of truth superseded by theory. See for example, *A Second Collection*, pp. 225–30, 275. The importance Voegelin attaches to the role of myth is already well established. For Voegelin's critical view of metaphysics, see *Anamnesis*, pp. 193–94.

138. *Order and History* V, p. 17.

139. Voegelin made this remark in a letter to David Walsh dated December 23, 1974 (Eric Voegelin papers, box 40, file 2, Hoover Institution Library Archives, Stanford University).

140. He made this remark in an earlier letter to David Walsh dated June 18, 1974 (Eric Voegelin papers, box 40, file 2, Hoover Institution Library Archives, Stanford University).

141. I must caution, however, that in regard to Voegelin this contrast should not be overblown since he always considered himself a scientist in the Aristotelian sense.

142. Paul Tillich has described this fundamental difference in terms of two distinct types of philosophy of religion. For him the approach to God in history has been either "ontological" or "cosmological." The first, "ontological," approach, represented by Augustine, stressed the immediacy of the knowledge of God that precedes any distinction between subject and object. This approach was generally dissolved in Christian history by the "cosmological" approach of Aquinas, which under the influence of Aristotle stressed the knowledge of sense perception and abstraction. As a result, God was known through a mediated, rational method which had the concomitant tendency to turn God into an object. Tillich argues for the recovery of the ontological approach because it alone gives philosophy a religious foundation. It must also serve as the basis for any cosmological method in a philosophy of religion. Although he does not use this language, Voegelin would be in basic agreement with Tillich's view. See Tillich's famous essay "The Two Types of Philosophy of Religion," in *Theology of Culture*, ed. Robert C. Kimball (New York: Oxford University Press, 1959), pp. 10–29.

143. *Order and History* IV, p. 228.

144. See "Quod Deus Dicitur," p. 378.

145. See especially *Order and History* IV, pp. 44–48.

146. Ibid., p. 45. For the negative connotations this word has carried in Voegelin's earlier work, see *Order and History* I, p. 376, where he speaks of "religion" as "the transformation of existence in historical form into the secondary possession of a 'creed' concerning the relation between God and man" that first appeared in the Book of Deuteronomy; and p. 288, where he is critical of the obfuscation caused by the discussion of "religion" and "religious phenomena" in regard not only to Israel but to Near Eastern history in general. He remarks that "one cannot repeat often enough that 'religion' does not occur

in the Bible." In *Order and History* II, where he addresses the question whether Xenophanes was a "monotheist," "polytheist," or "pantheist," he chastises those who would interpret a thinker according to that person's "religion" which is presumed to consist in the "adherence to a 'system' of propositions concerning existence and nature of god" (p. 179).

147. Doctrine is not entirely negative for Voegelin because he acknowledges that it has served to protect "an historically achieved state of insight against the disintegrative pressures" of cultural turmoil (*Order and History* IV, p. 43). But he also believes that it no longer serves this original function because in our time "the deforming doctrinalization has become socially stronger than the experiential insights it was originally meant to protect" (ibid., p. 58). For Voegelin's appreciation and analysis of Christian doctrine, see his important letter to Alfred Schutz (January 1, 1953), in *The Philosophy of Order*, ed. Opitz and Sebba, pp. 449–57.

148. Voegelin long ago expressed this uncertainty of faith in a controversial statement: "Uncertainty is the very essence of Christianity." This is so because in the dedivinization of the world "the world-transcendent God is reduced to the tenuous bond of faith, in the sense of Heb. 11:1, as the substance of things hoped for and the proof of things unseen. Ontologically, the substance of things hoped for is nowhere to be found but in faith itself; and, epistemologically, there is no proof of things unseen but again this very faith" (*The New Science of Politics*, p. 122).

149. The extent of Lonergan's affinity with Voegelin on this whole issue can be seen in his essay "Theology and Praxis," in *A Third Collection*, pp. 184–201. His only critical comment is the single sentence: "Now I think Voegelin's criticism of doctrines and doctrinization to be exaggerated" (p. 195). Given the backgrounds of the two thinkers, this comment can stand without further explanation.

150. Although sprinkled throughout his work, much of this theme in Lonergan lies buried in his obscure Latin treatises. These will soon appear in English as part of Lonergan's collected works. The "law of the cross" is discussed in the last section of *De Verbo Incarnato*, trans. and ed. Charles Hefling. For a helpful essay on this aspect of Lonergan, see William P. Loewe, "Lonergan and the Law of the Cross: A Universalist View of Salvation," *Anglican Theological Review* 59 (1977): 162–74. Two of Lonergan's students have briefly mentioned this lacuna in Voegelin's soteriology. See Fred Lawrence, "Voegelin and Theology as Hermeneutical and Political," in *Voegelin and the Theologian*, ed. Kirby and Thompson, pp. 314–54, at pp. 334–35; and Robert Doran, "Theology's Situation: Questions to Eric Voegelin," in *The Beginning and the Beyond: Papers from the Gadamer and Voegelin Conferences*, ed. Lawrence, pp. 69–91 at p. 75.

151. See "Wisdom and the Magic of the Extreme," pp. 335, 337. It is possible that Voegelin would have found Lonergan's language of the "law of the cross" too devotional and parochially Christian for his philosophic taste.

152. According to Eugene Webb, Voegelin gave precise affirmation to this in his unpublished "History of Political Ideas." In the section on "Luther and Calvin," Voegelin said that Hellenic civilization had no parallel to the principle enunciated in 1 John 4:8: "He who does not love, does not know God; for God is love." This is the experiential insight that Voegelin believed lies at the root of Christianity. It is the experience of *amicitia*, or mutual love between God and humankind that gives to faith its spiritual maturity. See Webb, *Eric Voegelin: Philosopher of History*, p. 189.

153. I do not mean to suggest that because Voegelin was not a confessional Christian theologian he missed the salvific nature of human love that is central to Christianity and symbolized by the cross. If the soteriological truth of love as the solution to the problem of evil (or as the personal foundation of order overcoming disorder) is revealed in the classic texts, then Voegelin, by his own principles, should have analyzed and incorporated it into his philosophy. The equivalent philosophic symbolism to the Christian experience of love found in the Gospels is located in certain key texts of Plato, such as *Symposium* 210a–212c and *Phaedrus* 250e–257b where Plato gives beautiful expression to the self-transcending, salvific nature of human love. From these passages the seeds of Christian love seem to be planted already in Plato. For all the deference he gives to Plato as the philosophic authority on the subject of human and divine order, Voegelin curiously refrains from any treatment of these passages in his writings. One can only guess that the reason Voegelin gave no mention to interpersonal love is perhaps that he wanted to focus on recovering the It-reality that must not be reduced to thing-reality, and he believed that concrete human love partakes too much of thing-reality. Another reason might be that because of his early reaction against the phenomenologists who attempted to understand the constitution of consciousness on the order of the interpersonal, he was biased against perceiving the revelatory qualities of the interpersonal. Nevertheless, the Christian teaching of incarnation would seem to denote the experience of human love as the inescapable medium and privileged locus for the revelation of divine love. The It-reality of divine presence is revealed through the concrete love of persons, whose thingly bodies incarnate their nonthingly souls.

It should be added that the analysis of the equivalent symbolisms of love in Plato and the New Testament is not enhanced by the conventional bifurcation of love into its allegedly irreconcilable forms of "agape and eros," such as argued in Anders Nygren's famous book by the same name.

154. Quoted in *Anamnesis*, p. 140. Voegelin states that this movement of the soul drawn by love toward God, captured in Augustine's symbol of

Exodus, is "the classical formulation of the material principle of a philosophy of history" (ibid.). This is so because St. Augustine "was well aware that the structure of history is the same as the structure of personal existence.... His conception of history as a tale of two Cities, intermingling from the beginning of mankind to its end, conceives it as a tale of man's personal Exodus written large" ("Immortality: Experience and Symbol," p. 262). Voegelin also treats this Augustinian symbolism of personal exodus in his essay "Configurations in History," originally published in *The Concept of Order*, ed. Paul G. Kuntz (Seattle: University of Washington Press, 1968), pp. 23–42; reprinted in *Published Essays (1966–1985)*, pp. 95–114, at 105.

155. Quoted in *Anamnesis*, p. 171. For a slightly different translation, see Albert Camus, *Notebooks: 1942–1951*, trans. Justin O'Brien (New York: Harcort Brace Jovanovich, 1965), p. 243.

6. The Theological Implications of Voegelin's Theory of Consciousness

1. Voegelin argues that the source of this method of theologizing can be traced back to the intermediary symbolism of Philo. Philo was the first to unite Scripture and philosophy through his allegoric method of interpretation which presupposed and engendered the problematic conceptions of Scripture as the word of God, philosophy as the handmaiden of Scripture, and the split between reason and revelation as well as reason and faith. On these presumptions, Philo laid the foundations for seventeen centuries of Judaic, Christian, and Islamic thought until Spinoza broke with this largely unconscious pattern in his *Tractatus Theologico-Politicus*. For Voegelin's discussion of Philo and the inadequacies of allegoresis, see *Order and History* IV, pp. 29–36.

2. "Responses at the Panel Discussion of 'The Beginning of the Beginning'" (transcription of Voegelin conference held at Boston College, March 25, 1983), in *The Beginning and the Beyond: Papers from the Gadamer and Lonergan Conferences*, ed. Lawrence, p. 101.

3. Once when asked about the meaning of Christianity in today's world, Voegelin bluntly answered with a statement reminiscent of Kierkegaard: "I have my doubts as to whether Christianity exists at all" ("Philosophies of History: An Interview with Eric Voegelin," p. 137).

4. See, for instance, "Equivalences of Experience and Symbolization in History," where he says that "the test of truth, to put it pointedly, will be the lack of originality in the propositions" (p. 122).

5. See *From Enlightenment to Revolution*, pp. 18–23, 34.

6. Ibid., pp. 22–23. One of Voegelin's critics representing Catholic orthodoxy has taken issue with this characterization of the Church. John Gueguen

in his review of this book rejected Voegelin's claim that Christian dogmatism was associated with the "dynamics of secularization" in the modern world. He accused Voegelin of having a "deficient Christianity," of being an inadequate and misleading guide to Christian truth, of confusing religious dogma with ideological dogma, and of taking a subversive attitude in regard to the Church's authoritative teaching. He said his "antipathy toward credal Christianity" was based in his "classical humanism," and although his is a great mind it too must "halt" before the mysteries of Christian doctrine and "the authoritative Church." See John Gueguen, "Voegelin's *From Enlightenment to Revolution*," *Thomist* (1978): 123–34.

7. Voegelin does recognize, however, that if spiritual reality is to survive in the world it must undergo the travail of its institutionalization. But he is more aware of the danger involved: "The prophets, philosophers, and saints, who can translate the order of the spirit into the practice of conduct without institutional support and pressure, are rare. For its survival in the world, therefore, the order of the spirit has to rely on a fanatical belief in the symbols of a creed more often than on the *fides caritate formata*—though such reliance, if it becomes socially predominant, is apt to kill the order it is supposed to preserve" (*Order and History* I, pp. 376–77).

8. *From Enlightenment to Revolution*, p. 21.

9. By "second naivete" Ricoeur means to designate a mode of hermeneutical reappropriation that must now come to life in the wake of the deficient "demythologizing" by the various historical-critical methods that since the eighteenth century radically critiqued the "first naivete" of simple, fideistic belief. In his earlier works Ricoeur cites Marx, Nietzsche, and Freud as the great modern debunkers who inherited this secularizing movement.

10. Ibid., p. 22.

11. The great political philosopher Leo Strauss, in spite of his astute diagnosis of the modern crisis, was an example of a thinker who maintained this very dichotomy between reason and faith, Athens and Jerusalem, philosophy and theology. Unlike Voegelin, who understood faith as trustful openness toward the divine ground that carries great epistemological status, Strauss understood faith as assent to religious propositions that are not evident to natural reason and thus inimical to philosophy. With his quasi-positivist understanding of philosophy Strauss had to reject revelation as a potential source of real knowledge. For an excellent comparison of these two thinkers, see James M. Rhodes, "Philosophy, Revelation, and Political Theory: Leo Strauss and Eric Voegelin," *Journal of Politics* 49 (1987): 1036–60. The correspondence between Strauss and Voegelin which illustrates this very discord has recently been published. See *Faith and Political Philosophy: The Correspondence between Leo Strauss and Eric Voegelin, 1934–1964* (University Park, Pa.: Pennsylvania State University Press,

1993). In addition to four previously published essays by Strauss and Voegelin which deal with revelation and reason, this volume includes comparative essays by James L. Wiser, Hans-Georg Gadamer, Stanley Rosen, Thomas J. J. Altizer, Timothy Fuller, Ellis Sandoz, Thomas L. Pangle, and David Walsh.

12. The most notable reviews by Voegelin's critics are Thomas Altizer, "A New History and a New but Ancient God?" *Journal of the American Academy of Religion* 43 (1975): 757–64, reprinted in *Eric Voegelin's Thought: A Critical Appraisal,* ed. Sandoz, pp. 179–88; Bruce Douglass, "A Diminished Gospel: A Critique of Voegelin's Interpretation of Christianity," in *Eric Voegelin's Search for Order in History,* ed. McKnight, pp. 139–54; John Gueguen, "Voegelin's *From Enlightenment to Revolution,*" *Thomist* 42 (1978): 123–34; John Hallowell, "Existence in Tension: Man in Search of His Humanity," *Political Science Reviewer* 2 (1972): 162–84, reprinted in *Eric Voegelin's Search for Order in History,* ed. McKnight, pp. 101–26; Thomas Molnar, "Voegelin as Historian," *Modern Age* 19 (1975): 427–29; Marion Montgomery, "Eric Voegelin and the End of Our Exploring," *Modern Age* 23 (1979): 233–45; Gerhart Niemeyer, "Eric Voegelin's Philosophy and the Drama of Mankind," *Modern Age* 20 (1976): 28–39; Glenn N. Schram, "Eric Voegelin, the Christian Faith, and the American University," *Dialogue* 16 (1977): 130–35; Harold Weatherby, "Myth, Fact, and History: Voegelin on Christianity," *Modern Age* 22 (1978): 144–50; and Frederick Wilhelmsen, "The New Voegelin," *Triumph* (January 1975): 32–35, revised form in Wilhelmsen's *Christianity and Political Philosophy,* chap. 7, "Professor Voegelin and the Christian Tradition" (Athens: University of Georgia Press, 1978), pp. 193–208.

13. The exception to this was his direct response to Thomas Altizer's review of *The Ecumenic Age* which among all the critical reviews was the most perspicacious and most tantalizing study of his work. Both essays were reprinted in *Eric Voegelin's Thought: A Critical Appraisal,* ed. Sandoz, pp. 179–97. Two excellent essays that judiciously respond to the issues raised by Voegelin's critics are Eugene Webb's "Eric Voegelin's Theory of Revelation" and James Rhodes's "Voegelin and the Christian Faith." Also of importance is William Thompson's very affirmative article on Voegelin's Christology, which answers many of the critics; see "Voegelin on Jesus Christ," in *Voegelin and the Theologian,* ed. Kirby and Thompson, pp. 178–221.

A review of all the critical literature is handily provided in John Kirby's essay "On Reading Eric Voegelin: A Note on the Critical Literature," in *Voegelin and the Theologian,* ed. Kirby and Thompson, pp. 24–60. Against Voegelin's Christian orthodox critics, Kirby concludes that, as a rule, they neglected Voegelin's other writings on Christianity and the New Testament, such as his essays on "Immortality," "History and Gnosis," and "The Gospel and Culture." Kirby finds that

these writers generally indicated little interest in Voegelin's philosophy of consciousness, of which his writings on Christ are expressly a part. The tendency to detach
certain "results" from Voegelin's analytical process (in this case results relating to
Christianity), and treat them as "positions" points, finally, to the great shortcoming
of all these critics without exception. Not one challenged the theory of noetic and
pneumatic differentiations of consciousness that underlay the investigations of *The
Ecumenic Age*. All attempts made thus far to advance serious criticisms of this volume
are burdened by the failure to confront the basic structure of Voegelin's approach
to the problem of the order of consciousness. (Ibid., pp. 38–39)

14. This response was the result of the papers delivered on Voegelin's
thought at the 1976 meeting of the American Political Science Association
in Chicago. These papers, including Voegelin's reply, were published by Ellis
Sandoz under the title: *Eric Voegelin's Thought: A Critical Appraisal*. A part
of Voegelin's illuminating response, entitled "Epilogue," is worth quoting
at length:

> The task of clearing up the antinoetic mess that has accumulated over the
> centuries in the contemporary science of man is enormous. It is not to be discharged
> by one generation of scholars who "think," and still less so by one man alone.
> Reading the essays in their finished form I had sometimes the feeling that my
> fellow symposiasts, perhaps in a state of enthusiasm engendered by the sense that
> something is done after all, underrate the magnitude of the task, a feeling fostered
> by the recurrent complaints about my failure to have dealt sufficiently with the
> complex of problems they comprehend under the topical head of "Christianity."
> The complaint, with its admonition to deliver the goods, implies the confidence
> that I can do everything that is supposed to be done. . . .
>
> If the published part of my studies on "Christianity" is less comprehensive than
> desired, the quite unmysterious reason is the quantity of the historical materials
> that have to be submitted to noetic analysis. Moreover, the topic "Christianity"
> is theoretically even more inadequate, if that is possible, than such other topics as
> "philosophy," "theology," "history," "religion," or "science," for it covers under its
> broad wing no less than the pneumatically formative force of the Western and Eastern
> *Christianitas* for the better part of two millennia, in both the Church formations and
> the sectarian movements, not to mention the successor movements of the modern
> ideologies. A study of "Christianity" is inextricably involved in the study of Western
> civilizational order since antiquity, in its phases of ecumenic, national, and ideological
> imperialism; and about this involvement I have had to say quite a bit in the course of
> my publications. The modernist topicality of "Christianity" as a "religion" among
> others, a topicality determined by a variety of polemical motives, may have been so
> dominant in the mind of the critics that it has obscured the fact of my dealing all
> the time with problems of "Christianity" when dealing with aspects of order which
> also may appear to fall under other topics. (Ibid., pp. 201–2)

15. When Voegelin speaks disparagingly of theology, it is because he identifies it with this derivative symbolism. Originally, he says, theology was a successful "amalgamate" of Christian revelation and postclassical *noesis*. But this success was purchased at the cost of noetic paralysis. "Since Philo, the theologians sought to assign to philosophy the role of theology's handmaiden" because they "saw the fullness of truth about God, man, and the world given by revelation, so philosophy needed to perform only the service of constructing the framework of *ratio* for revealed truth" (*Anamnesis*, p. 186). What emerged was the doctrinal subordination of philosophy to revelation and theology; a diminished *noesis* ensued. Noetic symbols were reduced to concepts of dogmatic metaphysics which weakened the critical effectiveness of noetic insight. See also ibid., pp. 87, 199; *Order and History* IV, p. 48.

16. In *The New Science of Politics* Voegelin made the bold statement that "uncertainty is the very essence of Christianity" (p. 122).

17. *The New Science of Politics*, p. 78; *Order and History* V, p. 71.

18. See *Order and History* II, p. 283.

19. See especially *Order and History* IV, pp. 242–44. But also see Voegelin's earlier discussion of the danger of "including the circumstances of revelation into its contents," a tendency which would lead to its "mortgage," as in the case of Israel's "parochialism" (*Order and History* I, pp. 369–72).

20. In this context, Voegelin expresses hermeneutical principles that appear closely allied with those of Hans-Georg Gadamer. Reacting against the "Romantic hermeneutics" of Schleiermacher and Dilthey, Gadamer argues that the interpretation of a text does not direct one to an author's mind that lies somewhere behind the text and where one could somehow find the author's real intention, and thus the real meaning of the text. Although Voegelin would not entirely agree with this view, he would certainly espouse Gadamer's hermeneutical maxim that what interpretation aims at is what unites both text and reader, i.e., the Question that the text addresses. See Gadamer, *Truth and Method*, pp. 362–79.

21. "Response to Professor Altizer's 'A New History and a New but Ancient God?'" p. 295.

22. We must not forget, however, that Voegelin, in his letter "On Christianity" to Schutz, expressed great admiration for the christological and trinitarian doctrines, insofar as these theological achievements were the perfect symbolisms for expressing "essential Christianity" even though they are rarely subjected to proper philosophical analysis. In his later life, however, his aversion to the codification of Christian truth in theological doctrine no doubt led to his familiar response to those who asked him about his "religious affiliation": "I am a pre-Nicene Christian."

23. This is essentially the view that Altizer, in his review, discerns in Voegelin, whom he says did not himself profess it in so many words. He

went on to suggest that because of this fundamental error, Voegelin believes that Christian theology has "misread" and "misidentified" the nature of Christ. Altizer's statement, imputing Voegelin, is provocative:

> Our greatest failure, theologically, is that we have failed to understand either the nature or the identity of revelation. Israel failed in its creation of Scripture. Christianity failed by identifying the transfiguring incarnation with the historical and dogmatic Christ. . . . The Incarnate Word is not a man; it is rather the eschatological movement of the Whole, of reality itself. Our consciousness including most particularly our historical consciousness, has issued from a split between the subject and the object of consciousness. The total reality that was once manifest as a process of transfiguration has evaporated in the hypostatized subject and object of our historical consciousness. Then the luminosity of noetic consciousness is deformed into an "anthropology" of intramundane man and a "theology" of a transmundane God, and the theophanic event is destroyed. The death of God, then, originates in Christianity, and it originates precisely in Christian faith in the transcendent God. So likewise, the modern revolt against God, the modern murder of God, is simply a development of the Christianity against which it is in revolt. May we not then conclude that it is the Christian Christ, the Christian Word, which is the most fundamental source of our crisis today? ("A New History and a New but Ancient God?" pp. 184–85)

24. The only exception can be found in Voegelin's unpublished "History of Political Ideas," under part 4: "Christianity and Rome," chap. 1: "The Rise of Christianity," where he takes up a political and historical examination of Jesus and the Gospel. This study is very pertinent for understanding the development of Voegelin's perception of Christianity and its origins from his early period. Right off he complains of the "insufficiency of critical exegesis of the gospels" before reviewing the state of historical science at the time (the 1930s) on the life and significance of Jesus. The manuscript is among the Eric Voegelin papers, boxes 57–60, at the Hoover Institution Library Archives, Stanford University.

25. "The Gospel and Culture," p. 198.

26. Ibid., p. 203.

27. Ibid., p. 173.

28. See "The Gospel and Culture," p. 189.

29. See "The Beginning and the Beyond," pp. 183–84.

30. "The Gospel and Culture," pp. 199–200.

31. Ibid., p. 201. This passage seems to direct as much criticism against the liberal "quest for the historical Jesus" movement of the nineteenth century as it does at the orthodox apologists who reject or ignore the advances of modern historical research. On the problems associated with "the historical Jesus" and

the "historicity of Christ," see the very important section in *Order and History* IV, pp. 259–66.

Voegelin's reading of the Gospel seeks to maintain the metaxic balance between the two extremes of "empirical fact" and "speculative dogma." As a result I believe he, along with Lonergan, would greatly applaud the work being done today in historical Jesus research, for advances in historical science provide Christian theology with the necessary anchoring in the historical reality of the past, spearheading the return from dogma to the reality of experience that Voegelin heralds. Though researchers and historians of the New Testament period prescind from meditative analysis of the theophanic reality symbolized in the texts, they nevertheless provide the important historical reconstruction for philosophers and theologians who take up the task of "faith seeking understanding" focused on Jesus the Christ. As we saw in discussing Lonergan's theological method, the manifold work of theology is most successful when its functional specialties operate interdependently in an integral whole.

Of the myriad works of scholars in historical Jesus research, the most important to appear recently in this country are John P. Meier, *A Marginal Jew: Rethinking the Historical Jesus* (New York: Doubleday, 1991); and John Dominic Crossan, *The Historical Jesus: The Life of a Mediterranean Peasant* (San Francisco: HarperCollins, 1991). Both of these very erudite and heavily documented works draw together the most recent advances in historical Jesus research. A derivative work for a more general audience that provocatively exploits some of this material is Steven Mitchell, *The Gospel According to Jesus* (New York: HarperCollins, 1991). The strength of Mitchell's work is his ability to draw on other religious traditions for "theophanic equivalences" in reconstructing and explaining the historical core of the Gospel story. Though Mitchell is not a Christian theologian his spiritually inspiring work is nonetheless limited by his Jeffersonian paring of the Gospels, the cut-and-paste procedure that, true to its Enlightenment bias, avoids the important christological symbols in the texts.

32. This can be read in light of his exegesis of Genesis chap. 1 in *Order and History* V, p. 21.

33. "The Gospel and Culture," p. 204.

34. "Immortality: Experience and Symbol," p. 78.

35. *Order and History* IV, p. 17.

36. The tendency to reduce Jesus to a disincarnate symbol is more true of modern theologians like Bultmann and Tillich. See Voegelin's provocative argument with Bultmann in his essay "History and Gnosis," in *The Old Testament and Christian Faith*, ed. Bernhard Anderson (New York: Herder and Herder, 1969), pp. 64–89.

37. *Order and History* I, p. 345.

38. Ibid.

39. "Wisdom and the Magic of the Extreme," p. 370. See also "Immortality: Experience and Symbol," p. 79, Voegelin's exegesis of the Chalcedonian Creed.

40. "The Gospel and Culture," p. 202.

41. See "The Beginning and the Beyond," p. 183; "The Gospel and Culture," pp. 192–93; "Wisdom and the Magic of the Extreme," p. 368; and "Response to Professor Altizer's 'A New History and a New but Ancient God?'" p. 294.

42. This for Voegelin is particularly true of Paul. See Voegelin's extended treatment of Paul's writings in chap. 5 of *Order and History* IV, "The Pauline Vision of the Resurrected," pp. 239–71.

43. "The Beginning and the Beyond," pp. 186–87. On the problems of the Fourth Gospel, see also *Order and History* IV, pp. 13–20.

44. Voegelin's aversion to classical Christology is further reflected in *The New Science of Politics*, where in reference to Nicea he uses the phrase "the sublimely meaningless *homo-ousios*," after which he declares that, "the problems of imperial theology, however, could not be solved by a linguistic compromise" (p. 100).

45. "The Beginning and the Beyond," p. 187.

46. *Order and History* IV, p. 259.

47. That the Patres did say too much seems to be Voegelin's view. For example, see ibid., p. 260, where he speaks about the dogmatic constructions of the early christological debates as changing the meaning of the "Christ" in the attempt to protect the unknown God in Christ from confusion with other theophanies.

48. Voegelin emphasizes the incongruity between the Christ of the christological dogmas and the Son of God found in the Gospels and Paul's letters. This is why in all his writings he does not rely on the language of doctrine. Even in discussing Christianity he never uses the secondary symbolisms and conceptual formulations of dogmatic theology, as the following sentence explains: "One can admire the technical perfection of the Definition of Chalcedon under the conditions of philosophical culture in the fifth century A.D. and refuse to use its language when speaking of 'Christ,' because the philosophical terminology of 'natures' has become inadequate in the light of what we know today about both classic philosophy and theophanic events" (ibid., p. 263).

49. "The Gospel and Culture," p. 210.

50. "Response to Professor Altizer," p. 294.

51. Ibid.

52. Voegelin's letter to Schutz, "On Christianity," in *The Philosophy of Order*, p. 454.

53. Ibid., pp. 454–55.

54. Ibid., p. 455.

55. *Order and History* V, p. 73.

56. Ibid., p. 96.

57. "The Gospel and Culture," p. 208.

58. On this, see Voegelin's analysis of the *Timaeus*, in *Order and History* V, pp. 91–107, along with his analysis of immortality based on the *Phaedrus* myth in "The Gospel and Culture," pp. 208–9, and in "The Beginning and the Beyond," pp. 212–27. In this latter essay Voegelin made the following, intriguing observation: "The function of the immortals in Plato's *fides* is equivalent to that of the visions of the resurrected Christ in the Christian *fides*" (p. 224).

59. *Order and History* V, p. 96.

60. See ibid., p. 98.

61. Ibid.

62. See *Order and History* IV, pp. 14–17, where in the section entitled "The Tension in the Gospel of John," Voegelin discusses the tension between the symbols Christ and Jesus, divine word and human word, and beginning and beyond, and also the ambiguities of Jesus' "I am" sayings.

63. In his review of Voegelin's *Autobiographical Reflections*, Paul Kuntz has recently drawn up his own interesting list of Voegelinian "commandments" for theology, morality, philosophy, and scholarship. See "Voegelin's Four Decalogues," *Intercollegiate Review* 26 (1990): 47–50.

64. The current work of many women theologians who attempt to balance the prevailing male images of God by recovering the lost feminine images would be a notable example of this reconstructive task.

65. On these particular themes three recent works are worth mentioning. Voegelin's contribution to the critique of modernity is contained in David Walsh's *After Ideology: Recovering the Spiritual Foundations of Freedom* (San Francisco: HarperCollins, 1990). Voegelin's early German works on modern race theory are analyzed in Thomas W. Heilke, *Voegelin and the Idea of Race* (Baton Rouge: Louisiana State University Press, 1990). Finally, Voegelin's writings on gnosticism, political ideology, and pneumapathology are studied in Michael Franz, *Eric Voegelin and the Politics of Spiritual Revolt: The Roots of Modern Ideology* (Baton Rouge: Louisiana State University Press, 1992).

66. This task will be greatly expedited by the publication of *The Collected Works of Eric Voegelin*. Louisiana State University Press is publishing Voegelin's *opera* in thirty-four volumes. As of 1993, four volumes have been published. These include *Autobiographical Reflections* (vol. 33); all of his late essays, some previously unpublished (vols. 12 and 28); as well as his previously unpublished essay on the nature of the law (vol. 27), a monograph written in 1957 for his students at Louisiana State University Law School. See *The Nature of the Law and Related Legal Writings*, ed. Robert Anthony Pascal, James Lee Babin, and John William Corrington (Baton Rouge: Louisiana State University Press,

1991). When complete in another decade or so, these volumes will contain a selection of Voegelin's most important correspondence, his book reviews, his multivolume "History of Political Ideas," all of his essays, miscellaneous papers, and a translation of all his early German works into English (which are the next volumes scheduled to appear). For a perspicacious review of the volumes at hand, including an instructive look at the prospective series and its problems, see James M. Rhodes, "On Voegelin: His Collected Works and His Significance," *Review of Politics* 54 (Fall, 1992): 621–47.

BIBLIOGRAPHY

Primary works of Voegelin and Lonergan are listed chronologically by publication date. Secondary works are listed alphabetically by author.

The most complete bibliography of Eric Voegelin's writings currently available has been compiled by the Eric Voegelin Institute at Louisiana State University under the direction of Ellis Sandoz. An up-to-date bibliography of secondary literature on Voegelin has also been compiled by the institute. Eric Voegelin's papers are now housed at the Hoover Institution Library Archives at Stanford University. Voegelin's collected works are being published in thirty-four volumes by Louisiana State University Press.

Bernard Lonergan's papers are housed at the Lonergan Research Institute at Regis College in Toronto. Most of his unpublished writings are duplicated at various Lonergan research centers throughout the world. Lonergan's collected works are being published in twenty-two volumes by the University of Toronto Press.

Eric Voegelin

PRIMARY WORKS

BOOKS

Voegelin, Eric. *Über die Form des amerikanischen Geistes.* Tübingen: J. C. B. Mohr, 1928.

———. *Rasse und Staat.* Tübingen: J. C. B. Mohr, 1933.

———. *Die Rassenidee in der Geistesgeschichte von Ray bis Carus.* Berlin: Junker und Dünnhaupt, 1933.

———. *Der Autoritäre Staat.* Vienna: Springer, 1936.

———. *Die politischen Religionen.* Vienna: Bermann-Fischer, 1938.

———. *The New Science of Politics.* Chicago: University of Chicago Press, 1952.

———. *Order and History.* 5 vol. Baton Rouge: Louisiana State University Press, 1956–87.

Vol. I: *Israel and Revelation.* 1956.

Vol. II: *The World of the Polis.* 1957.

Vol. III: *Plato and Aristotle*. 1957.

Vol. IV: *The Ecumenic Age*. 1974.

Vol. V: *In Search of Order*. 1987.

———. *Wissenschaft, Politik und Gnosis*. Munich: Kösel, 1959.

———. *Anamnesis: Zur Theorie der Geschichte und Politik*. Munich: R. Piper, 1966.

———. *Science, Politics, and Gnosticism*. Chicago: Henry Regnery, 1968. Includes: "Science, Politics, and Gnosticism" (*Wissenschaft, Politik und Gnosis*, trans. William J. Fitzpatrick); "Ersatz Religion: The Gnostic Mass Movements of Our Time" ("Religionsersatz: Die gnostischen Massen bewegunen unserer Zeit," *Wort und Warheit* 1 [1960]: 5–18, trans. Voegelin).

———. *Plato*. Paperback ed. of part 1 of *Plato and Aristotle* (1957). Baton Rouge: Louisiana State University Press, 1966.

———. *From Enlightenment to Revolution*. Ed. John Hallowell. Durham: Duke University Press, 1975.

———. *Anamnesis*. Trans. and ed. Gerhart Niemeyer. Notre Dame: University of Notre Dame Press, 1978. Paperback ed.: Columbia, Mo.: University of Missouri Press, 1990. Includes from the original German edition: "On the Theory of Consciousness" (1943); "Anamnetic Experiments" (1943); "What Is Right by Nature?" (1963); "What Is Nature?" (1965); "Eternal Being in Time" (1964); and "What Is Political Reality?" (1966).

———. *Conversations with Eric Voegelin*. Ed. R. Eric O'Connor. Thomas More Institute Papers, 1976. Montreal: Thomas More Institute, 1980. Includes: "In Search of the Ground" (1965); "Theology Confronting World Religions?" (1967); "Questions Up" (1970); and "Myth as Environment" (1976).

———. *Political Religions*. Trans. T. J. DiNapoli and E. S. Easterly, III. Toronto Studies in Theology, vol. 23. Lewiston, N.Y.: Edwin Mellen Press, 1986.

———. *Autobiographical Reflections*. Ed. Ellis Sandoz. Baton Rouge: Louisiana State University Press, 1989.

———. *Published Essays, 1966–1985*. Ed. Ellis Sandoz. *The Collected Works of Eric Voegelin*, vol. 12. Baton Rouge: Louisiana State University Press, 1990. Includes: "The German University and the Order of German Society: A Reconsideration of the Nazi Era" (1966); "On Debate and Existence" (1967); "Immortality: Experience and Symbol" (1967); "Configurations in History" (1968);"Equivalences of Experience and Symbolization in History" (1970); "On Henry James's *Turn of the Screw*" (1971); "The Gospel and Culture" (1971); "On Hegel: A Study in Sorcery" (1971); "On Classical Studies" (1973); "Reason: The Classic Experience" (1974); "Response to Professor Altizer's 'A New History and a New but Ancient God?'" (1975);

"Remembrance of Things Past" (1978); "Wisdom and the Magic of the Extreme: A Meditation" (1983); and "Quod Deus Dicitur" (1985).

————. *What Is History? and Other Late Unpublished Writings.* Ed. Paul Caringella and Thomas Hollweck. *The Collected Works of Eric Voegelin*, vol. 28. Baton Rouge: Louisiana State University Press, 1990. Includes "What is History?" (1963); "Anxiety and Reason" (1968); "The Eclipse of Reality" (1969); "The Moving Soul" (1969); and "The Beginning and the Beyond" (1977).

————. *The Nature of the Law and Related Legal Writings.* Ed. Robert Anthony Pascal, James Lee Babin, and John William Corrington. *The Collected Works of Eric Voegelin*, vol. 27. Baton Rouge: Louisiana StateUniversity Press, 1991.

————. *Faith and Political Philosophy: The Correspondence Between Leo Strauss and Eric Voegelin, 1934–1964.* Trans. and ed. Peter Emberley and Barry Cooper. University Park, Pa.: Pennsylvania State University Press, 1993.

ESSAYS

Voegelin, Eric. "Extended Strategy: A New Technique of Dynamic Relations." *Journal of Politics* 2 (1940): 189–200.

————. "The Growth of the Race Idea." *Review of Politics* 2 (1940): 283–317.

————. "Some Problems of German Hegemony." *Journal of Politics* 3 (1941): 154–68.

————. "Siger de Brabant." *Philosophy and Phenomenological Research* 4 (1944): 507–523.

————. "The Origins of Scientism." *Social Research* 15 (1948): 462–94.

————. "The Oxford Political Philosophers." *Philosophical Quarterly* 3 (1953): 97–114.

————. "On Readiness to Rational Discussion." In *Freedom and Serfdom*, pp. 269–84. Ed. Albert Hunold. Dordrecht: D. Reidel, 1961. Originally published as "Diskussionsbereitschaft." In *Erziehung zur Freiheit*, pp. 355–72. Ed. Albert Hunold. Zürich: Erlenbach; Stuttgart: Rentsch, 1959. Reprinted as "John Stuart Mill: Diskussionsfreiheit und Diskussionsbereitschaft." In *Anamnesis: Zur Theorie der Geschichte und Politik*, pp. 239–53. Munich: R. Piper, 1966.

————. "Industrial Society in Search of Reason." In *World Technology and Human Destiny*, pp. 31–46. Ed. Raymond Aron. Ann Arbor: University of Michigan Press, 1963. Originally published as "La société industrielle à la recherche de la raison." In *Colloques de Rheinfelden*, pp. 44–64. Ed. Raymond Aron and George Kennan. Paris: Calmann-Levy, 1960.

————. "Historiogenesis." *Philosophisches Jahrbuch* 68 (1960): 419–46. Reprinted in *Philosophia Viva: Festschrift für Alois Dempf*, pp. 419–46. Ed. Max Müller and Michael Schmaus. Freiburg and Munich: Albert, 1960.

Expanded and reprinted in Voegelin, *Anamnesis* (1966), pp. 76–116. Translated and further expanded in Voegelin, *The Ecumenic Age* (1974), chap. 1, pp. 59–113.

———. "Toynbee's *History* as a Search for Truth." In *The Intent of Toynbee's History*, pp. 183–98. Ed. Edward T. Gargan. Chicago: Loyola University Press, 1961.

———. "World Empire and the Unity of Mankind." *International Affairs* 38 (1962): 170–88.

———. "On Debate and Existence." *Intercollegiate Review* 3 (1967): 143–52. Reprinted in *A Public Philosophy Reader*, pp. 152–67. Ed. Richard J. Bishirjian. New Rochelle, N.Y.: Arlington House, 1978. Reprinted in *Published Essays, 1966–1985*, pp. 36–51.

———. "Immortality: Experience and Symbol." *Harvard Theological Review* 60 (1967): 235–79. Reprinted in *Published Essays, 1966–1985*, pp. 52–94.

———. "Configurations of History." In *The Concept of Order*, pp. 23–42. Ed. Paul G. Kuntz. Seattle: University of Washington Press, 1968. Reprinted in *Published Essays, 1966–1985*, pp. 95–114.

———. "History and Gnosis." In *The Old Testament and Christian Faith*, pp. 64–89. Ed. Bernhard Anderson. New York: Herder and Herder, 1969.

———. "Equivalences of Experience and Symbolization in History." In *Eternità e Storia, I valori permanenti nel divenire storico*, pp. 215–34. Ed. L. Paysan. Florence: Valecchi, 1970. Reprinted with minor changes in *Philosophical Studies* 28 (1981): 88–103. Reprinted in *Published Essays, 1966–1985*, pp. 115–33.

———. "The Eclipse of Reality." In *Phenomenology and Social Reality* (memorial volume for Alfred Schutz), pp. 185–94. Ed. Maurice Natanson. The Hague: Martinus Nijhoff, 1970. This essay is only the first 15 pages of the original manuscript. The full 70-page manuscript has been published in *What is History? and Other Late Unpublished Writings*, pp. 111–62.

———. "The Turn of the Screw." Contains: A Letter to Robert B. Heilman (November 13, 1947) and Postscript: "On Paradise and Revolution" (January 1970). *Southern Review* 7 (1971): 9–48. Reprinted under the title "On Henry James's *Turn of the Screw*," in *Published Essays, 1966–1985*, pp. 134–71.

———. "The Gospel and Culture." In *Jesus and Man's Hope*, pp. 59–101. Ed. D. Miller and D. G. Nadidian. Pittsburgh: Pittsburgh Theological Seminary Press, 1971. Reprinted in *Published Essays, 1966–1985*, pp. 172–212.

———. "On Hegel: A Study in Sorcery." *Studium Generale* 24 (1971): 335–68. Reprinted in *Published Essays, 1966–1985*, pp. 213–55.

———. "On Classical Studies." *Modern Age* 17 (1973): 2–8. Reprinted in *A Public Philosophy Reader*, pp. 257–65. Edited by Richard J. Bishirjian. New

Rochelle, N.Y.: Arlington House, 1978. Reprinted in *Published Essays, 1966–1985*, pp. 256–64.

———. "Philosophy of History: An Interview." *New Orleans Review* 2 (1973): 135–39.

———. "Reason: The Classic Experience." *Southern Review* 10 (1974): 237–64. Reprinted in Eric Voegelin, *Anamnesis*, pp. 89–115. Ed. Gerhart Niemeyer. Notre Dame: University of Notre Dame Press, 1978. Reprinted in *Published Essays, 1966–1985*, pp. 265–91.

———. "Response to Professor Altizer's 'A New History and a New but Ancient God?'" *Journal of the American Academy of Religion* 43 (1975): 765–72. Reprinted in *Eric Voegelin's Thought: A Critical Appraisal*, pp. 189–97. Ed. Ellis Sandoz. Durham, N. C.: Duke University Press, 1982. Reprinted in *Published Essays, 1966–1985*, pp. 292–303.

———. "Remembrance of Things Past." Chap. 1 of English trans. of *Anamnesis*. Ed. Gerhart Niemeyer. Notre Dame: University of Notre Dame Press, 1978; and Columbia, Mo.: University of Missouri Press, 1990, pp. 3–13. Reprinted in *Published Essays, 1966–1985*, pp. 304–14.

———. "Wisdom and the Magic of the Extreme: A Meditation." *Eranos Jahrbuch, 1977* 46 (1981): 341–409. Reprinted in *Southern Review* 17 (1981): 235–87. Reprinted in *Published Essays, 1966–1985*, pp. 315–75.

———. "On Christianity" and "On Gnosticism." Two letters in reply to Alfred Schutz, dated January 1, 1953, and January 10, 1953. In *The Philosophy of Order: Essays on History, Consciousness, and Politics*, pp. 449–62. Trans. Gregor Sebba. Ed. Peter J. Opitz and Gregor Sebba. Stuttgart: Klett-Cotta, 1981.

———. "In Memoriam Alfred Schutz." In *The Philosophy of Order: Essays on History, Consciousness, and Politics*, pp. 463–65. Trans. Gregor Sebba. Ed. Peter J. Opitz and Gregor Sebba. Stuttgart: Klett-Cotta, 1981. Originally published in *Anamnesis: Zur Theorie der Geschichte und Politik*, pp. 17–20. Munich: R. Piper, 1966.

———. "Epilogue." In *Eric Voegelin's Thought: A Critical Appraisal*, pp. 199–202. Ed. Ellis Sandoz. Durham: Duke University Press, 1982.

———. "Consciousness and Order: 'Foreword' to *Anamnesis*." *Logos* 4 (1983): 17–24. Trans. Voegelin. Originally appeared as "Vorwort." In *Anamnesis: Zur Theorie der Geschichte und Politik*, pp. 7–13. Munich: R. Piper, Verlag, 1966. Reprinted in *The Beginning and the Beyond: Papers from the Gadamer and Voegelin Conferences*. Supplementary issue of *Lonergan Workshop*, vol. 4, pp. 35-41. Ed. Fred Lawrence. Chico: Scholars Press, 1984.

———. "The Meditative Origin of the Philosophical Knowledge of Order." Trans. Fred Lawrence. In *The Beginning and the Beyond: Papers from the Gadamer and Voegelin Conferences*. Supplementary issue of *Lonergan Workshop*, vol. 4, pp. 43–51. Ed. Fred Lawrence. Chico: Scholars Press, 1984.

Originally published as "Der meditative Ursprung philosophischen Ord-nungwissens." In *Zeitschrift für Politik* 28 (1981): 130–37.

———. "Responses at the Panel Discussion of 'The Beginning and the Be-yond.'" In *The Beginning and the Beyond: Papers from the Gadamer and Voegelin Conferences.* Supplementary issue of *Lonergan Workshop*, vol. 4, pp. 97–110. Ed. Fred Lawrence. Chico: Scholars Press, 1984.

———. "Autobiographical Statement at Age Eighty-Two" (with responses to questions). In *The Beginning and the Beyond: Papers from the Gadamer and Voegelin Conferences.* Supplementary issue of *Lonergan Workshop*, vol. 4, pp. 111–31. Ed. Fred Lawrence. Chico: Scholars Press, 1984.

———. "The German University and the Order of German Society: A Re-consideration of the Nazi Era." Trans. Russell Nieli. *Intercollegiate Review* 20 (1985): 7–27. Originally published as "Die deutsche Universität und die Ordnung der deutschen Gesellschaft." In *Die deutsche Universität im Dritten Reich*, pp. 241–82. Ed. Helmut Kuhn, et al. Munich: Piper, 1966. Reprinted as "Universität und Öffentlichkeit: Zur Pneumopathologia der deutschen Gesellschaft." *Wort und Wahrheit* 21 (1966): 497–518. English trans. reprinted in *Published Essays, 1966–1985*, pp. 1–35.

———. "Quod Deus Dicitur." *Journal of the American Academy of Religion* 53 (1985): 569–84. Reprinted in *Published Essays, 1966–1985*, pp. 376–94.

———. "What is History?" (1963). In *What is History? and Other Later Un-published Writings*, pp. 1–51. Ed. Paul Caringella and Thomas Hollweck. *The Collected Works of Eric Voegelin*, vol. 28. Baton Rouge: Louisiana State University Press, 1990.

———. "Anxiety and Reason" (1968). In *What is History? and Other Late Un-published Writings*, pp. 52–110. Ed. Paul Caringella and Thomas Hollweck. *The Collected Works of Eric Voegelin*, vol. 28. Baton Rouge: Louisiana State University Press, 1990.

———. "The Eclipse of Reality" (1969). In *What is History? and Other Late Unpublished Writings*, pp. 111–62. Ed. Paul Caringella and Thomas Holl-weck. *The Collected Works of Eric Voegelin*, vol. 28. Baton Rouge: Louisiana State University Press, 1990.

———. "The Moving Soul" (1969). In *What is History? and Other Late Un-published Writings*, pp. 163–72. Ed. Paul Caringella and Thomas Hollweck. *The Collected Works of Eric Voegelin*, vol. 28. Baton Rouge: Louisiana State University Press, 1990.

———. "The Beginning and the Beyond: A Meditation on Truth." Aquinas Lecture, Marquette University, 1975 (1977). In *What is History? and Other Late Unpublished Writings*, pp. 173–232. Ed. Paul Caringella and Thomas Hollweck. *The Collected Works of Eric Voegelin*, vol. 28. Baton Rouge: Louisiana State University Press, 1990.

SECONDARY WORKS

Altizer, Thomas J. J. Review: Eric Voegelin, *Anamnesis*. *Journal of Religion* 59 (1979): 375–76.

———. "A New History and a New but Ancient God?" *Journal of the American Academy of Religion* 43 (1975): 757–64. Reprinted in *Eric Voegelin's Thought: A Critical Appraisal*, pp. 179–88. Ed. Ellis Sandoz. Durham: Duke University Press, 1982.

Anderson, Bernhard. "Politics and the Transcendent: Voegelin's Philosophical and Theological Exposition of the Old Testament in the Context of the Ancient Near East." In *Eric Voegelin's Search for Order in History*, pp. 62–100. Ed. Stephen A. McKnight. Baton Rouge: Louisiana State University Press, 1978. Originally published in an earlier form in *Political Science Reviewer* 1 (1971): 1–29.

Anonymous. "Journalism and Joachim's Children." *Time* (March 9, 1953): 57–61.

Bueno, Anibal A. "Consciousness, Time and Transcendence in Eric Voegelin's Philosophy." In *The Philosophy of Order: Essays on History, Consciousness, and Politics*, pp. 91–109. Ed. Peter J. Opitz and Gregor Sebba. Stuttgart: Klett-Cotta, 1981.

Caringella, Paul. "Eric Voegelin: Philosopher of Divine Presence." *Modern Age* 33 (Spring 1990): 7–22.

Cooper, Barry. *The Political Theory of Eric Voegelin*. Toronto Studies in Theology, vol. 27. Lewiston, N.Y.: Edwin Mellen Press, 1986.

———. "Voegelin's Concept of Historiogenesis: An Introduction." *Historical Reflections/Réflexions Historiques* 4 (1977): 231-50.

Corrington, John William. "Order and Consciousness/Consciousness and History: The New Program of Voegelin." In *Eric Voegelin's Search for Order in History*, pp. 155–95. Ed. Stephen A. McKnight. Baton Rouge: Louisiana State University Press, 1978.

Dahl, Robert. "The Science of Politics: Old and New." *World Politics* 7 (1955): 479–89.

Dallmayr, Fred. "Voegelin's Search for Order." *Journal of Politics* 51 (May 1989): 411–30.

Doran, Robert. "Theology's Situation: Questions to Eric Voegelin." In *The Beginning and the Beyond, Papers from the Gadamer and Voegelin Conferences*. Supplementary Issue of *Lonergan Workshop*, vol. 4, pp. 69–91. Ed. Fred Lawrence. Chico: Scholars Press, 1984.

Douglass, Bruce. "The Break in Voegelin's Program." *Political Science Reviewer* 7 (1977): 1–22.

———. "A Diminished Gospel: A Critique of Voegelin's Interpretation of Christianity." In *Eric Voegelin's Search for Order in History*, pp. 139–54.

Ed. Stephen A. McKnight. Baton Rouge: Louisiana State University Press, 1978.

Franz, Michael. *Eric Voegelin and the Politics of Spiritual Revolt: The Roots of Modern Ideology*. Baton Rouge: Louisiana State University Press, 1992.

Gueguen, John. "Voegelin's *From Enlightenment to Revolution*." *The Thomist* 42 (1978): 123–34.

Havard, William C. "Voegelin's Changing Conception of History and Consciousness." In *Eric Voegelin's Search for Order in History*, pp. 1–25. Ed. Stephen A. McKnight. Baton Rouge: Louisiana State University Press, 1978. Originally published in earlier form under the title, "The Changing Pattern of Voegelin's Conception of History and Consciousness." *Southern Review* 7 (1971): 49–67.

Hughes, Glenn. "Eric Voegelin's View of History as a Drama of Transfiguration." *International Philosophical Quarterly* 30 (1990): 449–64.

———. *Mystery and Myth in the Philosophy of Eric Voegelin*. Columbia: University of Missouri Press, 1993.

Keulman, Kenneth. *The Balance of Consciousness: Eric Voegelin's Political Theory*. University Park and London: Pennsylvania State University Press, 1991.

Kirby, John. "On Reading Eric Voegelin: A Note on the Critical Literature." In *Voegelin and the Theologian: Ten Studies in Interpretation*. Toronto Studies in Theology, vol. 10, pp. 24–60. Ed. John Kirby and William M. Thompson. New York and Toronto: Edwin Mellen Press, 1983.

———. *The Relation of Eric Voegelin's "What Is Political Reality?" to His "Order and History."* Unpublished Ph.D. dissertation, St. Michael's College, University of Toronto, 1980.

Kirby, John, and William M. Thompson, eds. *Voegelin and the Theologian: Ten Studies in Interpretation*. Toronto Studies in Theology, vol. 10. New York and Toronto: Edwin Mellen Press, 1983.

Kuntz, Paul G. "Voegelin's Four Decalogues." *Intercollegiate Review* 26 (1990): 47–50.

Lawrence, Fred. "On 'The Meditative Origin of the Philosophical Knowledge of Order.'" In *The Beginning and the Beyond: Papers from the Gadamer and Voegelin Conferences*. Supplementary issue of *Lonergan Workshop*, vol. 4, pp. 53–67. Ed. Fred Lawrence. Chico: Scholars Press, 1984.

———. "Voegelin and Theology as Hermeneutical and Political." In *Voegelin and the Theologian: Ten Studies in Interpretation*. Toronto Studies in Theology, vol. 10, pp. 314–54. Ed. John Kirby and William M. Thompson. New York and Toronto: Edwin Mellen Press, 1983.

Lawrence, Fred, ed. *The Beginning and the Beyond: Papers from the Gadamer and Voegelin Conferences*. Supplementary issue of *Lonergan Workshop*, vol. 4, Chico: Scholars Press, 1984.

McCarroll, Joseph. "Man in Search of Divine Order in History." *Philosophical Studies* 28 (1981): 15–45.

McKnight, Stephen A., ed. *Eric Voegelin's Search for Order in History*. Baton Rouge: Louisiana State University Press, 1978. Rev. and expanded edition, Lanham, Md.: University Press of America, 1987.

Molnar, Thomas. "Voegelin as Historian." *Modern Age* 19 (1975): 427-29.

Montgomery, Marion. "Eric Voegelin and the End of Our Exploring." *Modern Age* 23 (1979): 233–45.

———. "Eric Voegelin as Prophetic Philosopher." *Southern Review* 24 (1988): 115–33.

Neili, Russell. "Eric Voegelin's Evolving Ideas on Gnosticism, Mysticism, and Modern Radical Politics." *Independent Journal of Philosophy* 5/6 (1988): 93–102. Rev. version appeared as "Eric Voegelin: Gnosticism, Mysticism, and Modern Radical Politics." *Southern Review* 23 (1987): 332–48.

Niemeyer, Gerhart. "Eric Voegelin's Philosophy and the Drama of Mankind." *Modern Age* 20 (1976): 28–39.

———. "God and Man, World and Society: The Last Work of Eric Voegelin." *Review of Politics* 51 (1989): 107–23.

Nisbet, Robert. "Eric Voegelin's Vision." *Public Interest* 71 (Spring 1983): 110–17.

Opitz, Peter J., and Gregor Sebba, eds. *The Philosophy of Order: Essays on History, Consciousness, and Politics*. Stuttgart: Klett-Cotta, 1981.

Porter, J. M. "A Philosophy of History as a Philosophy of Consciousness." *Denver Quarterly* 10 (Autumn 1975): 96–104.

Rhodes, James M. "On Voegelin: His Collected Works and His Significance." *Review of Politics* 54 (Fall, 1992): 621–47.

———. "Philosophy, Revelation, and Political Theory: Leo Strauss and Eric Voegelin." *Journal of Politics* 49 (1987): 1036–60.

———. "Voegelin and Christian Faith." *Center Journal* 2 (Summer 1983): 55–105.

Sandoz, Ellis. "In Memoriam: Eric Voegelin." *Southern Review* 21 (1985): 372–75.

———. *The Voegelinian Revolution: A Biographical Introduction*. Baton Rouge: Louisiana State University Press, 1981.

Sandoz, Ellis, ed. *Eric Voegelin's Significance for the Modern Mind*. Baton Rouge: Louisiana State University Press, 1991.

———, ed. *Eric Voegelin's Thought: A Critical Appraisal*. Durham: Duke University Press, 1982.

Schram, Glenn N. "Eric Voegelin, the Christian Faith, and the American University." *Dialogue* 16 (1977): 130–35.

Sebba, Gregor. "History, Modernity and Gnosticism." In *The Philosophy of Order: Essays on History, Consciousness, and Politics*, pp. 190–241. Ed. Peter

J. Opitz and Gregor Sebba. Stuttgart: Klett-Cotta, 1981.

———. "Prelude and Variations on the Theme of Eric Voegelin." In *Eric Voegelin's Thought: A Critical Appraisal*, pp. 3–65. Ed. Ellis Sandoz. Durham: Duke University Press, 1982. Original shorter version published in *The Southern Review* 13 (1977): 646–76.

Thompson, William M. "Eric Voegelin: In Retrospect." *Religious Studies Review* 10 (1984): 29–33.

———. "Voegelin and the Religious Scholar: An Introduction." In *Voegelin and the Theologian: Ten Studies in Interpretation*. Toronto Studies in Theology, vol. 10, pp. 1–23. Ed. John Kirby and William M. Thompson. New York and Toronto: Edwin Mellen Press, 1983.

———. "Voegelin on Jesus Christ." In *Voegelin and the Theologian: Ten Studies in Interpretation*. Toronto Studies in Theology, vol. 10, pp. 178–221. Ed. John Kirby and William M. Thompson. New York and Toronto: Edwin Mellen Press, 1983.

Wagner, Helmut R. "Agreement in Discord: Alfred Schutz and Eric Voegelin." In *The Philosophy of Order: Essays on History, Consciousness, and Politics*, pp. 74–90. Ed. Peter J. Opitz and Gregor Sebba. Stuttgart: Klett-Cotta, 1981.

Walsh, David. *After Ideology: Recovering the Spiritual Foundations of Freedom*. San Francisco: HarperCollins, 1990.

Webb, Eugene. *Eric Voegelin: Philosopher of History*. Seattle: University of Washington Press, 1981.

———. "Eric Voegelin's Theory of Revelation." In *Eric Voegelin's Thought: A Critical Appraisal*, pp. 157–77. Ed. Ellis Sandoz. Durham: Duke University Press, 1982. Originally published in *The Thomist* 42 (1978): 95–110.

———. "Faith, Truth, and Persuasion in the Thought of Eric Voegelin." In *Voegelin and the Theologian: Ten Studies in Interpretation*. Toronto Studies in Theology, vol. 10, pp. 356–69. Ed. John Kirby and William M. Thompson. New York and Toronto: The Edwin Mellen Press, 1983.

———. "Metaphysics or Existenzerhellung: A Comparison of Lonergan and Voegelin." *Religious Studies and Theology* 7 (1987): 36-47.

———. *Philosophers of Consciousness: Polanyi, Lonergan, Voegelin, Ricoeur, Girard, Kierkegaard*. Seattle: University of Washington Press, 1988.

Weatherby, Harold. "Myth, Fact, and History: Voegelin on Christianity." *Modern Age* 22 (1978): 144–50.

Wilhelmsen, Frederick. "The New Voegelin." *Triumph* (January 1975): 32–35. Rev. and reprinted in *Christianity and Political Philosophy*, as chap. 7, "Professor Voegelin and the Christian Tradition," pp. 193–200. Athens: University of Georgia Press, 1978.

Wiser, James. "Eric Voegelin: A Study in the Renewal of Political Science." *Polity* 17 (1985): 295–312.

Bernard Lonergan

PRIMARY WORKS

Lonergan, Bernard. *Insight: An Essay in Human Understanding.* New York: Harper and Row, 1957.

———. *Verbum: Word and Idea in Aquinas.* Ed. David B. Burrell. Notre Dame: University of Notre Dame Press, 1967.

———. *Collection: Papers by Bernard Lonergan.* Ed. Frederick. E. Crowe. New York: Herder and Herder, 1967.

———. *Grace and Freedom: Operative Grace in the Thought of St. Thomas Aquinas.* Ed. J. Patout Burns. New York: Herder and Herder, 1971.

———. *Doctrinal Pluralism.* Milwaukee: Marquette University Press, 1971.

———. *Method in Theology.* New York: Seabury Press, 1972.

———. *Philosophy of God, and Theology.* Philadelphia: Westminster, 1973.

———. *A Second Collection.* Ed. W. F. J. Ryan and B. J. Tyrrell. Philadelphia: Westminster Press, 1974.

———. *Three Lectures.* Thomas More Institute Papers, 1975. Ed. R. Eric O'Connor. Montreal: Thomas More Institute, 1975.

———. *The Way to Nicea.* Trans. Conn O'Donovan. Philadelphia: Westminster Press, 1976.

———. *Understanding and Being: An Introduction and Companion to Insight.* The Halifax Lectures, 1958. Ed. Elizabeth and Mark Morelli. New York and Toronto: Edwin Mellen Press, 1980.

———. *Caring about Meaning: Patterns in the Life of Bernard Lonergan.* Thomas More Institute Papers, 1982. Montreal: Thomas More Institute, 1982.

———. *A Third Collection: Papers by Bernard J. F. Lonergan, S.J.* Ed. Frederick E. Crowe. New York: Paulist Press, 1985.

SECONDARY WORKS

Burt, Julian. "Lonergan Doctrine: Is It Orthodox?" *Homiletic and Pastoral Review* 86 (1986): 26–32, 50–53.

Byrne, Patrick H. "The Fabric of Lonergan's Thought." In *Lonergan Workshop*, vol. 6, pp. 1–84. Ed. Fred Lawrence. Atlanta: Scholars Press, 1986.

Corcoran, Patrick, ed. *Looking at Lonergan's Method.* Dublin: Talbot Press, 1975.

Crowe, Frederick E. *The Lonergan Enterprise.* Cambridge: Cowley, 1980.

———. *Old Things and New: A Strategy for Education.* Supplementary issue of *Lonergan Workshop*, vol. 5. Atlanta: Scholars Press, 1986.

Crowe, Frederick E., ed. *Spirit as Inquiry: Studies in Honor of Bernard Lonergan.* *Continuum* 2 (1964), special issue.

Doran, Robert M. *Psychic Conversion and Theological Foundations: Toward a Restructuring of the Human Sciences.* Chico: Scholars Press, 1981.

————. *Subject and Psyche: Ricoeur, Jung, and the Search for Foundations.* Washington, D.C.: University Press of America, 1978.

————. *Theology and the Dialectics of History.* Toronto: University of Toronto Press, 1990.

Drilling, Peter J. "The Pyramid or the Raft: Francis Schüssler Fiorenza and Bernard Lonergan in Dialogue about Foundational Theology." *Horizons* 13 (1986): 275–90.

Gregson, Vernon, ed. *The Desires of the Human Heart: An Introduction to the Theology of Bernard Lonergan.* New York: Paulist Press, 1988.

Hefling, Charles C. *Lonergan on Development: "The Way to Nicea" in Light of His More Recent Methodology.* Unpublished Ph.D. dissertation, Boston College, 1982.

————. *Why Doctrines?* Cambridge: Cowley, 1984.

Lamb, Matthew L. *History, Method and Theology: A Dialectical Comparison of Wilhelm Dilthey's Critique of Historical Reason and Bernard Lonergan's Meta-Methodology.* Missoula: Scholars Press, 1978.

Lamb, Matthew L., ed. *Creativity and Method: Essays in Honor of Bernard Lonergan.* Milwaukee: Marquette University Press, 1981.

Lawrence, Fred, ed. *Lonergan Workshop.* Vol. 1–9. Chico: Scholars Press, 1981–93.

McCool, Gerald A. "History, Insight and Judgment in Thomism." *International Philosophical Quarterly* 27 (1987): 299–313.

McShane, Philip, ed. *Foundations of Theology: Papers from the International Lonergan Congress, 1970.* Vol. 1. Notre Dame: University of Notre Dame Press, 1971.

————. *Language, Truth and Meaning: Papers from the International Lonergan Congress, 1970.* Vol. 2. Notre Dame: University of Notre Dame Press, 1972.

Mathews, William. "Lonergan's Quest." *Milltown Studies* (Spring 1986): 3–34.

Meynell, Hugo A. *The Theology of Bernard Lonergan.* Atlanta: Scholars Press: 1986.

O'Leary, Joseph Stephen. "The Hermeneutics of Dogmatism." *Irish Theological Quarterly* 47 (1980): 96–118.

Riley, Philip Boo, and Timothy Fallon, eds. *Religion and Culture: Essays in Honor of Bernard Lonergan.* Albany: State University of New York Press, 1987.

————. eds. *Religion in Context: Recent Studies in Lonergan.* College Theology Society Resources in Religion, vol. 4. Lanham, Md.: University Press of America, 1988.

Other Works Cited

Ancilla to the Pre-Socratic Philosophers. Trans. Kathleen Freeman. Cambridge: Harvard University Press, 1957.

Anselm, St. *Anselm of Canterbury,* vol. 3. Trans. and ed. Jasper Hopkins and Herbert Richardson. New York: Edwin Mellen Press, 1976.

——. *Basic Writings.* Trans. S. N. Deane. LaSalle, Ill.: Open Court, 1962.

Arendt, Hannah. "Philosophy and Politics." *Social Research* 57 (Spring 1990): 73–103.

Aristotle. *The Basic Works of Aristotle.* Ed. Richard McKeon. New York: Random House, 1941.

Augustine, St. *Confessions and Enchiridion.* Trans. Albert C. Outler. Library of Christian Classics, vol. 7. Philadelphia: Westminster Press, 1955.

Barth, Karl. *Anselm: Fides Quaerens Intellectum.* Trans. Ian W. Robertson. Richmond: John Knox Press, 1960.

Bergson, Henri. *The Two Sources of Morality and Religion.* Trans. R. Audra and C. Brereton. Garden City, N.Y.: Doubleday, 1935.

Bonaventure, St. *The Mind's Journey to God.* Trans. Lawrence S. Cunningham. Chicago: Franciscan Herald Press, 1979.

Buber, Martin. *Moses: The Revelation and the Covenant.* New York: Harper and Row, 1958.

Camus, Albert. *Notebooks: 1942–1951.* Trans. Justin O'Brien. New York: Harcourt Brace Jovanovich, 1965.

——. *The Rebel.* Trans. Anthony Bower. New York: Random House, 1956.

Cicero. *Tusculan Disputations.* Trans. J. E. King. The Loeb Classical Library. Cambridge: Harvard University Press, 1945.

Crossan, John Dominic. *The Historical Jesus: The Life of a Mediterranean Peasant.* San Francisco: HarperCollins, 1991.

Fiorenza, Francis Schüssler. *Foundational Theology: Jesus and the Church.* New York: Crossroad, 1984.

Frankfort, Henri, et al. *The Intellectual Adventure of Ancient Man.* Chicago: University of Chicago Press, 1946.

Friedlaender, Paul. *Plato: An Introduction.* 2nd ed. Trans. Hans Meyerhoff. Princeton: Princeton University Press, 1969.

Gadamer, Hans Georg. *Truth and Method.* 2nd revised ed. Trans. Joel Weinsheimer and Donald G. Marshall. New York: Crossroad, 1989.

Germino, Dante. *Beyond Ideology: The Revival of Political Theory.* Chicago: University of Chicago Press, 1967.

——. *Political Philosophy and the Open Society.* Baton Rouge: Louisiana State University Press, 1982.

Gilson, Etienne. *The Christian Philosophy of St. Thomas Aquinas*. Trans. L. K. Shook. New York: Random House, 1956.

———. *The Spirit of Medieval Philosophy*. Trans. A. H. C. Downes. New York: Charles Scribner's Sons, 1936. Reprint ed. Notre Dame: University of Notre Dame Press, 1991.

Heidegger, Martin, *Being and Time*. Trans. John Macquarrie and Edward Robinson. New York: Harper and Row, 1962.

Heiler, Friedrich. "The History of Religions as a Preparation for the Cooperation of Religions." In *The History of Religions*, pp. 142–53. Ed. M. Eliade and J. Kitagawa. Chicago: University of Chicago Press, 1959.

James, William. *Essays on Radical Empiricism* [and] *A Pluralistic Universe*. New York: Longmans, Green, and Co., 1947.

Jaspers, Karl. *The Origin and Goal of History*. Trans. Michael Bullock. New Haven: Yale University Press, 1953.

Knox, Ronald A. *Enthusiasm*. New York: Oxford University Press, 1961.

Leibniz, Gottfried Wilhelm. *Philosophical Writings*. Trans. Mary Morris. Everyman's Library, no. 905. New York: E. P. Dutton, 1934.

Meier, John P. *A Marginal Jew: Rethinking the Historical Jesus*. New York: Doubleday, 1991.

Mitchell, Steven. *The Gospel According to Jesus*. New York: HarperCollins, 1991.

Nietzsche, Friedrich. *The Use and Abuse of History*. Trans. Adrian Collins. Indianapolis: Bobbs-Merrill, 1957.

Plato. *Collected Dialogues*. Ed. Edith Hamilton and Huntington Cairns. Princeton: Princeton University Press, 1961.

Pascal. *Pensées*. Trans. W. F. Trotter. New York: E. P. Dutton, 1958.

Sokolowski, Robert. *The God of Faith and Reason: Foundations of Christian Theology*. Notre Dame: University of Notre Dame Press, 1982.

Snell, Bruno. *The Discovery of the Mind: The Greek Origins of European Thought*. Trans. T. G. Rosenmeyer. New York: Harper, 1960.

Tillich, Paul. "The Two Types of Philosophy of Religion." In *Theology of Culture*, pp. 10–29. Ed. Robert C. Kimball. New York: Oxford University Press, 1959.

Wagner, Helmut. *Alfred Schutz: An Intellectual Biography*. Chicago: University of Chicago Press, 1983.

INDEX OF NAMES

Abraham, 53–54, 85, 152, 242, 270, 290
Aeschylus, 63–64
Akhenaton, 52
Altizer, T., 255, 269, 284, 286, 290, 291, 294, 311, 313, 314, 316
Anaxagoras, 65
Anaximander, 96, 281, 285
Anderson, B., 269, 315
Anselm, St., 8, 11, 73, 137, 151–56, 159–60, 210, 220, 256, 272, 274, 289, 291–92
Aquinas, St. Thomas. *See* Thomas Aquinas, St.
Archimedes, 291
Arendt, H., 272
Aristotle, 6–8, 20, 26, 38, 42, 49, 57, 60, 67, 75–78, 90, 96, 99, 100, 102, 104, 108, 129, 158, 175, 176, 208, 216–18, 227, 250, 256–58, 261, 271, 275, 278, 282, 289, 291, 297, 306
Arius, 244
Augustine, St., 13, 35, 43, 61, 71, 83, 88, 102, 175, 210, 222, 253, 263, 264, 278, 288, 306, 308–9

Barth, K., 152, 291
Bergson, H., 19, 26, 97, 262, 278
Bonaventure, St., 115, 134–36, 287
Buber, M., 270
Bueno, A., 262
Bultmann, R., 315
Burt, J., 302
Byrne, P., 294

Camus, A., 19, 222, 278, 309
Caringella, P., 255, 267, 285
Christ, 42, 55, 64, 79, 92, 101, 103, 108, 136, 137, 142, 143, 152, 153, 160, 163, 164–65, 205, 217, 221, 232, 233, 235–47, 251, 253, 278, 289, 290, 294, 311, 312, 314–17. *See also* Jesus
Cicero, 155, 219, 279
Clapham, L., 269
Clauberg, J., 291
Comte, A., 41, 106
Cooper, B., 265, 280
Corcoran, P., 295
Corrington, J. W., 276
Crossan, J. D., 315
Crowe, F. E., 295, 297, 298
Cunningham, L., 287

Dahl, R., 267
Dahllmayr, F., 285
Denzinger, H., 290
Descartes, R., 7, 28, 137, 172, 210
Dilthey, W., 313
Doran, R., 301, 307
Douglass, B., 275, 311
Drilling, P. J., 300

Einstein, A., 284
Elijah, 85
Euripides, 63–64

Fallon, T., 295, 303
Fiorenza, F. S., 299–300
Fitzpatrick, W., 278
Franz, M., 317
Freeman, K., 280
Freud, S., 19, 34, 264
Friedlaender, P., 277

Gadamer, H. G., 174, 259, 267, 284, 296, 304, 305, 307, 309, 311, 313
Gaunilo, 154
George, S., 19
Germino, D., 260, 262

Gilkey, L., 295, 300
Gilson, E., 152, 157, 158, 291–93
Gregson, V., 295
Gueguen, J., 309–11

Hallowell, J., 311
Havard, W. C., 276
Hefling, C. C., 303, 307
Hegel, G. W. F., 8, 9, 95, 106, 127–32, 141, 275, 281, 286, 287
Heidegger, M., 9, 97, 175, 180, 256, 278, 285, 296
Heilke, T., 256, 259, 317
Heller, F., 301
Heraclitus, 62, 63, 65, 90, 222, 272, 293
Herodotus, 66
Hesiod, 59–61, 132–36, 159, 161, 227, 270, 286–87
Hitler, A., 243
Hobbes, T., 278
Homer, 58–61, 64, 106, 132, 140, 161, 270
Hughes, G., 283
Hume, D., 26
Husserl, E., 27–30, 34, 45, 137, 178, 213, 263, 304, 305

Isaiah, 54, 85, 283

James, W., 24–27, 34, 262
Jaspers, K., 19, 50, 92, 94, 279–80
Jeremiah, 20, 54, 85, 86
Jesus, 44, 55, 137, 143, 145, 152, 164–68, 231–33, 236–46, 251, 257, 282, 289, 294, 299, 311, 314, 315, 317. *See also* Christ
Joachim of Fiore, 261, 267
John the Evangelist, St., 85, 92, 131, 142, 163, 221, 241, 251, 252, 277, 289, 298, 308
John XXIII, Pope, 205, 296
Jung, C. G., 34, 264, 265, 274, 286, 301

Kant, I., 9, 24, 128, 172, 181, 256, 296
Kelsen, H., 19
Kierkegaard, S., 19
Kirby, J., 255, 257, 276, 277, 307, 311
Knox, R. A., 278
Kuntz, P. G., 309, 317

Lamb, M. L., 295

Lawrence, F., 259, 267, 284, 287, 294, 304, 307, 309
Leibniz, G. W., 32, 97, 134–36, 287
Leo XIII, Pope, 296
Loewe, W. P., 307

McCarroll, J., 259, 275
McCool, G., 296–97
McKnight, S. A., 311
McShane, P., 295
Mark the Evangelist, St., 260
Marx, K., 19, 41
Mary (Mother of Jesus), 44, 243
Mathews, W., 301
Matthew the Evangelist, St., 164, 165, 166, 168, 293
Meier, J. P., 315
Meynell, H. A., 295
Migne, J. P., 291
Mitchell, S., 315
Molnar, T., 311
Montgomery, M., 258, 311
Moore, H., 170
Morris, M., 287
Moses, 52–55, 64, 85

Neili, R., 267
Newman, J. H., 297
Newton, I., 128, 284
Niemeyer, G., 285, 311
Nietzsche, F., 1–3, 278
Nisbet, R., 262
Nygren, A., 308

O'Donovan, C., 298, 302
O'Leary, J. S., 302
Ockham. *See* William of Ockham
Opitz, P. J., 268, 288, 307
Origen, 103

Parmenides, 61, 62, 65, 66, 85, 128, 134, 136, 140, 271, 292
Pascal, B., 87, 88, 279
Paul of Tarsus, St., 13, 42, 62, 100–102, 105, 106, 108, 117, 132, 136, 138, 160, 166, 167, 217, 233, 240, 241, 277, 282, 293, 316
Peirce, C. S., 25
Peter, St., 132, 164, 294
Philo Judaeus, 309

Pilate (Roman governor), 165
Plato, viii, xii, 4, 7–11, 16, 20–23, 26, 27, 29, 31, 40, 42, 44, 50, 55, 57–59, 62, 63, 65–78, 82, 85–87, 90, 96, 99–102, 104, 105, 108, 112, 115, 117, 118, 120, 123, 124, 126, 129–31, 134, 136–49, 154–61, 163, 167–69, 216, 217, 218, 221, 223, 227, 228, 244–46, 254–61, 271, 273, 274, 277, 278, 280, 284, 285, 287–94, 304, 308, 317
Porter, J. M., 264, 276
Protagoras, 65
Pyrrho of Elis, 78

Rahner, K., 178
Rhodes, J. M., 264, 310, 311, 318
Ricoeur, P., 230, 301, 310
Riley, P. B., 295, 303
Russell, B., 19

Sandoz, E., 258, 262, 267, 269, 279, 282, 284, 294, 311, 312
Scheler, M., 34
Schelling, F., 24, 32, 38, 39, 89, 155, 273
Schleiermacher, F. E. D., 3, 313
Schmitt, F., 292
Schram, G. N., 311
Schutz, A., 24, 27, 43, 44, 136, 137, 243, 263, 265, 266, 268, 288, 307, 313, 316
Sebba, G., 259, 266–68, 288, 307
Siger de Brabant, 256
Snell, B., 302, 305
Socrates, viii, 11, 22, 57, 66–70, 75, 78, 82, 85, 245, 248, 254, 271, 280, 282

Sokolowski, R., 288–89
Solon, 60
Spengler, O., 92, 94
Spinoza, B., 9
Strauss, L., 310, 311

Thomas Aquinas, St., 6, 43, 61, 79, 117, 151, 157, 172, 175–77, 187, 218, 231, 232, 252, 285, 287, 290–91, 296, 299, 304, 306
Thompson, W. M., 255, 277, 304, 307, 311
Thucydides, 66
Tillich, P., 189, 300, 306, 315
Toynbee, A., 92, 94, 279
Tracy, D., 300
Tyrtaeus, 60

Urban II, Pope, 292

Voegelin, L., 258

Wagner, H., 265–66, 268
Walsh, D., 304–6, 311, 317
Weatherby, H., 311
Webb, E., 259, 266, 282, 308, 311
Weber, M., 19
Whitehead, A. N., 33, 240, 264
Wilhelmsen, F., 311
William of Ockham, 256
Wiser, J., 311
Wittgenstein, L., 19, 124

Xenophanes, 60, 61, 66, 69, 307

Zoroaster, 305

INDEX OF SUBJECTS

absolute knowledge, 129–30
absolute reality, 129
abstract experience, 48
abstraction: automatic process, 176; from
    normal experience, 30
Academy (Athens), 75
actualization of relation, 49
adoptionism, 244
aeons, 76
Aeterni Patris (Leo XIII), 296
affectivity, Lonergan, 217
agape, 308
agathon (the Good), 69, 72, 120
age: of human being, 162; immediacy,
    202
agent intellect, 218
aggiornamento, 205
aleithos logos, 105
alienation, 111, 234
allegoresis, 309
ambiguity: Bonaventure, 134–35;
    compact use of language, 157; Hesiod,
    134; Leibniz, 135–36; symbolic, of
    divine presence, 122–27
American philosophers, 26
amicitia, 308
amor sui, 278
analogia entis, 232, 252
analogy, 200
analysis by association, 258
anamnesis, 3; anamnetic experiments, 27,
    35; anamnetic recovery, 100; compact
    language, 123; deciphering, 72;
    German context, 127–32; Voegelin
    on, 57
Anamnesis (Voegelin), 23, 116, 255, 261,
    263, 264, 265, 276, 303, 313
Ancilla to Pre-Socratic Philosophers
    (Freeman), 288

an est? 176
anima animi, 61
answers, Lonergan, 179
anthropogony, 94
anthropological principle, 68, 70
anthropological truth, 41–42, 136–37
anthropology: contemplation, 76;
    Lonergan, 172–78; Voegelin, 254
anthropomorphism, 60–61, 305
apeiron, 96, 101; apeirontic depth, 87, 90
apodictic beginning, 29
apophatic theology, 252
aporia, 78
appearance, transparence turns to, 28
appropriating mind, 177
a priori facticity, 177
arete, 74
articulate experience, 129
aspernatio nationis, 279
astrophysical universe, 284
Athens, 57, 63, 64–65, 66, 67, 68, 69,
    71, 154, 231. *See also* Greece
attending to oneself, as knowing, 174
attunement, 5, 49
Austria, 18, 259
authenticity: Christianity, 203;
    conversion, 189; freedom and
    the human good, 184–87
authentic philosophy, 283
authentic subjectivity, 173, 178
authentic theology, 208
authority: in the Church, 228–29; in
    society, 63
Autobiographical Reflections (Voegelin), 258,
    317
autogenesis, 287
awareness: tension between two poles of
    being, 81; Voegelin, 217
axis-time, 50, 92, 94

Babylon, 52
balance: of consciousness, 101, 109–13,
    162; intentionality and luminosity,
    250; language of reality, 140; loss of,
    99; noetic, 215; noetic and pneumatic
    differentiations, 248
baptizing Plato and Aristotle, 90
beatific vision, 153–54
becoming, 140; being and, 149, 254;
    historiogenesis, 96
beginning (the beginning): and beyond,
    110, 121, 148; God of the beginning
    and God of the end, 150, 240
The Beginning and the Beyond (Lawrence),
    305
behavior, disordered existence, 89
being: all being is symbolic, 27; analogy
    of, 61; Aquinas, 157; awareness and,
    44, 149, 254; being-becoming-space,
    147; conversion, 189; eternal, 81–82;
    knowing and, 210; leaps in, 50–51;
    levels of, 32–33; Lonergan, 207;
    Lonergan and Voegelin, 234; love of,
    57–58; meaning and, 234; objectively
    known, 210; order of, 46; quaternian
    structure of, 49; singular, 140; thing
    and, 156; understanding, 180
Being and Time (Heidegger), 296
being-in-love, 199, 203
being-in-the-world, 173
being-things, 119
belief: knowledge, 207; Lonergan, 206;
    perfection, 245
beyond (the beyond), 9–10, 68, 73–74;
    and the beginning, 121; beyond the,
    160; consciousness and, 173; Christ,
    167; differentiation, 140; divine, in
    time, 236; God beyond the gods,
    108; God of the, Hesiod, 133; in
    history, 118; Jovian, 132; moving
    beyond structure, 109–10; mystery
    of the, 252; nonpresent, one beyond
    the many, 218; presence of the, 119;
    soul's movement, 89; of things, 146
Beyond Ideology (Germino), 260
bias, 175, 185, 190
Bible, 155; Colossians, 166, 240;
    Deuteronomy, 306; Exodus, 52;
    Genesis, 120; Gospel, 205, 236–38,
    314; Hebrews, 112, 307; John, 131,

142, 164, 165, 168, 221, 240, 242,
    245, 252, 289, 308; Matthew, 293;
    New Testament, 163, 231–32; Psalms,
    154, 170; Romans, 166
biblical personalism, 207
biography, 165, 263
breakthroughs in history, 93
burden of history, 1–2

carriers of divine reality, 54
catharsis, 68, 222
Catholic philosophy, 268
causality, 135, 141
cave, parable of the, 69
Chalcedon, Council of, 240, 241, 316
Chalcedonian Creed, 168
children, Father-Mother-Offspring
    (*Timaeus*), 149
China, 107
chora (space), 146
Chosen People, 54, 64
Christian philosophy, 227–28
Christianity, 47; Christian vision,
    163–70; classical philosophy and,
    289; conversion, 188–89; *ecumene*,
    107–8; ecumenic religion, 99; faith
    and reason, 251; faith and vision in
    Christian context, 150–70; Lonergan
    and Voegelin, 220–21; meditation,
    28; metaphysics, 41; monopoly of
    revelation, 13; Pauline vision, 102;
    Republic, 69; return to Platonic
    myth, 136–37; Roman Empire, 40;
    Voegelin, 5, 6, 16, 79, 135, 227–47,
    312
Church: authority, 204, 228–29;
    Lonergan, 205; monopoly of
    revelation, 126; and revelation, 12;
    Voegelin, 229
circumstances of revelation, 313
civitas Dei, 70–71
Civitas Dei (Augustine), 102
clarity in symbolization, 137
classicism, absolutist view of culture, 212
classicist theology, 198, 206
clearing in existence, 285
closed self, 26
cloud of unknowing, 202
The Cloud of Unknowing, 35, 116
concrete experience, 34

cogito, 173
cognitio fidei, 159
cognition: cognitional intentionality,
    15, 201; expansion of the cognitive,
    184; Lonergan, 173; Lonergan and
    Voegelin, 214
collective unconscious, 72
common sense, 189–90
communion, pattern of experience, 201
community: Heraclitus on, 62; *homonoia,*
    55; of pathos, xii; reality of, 71
compact symbols, 145
compact to differentiated forms, 46, 47
compact use of language, 157
compactness of the social collective, 94
comprehending story, 122
concepts: conceptualist extrinsicism,
    210; conceptualist reductionism of
    doctrine, 220; data of the senses, 175;
    insight and, 179
concrete experience, 48
conduct of life, 184
conscience: consciousness of, 185
consciousness, 45, 58, 91; affective, 203; *a
    priori* structure, 207; balance of, 109–
    13; beyond in, 118; concrete reality,
    151; conscious existence, 23; constant
    of, 145; and conversion, 190–92; data
    of, 187; differentiating, 14–15, 200;
    divine presence, 233, 238; ecumenical,
    107; ever-questioning, 249; exegesis
    of, 116; experiencing, 95; experiential
    basis of, 127; foundational starting
    point, 247; *Gegenstandsformlichkeit,*
    304; hardening of, 9; horizon, 181;
    intentional, 156, 178, 213, 250; levels
    of, 183, 196–97, 214; as luminosity,
    230; luminosity of, 146; meditative
    analysis of, 137; paradox of, 118;
    participatory character of, 133;
    perversion of, 125; of principles, 39;
    questioning, 96; radical philosophy
    of, and reality, 119; response to the
    Question, 112; spiritual, 73; splitting,
    128; structure, 104, 172; subject as
    subject, 174; subjective, 204; time
    dimension, 263; transcendence, 8,
    195–96; two types of, 7; Voegelin on,
    3, 82, 227–54
conservatism, 257

constants: experience and symbolization,
    141; nature of human beings, 281
constitutional community, 53
construing of a field of study, 89
contemplation, life of (*bios theoretikos*), 76
content: of revelation, 233–34; of the
    quest, 153
context, truth, 204
contingent things, 135–36
controversy, language, 216
Conversations with Eric Voegelin
    (O'Connor, ed.), 261
conversion: consciousness, 183;
    Lonergan, 217; love, 221; luminosity,
    215; *periagoge,* 57; Plato on, 20;
    transcendence and, 16; Voegelin, 250
coredeemers of humankind, 243
corpus mysticum, 290
cosmic cycles, 74
cosmic divine world, 51
cosmogonic myth, 110–11
cosmological civilization, 51
cosmological myth, 59, 64, 84, 139, 216
cosmological truth, 41–42
cosmopolis, 304
cosmos: *aition* of the, 148; beginning,
    140; Christ, 242; cosmic fides, 167;
    full of God, 158; lastingness of,
    110; object in space, 147; Plato's
    faith, 137; Plato's focus, 245;
    primary experience, 105; structure,
    168; tensionally structured, 148;
    transcendence, 52
counterpositions, 173
covenantal order of existence, 54
creation: salvation, 245; *Timaeus,* 142
creator-god, 110, 163
creatureliness, 21
credo ut intelligam, 73, 151
Creed, 153, 168
critical realism, 173
Critique of Pure Reason (Kant), 128
Cronos. *See* Kronos
cult of Greek democracy, 63
culture: breakthroughs in consciousness,
    85; classicism, 212; cultured
    despisers, 228; deculturation, 234–35;
    development, 205; theology and, 253;
    transcultural base, 195
Cur Deus Homo (Anselm), 292

daimonios aner, 170, 228
death, 170; *Gorgias*, 68; Lonergan and
    Voegelin, 221; resurrection, 244. *See
    also* life and death
decision, 64
deculturation, 234
De Deo Trino (Lonergan), 302
deductivism, 205
deformation: doctrinal, 161; Gospel, 237;
    reality, 110; theology, 249
Demiurge, 73, 110, 141, 148
demonic drive, 64
demythologizing, 310
depositum fidei, 228
depth psychology, 129
desensualization of the myth, 50
desire: to know, 180, 186, 201, 215; for
    understanding, 190
development: culture and doctrine,
    205–6; movement of consciousness,
    184
De Verbo Incarnato (Lonergan), 307
dialectic, 20, 206
dialogues, Plato and Aristotle, 67
dianoetic virtue, 77
differentiation: beginning and beyond,
    120; beyond, 140; breakthrough to,
    51; Christ, 243; Christian, 43, 288;
    compact to differentiated forms, 46;
    consciousness, 14, 84, 95, 109, 129,
    193–94, 200, 207, 211, 214–15;
    context, 139; of conversions, 189;
    experiences, 47–48; historical, 40;
    interiority, 174; language, 90; level of
    consciousness, 73; *metaxy*, 96; New
    Testament, 232; Olympian gods, 133;
    Platonic myth, 136; predifferentiatied
    oneness, 216; process of experience,
    122; reality, 145; spiritual experience,
    105; symbolisms, 49; of truth, 166
Ding-an-sich, 128
Dionysiac component in tragic existence,
    64
The Discovery of Mind (Snell), 305
distancing remembrance, 123
distentio animi, 83
diversification: divine presence in history,
    158; objectification of human spirit,
    182
divine (the divine): beyond, 104–5;

divine-human encounter, 125–26,
    162, 248; divine-human process, 109;
    giving-and-commanding pole, 85,
    86; ground, 22, 241; in history, 69,
    152, 158; incarnation, 103; love, 200;
    paradigm, 142; participation in, 62;
    Platonic myth and, 44, 139; presence,
    117, 119, 142, 152, 158, 166; reality,
    219; reality from the beyond, 130–31;
    reality, of the ground, 82; reality, of
    the Idea, 72; self-communication,
    208; symbol and, 122–27, 150; truth,
    250
doctrinalization, 88: hypostatizing,
    6; meditation and, 230; suspect
    symbolism, 241
doctrine: deformations, 161; fossilization,
    finality, 249; Lonergan, 198, 203–
    9; Lonergan and Voegelin, 220;
    modernity, 100; theology, 155; and
    ultimate truth, 11
doctrinization, 9
dogma, 204; faith, 229; Voegelin, 160,
    234
dogmatic theology, 206
dogmatism, 6, 116
dogmatomachy, 281
doxa, 48, 156, 271
doxic conception of truth, 249
drama: comprehending story, 122; Israel
    and Revelation, 56; participation,
    238. *See also* tragedy
drawing (*helkein*), 85
dualism, 251

ecclesiastic statesman, 74
ecstasy, 185, 217
The Ecumenic Age (Voegelin), 23, 24, 42,
    82, 84, 89, 91–101, 110, 112, 113,
    117, 136, 231, 269, 279, 280, 282,
    311
education/*paideia*, 22, 67
egophanic pursuit of absolute knowledge,
    123
egophanic revolt, 105
Egypt, 52, 280
empire: ecumenic age, 97–98;
    historiogenesis, 94; unity of
    humankind, 106–9
empiricism, 25–26, 176, 205, 248

Enchiridion (Denzinger), 290
engendering experience, 48
English philosophers, 26
enlightened rationality, 65
Enlightenment, 7–9, 22, 126, 177–78, 315
Enthusiasm (Knox), 278
Enuma elish, 52
epekeina, 10
epic poetry, 58
epistemology: Kant, 172; Lonergan, 176; Lonergan and Voegelin, 210
epoch, 109, 137, 215, 261
equivalence: experience, 92, 244; *fides quaerens intellectum*, 288; meanings, 211; symbolisms of love, 308; theory, 83–84
equivalents, 95–96, 129, 209
Eric Voegelin, Philosopher of History (Webb), 266, 308
Eric Voegelin's Thought (Sandoz), 312
eros, 301, 308
erotic love, 67
erotic mania, 274
eschatological direction, 108
eschatological symbol, 107
Essays on Radical Empiricism (W. James), 25–26
esse, 156; and *est*, 175
essence, and objective truth, 124
essential Christianity, 44
eternal being, 81–82
eternal life, 244
eternal now, 134
eternity, time and, 141–43
ethics, sophists and, 65
Ethics (Aristotle), 77, 91
Evangelists, 282
evocative truth, 160
excellence, Aristotle, 77
exclusivity, Jesus, 251
exigencies, Lonergan, 300
existence: "clearing in existence," 285; historical, 23; of love, 202–03; metaxic structure of, 153; mystery of, 32; philosopher's, 162; Plato on the beyond, 10; structure of, 145; tensional nature of, 122; truth and, 187, 208; Voegelin on reality, 20
existential openness, 217

existential order, 211
existere, 156
Exodus within reality, 106
experience: awareness of being, 23; compact experience, 49; concrete, 25–26; consciousness, 179; constants of, 84; differentiated, 59; equivalent, 244; experiential analysis, 103–4; experiential basis of consciousness, 127; experiential exegesis, 45, 233, 248; experiential grounding of faith, 208; experiential regeneration, 100; experiential theology, 237; human, 247; knowing, 181–82; Lonergan, 180; massively possessive, 112; mediated, 111; modes of, 110; nonexperientiable reality, 117–18; paradoxic structure of, 219; personal, 207; religious and intellectual, 217; religious, 228; self-transcending, 198; truth of reality, 125; Voegelin and Lonergan, 15; Voegelin's background, 18
expressive symbols, 124
extendedness, 264
extracosmic god, 242
extrinsicism, 210

faith: history, 233; Lonergan, 203; Lonergan and Voegelin, 220, 232; Nicea and Chalcedon, 241; objective events, 13; one true faith, 249; Plato, 75; and reason, 7, 112, 154, 250–51, 252; and understanding, 144; and vision in Christian context, 150–70; Voegelin, 231
Faith and Political Philosophy (Strauss and Voegelin), 310–11
Father-Mother-Offspring (*Timaeus*), 149
Father of Christ, 164, 246
fides, 160–61, 242, 245, 246
fides caritate formata, 310
fides quaerens intellectum, 12, 16, 139, 140, 144, 150, 156, 158, 161, 220, 252, 253, 274, 288
Fides Quaerens Intellectum (Barth), 152
first naivete, 230
flight from transcendence, 65
flowing presence, 83
flux of divine presence, 134

focused perception, 29
folly, 154, 155–56, 159
forma naturalis, forma supernaturalis, 243
formation-deformation, 130
foundationalism, 4–5
foundational theology, 15, 171–225
Foundational Theology (Fiorenza), 299
foundations, Lonergan's method and, 194–203
freedom, and the human good, 184–87
friendship, 42
From Enlightenment to Revolution (Voegelin), 267, 310
fulfillment, love and, 200
fullness of God's presence in Christ, 240
fullness of Passion and resurrection, 166
future: consciousness, 30; Lonergan, 196; past and, 121

Gegenstandsformlichkeit, 304
Geist and *nous*, 131
geographical expanse, 107
German philosophy, 127–32, 175
Germany, 8
gnosticism, 40, 95, 111, 242, 252, 267
God/gods: Anselm, 154, 156; beyond the gods, 108; beyond the personal God, 250; Christ, 242; Christianity, 158; cosmological myth, 47; death of, 8–9; equivalents, 96; extracosmic god, 242; falling in love with, 199; and *Geist*, 131; "God is the measure of the human being," 20; history, 236–37; human beings and, 83; image of, 246; intention in meditation, 35; *Laws*, 74–75; Leibniz, 135; Lonergan and Voegelin, 213–14; love, 188, 195; male and female images, 317; meditation, 35; mode of thingness, 157; multiple quests, 144–45; *nous*, 22; as object, 306; Olympian, 132–33; openness towards, 112; plurality of, 32; *Proslogion*, 152; St. Paul, 167; self-communication, 208; Son of God, 163, 165; true theology, 69; and universe, 113; unrestricted act of understanding, 182; voice, 126; word of, 10–11; world-transcendent, 51
The God of Faith and Reason (Sokolowski), 288–89

good (the Good)/*agathon*, 69, 72, 120
good and evil: empires, 99; task of theologian, 249; the Question, 112
good polis, *Republic*, 70
Gorgias (Plato), 22, 68–69, 70
The Gospel According to Jesus (Mitchell), 315
government/*politeia*, 70
grace: conversion, 199, 253; in death, 221–22; *gratia operans*, 299; nature and, 208; sanctifying, 187–88; transcendance and, 136–37
Grace and Freedom (Lonergan), 299
grasping the point, 176
Greece, 50, 56–66, 84, 86, 93, 108, 132, 139
Greek philosophy, 41, 47, 90–91, 244, 251
ground of all being, 88, 117
groups, group bias, 185

habitus, 299
happiness/*eudaimonia*, 76–77
hardness of heart, 203
hears God's voice, 126
heart to heart experience, 207–8
height and depth, 129–30, 201
helkein, 85, 251
heresy, 257, 268
hermeneutics, 24, 178, 192, 194, 209, 249, 313
heuristic structures, 182
high Christology, 251, 289
historical Jesus, 314–15
historicism, 174
historiogenesis, 93–97
history, 37–80; abusers of, 3; Aristotle, 76; burden of, 1–2; Christ written large, 239; classicist model, 204; directions in historical process, 215; discovery of mind, 211; divine presence in, 152, 158; faith, 233; fulfillment of, 105–6; God revealed in, 235; Greek historiography, 66; historical existence, 23; historical form of the people, 55–56; historic form, 51; historicity of Truth, 78; historiogenetic conception of, 24; historiography, 91; intelligibility, 206; mysterious in, 3–4; pleuromatic

presence of Christ, 169; pragmatic, 99; process of, 14; revelation in, 165; theory of equivalence, 84; *Timaeus*, 72; tragedy and, 64; transfiguration, 283; unilinear image of, 13; Voegelin's contribution, xi–xii; *zetema* advancing through, 90

History of Christian Philosophy in the Middle Ages (Gilson), 291

holiness, 190, 199

Holy Spirit, 243

homoousios, 205

hope, the Question and, 112

horizons: consciousness, 181; contemporary, 152; intentionality, 215; Lonergan, 195; love, 200; of reality, 34; restriction of the, 19; self-appropriated interiority, 192; subject as subject, 174

hubris, 278

human beings: all-too-human-image, 145; authentic humanity, 57; Christ, 238; consciousness, 34, 73; coredeemers, 243; experience, 247; God, 83; human nature, 104; human seeking-and-receiving pole, 85–86; integration of human living, 185–86; Lonergan, 192; Lonergan and Voegelin, 219; love, 199–200; mature, 77; method in theology, 205; nature of, 47; participation in eternal being, 81; philosophical orientation, 62; Platonic myth, 136; puppets of the gods, 112; transpolitical end, 71; unity of humankind, 106–9; words do not mean, persons mean, 177

humility, intellectual, 13

hyperouranion, 105

hypostasis, 125, 205; hypostatic distortion, 13; hypostatic union, 168; hypostatization, 48, 88, 123; hypostatized symbols, 251; hypostatizing doctrininalization, 6; hypostatizing objectification, 213

I (*Ich*): "I am" sayings, 317; "*Ich*" philosophy, 286; *Ich* seeking identity, 128; "I" of Jesus, 239, 307; symbols, 30

Idea: naked reality of, 74; Plato and Aristotle, 76; soul and, 71

idealism, 25, 128, 172, 176

identity, levels of being, 33

ideology: history of ideas, 37–38; unity of knowledge, 2; Voegelin, 211, 234

illative sense, 297

illumination, 86; illuminated dimension of consciousness, 31; illuminated experience, 46; *illuminatio divina*, 218; inner, 30

image/*eikon*, 166; reality and, 124

imagination: comprehending reality, 124–25, 141; imaginative oblivion, 7, 127–32; imaginative symbolization, 143; imaginative vision, 159; intellectual conversion, 189; reflective distance, 123; symbolic, 130, 135

imago Dei, 192, 194

immanence: cosmological myth, 47; experience, 82; ideology and, 40–41; immanentist metaphysics, 78; immanentized understanding, 256; intelligibility, 206; knowing, 173; levels of consciousness, 33; Lonergan and Voegelin, 218; meaning of Christ, 246; *Republic*, 70; source of transcendence, 182; transcendence and, 52–53, 59, 75–76

immanentize the eschaton, 41, 252, 257

immediacy, 201–2

immortality, 101; human beings, 62; immortalization, 100, 244

imperial symbolization, 52

imperialism, 91–92

In-Between reality, 151, 234

in-between structure of human experience, 210

incarnation, 43, 166–68; Christ, 242; Jesus, 241; once-and-for-all event, 251; transfiguration, 236; Voegelin, 238

inclusivism, 249

indelible present, 134

index (symbol), 277

index of experience, 82

individual human personality, 54

ineffable divine beyond, 252

ineffable silence, 148

infinite: consciousness and the, 31; finite

and, 50; being, 82; truth, 79; yearning
for, 248
inner dimension, 62
inner word, 177, 200–201
inquiry, 151; critical realism, 173;
inquiring mind, 177; questions,
204; and theology, 12; Voegelinian
theology, 247; *zetema*, 58
inrush of foolishness, 159
In Search of Order (Voegelin), 14, 23, 24,
113, 115, 117–50, 156, 270
Insight (Lonergan), 175, 183, 184, 186,
187, 188, 295, 296, 297, 299, 305
insight: doctrinal development, 206;
experiential insights, 235; and
institutions, 123–24; Lonergan,
175–76; self-transcendence, 185
institutionalization, 310
integration, higher, 186
intellect: agent intellect, 218; grasp of
being, 61; intellectual conversion,
189, 191; intellectual thinning out,
76; subject as, 183
intellectualism, 182
intelligibility: immanent historical
process, 206; Lonergan, 180–81; quest
for the intelligible, 177; reality, 181;
intentio animi, 28
intentionality, 73; analysis, 183, 188;
Anselm, 156; cognitional, 15, 201;
of consciousness, 146; German
context, 127; Husserl, 304; intentional
consciousness, 178, 220; intentionalist
entity, 133; language, 213; Lonergan,
181; in love with God, 188;
luminosity, 214, 216; paradox of
consciousness, 118
intention in meditation, 35
interiority: differentiation, 174; Lonergan,
177; normative structure of, 185
interpenetration of beings, 82
interpersonal love, 309
interpretation, Gadamer, 313
interpreter vs. thinker, 116
intersubjektive, 265
intracosmic gods, 140
intuition, 128
invisible measure, 65
Israel, 47, 50, 51–56, 61, 63, 64, 71, 84,
86, 93, 108, 236, 240, 251

Israel and Revelation (Voegelin), 51–55,
239, 269
Itinerarium mentis in Deum (Bonaventure),
135
It-reality, 128, 142, 161, 230, 236, 244,
253, 308

Jerusalem, 231
Judaism, 188–89, 240
judgment: of the dead, 68; future, 196;
knowledge and, 179; Lonergan, 180
justice: *dike*, 63–64; *Gorgias*, 68

kataphatic mode of theology, 252
kerygmata, 233
knower and known, 26, 45, 129
knowing: and being, 210; human, 173;
intellectual conversion, 189; and love,
201; subject, 174; Lonergan, 175;
reality as a nonthing, 118
knowledge: belief and, 207; egophanic
pursuit of absolute, 123; *episteme*,
69; experience of process, 31; faith
and reason, 154; and ignorance, 82;
Lonergan and Voegelin, 211, 220;
love precedes, 191–92; mystery, 199;
the Question, 62, 112, 217–18; of
reality, 25; and soul, 65; and truth,
78; unity of, 2
known unknown, 181, 199, 202
Krisis der europäischen Wissenschaften
(Husserl), 263
Kronos, 74

language, 110–11, 172; analogy, 252;
Anselm, 156; of Christianity, 230;
compact, 140; conditions of the
world, 138; deformation, 8, 116–17;
differentiated, 90; economy of
analytical terms, 34; equivalence,
84; experience and symbolization,
134; index, 277; ineffable effable,
148; inner word of, 200; inrush
of foolishness, 159; of intention,
213; limits of, 118; Lonergan and
Voegelin, 15, 214–15; love language,
232; mediating, 234; meditative
exegesis, 48; metaphysics, 6–7, 8;
modern philosophy, 210; of nature,
104; paradoxic structure of, 216;

and structure, 120; symbolic, 29;
symbols, 45; theophanic experiences,
245–46; theoretical, 205; *Timaeus*,
141; transcendence, 230–31
law, 54; of the cross, 307; law making,
77; philosophers and, 228; Plato on,
63; *Statesmen*, 72; transcendence, 65
Laws (Plato), 20, 22, 74, 75, 76, 85, 111,
118, 131, 154, 161, 162
leap in being, 47, 50–51, 56, 71, 100,
109
liberalism, 257
liberation, 52
liberty, 186
life and death: death of God, 8–9;
Nietzsche as philosopher, 3; Voegelin
on, x
limit experience, 29
linear history, 95
linear progression, 287
literalist deformation, 232
liturgy, 63
Logik (Hegel), 131
logos, 55, 61, 66, 139, 243
logos basilikos, 72
logos spermatikos, 236
Lonergan, Bernard: anthropology,
172–78; church, 205; cognition,
177; comparison with Voegelin,
209–26, esp., 223–25; conversion,
187–94, 192, 253; desire to know,
180, 186; development of doctrine,
206; differentiated consciousness,
207; doctrine, 203–9; faith, 203;
foundational theology, 171–225;
intentional consciousness, 250;
interiority, 174; meaning, 202;
moving viewpoint, 183; mysticism,
202; nature and grace, 208; pluralism,
193; revelation, 302; subject as
subject, 174; subjectivism, 172;
theological method and foundations,
194–203; theory of consciousness,
15; transcendental Thomist, 175;
transcendental method, 178–84
The Lonergan Enterprise (Crowe), 298
looking, Lonergan, 211
love: of being, 57–58; and belief, 207;
erotic, 67; existence of, 202–3; of
God, 55, 86–87; God's saving, 244;

Lonergan and Voegelin, 221–222;
"love language," 232; pleromatic,
of Christ, 247; precedes knowledge,
191–92, 200; *Republic*, 71; without
restriction, 188, 199; revelation of
Christ, 164; total self-surrender, 190;
Voegelin, 308; way up, way down,
184; of wisdom, 62
luminosity, 118, 137; consciousness, 146;
consciousness as, 230; of consciousness, 250; intentionality, 214; luminous event, 159; luminous process of
consciousness, 83; truth, 162

mache athanatos, 163, 166
madness/*mania*, 71
magisterium, 229
Marxism, 41
mass murder, 18
materialism, consciousness, 25
meaning: and being, 234; of Christ,
235–47; church, 229; context, 206;
doctrine, 205; equivalent meanings,
211; existential, of experience, 248;
immediacy, 201–2; interiority, 188;
Lonergan and Voegelin, 209; noetic
control, 105; realms of, 300; single
line of, 94; Voegelin, 230; words do
not mean, persons mean, 177; world
of meaning, 30
measure: divine measure, 20–21; God
is measure of all things, 75; man is
measure of man, 65
mediation, 50, 202
meditation, 27–28; ascent, 156;
confrontation, 5; and doctrinalization,
230; exegesis, 48, 103–4; intention
of consciousness, 33; knowledge and,
159; reading, 147; reflective distance,
250; theology, 249; transcendence,
35; Voegelin's style, 116
medium inter fidem et speciem, 292
memory, 30
Memphite theology, 52
metacontextual theological method,
194–95
metalepsis, 233, 251; character of quest
for truth, 123; experiences, 124;
participation, 151; reality, 156
metanoia, 187

metaphysics, 6–7, 8, 44, 264; Greek and Christian, 41; immanentist, 78; investigating reality, 10; Lonergan, 173; noetic analysis, 136; process, 33; propositional, 158; theology, 207
Metaphysics (Aristotle), 297
metatastic expectations, 106
metatastic faith, 57
metaxy, 14, 21, 23; experience of consciousness, 130; history, 216; imminent *parousia*, 105; in-between reality, 82; Jesus, 246, 251; pneumatic vision, 168; quest for truth, 145; structured movement, 120–21; subject and object, 103; symbols and, 125, 212; tension in life of mystics, 89; unknown God, 164; word, 236
method: Lonergan, 171, 188, 194–203; transcendental method, 178–84; Voegelin's theological method, 151–63
Method in Theology (Lonergan), 187, 197, 203, 204, 206, 207, 214, 217, 298, 300
micropolis, 70
Middle Ages, 6, 9, 152
middle, as starting point, 121
millenial constant, 95
mind: discovery of, 205; eros of the heart, 201; getting along without, 232; knower and known, 26
Minoan civilization, 56
miraculous events, 233–34
modernity, 212, 267
Monadologie (Leibniz), 135
monarchy, 52, 53; king lists, 95; philosopher-king, 63, 66, 74
monogenes, 142, 147–48, 168
monosis, 142, 147
moral conversion, 190, 191, 198
morbus animi, 155, 279
mortgage of metaphysics, 264
mortgage of the Chosen People, 64
mortgage of the polis, 71
Mother-god (*Timaeus*), 149
movement, 75; Anselm's quest, 153; assent/ascent, 155–56; conversion moves, 190; experience to consciousness, 180; faith and understanding, 138, 144; toward

God, 157; of love, 222; *mythos* to *logos*, 232; *psyche*, 118; pulls, 150; of reality, 107; of the soul, 253; of the soul toward ultimate reality, 85; soul toward the beyond, 168; structure and, 124; structured, 121; theology, 196
multiple worlds, 142
Munich, University of, 276
murder, 18, 259
Muses, 132
mystery/*apeiron*, 101; of the beyond, 252; divine beyond, 143; divine presence, 238; and doctrine, 10; drama of human history, 109; erotic relationship, 68; existence, 32, 96; God beyond the personal God, 250; historical process, 106; order of being, 46; paradoxic penultimacy, 148; philosopher's quest, 117; Plato, 145; of the process, 111; the Question, 11; religions, 61; symbols, 233; tetragrammatic depth, 117–18
Mystery and Myth in the Philosophy of Eric Voegelin (Hughes), 283
mysticism, 42; Christianity and Platonism, 218; Lonergan, 202, 216; Lonergan and Voegelin, 250; mystical theology, 237, 253; mystics and *metaxy*, 89; *via negativa*, 116
myth: Aristotle, 78; classical Greek, 132; cosmic cycles, 74; cosmological and philosophical, 139; finite process, 31; gods, 72; Lonergan, 305–6; metaphysics, 59; objects, 304; Plato, 161; Platonic philosophy, 137; reified or hypostatized, 38; as scientifically worthless, 131; theology, 144; *Timaeus*, 73; Voegelin, 230

nabal, 154
naivete, 230
National Socialism, 18, 41, 259
natural reason, 7, 128, 150
nature: and grace, 208; theophany, 103
nazism. *See* national socialism
Near East, 37, 51
necessity, 131
new age, 169
new and old, revelation, 92

The New Science of Politics (Voegelin), 22–23, 24, 25, 37–43, 112, 136–37, 257, 267, 307, 313
new world order, 2
Nicea, Council of, 241
Nicomachean Ethics (Aristotle), 77
nihilism, 29
noetic: analysis, 136; beyond, 133; consciousness, 21, 131; control, 86, 245; guidance, 138; paralysis in theology, 313; response, 11; revelation, 248–49; search for divine ground, 241; speculation, 159; theology, 6; truth, 126; vision, 161, 162, 168
nonexistent origin of all things, 96
normativity, conversion, 199
nosos, 155
nothing, 32
noumena of consciousness, 33
nous, 7, 61, 75, 77, 126, 131, 136, 169; *nous-in-psyche-in-soma*, 147
numerical connotation, 142

object: intended, 213; noetic search, 218; over against itself, 34; subject and, 26; and subject, 146; symbols and concepts, 119; time and eternity, 82
object-forming character of consciousness, 304
objectification of conversion, 198
objectifying consciousness, 73
objective: footing for the quest, 121; truth, 124; as word, use of or taken as, 290
objectivism, 207, 210
objectivity: authentic subjectivity and, 173; of human knowing, 180; and subjectivity, 203–4;
oblivion, 285
Offspring, Father-Mother-Offspring (*Timaeus*), 149
oikoumene, 106, 108, 130
okeanos, 106, 108
The Old Testament and Christian Faith (Anderson), 315
Olympian gods, 58
omphalos, 51, 52
one beyond the many, 218
oneness, divine reality, 142–43

ontic constants, 97
ontological proof, 152
ontology: Aristotle, 76–78; human development, 33; metaxy, 83; "onto-theo-logy," 296; symbols, 232, 235; truth of existence, 100
openness: to being, 62, 179; consciousness, 89; Lonergan and Voegelin, 217–18; self, 26; soul, 19; theophanic field, 241
opinion, 234, 271–72; climate of, 22; *doxa*, 69
opsis, 159
order and disorder, 21, 23; beginning and end, 150; of existence, 96; Lonergan and Voegelin, 209, 210; *monogenes*, 142–43; order of history, 23; Pauline vision, 102; regenerative force, 67; remembrance, 133; Voegelin on history of ideas, 38
Order and History (Voegelin), 14, 24, 40, 44–50, 81, 120, 137, 138, 267, 274, 276, 277, 279, 281, 283
origin/*arche*, 96
Orphism, 271
other-worldly love of God, 200
outside, known from the, 209

paganism, 158
painting, consciousness, 29–30
paleolithicum, 269
paraclete, 132
paradigm, 140, 142
paradigmatic order of the beyond, 73–74
paradox, divine presence, 122
Parmenides (Plato), 157, 292
parousia, 102, 105, 119, 133–34
participation: in being, 56, 211; in consciousness, 128, 132; in the divine, 62; drama of, 238; eternal being, 81; human mortality, 168; Lonergan and Voegelin, 209, 219; metaleptic, 87, 251; in the *metaxy*, 96; in reality, 20, 161; in the whole, 46
past: consciousness, 30; and future, 121; Lonergan, 196
patterns of experience, 182–83
Peloponnesian War, 65–66, 67
perception: concrete experience, 34; empiricism, 248; stream of, 25; stream

theory of consciousness, 29; things known through, 82
performance, consciousness, 179
periagoge, 130, 131
periechon, 143, 147
periodization, 92
personal facticity, 234
personalism, 207
personalization of the divine *parousia*, 245
persuasion (*peitho*), 21
Phaedrus (Plato), 71–72, 105, 274, 317
phantasm, 176
phenomenology, 308; Husserl, 29; Lonergan, 178; meditation, 28
phenotypes, 93
Philebus (Plato), 82
philia, 68
philodoxers, 41, 261
philosophers: discourse, 216; and law, 228; missionary impulse, 99; mystic, 63; myths and, 50; Pauline vision, 102; pre-Socratic, 60; quest, 117, 126–27; sophists, 65; task, 110; Voegelin, 5
philosophy: abolition of, 130; endless inquiry, 89; and mysticism, 116; and myth, 139; remedial function, 57; revelation and, 84; theology, 158, 212, 273; Voegelin's, of consciousness, 227–54; Western, 207
Philosophy of History (Hegel), 95
Philosophy of Order (Opitz & Sebba), 267, 288, 307
physics, theoretical, 284
"place," 148
Plato and Aristotle (Voegelin), 57
pleroma, 167
pleromatic presence, 143, 243
pluralism: conversion, 192; Plato, 145
A Pluralistic Universe (W. James), 25–26
plurality: of histories, 107; of quests, 121; of views, 205
pneuma, 167
pneumapathology, 89, 155
pneumatic: consciousness, 105; differentiation, 143; experience, 85, 221; experience of God, 163; revelation, 101, 248–49
poetry, 58, 68, 69
polis: Aristotle, 76; "the human being writ large," 20; *Laws*, 74–75; *Phaedrus*,

72; *Republic*, 70; second best, 74
political friendship, 77
political prisons, 18
political science: *The New Science of Politics*, 38; theology, 255
Politics (Aristotle), 77, 91
politics: restorative enterprise, 23; sophists, 65; Voegelin's background, 17–18; wisdom, 21
positivism, 211
power: quest for, 123; sense of, 124
practical living, 76
pragmatic (the pragmatic), 76; history, 99
prayer, 153
pre-Nicene Christian, 313
pre-Socratic philosophers, 60
pre-Socratic thinkers, 271
prediffferentiatied oneness, 216
Principes de la nature et de la grâce fondés en raison (Leibniz), 135
prior word, 200–201
process metaphysics, 33
process of revelation, 109
process theology, 32–33
projection of human images, 60
proof/*probatio*, 154
prophets, 53–54, 71, 86, 126
proportionate being, 181, 298
propositions, 99, 126: dogmatic, 249; knowledge, 234; language, 160; Lonergan and Voegelin, 220; metaphysics, 158; proof or nonproof, 154; theology, 155; Voegelin on Hegel, 131
Proslogion (Anselm), 152, 153, 154, 155, 155, 292
prudential wisdom, 77
psyche, 59, 90, 105, 118
psychic conversion, 301
psychic depth, 129
psychoanalysis, 129
psychologism, 172–73
psychology, 188, 231, 265
Pythagoreanism, 271

quest: for the intelligible, 177; for truth, 121, 126–27, 130–31, 144, 148, 161, 169, 246. See also philosophers, philosophy
Question (the Question), 111–12

question and answer, 96–101, 205–6
questions: *diaporein*, 87–88; Lonergan,
   176, 181, object, 213; primordial
   wonder, 179
quid est? 176

race, 18
ratio fidei, 291
rationalism, 230; demythologization, 32;
   philosophy and myths, 50
rational quest, 88
reading and interpetation, 147
realism, 173
reality, 247–48; already out there now
   real, 176, 190–91; being and, 135; of
   a community, 71; cannot be proved,
   155; cosmos, 142; divine, 61; eclipse
   of, 88, 89; eschatological *telos*, 102;
   foundational, 198; headed beyond
   itself, 100; Hesiod and remembrance,
   132–34; horizon of, 34; and image,
   124; imagination and, 124–25; in-
   between, 151; in-between structure,
   234; intelligibility, 181; it-reality, 119;
   language and, 160; levels of, 73, 213;
   luminosity, 118–19; metaleptic, 87;
   nonexperientiable, 117–18; nonthing,
   146; objective; 204; partaking, 149;
   participation in, 161; behind symbolic
   language, 233; spoken word, 120;
   subjective, 172; truth and, 128–29
reason: Anselm, 153–54; Aristotle, 77;
   attunes us to God, 22; consciousness,
   21; faith, 250–51, 252; Homeric epic,
   58- 59; life of, 261; noetic philosophy,
   86; ordering human experience, 49;
   and revelation, 7, 126, 219. *See also*
   natural reason
reborn soul, 69
reconstructive theology, 235
recovery, hermeneutics of, 24
redemption, myth and, 42
reductionism, 34, 220, 290
reference, 146
reflection: consciousness, 34–35;
   subjective acts of, 128
reflective distance, 111, 123, 128, 133:
   Anselm, 152; Christ, 246; in language,
   141; meditation, 250

Reformation/Counter-Reformation,
   204–5
reification of language of myth, 48
relation: actualization of, 49; experienced,
   26; human and divine, 42
religion: *ecumene*, 107; empires and, 99;
   faith, 203; Lonergan's transcendental
   method, 194; love, 200; religious
   conversion, 190–99, 207; religious
   experience, 188; religious harmony,
   145; religious pluralism, 143;
   religious wars, 229; study of, 248;
   transcendental method, 182; as a
   word, 219, 306
remembrance: Hesiod and, 132–34;
   reflective distancing, 123; Voegelin,
   138
renewal, new type of foundation, 172
representation, 61, 64
Republic (Plato), 20, 22, 67, 69, 74, 76,
   82, 85, 154, 155, 159, 254, 273, 293
resistance, hardened, 154
responsibility, Lonergan, 185, 186
restriction of the horizon, 19
resurrection: of the body, 244; Christ,
   278; Pauline experience, 282
retheoretization, philosophy of history,
   92
return to a consciousness of principles, 39
revelation: Aquinas, 157; Christ, 164;
   content, 118, 233–34; demarcation,
   92; doctrine and, 103; experience,
   233; *Gorgias*, 68–69; Gospel as event,
   238; Heraclitus, 62; in history, 13,
   239; language and, 125; Lonergan,
   214, 302; monopoly of, 9; natural
   reason, 126; noetic, 104, 168; one
   does not abolish another, 108;
   participation in, 117; and philosophy,
   84; Plato, 159; Platonic, 163; reason
   and, 7, 219; revelatory appeal, 12;
   Strauss, 310; symbols and myth, 232;
   truth, 212–13, 250; unrevealed reality,
   143; Voegelin, 145, 236, 248
revelatory role of the experiences of the
   wise, 39
revolt: against oblivion, 138; Promethean,
   111

salvation, 150; creation, 245; *Geist* and,

131–32; history, 13; beyond history,
41; Lonergan, 187; Lonergan and
Voegelin, 221
sameness (equivalence), 84
saving tale, 169, 293
savior (title), 247
savior-god, 163
scholasticism, 175
school philosophies, 18–19
school theology, 237
science, 128; of being, 157; Lonergan,
174; Lonergan and Voegelin, 212;
mathematized sciences, 135; *The New
Science of Politics*, 38; scientism, 212;
scientists, Voegelin, 306
scotosis, 8, 303
scripture, 234; fixed canon, 99; Pauline
vision, 102–3; protective device, 126.
See also Bible
secondary symbols, 232
A Second Collection (Lonergan), 301, 306
second coming of Christ, 13, 101
second immediacy, 202
second naivete, 230
second realities, 23, 130
secularization 229, 310
secular process of destruction, 9
seeking/*zetein*, 87
self: pseudo-grounds, 88; self-
transcending, 25
self-appropriation, 192, 250
self-authentication, 193
self-communication, 208
self-conscious *psyche*, 60
self-determination, 187
self-presence, 174
self-revelation, 182
self-surrender, 190, 199, 202
self-transcendence, 181, 184, 189, 191,
198, 200, 208, 209, 210
self-transcendent knowledge, 180
self-transformation, 187, 191
self-understanding of man, 61
self-validation, 188
sensorium of transcendence, 54, 59, 62
sentiments, 267
Seventh Letter (Plato), 124, 294
shepherd-god, 74
silence, of God, 148
sin, of bias, 185–86

skepticism, 25, 78
social conditions, authenticity, 185
social science, 39
society: cosmological societies, 93;
disengagement of the soul from, 70;
life of reason, 261; political realm,
63; self- interpretation, 40; sophists'
discourse, 65
soma/body, 140–41
Son of God, 142
sophists, 20, 64–65, 69, 154, 155
soteriological truth, 42, 136–37
soul: Aristotle, 78; divine meditation,
12; ensouled cosmos, 75; full
differentiation, 68; Greek experience,
48; ideology, 20–21; immortality,
55; knowledge and, 65; *morbus animi*,
155; movement of, 62, 85; open, 19;
order of the, 68, 70; and society, 74;
struggle in tragedy, 64; transcendence,
39, 232
space, 146: meaning, 30; mother or
nurse, 149
specialization, theology, 196
speculation, 128
Spirit (paraclete), 132
The Spirit of Medieval Philosophy (Gilson),
152
spirituality: expansion of the spiritual
horizon, 91; holiness, 190, 199;
homonoia, 108; inner word of religion,
200; order and the spiritual realm, 98;
parallel spiritual movements, 94–95;
recovery of spiritual insight, 103;
spiritual ascent, 254; spiritual grasp
of the whole of being, 49; spiritual
outbursts, 91–92; spiritual person, 20;
spiritual realm, 82; spiritual reform,
66; tension in West, 229; Voegelin,
230
spoudaioi, 20, 77
Statesman (Plato), 72, 74
stoicism, 78, 99, 234, 256
stories of God, 149
story of reality, 137
stream of perceptions, 25
stream theory, 27, 29
structure: everlasting, of consciousness,
104, 172; of cosmos, 141; evocation
of, 120; moving beyond, 109–10;

Study of History (Toynbee), 279
subject: as intellect, 183; and object, 26, 146; as subject, 174
subjective acts of reflection, 128
subjectivism: Lonergan, 172, 210
subjectivity, 28, 203–4
sufficient reason, 135–36
Sumeria, 95
superbia, 278
symbolism: Church and, 230; Hesiod, 133; historiogenesis, 93–94; secondary, 34; suspect, 241; transcendence, 252
symbolization: equivalent, 209; God/gods, 61; religious conversion, 190
symbols: accumulated, 100; all being is symbolic, 27; clarity in, 137; Dionysiac ascent to God, 69; divine, 134; evocative truth, 160; experiences of reality, 23; image of God, 246; luminative, 147; mystery, 233; mythic symbols, 50; ontic context, 28, 31; ontology, 232, 235; Pauline vision, 102–3; search for the divine ground, 84; symbolic ambiguities of divine presence, 122–27; truth, 11, 79; Voegelin on, 165
Symposium (Plato), 82, 308
system to end all systems, 129

tabula rasa, 28
temporal being, 81
tension: Demiurge and cosmos, 149; insight and questions, 179; order and, 23; tensional pressure, 145; thought and being, 140
tetragrammatic depth, 118
theocracy, 270
theogony, 94
Theogony (Hesiod), 59, 132, 159
theologians, 4, 5; experiences of conversion, 193; recovering lost feminine images, 317; subjectivity, 208; Voegelin's work, 254
theological philosophy, 6
theology: Aristotle, 60; foundational, 171–225; horizons, 192; Lonergan's method and foundations, 194–203; noetic paralysis, 313; philosophy,

212; Plato, 65, 138; renewal, 204; *Republic*, 69; types of, 155; Voegelin's references, 4; Voegelin's method, 151–63, 247–54; word and, 10
Theology of Culture (Kimball), 306
theophanic: equivalences, 315; events, 91–92, 151; experience, 84, 86, 236
theophany, 3, 11, 100, 101, 103, 106, 110, 125
theopolitical constitution of Israel, 53
theoretike energeia, 49
theory: of consciousness, 27; retheoretization of, 39
theotes, 166
therapeutic function of philosophy, 22
things, 140; and being, 156; resistance to differentiation, 145–46; thing-in-itself, 27; thing-reality, 128, 150, 309; thingliness, 148
thinker vs. interpreter, 116
thinking and being, 140
A Third Collection (Lonergan), 307
thought and language, Lonergan and Voegelin, 232
t'ien-hsia/all under heaven, 107
Timaeus (Plato), 72–73, 74, 104, 115, 130, 136, 137–40, 142, 147, 149, 159, 257, 274, 290, 292, 304, 317
time: dimension of consciousness, 263; *eikon* of eternity, 141–43; flow of, 30; history and, 91; timeless *metaxy*, 83; truth becomes historical, 79
totalitarianism, 2, 20–21
Tractatus-Theologico-Politicus (Spinoza), 309
tradition: reaction and, 28; traditional Christian thought, 231
transcendence: Aristotle, 78; being, 181; cautious use of symbolism, 252; consciousness, 195–96; cosmological myth, 47; experience of, 81–82; form of consciousness, 128; hermeneutics, 194; horizon, 193; human-divine relationship, 42; immanence and, 52–53, 59; immanentized version of, 88; knowledge and, 62; language, 230–31; levels of consciousness, 196–97; Lonergan and Voegelin, 209, 213, 215; love, 199; meditation and, 10; myths and, 31–32; necessity of, 192; order, 11; process theology, 32;

radical, of divine being, 52; source
of political order, 39; theology, 202;
transcendental method, 178–84, 217;
Voegelin and, 118
transcendentalism, order of symbols,
28–29
transcultural base of universal
communication, 194–95
transfiguration, 100–6; of all things
in cosmos, 252; history, 169, 283;
incarnation, 236; 243; ultimate, 110
transformation of nature, 187
transpersonal Word, 201
transpolitical end of the human being, 71
Trinity, 243
truth: deformation of, 124, 220;
differentiation of, 166; doctrine, 206;
evocative, 160; of existence, 187;
existence in tension, 61–62; as a
given, 206; incarnate, 163; insight,
179; judgment, 175; knowledge and,
78; luminosity, 162; philosophy and
ideology, 58; philosophy and myth,
50; possession of whole truth, 143–44;
quest for, 250; and reality, 128–29;
or revelation, 212–13; symbolic,
249; symbols and, 11; theology, 155;
transcendence and, 79; universality of,
209; to value itself, 190; Voegelin on
dogmatism and, 6
Truth and Method (Gadamer), 313
turning around/*Umkehrung*, 130
Tusculan Disputations (Cicero), 155, 279
Two Sources of Morality and Religion
(Bergson), 26

Über die Form des amerikanischen Geistes
(Voegelin), 25
ultima solitudo, 202
ultimate Beyond, 133
ultimate concern, 189
ultimately penultimate, 148
uncertainty, essence of Christianity, 307,
313
unconscious, 34, 72
understanding: being and, 180;
consciousness and, 174–75; a doctrine
and, 206; faith and, 144; God, 176;
immanentized, 256; Lonergan, 180,

190; *Proslogion*, 153; theophanic
event, 86
unilinear construction of history, 93
uniqueness of Jesus the Christ, 242–43,
251
United States, 24, 25
unity: empire and, 98; of knowledge, 2;
of humankind, 106–9; religious love,
200
universal communication, 195
universality, *ecumene*, 107
universe: God and, 113; symbol, 284
unknown God, 104, 118, 164, 236–37,
240, 242, 245
unknown unknown, 181
unoriginality, 228
unseemly gods, 60
untutored desire to understand, 305

values, moral conversion, 190, 191
verification, conversion, 199
vice, disordered existence, 89
violence, 2, 18, 259
virtues: dianoetic, 77; theological, 62
vision: anamnetic recovery, 12; Christian,
163–70; faith and, in Christian
context, 150–70
visionary experience of transcendence,
218
Voegelin, Eric: abolition of history,
169; anamnetic experiments, 35;
Anselm, 156; Aquinas, 157; Aristotle,
76–77; Augustine, 137; authority,
228; authors of Genesis, 120;
autobiography, 24; breakthroughs in
history, 93; Christ, 165, 244; Christian
symbols, 166–67; Christianity, 312,
314; Christology, 240–41, 242;
constitution of reason through
revelation, 87; contemplation, 49;
conversion, 252–53; cosmological
myth, 47, 84; culture, 234–35;
differentiation of experiences, 48;
disordered existence, 88; dogma, 160,
234; dogmatism, 26; early writings,
17–35; *ecumene*, 106; *Ecumenic Age*,
109; empiricism, 248; experiential
analysis, 103–4; faith, 249; faith
and hope, 112–13; God, 9; Hegel,
127–32; "historical form of the

people," 55–56; history, 95, 108; history of ideas, 37–38; Husserl, 305; ideology, 234; ideology and philosophy, 57; incarnation, 238; *Israel and Revelation*, 53; It-reality, 119, 244; Jesus, 241, 242, 243, 251; language, 246; *Laws*, 74; Lonergan compared to, 198, 209–26; love, 308; meaning of Christ, 235–47; meditative process, 27–28; metaphysical language, 8; *metaxy*, 233; method, 4–5; modernity, 100; noetic experience, 82; Olympian gods, 132; ontology and symbols, 232, 235; order, 21; *Order and History*, 45; *Parmenides*, 61; Pauline vision, 102; philosophizing, 43; philosophy of consciousness, 33; Plato, 141–42; Platonic theology, 11; progress of a philosopher, 90; reason and revelation, 87; reconstruction of philosophy, 5; reflective distance, 111–12; remembrance, 138; return to the Platonic myth, 136–50; revelation and faith, 12; self, 26; Socrates and Plato, 67; style, 115–16; study of Voegelin's work, 253–54; theological method, 151–63; theory and history, 40; theory of consciousness, 15; Thucydides, 66; *Timaeus*, 72; tragedy as liturgy, 63; transcendence, 32; truth of existence, 86; two types of consciousness, 7; unconscious consciousness, 130; Voegelin's

philosophy of consciousness, 227–54; Voegelinian theology, 247–54
Vorhandenheit, 175, 296

war, 66, 229
The Way to Nicea (Lonergan), 298, 302
way up, way down, 184
well known but not known well, 25
western civilization, xi, 1, 18, 29, 229, 234, 254, 312
What is History? (Voegelin), 284
"Who is this God?" 118, 134–36
Why Doctrines? (Hefling), 303
will to power, 98, 278
wisdom: *Laws*, 75; politics and, 21; *sophon*, 62; Voegelinian theology, 16
wonder: primordial, 179; *thaumazein*, 87
word: Christ, 241; truth of the, 162; words do not mean, persons mean, 177
Works and Days (Hesiod), 59
world history, 71
The World of the Polis (Voegelin), 56, 270, 282
World Technology and Human Destiny (Aron), 260
world-transcendent God. 51

Yahweh, 53, 55

zetema, 90, 117, 118
zetesis, 251
Zeus, 74
Zuhandenheit, 296

ABOUT THE AUTHOR

Michael P. Morrissey is an Assistant Professor of Theology at the University of St. Thomas, St. Paul, MN. He received his Ph.D. at the Graduate Theological Union, Berkeley, Cal., and has published a number of articles on religion and spirituality.